The Lorette Wilmot Library
Nazareth College of Rochester

DEMCO

Transatlantic Insurrections

Transatlantic Insurrections

British Culture and the Formation of American Literature, 1730–1860

PAUL GILES

PENN

UNIVERSITY OF PENNSYLVANIA PRESS   Philadelphia

Copyright © 2001 University of Pennsylvania Press

Printed in the United States of America on acid-free paper

10 9 8 7 6 5 4 3 2 1

Published by
University of Pennsylvania Press
Philadelphia, Pennsylvania 19104-4011

Library of Congress Cataloging-in-Publication Data

Giles, Paul.
    Transatlantic insurrections: British culture and the formation of American literature,
    1730–1860 / Paul Giles.
        p. cm.
    Includes bibliographical references (p.   ) and index.
    ISBN 0-8122-3603-3 (cloth : alk. paper)
    1. American literature—English influences. 2. American literature—Colonial period, ca.
    1600–1775—History and criticism. 3. American literature—Revolutionary period,
    1775–1783—History and criticism. 4. American literature—19th century—History and
    criticism. 5. American literature—1783–1850—History and criticism. 6. United
    States—Civilization—British influences. 7. English literature—Appreciation—United
    States. 8. United States—Relations—Great Britain. 9. Great Britain—Relations—United
    States. I. Title.
    PS159.G8G52001
    810.9—dc21   00-069088

810.9
Gil

Contents

All kinds of reasoning consist in nothing but a *comparison*, and a discovery of those relations, either constant or inconstant, which two or more objects bear to each other.

Hume, *A Treatise of Human Nature*, 1739

Master: I doubt that there can be anywhere under God's heaven another head which contains as many paradoxes as yours.

Jacques: What harm is there in that? A paradox isn't always a lie.

Diderot, *Jacques the Fatalist*, c. 1780

Introduction
British-American Literature:
Paradoxical Constitutions, Civil Wars

The purpose of this book is to read British and American literature comparatively. My argument will be that the development of American literature appears in a different light when read against the grain of British cultural imperatives, just as British literature itself reveals strange and unfamiliar aspects that are brought into play by the reflecting mirrors of American discourse. It is, by now, an academic commonplace to acknowledge how national ideals, and the "canonical" models of aesthetic expression that support them, should be seen as highly politicized entities, laden with ideological implications of all kinds. What may not be so apparent is the way such formal and ideological dimensions are apt chameleonically to change their shape when refracted through a spectrum of alternative cultural traditions. To read national literatures in a transnational way is thus to suggest the various forms of contingency that have entered into the formation of each naturalized inheritance.

One reason for focusing upon British and American cultures in the eighteenth and nineteenth centuries is to show how the emergence of autonomous and separate political identities during this era can be seen as intertwined with a play of opposites, a series of reciprocal attractions and repulsions between opposing national situations. Over recent years, there have been many critical studies which have considered the evolution of literary traditions as postcolonial phenomena, whereby a developing culture defines itself in opposition to some oppressive power which nevertheless continues to haunt it. This particular approach is different, however, in that the fulcrum of my study is a civil war: not the American Civil War, but that earlier internecine conflict which, because of its outcome, subsequently became known as the American Revolution. (In his early *History of the American Revolution*, published in 1789, the republican David Ramsay described the recent bloody event in terms of "the horrors of a civil war," as though either appellation were valid.)[1] My argument starts some fifty years before and ends about eighty years after the Revolution, and I want to suggest how during this period British and American literature became kinds of "secret sharer" (to appropriate the title of a Joseph Conrad short story), twisting and intertwining with each other in mutually disorienting ways. Whereas Simon Gikandi sees "the paradox of Englishness" as its "need to define the national character against a colonial other that it must then disown," I will argue that such disavowal became more difficult to sustain in the context of the American Revolution precisely because it was a family quarrel which the British lost.[2] Most scholars considering American culture in the light of postcolonial theory have posited hierarchical divisions and antagonisms between the different sides of the Atlantic: Jennifer DeVere Brody, for instance, has discussed ways in which the "high" moral superiority of Victorian English culture defined itself against what could be categorized as "low" and American.[3] What I want to suggest, however, is that in these years on either side of the Revolution British and American cultural narratives tended to develop not so much in opposition but rather as heretical alternatives to each other.

While most postcolonial accounts of literature are concerned at some level with questions of ethnocentric consciousness and conflict, then, my reading of British-American culture will revolve around the more discomfiting figures of mirroring and twinning, where mutual identities are not so much independently asserted but sacrilegiously travestied. To some extent, this approach follows in the theoretical path outlined by Edward Watts, who has argued that American culture at the turn of the nineteenth century was not simply "anticolonial" in the sense of seeking to resist a hegemonic British power, but rather embodied many of the internal contradictions of a settler culture that saw itself as "both colonizer and colonized at once." Watts describes this as a Second World, rather than Third World, form of postcolonialism: instead of the "narrow binaries" pitting oppression against emancipation, the "bifocal" aspects linked to divisions within post-Revolutionary America produced a culture that looked in different directions simultaneously.[4] I want to push this argument further, though, by also examining how the American Revolution was refracted within British writing, as well as by considering the implications of this transatlantic rupture for the subsequent formation of "British Literature" and "American Literature" as supposedly discrete categories. The methodology here will tend more toward the comparative than the postcolonial, in Watts's sense of that term, since I am concerned with American literature not as subordinate to an imperial British literature, but rather as something that develops in parallel to it. My focus will be on points of transnational convergence and interference that arise out of works incorporating their own particular local perspectives.

One theme of this book will concern ways in which the sense of an insurrectionary division from within is expressed tropologically in literary texts of this period through various figures of paradox. The logic of paradox, as outlined here, opens up prospects of division and dualism, evoking instances of self-contradiction where materially embodied texts fail to coincide with their own ideological designs. By reading British and North American cultures against each other, I hope not only to highlight the constricting parameters of their ideological "norm," but also to illuminate more complicated occasions when they traverse each other and become uneasily aware of their own potential reversibilities. I intend to examine various manifestations of this paradoxology in North Atlantic culture between the 1730s, when Alexander Pope's fame was at its height, and the 1860s, when Anthony Trollope was publishing his most famous novels.

One of the general inferences I wish to draw from these discussions of American literature as a "bifocal" phenomenon is that British elements in its constitution have remained relatively unacknowledged over the past fifty years. There are many reasons for this erasure of a British cultural matrix, but one in particular has been the professional institutionalization of Transcendentalism as a touchstone for American cultural identity. In "A Plea for Captain John Brown," for example, Henry David Thoreau claims it was the transcendence of legalistic categories that made Brown "the most American of us all," and he goes on to underline Brown's equation of personal independence and national identity by punning on the word "constitution": "It is," he writes in 1859, "the difference of constitution, of intelligence and faith, and not streams and mountains, that make the true and impassable boundaries between individuals and between states."[5] By aligning the constitution of human character with the constitution of America, Thoreau chooses to emphasize the "impassable boundaries" guarding the autonomy of both.

In literary criticism of the mid-twentieth century, when American literature was coming to occupy a more prominent place on academic agendas, Thoreau's kind of cultural nonconformity was valorized by classic critical texts promoting ideologies of westward pastoralism (Leo Marx, *The Machine in the Garden*), organic democracy (F. O. Matthiessen, *American Renaissance*), and natural exclusivism (Henry Nash Smith, *Virgin Land*). All of these works, in their different ways, tended to reinforce a myth of the United States as an integral and separate country, a nation set apart from the old laws of Europe. The limitations (and the strengths) of this "myth and symbol" school are by now an old story, and I do not intend to rehearse these issues in detail here, except to note how their essentialist theses about what might constitute a "genuine" American literature were predicated implicitly upon the attempt to establish the kind of "metaphysical paradigms," in Gregory Jay's term, characteristic of historiography informed by a theological or quasi-theological perspective.[6] The "spirit" of freedom considered to be synonymous with American national culture during the 1950s was, in part at least, an extrapolation from religious assumptions about the destiny of the soul. As Donald E. Pease and others have said, in these assumed ideal orders of American literature put forward during the years after World War II, it is not hard to infer traces of Cold War rhetoric, the providential people of plenty cherishing their birthright of freedom and self-determination.[7] Nor is it difficult here to make out the influence of Northrop Frye, whose synthetic categories of myth stood ready to infuse the inchoate material world with a breath of universal spirit.

These mythic accounts of American literature occupying its own separate sphere can be seen as a culmination and continuation of attempts earlier in the twentieth century to define an Americanist field specifically against the oppressive weight of British cultural hegemony. We see in embryonic form the nationalist agendas of American studies through the implicitly—and sometimes explicitly—antagonistic tone toward Britain disseminated by groups like that centered around the journal *Seven Arts* around the time of World War I. This movement, marshaled by Van Wyck Brooks and Waldo Frank, declared itself impatient of the genteel snobbery practiced by Ivy League anglophiles, and it sought instead to place emphasis upon what it saw as the vernacular or Whitmanian impulses within American life and art, the native strengths of writing in the American grain. The most vehement statement of this position came in Randolph Bourne's 1916 essay, "Trans-National America," which inveighs against "the ruling class of Anglo-Saxon descendants in these American States" and complained of how "English snobberies, English religion, English literary styles, English literary reverences and canons, English ethics, English superiorities, have been the cultural food that we have drunk in from our mothers' breasts." Bourne specifically takes issue with what he conceives as the English tendency to think of Americans "incorrigibly as 'colonials,'" and his essay anticipates what Caren Irr has described as the "exemplary response" to a postcolonial situation among radical American critics during the 1920s and 1930s, who sought imaginatively to map out a distinct, coherent national culture as a counterpoint to more general humanist assumptions of cultural hierarchy, assumptions which were too often based on Anglo-Saxon traditions.[8]

This interweaving of literary analysis with nationalist agendas in the interwar period reaches its apogee in F. O. Matthiessen's *American Renaissance*, published in 1941. Matthiessen follows the example of Coleridge in attending closely to questions of language and symbolic form, but he also strives to insert his close readings of Emerson, Whitman, Thoreau, Hawthorne, and Melville into a synthetic, prophetic interpretation of American culture. The Harvard critic proposes to validate his five canonical figures as equivalent in status to writers of the English Renaissance—Shakespeare, Jonson, Webster, Donne and Browne—but he introduces a comparative dimension only to suppress it, since he is concerned above all to position himself in opposition to British literature. As I shall argue later, while more recent American critics have rejected the narrow dimensions of Matthiessen's literary canon, they have often reproduced his ideology of cultural nationalism in a different guise. For instance, as Lawrence Buell observes: "In Harold Bloom's theory of American poetic succession, no foreign power disrupts the symposium once Emerson enters it; British and American literary histories are kept rigorously distinct."[9] In Bloom's world, once again, the hypostatization of Transcendentalism as a nationalist idiom works to consolidate the demarcation of American literature as a constitutionally separate domain.

Across different generations, then, Bourne, Matthiessen and Bloom saw themselves as attempting to modernize and to democratize the study of American culture, to move it away from an obsequious dependence on British models. One irony here is that this emphasis on what F. R. Leavis referred to dismissively as "the Americanness of American literature" was itself partly a reaction against the fact that the field in its first professional incarnation had actually been conceived as a comparative discipline.[10] The first American literature group that convened at the Modern Language Association in 1926 maintained that Americanists should not become sidetracked into narrowly nationalistic concerns, but should focus instead upon relationships between American literature and its European counterparts; and a similar attitude prevailed when the first formal American literature section of the MLA was created in 1930. The inaugural issue of their celebrated journal, *American Literature*, was published in March 1929, and it featured an explicitly comparative essay by George E. Hastings, "John Bull and His American Descendants," which was concerned to read John Arbuthnot's *History of John Bull* alongside Francis Hopkinson's political allegory, *A Pretty Story*. A similar comparative emphasis manifested itself in subsequent issues: for example, the second number, two months later, included an article on "Some German Surveys of American Literature" and another piece on Whitman's relationship with Edward Dowden, Professor of English at Dublin in the 1870s. These early academic movements were orchestrated by scholars such as Jay B. Hubbell, Norman Foerster, and Robert E. Spiller; it is not coincidental that they took place during an era of high modernism, the late 1920s, when there was a tendency among many literary intellectuals to follow the example of Idaho native Ezra Pound in taking "provincialism" to be "the enemy" and in assuming that national literatures were most effective when understood in the light of each other.[11]

We see a legacy of this modernist idealism in the recent work of William C.

Spengemann, who argues, not unlike Pound, that "the history of what we call American literature" should be seen as "inseparable from the history of literature in English as a whole."[12] Spengemann believes that the English language is the entity holding this entire Anglo-American field together, and he is scornful of attempts to classify Benjamin Franklin, say, or Henry James as either "British" or "American" writers, given the propensity of these authors to cross national boundaries with disarming facility. Franklin's *Autobiography*, Spengemann writes, is generally "considered an American work, on the assumption that anything done by an American is itself American," despite the circumstances of it being "begun when Franklin was still a loyal British subject; written in English, not American; modeled avowedly on the styles of Bunyan and Defoe and on the genre of advice to apprentices; prompted initially by demands from London editors; composed largely in Europe; and published first in a French translation, in Paris."[13] Yet to point out the arbitrary way in which national literary traditions have been defined, as Spengemann does so well, is not necessarily to invalidate the usefulness or pertinence of such distinctions. William Faulkner and Arnold Bennett both wrote in English, but Mississippi is not the same place as Stoke-on-Trent, and some recognition of the substantial differences in their respective material cultures may help a reader to grasp how these fictional representations work. Spengemann's approach involves a mode of linguistic idealism whereby narrower nationalist idioms are cast aside as misleading or irrelevant, but this can work implicitly to shore up a style of cultural transcendence which would effectively proscribe the disruptive discontinuities of social formation and political change.

Where this thesis does seem most effective, though, is in relation to the area traditionally defined as "early American literature"—a category Spengemann suggests should be renamed "the literature of British America," on the grounds that even the phrase "American literature" did not come into being until the post-Revolutionary 1780s. He points out that Americanists have been so intent upon trying to identify what is specifically "American" about their chosen texts that they have too easily aligned seventeenth-century typology with nineteenth-century symbolism as different temporal modulations of one ideal American tradition. This has meant the metaphysical ingenuities of Edward Taylor, for instance, have been read as anticipating those of Emily Dickinson, while conversely "figures who cannot be made into forebears of the nineteenth century," poets who resist being requisitioned as patriotic precursors of the great American renaissance, "are largely ignored."[14] The different political circumstances appertaining to America before the 1780s, the fact that it was still a colonial outpost of the Crown, lend Spengemann's arguments a direct plausibility in this area which they sometimes strain to achieve in other contexts. Such a conception of "British America" becomes still more resonant if we follow the historical line of John M. Murrin, who argues it was through "closer and continuous contact with metropolitan England—London culture and the central government" that the American colonies became "more like each other" during the eighteenth century. In Murrin's view, it was British imperial ambitions that served as the "main counterpoise" to regional diversity in the American colonies, so that, paradoxically, they began to acquire structural similarities and a greater sense of American identity precisely through their subaltern relationship with Great Britain.[15]

The institutional histories of "English literature" and "American literature" have been amply covered elsewhere, but my general point is that recent understandings of these subjects have often been framed, covertly if not overtly, by particular sectional interests which have tended to occlude the more disruptive forces of interference and alterity.[16] The retrospective fabrication of national tradition becomes a reverse projection whereby utopian hopes for the future are displaced back into an idealized version of the past. In 1961, for instance, Raymond Williams wrote of his belief that a nation's culture "both organizes and continues to express a common meaning by which its people live." Williams elaborated:

In many societies it has been the function of art to embody what we can call the common meanings of the society. The artist is not describing new experiences, but embodying known experiences. There is great danger in the assumption that art serves only on the frontiers of knowledge. It serves on those frontiers, particularly in disturbed and rapidly changing societies. Yet it serves, also, at the very centre of societies. It is often through the art that the society expresses its sense of being a society.[17]

As with Matthiessen, we may sense lurking in Williams's view of artistic representation a myth of Eden and the Fall, a shadow of the ideal organic community that appears to constitute an imaginary paradise lost. The issue here is not, of course, to attempt to imagine some impossible place "beyond" ideology, an arena where literary response might transcend the partiality and limitations of cultural politics. What I am suggesting, however, is that those perceptions of "common meanings" have too often tended to privilege versions of the literary canon that work simply to underwrite forms of national or political identity. Ideas of what might constitute common meaning naturally differ, but any text that might interfere with such designs comes to be treated with suspicion. All this constitutes, on a grand scale, what Werner Sollors has called the mystique of "insiderism," the pastoralization of an "'in-group' vantage point," centered around "the old ethnic ontologies of 'authentic cultures.'"[18] This was the mythical insiderism that would claim only those located in a privileged position inside some particular culture should be qualified to speak about it. Within this circle, no aesthetic judgment could finally be open to contradiction, since it would be protected by that over-arching moral metanarrative to which the critic subscribes.

*   *   *

It is in a move to disrupt this self-perpetuating interaction between aesthetic responses and ethical assumptions that I am proposing here to set up a frame-work where the emergence of American literature can be re-read in the light of British culture and vice versa. By problematizing the boundaries of "American literature," it may be possible to bring to the surface some of those issues that critical narratives based upon a coherent teleology of national identity necessarily leave out. In interrogating associations between the construction of national mythologies and the institutionalization of literary canons, I am following in the theoretical path of recent critics such as Robert Weisbuch, Paul Gilroy, Michael Warner, Myra Jehlen, and Jim Egan, all of whom have sought to reposition the emergence of American literature within a transatlantic context, even though this particular work approaches the subject in another way.[19]

In *Atlantic Double-Cross* (1986), Weisbuch takes his direction from Harold Bloom as he describes how American authors in the "age of Emerson" sought deliberately to defend their imaginative scope against the more stifling modes of British empiricism. In Weisbuch's eyes, the American authors of this period were aggressively inventing a new style of writing where "ontological insecurity be-comes epistemological experiment": Melville, for example, is said to have pro-duced his short story, "Bartleby, the Scrivener" (1853), as a direct critique of the representation of the legal system in *Bleak House*, first published by Dickens in serial form a year earlier. Melville, argues Weisbuch, "implicitly yet fiercely at-tacks a kind of cowardly refusal on Dickens's part to dig for disturbing, obscure truth": whereas Dickens's representation of the court of Chancery relapses fi-nally into a sentimental complicity with English social values, Melville's Bartleby stands out in a more principled rejection of property and propriety.[20] Yet while Weisbuch's account of these crosscurrents is often very insightful, one effect of his analysis is to reinforce a doctrine of American romanticism, where the followers of Emerson strive to transcend the "low common sense" of British literary and philosophical perspectives by invoking an emancipatory form of idealism, what Weisbuch describes as a "reverse verisimilitude, life modeled on the mind's de-sign." Another consequence of this kind of antithesis is to leave the conceptual parameters of British literature relatively intact; indeed, Weisbuch argues that

"The Americans matter far less to their British contemporaries than the British do to the Americans."[21] By contrast, my aim in this project is to highlight some of the contortions and reversals that emerge within both national traditions when they are brought into dialogue with each other. The emphasis here is upon neither consolidating nor ignoring nationalism as a principle in the formation of cultures, but upon ways in which the definitions of such cultures becomes twisted and grotesquely perverted through various forms of entanglement with opposing centers of gravity.

Paul Gilroy's *The Black Atlantic* (1993) has been one of the most influential attempts of recent years to map out an "alternative to the nationalist focus which dominates cultural criticism," a focus he equates with "the tragic popularity of ideas about the integrity and purity of cultures."[22] (In an earlier work, published in 1987, Gilroy specifically indicts the collusion of Raymond Williams with these racial theories of "national belonging."[23]) Rather than romanticizing categories like "race," "people" or "nation," Gilroy seeks to foreground the "rhizomorphic" quality of diasporic formations predicated upon "mutuality and reciprocity," the "transnational structures of circulation and intercultural exchange."[24] As a manifesto, this is excellent; but it is at times curiously reminiscent of the writings of Enlightenment philosophes, with its vision of how a seamless cosmopolitan world of exchange might gradually supersede "overintegrated conceptions of pure and homogeneous culture." Gilroy is right to see the pressures of globalization and cultural hybridity as a means of destabilizing the pernicious force of organic national ideals, rooted as they are in particular forms of racism and "ethnically cleansed canon-building operations"; but it is less clear that the intercalation of literary and national narratives could so easily be wished away or written off merely as a regrettable by-product of the infamous "canon wars" in twentieth-century academia.[25] In retracing British and American literary history from *The Dunciad* and *The Anarchiad* through to Washington Irving and Anthony Trollope, it becomes clear that questions of national identity and attachment to imagined communities are sedimented, often in opaque and unconscious ways, within these works.[26] Consequently, challenges to such identity and affiliation tend to produce more violent textual ructions and figurative displacements than are suggested within the mobile rhetoric of *The Black Atlantic*, and Gilroy's utopian agenda becomes even more apparent in his most recent work, *Against Race* (2000), which seeks altogether to renounce race and nation as the basis for identity and to imagine a mode of "planetary humanism," a "heterocultural, postanthropological, and cosmopolitan yet-to-come."[27]

Although Gilroy's work has emerged from a line of British cultural studies more obviously connected with sociology rather than aesthetics, it helped to shape the thematic direction of *The English Literatures of America, 1500–1800*, a highly influential anthology of writings produced in 1997 by Myra Jehlen and Michael Warner, which sets out to treat pre-Revolutionary Atlantic culture as all of one piece. Again, this anthology opens up a wide range of new materials for academic discussion, and this in itself provides a welcome antidote to more standard accounts of early British and American literature. Through the book's very emphasis on diversity and heterogeneity, though, there appears to be sometimes a danger of glossing over the sharper points of difference within this Atlantic world. Discussing seventeenth-century Virginia, Jehlen writes of how a "creole culture appears as the system of English ways adapts in the New World to an alternative way of life"; but the anthology as a whole is not quite so illuminating on areas where such adaptations were harder to accommodate.[28] Dissensus, in other words, is embraced more readily than division. In part, this is because the hegemonic status of British literature, especially in the eighteenth century, has been partially suppressed here: Pope is only notionally represented, and this means the unbalanced circulation of power between opposing sides of the Atlantic remains relatively occluded. Jehlen and Warner seek to intervene within contemporary debates about the canon in the way their anthology finds space for marginalized voices, but it tends to understate the ways in which American writers were being forced to negotiate a rhetorical position for themselves within complex and unequal networks of transatlantic privilege. There have been various other moves recently to expand the "Early American Canon," to move it away from an "Anglo-oriented 'agenda'" by embracing works from sources other than New England male intellectuals.[29] While these interventions are timely and important, they too risk seeking to erase the specter of imperial power simply by ignoring it.

Such power plays were by no means confined to the region of New England, which was anyway less "Anglo-oriented" in some respects than other colonies. A writer like William Byrd II, for example, was not simply offering a direct account of his hybridized cultural experience within the creole world of Virginia in the 1720s, but rather engaging in elaborate textual play between the colloquial dialects of rural America and the supposedly masterful language of London. Byrd thus appropriates the idea of a dividing line as a formal principle within his writing, allowing the idea of a distant rhetorical authority to shadow and ironize his autochthonous texts, even as he uses colloquial Americanisms to transgress knowingly against the standards of British imperialism. It is this sense of doubleness and duplicity that many American writers of this time skillfully work with; these, however, are precisely the kinds of formal relations that can be understood only by reading British and American literatures in parallel. To restore an American dimension to British literature of this period is to denaturalize it, to suggest the historical contingencies that helped formulate the dynamics of Augustan order and imperial control. Conversely, to restore a British dimension to American literature is to politicize it: to reveal its intertwinement with the discourses of heresy, blasphemy, and insurrection, rather than understanding that writing primarily as an expression of local cultures or natural rights.

This is not, of course, to imagine that the different regions of America were culturally homogeneous, or that they reflected British traditions in exactly the same way. Describing variations between the New England and Chesapeake colonies in the seventeenth century, Jack P. Greene observes how it "is hardly possible to conceive how any two settlements composed almost entirely of Englishmen could have been much more different": New England more traditional, communal, and hierarchical; Chesapeake more secular, materialistic, and individualist in orientation.[30] My argument, however, concerns not so much the social and economic relations between Britain and its erstwhile colonies, but rather ways in which a reverse projection of Britain manifests itself in the consciousness of American writers, just as the prospect of America produces various forms of disturbance within English texts. Byrd's Virginia, Dwight's Connecticut, and Irving's New York all refract the world of old England in a different manner, but in each case we see at work an implicit double perspective which serves to formulate the indigenous culture comparatively, in terms of what it is not. This mirrors what Greene and J. R. Pole have referred to as "the larger picture" within "colonial British-America," where, for all the variations among different regions, "their status as colonies meant that they were subjected to a common imperial policy and operated within a roughly similar political framework."[31] The general point here turns upon ways in which British and American cultures in this pre-Revolutionary period were symbiotically intertwined. Jim Egan has observed how the English community in seventeenth-century New England understood itself as the very embodiment of "Englishness," so that the disputes which inevitably began to emerge there over the nature of government—controversies attributed by John Winthrop to corrupting forces back in England—could aptly be described in terms of an "insurrection," an "inversion—or antibody if you will—capable of undermining the health of the body politic from within."[32] Consequently, to describe the formation of an identifiably American culture as predicated upon indigenous conceptions of native "experience" is, at best, misleading. Early American experience was a duplicitous and frequently paradoxical business.

In light of this complex kind of political framework, the comparative methodology here should be seen as significantly different from that quest for that "ideal universality," in René Wellek's phrase, characteristic of comparative literature when the subject began to flourish in the American academy during the 1950s. Wellek, a prominent figure in this old comparative literature school, used to complain reasonably enough about "the narrow nationalism of much nineteenth-century scholarship," pointing out how this conception of literature as expressing a national spirit developed only in the wake of the patriotic political movements of the late eighteenth century, with their romantic attachment to the inherent values of the native soil.[33] Yet, by one of the ironies associated with comparative literature, it was this rise of nationalism that initially formed the basis for a more internationalist approach, as Goethe and others sought to establish dialogues between the local and the universal so as to circumvent the theoretical parameters of newly emerging national identities.[34] In recent times, comparative literature has come to be associated more frequently with notions of relativism or skepticism: it induces a "broader vision," claimed comparativist Jonathan Culler in 1986, which "exercises a critical demystificatory force on the cultural pieties of a nation." In 1990, Earl Miner's treatise comparing European and Japanese cultures similarly concluded: "The great gain for intercultural comparative study is that it avoids taking the local for the universal, the momentary for the constant, and, above all, the familiar for the inevitable."[35] We can no longer talk simply about "French" or "British" or "American" literature; but we can map out cross-cultural force fields in what Edward Said calls a "contrapuntal" way, so as to circumvent the various binary oppositions that still operate on the boundaries of national identity. The goal is not to be all-encompassing but, in Said's words, to "move beyond insularity and provincialism."[36]

This is why the idiom of comparativist defamiliarization generally finds itself at odds with the more mimetic strategies endorsed by many practitioners of American studies. Fredric Jameson—who, as an American specialist in French literature, also emerges from a comparativist background—has written of the "fundamental" tension between comparative literature and "fields of study for which the term 'area studies' seems the most appropriate."[37] As Jameson notes, the "relationality" implied by the former works against the "disciplinary autonomy" demanded by the latter; moreover, the exclusive emphasis placed by area-based academics upon (for example) the American elements in American studies serves to ensure this area becomes increasingly inward-looking and self-defining the more successful and coherent it becomes. Jameson finds such scholarly perimeters peculiarly inappropriate in this developing age of "global culture," where multinational capitalism and communications are rendering the idea of independent cultures and clear national boundaries increasingly problematical. This is not to say local issues have become irrelevant or unimportant; it is, though, to refuse "the temptation of isolationism and specialisation" and to move instead toward what Jameson calls *an internationalization of national situations*—a cultural internationalism which, owing to its keener sense of its own internal national situation, is first and foremost attentive to the structural and historical difference of the national situation of other countries, and reads their culture off that, just as its therapeutic distance from its own culture is acquired by its recognition of its own structural limits and peculiarities. This programme also includes a healthy curiosity about the projects and priorities of intellectuals in other countries (along with a healthy relativism with respect to our own), which is a form of recognition and respect.[38]

Though Jameson is careful here to avoid undermining altogether the validity of local situations, this general shift from nationality to estrangement, from thematic content to global form, necessarily problematizes those conceptual categories bound up with custom and locality: ethos, ethics, ethnicity. This in turn casts disconcerting shadows over academic discourses bound up with narrowly de-fined areas of indigenous principle.

A brief consideration of John Carlos Rowe's *At Emerson's Tomb*, published in 1997, might help to clarify some of these tensions between comparativism and area studies which Jameson talks about. Taking issue with "the Emersonian tradition of 'aesthetic dissent'" which has dominated American literature, Rowe seeks to introduce various "supplements"—represented here by the narratives of Frederick Douglass and Harriet Jacobs—that might "provide a cultural founda-tion for utopian ideals of equal justice and opportunity."[39] He cites with approba-tion the moves of Eric J. Sundquist and Paul Lauter to read less celebrated books alongside famous canonical texts, saying he "would describe this sort of literary criticism as *comparative*, even if it deals primarily with U.S. works and cultures." Rowe then goes on to outline his plan for reading comparatively three established literary traditions—European-American, African-American and American wom-en's writing—so as to look for points of incompatibility as well as intersection between them.[40] But while this strategy may be valuable in itself, it is hard to think of it as "comparative" in any meaningful sense, since Rowe's agenda in-volves less a transnational displacement of Emersonian dissent than the recuper-ation of U.S. minority cultures into a very familiar paradigm of self-reliance.

To regard comparative criticism as synonymous with the circumference of "U.S. works and cultures" is, therefore, to risk reproducing the most predictable kind of American cultural hegemony. This is where the influence of much earlier critics like Bourne and Matthiessen still manifests itself in American literary studies. It is not, of course, that the canonical texts advocated by these famous scholars have remained unchallenged, rather that their affiliation of "American" modes of expression with particular models of national consciousness has led to similar cultural values being displaced onto different kinds of narrative. The forms of idealism once associated exclusively with Emerson and Thoreau are now relocated in the figures of Douglass and Jacobs. Within this constitutionally liberal domain, the talismanic figure of heterogeneity and the imperative of multiple voices are valorized by being incorporated within the charmed circle of national protectionism.

By examining various facets of the interaction and intersection of British and American writing around the time of the Revolution, I hope to elucidate the inchoate nature of texts in which conceptions of national identity were much more divided and unstable. One of the complaints often made about the comparative method in general is that it produces, in Peter Carafiol's words, "accounts that leave the essentials of the tradition in place, particularly the faith that there is a distinct American literary tradition (portrayed in familiar terms) that can be compared to other coherent traditions."[41] But the logic of paradox here is designed specifically to counter a simple reproduction of such essentializing idioms. Rather than just playing off an "American" Washington Irving against an "English" Jane Austen, this paradoxical perspective works to transform both sides of the equation equally, representing a different Austen in the light of Britain's conflict with America and a different Irving in the light of his nostalgia for England.

Over the last few years, there have been various manifestos calling for a movement beyond the circumference of the national boundaries traditionally deployed as an explanatory context for American works. To take just one example, the September 1998 issue of *American Literature* featured an essay by Lawrence Buell suggesting that "a modest—but certainly not at all trivial—first step that would test Americanists' powers of stretchability would be for U.S. literary studies to make the 'Atlantic culture' move more than it does."[42] As an abstract principle this may be admirable, but in practice such impulses toward internationalism have consorted uneasily with powerful attachments to notions of local or national identity, both in the era of the American Revolution and today. Consequently, as we shall see later, a twenty-first-century version of comparative literature needs to situate itself on a dangerous and uncomfortable boundary where residual assumptions about autochthonous identity are traversed by something different.[43] This line of approach involves not simply an easy elision of the national into the transnational, but rather a consideration of various points of friction where these two discourses intersect. From this perspective, the cultures of Britain and America do not so much define themselves against each other as surreptitiously twist each other into strange, apparently unnatural forms.

In the chapters that follow, I trace the paradoxical interplay between American and British cultures from the earlier part of the eighteenth century, when the New England colonies were starting to drift away from their Puritan moorings, through until about the middle of the nineteenth century, which was the last time Britain was roughly equivalent to the United States in terms of population and economic power.[44] My chronological boundaries are relatively fluid: in 1730, Pope was writing his *Essay on Man*, which was to become his most influential work in America, while 1860 saw the publication of Hawthorne's last novel, *The Marble Faun*, and the serialization of *Framley Parsonage*, the fourth in Trollope's *Chronicles of Barsetshire*. I discuss a few texts that fall outside these parameters, particularly novels published by Trollope in the 1860s and 1870s that offer illuminating comparisons with Hawthorne's works; but these dates should give a fair indication of my interests, which are mainly in the antebellum period. In chapters 1 and 2, I explore how Pope's neoclassicism was imitated and reimagined in pre-Revolutionary New England; in chapters 3 and 4, I examine the involvement of Franklin and Jefferson with European writers; in chapters 5, 6, and 7, I focus on the long aftermath of the American Revolution, so as to consider how competing versions of racial and national identity emerged from within various circuits of transnational exchange. In all of these analyses, my purpose is to bring literary and generic models into a suggestive dialogue with cultural and historical contexts, working on the understanding that (for instance) Jefferson's approach to political notions of national sentiment and the American sublime would have been intellectually inflected by his interest in the writings of Thomas Paine, Edmund Burke, or, his favorite author, Laurence Sterne. Similarly, my consideration of how Hawthorne and Trollope approached the Victorian conception of the family romance is conditioned by the relocation of this genre within a post-Revolutionary context, where both authors can be seen as responding belatedly to the trauma of a British civil war. As Hawthorne made explicit in his introduction to *The Scarlet Letter*, the consolidation of national identity as an extension of familial feeling and inherited custom was shadowed at this time by uncomfortable memories of consanguineous conflict.

It would be foolish not to be aware of the many absences and elisions circumscribing this account of reciprocal transatlantic influences over the course of some 130 years. However, my concern has been not so much with history as such, but with the consequences and implications of history's displacement into narrative forms, forms used to underwrite and valorize particular versions of national identity. I am aware that most of the authors discussed here enjoy some kind of canonical status within their own native tradition, but it is often a cloudy or partial status: the Connecticut Wits are almost invariably thought of as reactionary and tedious, and are rarely examined for their comic potential; Franklin and Jefferson are seen primarily as politicians rather than as writers of satire or sensibility; Austen, Irving, and Trollope have been frequently patronized as genteel and conformist. I have, therefore, chosen to place various categories and authors commonly kept apart into heterodox juxtaposition in the hope of disturbing some of these preconceptions, while also considering how these celebrated figures relate to less illustrious writers such as Gilbert Imlay and Olaudah Equiano. Through a strategy of reading British and American authors against each other, my purpose has been not so much to chart a network of direct influences, but rather to elucidate some of those blindspots commonly overlooked within a trajectory of grand national narratives. Unobstructed teleologies of national identity often obscure more than they reveal, and one reason for the invocation of this paradoxical America is to acknowledge, as the Renaissance cartographers recognized, not only how the flat geographical maps of the Earth had been altered by the appearance of this new continent, but also how the particular perspective of the Old World in relation to itself was being thrown disconcertingly into relief.

Chapter One
The Art of Sinking
Alexander Pope and Mather Byles

The English poet most often seen as giving sustenance to the literature of early America is John Milton. According to Jay Fliegelman, Milton's Adam became idealized in America as a heroic rebel against authority, while the quest in *Paradise Lost* to establish a human rather than divinely ordained Eden was seen as a correlative to the American impulse to escape British oppression.[1] This, of course, is to understand Milton as a poet of the sublime, a prophetic harbinger of freedom: "Milton's great and distinguished excellence," wrote Hugh Blair in 1784, was his "sublimity." Subsequently, George F. Sensabaugh has described how, in this revolutionary era, Milton's capacity for transcendence was appropriated to provide intellectual justification for the rising glory of America.[2] In the proclivity within his political writings to question the legitimacy of authority while emphasizing the self-regulating character of dissent, Milton became institutionalized as an avatar of the emerging republicanism and romanticism of the new nation. Thus, K. P. Van Anglen characterizes ways in which Milton anticipates the Transcendentalist doctrines of Emerson and Thoreau, while Keith W. F. Stavely even more explicitly aligns the influence of Milton with what he calls "a coherent ideology of Puritan radicalism" running through from the theocratic framework of seventeenth-century New England to its more secularized manifestations in nineteenth-century American literature.[3] Harold Bloom, similarly, finds his chosen "strong" writers in the American poetic pantheon—Emerson, Whitman, Stevens—to be arguing implicitly with the patriarchal "shadow of Milton" through an intertextual "anxiety of influence."[4]

A poetic teleology linking Milton with Whitman, however, bears uncomfortable similarities to Perry Miller's construction of an American intellectual tradition running from seventeenth-century Puritans through Jonathan Edwards to Emerson and the romantics. This works to privilege certain kinds of progressive thought, to equate American culture with the impetus of what Emerson called "an original relation to the universe," and to see the crucial tension within American culture as a perpetual conflict between authority and self-legitimation, the old light versus the new.[5] This leads to the ironic situation, as Sacvan Bercovitch and others have noted, whereby strategies of dissent become a ritualistic convention in themselves; it also helps to account for the tired dichotomy between subversion and containment that runs throughout New Historicist criticism, where apparently radical positions outside social conventions are revealed as already incorporated within and therefore complicit with them.[6] This conceptual axis of originality and incorporation is dependent upon what Vincent Carretta has called a "Whig interpretation of literature," which, he argues, "operates just as strongly as a Whig interpretation of history to distort our view of the past."[7] Just as E. P. Thompson and his school of historians looked back to the eighteenth century for gleanings of radical dissent, so even the most sympathetic literary historians of this period have lamented the "excruciating" nature of American poetry in the eighteenth century, its conservative reproduction of a "neoclassical imitativeness that retarded American belles lettres in general during this period."[8]

My purpose in these first two chapters is to challenge such assumptions by reexamining American poetry of the eighteenth century in the light of Alexander Pope rather than Milton. The poets I have chosen mainly to focus upon, Mather Byles and John Trumbull, tend to follow Pope in their willingness to embrace contraries, to explore contradictions, rather than attempting to sublimate them into a struggle between the forces of light and darkness. There are, of course, other figures I might have chosen: Joseph Green or Francis Hopkinson, for example, or other Connecticut Wits like David Humphreys. As Michael Warner has observed, eighteenth-century Anglo-American poetry "still awaits a systematic treatment," and my intention here is to offer indicative readings rather than impose canonical judgments.[9] Nevertheless, both Byles and Trumbull testify to the significance of Pope in America in the way they reflect some of the elaborate paradoxes in eighteenth-century North Atlantic culture. In particular, they recognize, with some discomfort, that scientific changes and various forms of insurrection from within the framework of the body politic were creating a situation within which ideas of social order and cultural authenticity were becoming subject to violent fluctuation.

One theory of Pope's influence in America is that it was evident more in the engaged, journalistic verse that preceded the Revolution: "If Americans wrote for the age in Popean couplets," argued Sensabaugh, "they aspired to write for the ages in Miltonic language and style."[10] Again, though, this would seem retrospectively to be approaching Pope from a post-romantic perspective, assuming a division between common politics and an aesthetics of the sublime that would not have been obvious at the time. Indeed, while it may seem strange today to begin a study of American literature with a discussion of Alexander Pope, to Americans of the eighteenth century such a lineage would have seemed not only natural but inevitable, since Pope's writings were enormously popular in America during this era. All of the colonial leaders admired him: Benjamin Franklin particularly enjoyed reading Pope's letters; Thomas Jefferson recorded choice quotations from the great man's poetry in his commonplace book; George Washington owned the collected works in six volumes, together with separate editions of Pope's translations of the *Iliad* and *Odyssey*.[11] Within the revolutionary era, Pope's works accomplished the difficult feat of appealing to those on either side of the political spectrum. Jonathan Odell, as a staunch Tory and Loyalist, cherished Pope as an emblem of social stability and traditional hierarchy: in 1768, he contributed to the *Pennsylvania Chronicle* a panegyric to Pope's garden at Twickenham, where the English poet's "unostentatious seat" came to appear as a model of divinely sanctioned order, while the "deathless song" of the verse itself showed "divinely justified / The ways of GOD to man."[12] Conversely, revolutionary spirits such as Philip Freneau and Joel Barlow were also great admirers of Pope's genius: Barlow visited Twickenham in homage during his radical years as an honorary French citizen, declaring how "None of the temples and palaces of Europe have forced themselves upon me with such silent veneration and respect as I felt on entering the simple garden of Pope." Despite their very different political positions, Barlow shared with Pope a sense of antagonism toward the climate of financial corruption and venality that both poets regarded as a threat to the "natural" order of society.[13] For Pope, of course, this order was aristocratic; for Barlow, democratic.

It was not until the nineteenth century that Pope's star in America began to dim. For the Federalist mind of John Sylvester John Gardiner in 1806, Pope could still represent a conservative bulwark against impending chaos, despite the poet's loss of reputation in recent years:

It has been the fashion of late years to depreciate the poetical merit of Pope, and to exalt, in strains of lavish encomium, the mushroom poetasters of the day. . . . These gentlemen require originality at the expense of whatever absurdity. . . . But true taste admires nature only in her charms, not in the gross. . . . High, masterly execution is what constitutes a preeminent writer. He exhibits the best thoughts, exprest in the best manner.[14]

Yet the overtones of cultural elitism here—"masterly execution," "the best manner"—imply just those ways in which Pope's style was increasingly being resisted at this time. For Richard Henry Dana Sr., writing in the *North American Review* of 1819, Pope altogether lacked the requisite poetical qualities of pathos and sublimity; his language comprised merely "cold abstractions," lacking any emotive "attachments or association." Indeed, wrote Dana, as if to clinch his argument, "The truth is, Pope had no more idea of a poetical language than a Frenchman." Unlike Barlow, Dana viewed Pope not so much as a social satirist but in the light of emerging ideologies of romanticism and nationalism, where poets were supposed to discover some "organic" relationship to their native traditions. Stylistically, he found Pope too neoclassical and impersonal to fit that particular mold.[15]

Dana's response was predictable enough in terms of how nineteenth-century aesthetics were developing, and it betokens a general shift in critical sensibility during this century, a shift by no means confined simply to America. In 1880, Matthew Arnold was to spurn Pope's "style of versification" as having been "conceived and composed" in his "wits," whereas "genuine poetry," said Arnold, should be "conceived and composed in the soul."[16] But Dana's response is also interesting because it so clearly foreshadows the intellectual prejudices of later American scholars against Pope's kind of neoclassical idiom. Between the wars, Pope was being rehabilitated in England by T. S. Eliot, who declared "no person of our time can be said to know what poetry is unless he enjoys the poetry of Pope as poetry"—for its precise language and autotelic form, that is, rather than for any emotional "effect."[17] On the other hand, Vernon Louis Parrington in 1925 was still finding Pope's satire to be "mean and vindictive," and he went on to dismiss the Connecticut Wits, the most famous of Pope's poetic followers in America, as "the literary old guard of eighteenth-century Toryism, the expiring gasp of a rationalistic age, given to criticism, suspicious of all emotion, contemptuous of idealistic programs."[18] Some sixteen years after Parrington, F. O. Matthiessen echoed his countryman's romantic idealism when he accused these eighteenth-century "followers of Pope" of ignorance about how "poetic rhythm was an organic response to the centers of experience—to the internal pulsations of the body, to its external movements in work and in making love, to such sounds as the wind and the sea." For Matthiessen, the intellectual originality of Transcendentalism appeared as a necessary, indeed overdue antidote to the desiccated circumstances of post-Revolutionary American culture. "Pope was still the great poet in the Cambridge that Holmes and Lowell knew as boys," he observed, but, fortunately for the development of American literature, Emerson perceived the deficiencies of such "correct and bloodless gentility" and set the national culture on a new path.[19]

As Lydia Dittler Schulman has remarked, it is interesting that the most vehement opponents of Milton's poetic style among twentieth-century American writers have been expatriates like Eliot and Ezra Pound, who also chose to distance themselves from America's republican political tradition.[20] Eliot's marked preference for Pope rather than Milton can be seen as the corollary of our now traditional academic association of American poetry with the practice of romanticism, an affiliation that has served to marginalize those different aesthetic models that were so popular throughout the eighteenth century. This has created the critical opposition familiar to us today whereby Pope and Eliot are represented as the formal, conservative antithesis to an American literary republicanism which, inspired ultimately by Milton, runs through Emerson and Whitman into the radical poetics of the twentieth century. Yet, to see Pope in this way as an agent of reaction is to oversimplify, for to review his poetic legacy in America during the years leading up to the Revolution is to reconstitute a situation where aesthetic effects were bound up more explicitly with current events and political choices. Rhetorics of republican integrity or romantic sublimity were foreign to most eighteenth-century poets, who reveled in a world that was both fractured and fractious.

Under these circumstances, it may seem strange that revisions of the American literary canon under the aegis of New Historicism in its various forms should have paid so little attention to the intensely political and popular poetry of the eighteenth century.[21] Whereas innumerable arguments have been made for the novels of Harriet Beecher Stowe and Louisa May Alcott on the basis of their social and cultural significance, the same service has not been performed for John Trumbull's 1782 mock-epic poem *M'Fingal*, which went through twenty-three editions in forty years, nor for the widely-read *Anarchiad*, composed by Trumbull and others, which appeared in twelve numbers in the *New Haven Gazette* and the *Connecticut Magazine* between October 1786 and September 1787 and which exercised an important influence upon the Constitutional Convention at Philadelphia. Trumbull's poetry, in fact, enjoyed a similar kind of relationship to the time of the American Revolution as did *Uncle Tom's Cabin* to the Civil War era, but the authors' subsequent reputations in the annals of American literature are nowhere near equivalent. There are various fairly obvious reasons for this, including the fact that prose fiction, especially prose fiction with a clear moral message, is generally easier than poetry to assimilate within parallel discursive frameworks. Moreover, as John P. McWilliams, Jr., has pointed out, in a situation where the New Critical ideals of well-wrought urns and close textual readings are still so prominent, it is difficult to persuade students of poetry to engage with the prolix allusiveness of a Trumbull or a Timothy Dwight.[22] But some of this resistance may also be ideological. Whereas Stowe and Alcott merge nicely with a refurbished version of transcendental optimism—a traditional American idealism modulated to take account of gender and racial differences—the satire of Trumbull and Dwight remains less easy to incorporate: more edgy, more self-contradictory, less reconciling. To trace Pope's poetic legacy throughout eighteenth-century America is to recover an art located firmly within the public sphere, a discourse engaged overtly with political events. Yet the genius of this kind of writing was developed within a complex aesthetic framework of the paradoxical and burlesque, a skeptical framework that came largely to be smothered by subsequent naturalizations of romanticism as nationalist ideology.

*   *   *

Pope himself has always been a slippery figure to write about, a poet often regarded in his own time as ultraconservative, yet whose very anachronisms suggest his poetry's irrepressibly ludic quality, its deliberate transgression against a world of empiricism and ethics. On the surface, of course, Pope represents the epitome of common sense and good taste: in "Epistle to Dr. Arbuthnot," the author plays off the inclinations of "Sporus" (Lord John Hervey) for "Fancy's maze," "vile Antithesis" and "see-saw" wit against the more "manly" poet who "stoop'd to Truth, and moraliz'd his song."[23] Simply to invert this dichotomy, to claim Pope was "really" more attracted by wit than morality, would be too simplistic. Yet the brilliance of Pope's art lies in the way these two qualities clash up against each other: sense and sensibility are continually pressuring and interfering with each other, thereby creating a poetic world balanced dangerously on a knife-edge between the decorous and the duplicitous. The tantalizing pleasures of Pope's style derive from a delight in breaching decorum, in transgressing against formal codes of behavior, codes which, however, never cease to exist. The Victorian sense of Pope as a conservative figure was generally superseded in the late twentieth century by an acknowledgment of how his art, as Helen Deutsch said in 1996, "has something of the monstrous and the illicit in it."[24] In fact, though, Pope's poetry can be categorized finally as neither reactionary nor radical, neither light nor dark, since it operates in an ambivalent area where both sides of this equation are present simultaneously. Hence Pope's frequent use of pun, paradox, and oxymoron; he invents a world where, as the "Epistle to Lord Cobham" puts it, "puzzling Contraries confound the whole" (65), where social facades can belie private motives. In "Epistle to Dr. Arbuthnot," the author looks down on those who "Damn with faint praise, assent with civil leer" (201); but the way this grotesquely humorous phrase twists itself back oxymoronically within the conventional form of the iambic pentameter implies how Pope's subversive energies achieve their pleasantly rebarbative force from rubbing up against polite society, rather than trying to rub it out. Pope neither moralizes in the pure sense, nor simply allows his ludic qualities free play; the pleasure of his texts arises from the way in which ethics and aesthetics come together in a precarious balance, the way his double-edged discourse locates itself precisely on a boundary between official propriety and improper transgression.

Many recent treatments of Augustan poetry have considered it as "an arena of ideological conflict," refracting various cultural tensions in eighteenth-century England.[25] However, Pope's relationship with both Augustan England and Puritan America was also modulated crucially by theological differences which emerged out of his Roman Catholic cultural background. Though of course Catholics were no longer actively persecuted in eighteenth-century England, the anti-Catholic laws still compelled Pope to live at least ten miles outside London, and this, argues Pat Rogers, would have induced in the poet "a consciousness of exclusion and exile," a sense that he was being pushed both geographically and metaphorically away "from the centre of things."[26] Consequently, Pope's universe never coincided unproblematically with those "imperial thematics" David S. Shields locates within the Augustan idioms of early eighteenth-century British verse, and which Joseph Roach associates specifically with Pope.[27] The sumptuous qualities of Pope's imagery relate not so much to self-centered appropriations based upon political or economic hegemony, but rather to the compulsions of witty extravagance, in the etymological sense of that word: a mode of transgression, a wandering outside and beyond. The circular motions of Pope's art thus turn not so much upon the expansive circuits of imperialism, but upon fictions of Catholic universalism, where no standpoint is allowed to remain undisturbed by its contrary. It is, for example, this catholicized version of universalism, centered around a paradoxical fusion of opposites, that informs the antagonism toward slavery expressed most explicitly in *Windsor-Forest* (1713). Pope here envisions a world of "order in variety," where apparent antitheses are found to be mutually complementary: "tho' all things differ, all agree" (15–16). Consequently, he disavows the categorical distinctions and binary divisions on which racial theory is predicated, evoking instead a metaphysical reconciliation of opposites, where "blended lie th' oppressor and th' opprest!" (318).

This is not reductively to rationalize Pope's perceptions of social and political difference simply in terms of the "Catholic" framework of his ideas.[28] Yet, there is an important sense in which the legacy of Pope crucially reorients eighteenth-century American poetry away from what Stavely calls "the radical Protestant tradition" toward a form of cultural catholicity which incorporates powerful elements of paradoxical comedy and the burlesque. This comedy is not just a stylistic phenomenon, but a mode of ideological difference which introduces shadows of alterity into the protected realms of American culture. In one of his attacks on Pope, John Dennis argued that the English poet "knows not his own mind, and frequently contradicts himself"; but this is actually a perceptive observation on the part of his famous enemy, for Pope's literary idiom embraces contradiction, antithesis, and paradox as a stylistic response to a circular universe that denies the possibility of ultimate logical coherence or philosophical closure.[29] Abhorring the seventeenth-century Cartesian attempt to reduce the world to an externalization of human reason, Pope juggles his paradoxical discourse so as to undermine the structures of rationalism and civilization, thereby permitting a representation of human folly (sexuality, scatology, and so on) as well as more conventional forms of human wisdom. In *The Praise of Folly* (1511), Erasmus, who was one of Pope's favorite authors, effectively revived this classical genre of adoxography, described by Emrys Jones as a "perverse or paradoxical *encomia*," involving "the rhetorical praise or defence of things of doubtful value."[30] For Pope, the willing embrace of scatology and absurdity on the part of Erasmus was a mark of his universalist spirit of toleration, his capacity to embrace diverse and contradictory positions. In a letter to Jonathan Swift, in fact, Pope paid homage to the Dutch writer by describing himself as "of the Religion of Erasmus, a Catholick."[31]

It is also interesting retrospectively to note how *The Praise of Folly* was published only five years before the appearance of Thomas More's *Utopia*, in 1516. Erasmus and More, who were friends, were both philosophically influenced by the specter of a new land to the west that was being explored as they were writing in the early sixteenth century. Erasmus describes his narrator as someone originating from the "Fortunate Isles," considered at that time to be part of the mysterious American continent, and he presents his ideas as directed against the orthodoxies then prevailing in Europe, just as More's *Utopia* works as an implicit critique of Old World models.[32] But while the discourse of utopianism subsequently became closely associated with American cultural values in many different ways, the discourse of adoxography did not. More's visionary humanism came to run in parallel with the American dream, whereas Erasmus's burlesque catholicity, on the whole, could not be reconciled with American liberal ideals. The reasons for this, I would suggest, can be seen as analogous to reasons why the poetry of romanticism became canonized within the framework of American literature while Pope's style of neoclassical paradoxology failed to achieve such a status. After the Revolution, in particular, conversion narratives, rather than perversion narratives, could be integrated most easily into the progressivist discourse of the national sublime.

Pope and his American followers, however, do not fit comfortably into this category of the sublime. After Erasmus, the most prominent intellectual influence on this double-edged school of poetry was the work of Montaigne, whose essay "Of the Inconsistency of Our Actions" was thought by Pope to be the best thing which the French philosopher wrote.[33] Both Erasmus and Montaigne worked from a position of Catholic skepticism, recognizing how the old systems of medieval theology had been broken up by the new Renaissance fields of empirical learning, but maintaining a strongly anti-dualistic outlook that resisted any Faustian aspirations toward intellectual self-reliance. Describing himself as a "very earthy person," Montaigne wrote of how "transcendental humours frighten me, like lofty and inaccessible heights"; and he urged the most exalted personages to recognize how "in the world it is still our own bottom that we sit on." Montaigne equated this condition of human fallibility with an ontological inability to achieve rational finality within the sphere of knowledge: "Only fools are certain and immovable," he wrote.[34] It was this kind of radical challenge to any kind of dogma, including Church dogma, that caused Montaigne's *Essays* to be placed on the Index in 1676. The Frenchman's philosophical skepticism was also strongly influenced by explorations of the New World that were being undertaken at the time he was writing: according to R. A. Sayce, America was "part of Montaigne's world-view . . . a key-point in his moral relativism."[35] Like Pope, Montaigne was interested in how projections of the other—particularly, in his case, American Indians—appeared as an alternative to the entrenched customs of European civilization.

The point here is not that Pope was attracted to orthodox Catholicism—as Samuel Johnson noted, the "zealous Papists" had no time for him, nor he for them—but rather that he was influenced by Catholic renegades like Erasmus, Montaigne, and also Pascal, all of whom rejected the strictures of Church theology while maintaining a cagey, fideist relationship with a transformed version of Catholic ideology.[36] From this perspective, Pope's renowned capacity for duplicity and stratagems, his "general habit of secrecy and cunning," as Johnson put it, might be traced not just to the insecurity of his own social position in eighteenth-century England, but to a more abstract and conceptual awareness of how any given position he might assume on a particular matter was, through the burlesque medium of cultural catholicity, prone to ironic reversal.[37] In the prefatory "Design" to *An Essay on Man* (1733–34), Pope claims the merit of the piece comes "in steering betwixt the extremes of doctrines seemingly opposite"; and though this has sometimes been interpreted as the search for some stabilizing moral anchor or golden mean, the general effect of *An Essay on Man* is rather to delight in balancing off contraries, inverting doctrinal theories, while declining to reach any firm resolution.[38] As David B. Morris observed, "paradox is the poem's governing trope, not merely a stylistic feature. . . . for Pope, paradox is his way not of recommending or embellishing truth but of recognizing and expressing it": each term within his paradoxical equations modifies its counterpart, thereby creating a systematic cycle of transgression against the boundaries of empirical logic and reason. Much to the disgust of Johnson, who complained about the poem's "vulgarity of sentiment," Pope abjures the prospects of rational closure and chooses to delight instead in the pleasures of adoxography.[39]

Fittingly, *An Essay on Man* engendered the only explicitly theological controversy concerning Pope's poetry during his lifetime, when in 1737 the Jesuit order officially retracted its good opinion of the poem. In the same year, a Swiss Protestant theologian, Jean-Pierre de Crousaz, discovered dangerous heresies and contradictions within Pope's text, indicating how the poem tended toward an outlook of fatalism rather than being underpinned by the dogmas of orthodox Christianity.[40] The theologian's sense of disquiet was not misplaced: *An Essay on Man* derives much of its radically ambiguous quality from a secularized form of Catholic universalism that refuses to leave any sectarian position unchallenged by some heterodox alternative, some circuit of alterity. This effectively subverts traditional Protestant understandings of religious morality, and it has significant implications for the way Pope's style was disseminated within the more austere, conventional communities of eighteenth-century America. The thrust of Pope's epic poem is how each element within creation should be seen as part of a greater whole, how all things should be understood in terms of degree and their position relative to other objects and events. This mode of catholicity can be seen directly to contradict the dualistic eschatologies of American Puritanism, where good and evil, spirit and matter, appeared to be irredeemably sundered. In Pope's eyes, no individual category or privileged spirit can present itself as purely autonomous or self-authenticating:

> The good must merit God's peculiar care;
> But who, but God, can tell us who they are?
> One thinks on Calvin Heav'n's own spirit fell,
> Another deems him instrument of hell;
> If Calvin feel Heav'n's blessing, or its rod,
> This cries there is, and that, there is no God.
> What shocks one part will edify the rest,
> Nor with one system can they all be blest. (IV, 135–43)

It is no coincidence the author chooses in this passage to focus upon Calvin. The Calvinistic emphasis upon special signs of divine election and self-justification is trumped, in Pope's perspective, by a larger scheme in which the polarities of Manichaean consciousness come to be invalidated by a universe of partiality and relativism:

> Slave to no sect, who takes no private road,
> But looks thro' Nature, up to Nature's God;
> Pursues that Chain which links th'immense designs,
> Joins heav'n and earth, and mortal and divine. (IV, 331–34)

It is, therefore, a misconception to insist upon Pope's reactionary adherence in this poem to some feudalistic notion of a "great chain of being." What is at issue is not so much hierarchy as reciprocal processes of intersection and transference, the ways in which any claim to independent human reason must always be held in check by a recognition of the incorrigibly mixed nature of mankind. This is where Pope's intellectual debt to Erasmus and Montaigne becomes most apparent:

> Man's superior part
> Uncheck'd may rise, and climb from art to art:
> But when his own great work is but begun,
> What Reason weaves, by Passion is undone. (II, 39–42)

According to the Jesuit philosophers, Cartesian rationalism erroneously attempted to divide spirit from body, mind from matter. This tended to foster the kind of dualism whereby man sought to transcend his lower being and aspire toward some kind of celestial status—the idea of "angelism," in Scholastic terms—without duly recognizing how the human condition is necessarily bound to the spheres of terrestrial limitation, spheres which cannot ultimately be overcome by the intellect of man.[41]

This is a theme Pope deals with more explicitly in book 4 of *The Dunciad* (1742), where one of the author's footnotes specifically names Descartes as the kind of reasoner inclined to "See all in *Self*, and but for self be born" (IV, 480). This establishment of "Self-love" as the "sole Principle of Action," continues Pope in another pietistic footnote to line 501, "is vain, wrong, and destructive to the happiness of mankind." This helps to clarify the aspects of Pope's poetry which the Protestant scholar, de Crousaz, found so off-putting. The Puritan emphasis upon predestined forms of divine election, and the more general Protestant imperative of moral independence and clearcut ethical choice, is dissolved by Pope into a world where nothing is ever quite black or white but rather infinite shades of gray. Faithful to his Catholic sensibility, if not to its theological sense, Pope sees various forms of grace inhering immanently within the natural world of creation, even in its postlapsarian state. Unlike Michael Wigglesworth or Jonathan Edwards, he does not regard such grace or gracefulness as a transcendent category to be wrought from outside by some kind of divine and supernatural light.

In considering, then, how the influence of Pope manifested itself in the New World, we encounter a series of disjunctions and apparent contradictions. While Pope's work appears in some ways to epitomize the virtues of reason and decorum, it also embodies an irrational and at times obscene force which runs alongside its veneer of politeness. While the poetry also seems to promote the values of moral order, this is countered by a concurrent subtext of the heterodox and grotesque, where any given position is liable to find itself stood on its head. In this sense, Pope introduces into the American scene a different way of looking at the world, one that quizzically interrogates the precepts of the Miltonic sublime by its elaboration of paradoxical continuities rather than radical schisms. Whereas the elegist for Lycidas sung of "fresh woods, and pastures new," Pope celebrates instead the more devious pleasures of imitation and transgression. Pope's discursive system of doubleness and division consequently stands as both a challenge and a potential threat to the American provincial world of civic modesty and ethical integrity.

*   *   *

How exactly did such languages of adoxography play themselves out in colonial America? We know *An Essay on Man* was by far the most popular of Pope's works in America, being reprinted some 160 times between its first appearance there in 1747 and the mid-nineteenth century. Perhaps, as Agnes Marie Sibley has argued, most Americans looked on it as a straightforwardly moralistic and Christian work rather than one contaminated with any hint of structural irony or (in Elwin Courthope's useful phrase) "Catholic Deism."[42] In his analysis of Enlightenment learning in America, Henry F. May acknowledges the vast popularity of *An Essay on Man*—a poem that was constantly being quoted—yet ultimately he finds it "hard to explain this fact except as a sheer triumph of style. Its combination of supreme complacency with cosmic doubt is not the sort of doctrine usually appreciated in America."[43] Nevertheless, May's own quantification of the books in eighteenth-century American libraries offers some indications that New World intellectuals of this time may not have been so averse to skeptical writings as we sometimes imagine. Concluding their bibliographical survey, Lundberg and May note how it is "surprising to discover the great popularity among American republicans and Protestants of such monarchical historians as Hume and Voltaire, and of such religious and moral sceptics as Gibbon and Chesterfield."⁴⁴ It is, of course, impossible to know exactly how the more heterodox aspects of Pope were understood in eighteenth-century America. Still, by looking closely at a number of American poets who were heavily influenced by his style, we will be able to see how this idiom of material bathos and radical desublimation worked its way into the annals of American literature in the years leading up to political independence. By subverting Puritan eschatologies, Pope instituted an American poetic tradition of comic, carnivalesque scatology, albeit one which failed to survive the purifying fires of the Revolution.

Mather Byles, for instance, was an American follower of Pope whose literary reputation could hardly be lower than it is today. In his own time, however, Byles was one of the best known and most widely recognized writers in colonial New England. He was descended from the famous Boston Mathers: his uncle, Cotton Mather, supervised his education, and he also benefited from inheriting the extensive library accumulated by the Mather dynasty.⁴⁵ Nor was Byles slow to recognize the advantages of his elevated social position, allying himself by marriage to the niece of Jonathan Belcher, an opulent merchant who, by adroit political management while on a visit to England, had succeeded in getting himself appointed Governor of Massachusetts. It was Belcher who helped to build the Hollis Street Congregational Church in Boston, of which Byles was ordained pastor in 1733. He stayed in this position for over forty years, entertaining scant regard for the Great Awakening—his temperament, says C. Lennart Carlson, "was too aristocratic for that, his attitude too ironic"—and eventually antagonizing American patriots with his openly royalist attitudes.⁴⁶ In 1777, at a Special Session of the Peace in Boston, Byles was tried and convicted of disloyalty to the state, though because of his advanced age he was imprisoned for only a short time before being allowed to return home. His son, Mather Junior, fled in 1776 to Halifax, Nova Scotia, where he entered the ministry of the Anglican Church, but Byles himself remained in Boston until his death in 1788 at the age of 81. He was, by this time, a scorned and broken figure, overtaken by the march of events, and as much out of favor artistically as he was politically. Indeed, his reputation has never recovered from these multiple traumas. Even after he was dead, wrote his biographer, the name of Byles "continued to stand . . . as a synonym for disloyalty and treachery of the basest kind."⁴⁷

Byles's literary career began in 1727, two years after he left Harvard, when he began publishing poetry and prose in the *New-England Weekly Journal*. It was at this time that he began openly courting Pope, writing four letters to the English poet between 1727 and 1736, though he received but one in reply. Even now, these letters make painfully embarrassing reading, with Byles moving from a tone absurdly obsequious ("We pay you a deference and veneration belonging to a Race of Superior Beings, and you appear to our Imagination, like so many Deities in Human Shape") to one plangent and wheedling ("It is now several years since I boldly introduced myself to your notice; since which time I have written several replies to the only Answer I ever received from you, till at last, I concluded your Silence forbid my pressing the Matter any further").[48] To be sure, it was in the character of Byles to be "sycophantic," as John Seelye observes, but it is too easy to elide this moral judgment into an aesthetic critique and equate sycophancy in social life with imitation in poetics.[49] Byles did work with imitation—his poems pay tribute to Pope, Milton, King George II, and various Massachusetts dignitaries—but he is always interested in how these processes of reflection involve a confluence of perspectives whereby his own text relates to the prior model. In this sense, we can see how Byles's poetry plays in a manner both baroque and meditative with the whole idea of reduplication.

Naturally enough, such self-abasing tendencies have not endeared Byles to more traditional critics of American literature. Expressing a characteristic disdain for the lack of an identifiably nationalist agenda within his work, Benjamin T. Spencer in 1957 dismissed the Boston poet as engaged merely in an "excessive yet narrow and modish adulation of current English literary fashions which could have little relevance to the temper of American life." For Spencer, such misplaced yearnings for "Augustan elegance" display "the pervasive distaste of his time for the indigenous tradition which had been assuming substance and shape in the seventeenth century."[50] This, of course, represents the classic Cold War reading of American culture as founded upon an ethic of natural originality running from the Puritans through to Emerson, with the artificial designs of eighteenth-century poetry appearing only as an odd discontinuity within this lineage. It is a misleading configuration for many reasons, but in the case of Byles specifically it would altogether marginalize the sophisticated manner in which the poet negotiates with imitation and intertextuality, the ways he elevates this style of reflection into a metaphysical principle.

Altogether unaware of the independent spirit of romantic poetics, Byles explores the abstract idea of contiguity, the medium through which an event comes to be refracted and transmitted into other areas. Just as the seventeenth-century New England poets sought to establish a covenant between the human and the divine, so Byles endeavors to establish a covenant between eminent human personages and the civic life of eighteenth-century Massachusetts. In "Written in Milton's *Paradise Lost*," for example, Byles laments his own artistic inadequacies in the face of Milton's genius, yet he still hopes his text might catch an echo, however faint, of Milton's heroic strains:

Had I, O had I all the tuneful Arts
Of lofty Verse; did ev'ry Muse inspire
My flowing Numbers and adorn my Song!
Did Milton's fire flash furious in my Soul;
Could I command the Harmony, the Force,
The glitt'ring Language, and the true Sublime
Whose mingled Beauties grace his glowing Lays . . .
His mighty Numbers tow'r above thy Sight,
Mock thy low Musick, and elude thy Strains. (25)

George F. Sensabaugh sees Byles as straining toward a condition of poetic sublimity through his imitations of Milton, but falling back defeated into "conventional Augustan patterns and forms."[51] This, I think, is to ignore the more selfconscious aspects of Byles's art. Rather than simply relapsing into a neoclassical idiom, he deliberately exploits this alternative vantage point to address his own sense of distance from the "lofty" Milton, thus foregrounding the very absence of sublimity implicit in his own act of imitation. The force of Byles's verse involves an awareness of the disjunction between Milton's "mighty Numbers" and his own "low Musick," along with a recognition of the ironies that result from this juxtaposition.

It would be easy enough to call this a provincial art, aware of its own marginality. David S. Shields has commented upon the colonial sensibility in Byles, his sense of being incorporated within an "imperial contract" whereby his native Boston could be boosted into a city of Augustan splendor only through a system of mercantile exchange and power relations that recognized, culturally and economically, the subordination of Massachusetts Bay to London. This may be true enough, but, as Shields went on to remark, the more interesting question, the one that "has not yet been posed properly," is precisely how these "imperial legacies" have contributed to "the self-understanding of the United States."[52] In the twentieth century, the colonial environment in America was depicted as haunted by the ghosts of British cultural authority and custom in a generally negative fashion, and this is one of the reasons Byles is as unpopular in the United States at the beginning of the twenty-first century as he was at the end of the eighteenth. In a parallel way, the familiar romantic and nationalist line on Byles has indicted him for a kind of creative inadequacy, what Harold Bloom would call an oedipal belatedness: the fact that he was not a Mather, not an originator, merely a follower. In fact, however, Byles's texts mediate the aesthetics and problematics of imperialism in a more ingenious, provocative manner than these terms of simple degeneration would imply. In acknowledging his own ontological absence from any cultural or metaphorical center, Byles invents an art directed more toward the bathetic than the sublime, an art which in fact punctures the idea of sublimity by exposing it to the ironic conditions of time, distance, and loss.

In his poem "On the Death of the Queen," for instance, Byles focuses on the iconography of royalty as it appears from a distant country and contemplates how the "far-beaming" crown of Queen Caroline reproduced and "flash'd" its image over the seas separating Britain from America:

> But, BELCHER, first in Grief as in Command;
> With early Zeal you kiss'd her beauteous Hand;
> Your Honours to the destin'd Queen you paid,
> Ere the Crown flash'd, far-beaming, on her Head. (84)

This is royalist in tone, of course, and it also specifically highlights colonial deference, with Belcher, governor of Massachusetts, paying homage in person to the queen of England. Equally significantly, though, the poem focuses upon light traversing distances across a spinning globe, suggesting how the general circuits of communication operated in this new scientific age of the Enlightenment, and how systems of cultural and political meaning came to be disseminated within that context. Byles was fascinated both with the physical attributes of time and space and with the ways in which such dimensions are projected within the human consciousness; it is, therefore, not surprising to learn from Byles's biographer that an inventory of the poet's effects after his death included "geographical maps, many perspective glasses, microscopes, mathematical instruments, globes, a microscope pyramid, solar pyramid, universal pyramid, an opaque pyramid, a magic lanthorn and apparatus, a prism, camera obscura, pyramidical camera, 'turcle' shell burning glass, thermometers and a barometer, half-hour glasses, reflecting telescopes, silver coins, and valuable prints."[53] Whereas Byles's Puritan forebears prided themselves upon their capacity to internalize the material world through the travails of biblical scholarship, the eighteenth-century poet finds himself less sure of the spirit's superiority to all it surveys, and so his works negotiate an uneasy, awkward balance between mind and matter. Byles's poems thus comprise a literary equivalent to all of these optical instruments in his collection, and in their ingenious meditations upon the possibilities and parameters of language and representation they introduce a ludically self-reflexive element into American literature. Some Enlightenment philosophers saw such optical processes as a vehicle for locating supposedly objective perspectives, a way of scientifically dismantling the old systems of mythology and religion so as to probe a more impersonal truth.[54] By contrast, Byles as a poet above all alert to the possibilities of language chooses to emphasize the refractory capacities of these new instruments, prismatically circumventing any stable source of light by his projection of a world that is always in the process of turning.

As William C. Spengemann observes, there is always a danger of attempting to justify early American writing by imposing retrospective analogies that imply, misleadingly, some form of intellectual coherence within the American tradition.[55] Spengemann's warning is well taken, but it may still be worth mentioning—even if in an appropriately provisional way—the name of John Ashbery in connection with Mather Byles. Granted, the differences, historical and otherwise, between these two writers are almost too huge to contemplate; but Byles's poem "To Pictorio, on the Sight of his Pictures" does consider the reciprocal interactions between painting and poetry, in a way not dissimilar to the manner in which Ashbery's "Self-Portrait in a Convex Mirror" renegotiates the visual significances of Parmigianino. This will, I think, give some hint of the kind of poet Byles was. He is not sycophantic simply for the sake of it, he also writes about the necessarily imitative dynamics of poetic creation:

> Each year, succeeding, the rude Rust devours,
> And softer Arts lead on the following Hours;
> The tuneful Nine begin to touch the Lyre
> And flowing Pencils light the living Fire;
> In the fair Page new beauties learn to shine,
> The Thoughts to brighten, and the Style refine. (90)

A sense of poetic self-consciousness was common enough back in seventeenth-century New England, where various riddles, acrostics, and anagrams testified to the poet's hermeneutic quest to decipher the divine revelations at the heart of scripture. Byles's playful art, however, is oriented more toward material surfaces and worldly events:

> Let thy soft Shades in mimick figures play.
> Steal on the Heart, and catch the Mind away.
> Yet Painter, on the kindred Muse attend,
> The Poet ever proves the Painter's Friend. (92)

Again, friendship involves an abstract principle of mutual interaction and refraction, not just the grubbier business of back-scratching.

For a more celebrated example of fellowship working as a form of intertextuality during the neoclassical era, we need only recall Pope's "Epistle to Mr. Jervas," published in 1716. This poem, which celebrates the work of Charles Jervas—a portrait painter from whom Pope took lessons—was written as a prologue to Dryden's translation of Du Fresnoy's *Art of Painting*. Pope, like Byles, meditates here on "the mimic face" (6) of both painting and poetry, describing not only how each art reflects and refracts the other, but also how they both enjoy a mirrored relationship with aesthetic models and theories from the past:

> Smit with the love of Sister-arts we came,
> And met congenial, mingling flame with flame;
> Like friendly colours found them both unite,
> And each from each contract new strength and light.
> How oft in pleasing tasks we wear the day,
> While summer-suns roll unperceiv'd away?
> How oft our slowly-growing works impart,
> While images reflect from art to art?
> How oft review; each finding like a friend
> Something to blame, and something to commend? (13–22)

For Pope, as for Byles, the contiguity of friendship becomes associated with the proximate relations of different aesthetic forms. This involves not so much a personal relationship as its simulacrum, the transposition of human identities into forms of aesthetic exchange.

This representation of what is preestablished, the "anxieties of indebtness" incumbent upon a condition of "belatedness," would make Byles something other than a "strong" poet, in Harold Bloom's sense of the term. In V. L. Parrington's eyes, similarly, Byles was nothing more than a "dilettante," a self-indulgent refurbisher of second-hand goods.[56] Yet Byles's poem "Eternity" is, in its idiosyncratic way, an ambitious work that involves a fascinating blend of Puritan spirituality with the machinery of rationalist science. The poem starts by rejecting conventional scenes of classical pastoral in favor of the light of divine science, wherein God is depicted as a kind of zany mechanic, regulating the universe according to some inscrutable scheme based around the gravitational forces of Newtonian mechanics:

> No more of murm'ring Streams, or shady Groves,
> Of fleecy Flocks, or of their Shepherds Loves . . .
> A nobler Subject asks th'advent'rous Song;
> Scenes of eternal Wonders court my Eyes,
> And bid the Muse on soaring Pinions rise . . .
> ETERNITY, O thou unfathom'd Deep,
> In thy dark Womb, what hidden Wonders sleep?
> How am I lost in thee! who can explain
> The past Revolvings of thy mazy Reign? (106–7)

One intriguing aspect of this text is the way it deliberately problematizes the position of the devotional subject, confronting him with the disorienting, enigmatic systems of Enlightenment cosmology. We see here the poet's familiar tele-scoping of time and motion, travel and space; yet the peculiar strength of this poem derives from the way these physical dimensions are placed implicitly in conflict with both the idea of Christian transcendence and the authorial pursuit of epistemological control:

> Or who his Mind is able to dilate
> To the long Periods of thy future Date?
> Strange Labyrinths my puz'led Soul confound,
> And winde mysterious in an endless Round.
>
> Before this System own'd the central Sun;
> Or Earth its Race about its Orbit run,
> When Light ne'er dawn'd, nor Form display'd its Face,
> But shapeless Matter fill'd th' unmeasur'd Space. (107)

Displacement, metaphysical as well as linguistic, is the key figure here. As the Puritan cosmology is reconfigured within a mechanistic idiom, Byles envisions a faceless solar system, a universe filled incongruously with "shapeless Matter."

In the last section of "Eternity," the pastoral mood which the poet deliber-ately abjures in the first few lines becomes reconstituted, though now in a more aesthetically conscious and reflexive manner. Whereas the "shady Groves" of the pagan paradise lost were simply part of a bookish classical formula, this rejuve-nated form of Christian pastoral is held tantalizingly in suspense just beyond the poet's sensory capacities. It is, therefore, constructed as a metaphorical land-scape, an emblem of the paradise which intersects paradoxically with Earth, just as eternity, in Byles's conception, intersects paradoxically with the world of hu-man time:

> Far other Scenes my joyful Lays invite,
> And heav'nly Visions swim before my Sight,
> I hear soft Musick glide along the Air,
> And Songs of Seraphs echo in my Ear.
> I see the pious Souls with Pleasure crown'd,
> And o'er the holy Hills Delights abound.
> But Oh! the Raptures which my Powers confess
> When JESUS shines in his refulgent Dress!
> From his wide Wounds perpetual Streams of Light,
> For ever rush, and strike the dazzled Sight. (110)

Byles here emphasizes especially the ocular perspective of his narrator as ter-restrial onlooker: "heav'nly *Visions* swim before my *Sight*," "I *see* the pious Souls," "perpetual streams of Light . . . strike the dazzled *Sight*," and so on. The poem revolves around a series of transferences between different states of being, the material and the spiritual, with what is transcendent—"o'er the holy Hills"—becoming refracted, as through a glass darkly, within the linguistic medium of the poet. Again, this work illustrates the aesthetically self-conscious aspects of Byles's poetic technique, as he casts off the traditional forms of pastoral only to reinvent them in a more tricksy, self-reflexive manner.[57]

It is this sense of a paradoxical conjunction between spirit and matter, between the sublime and the bathetic, which permeates all of Byles's poetry. Throughout his work, the materialist conceptions of this new Enlightenment world feature as odd, partly comic obstacles to older spiritual designs, bizarre entities which strangely resist assimilation within the more familiar tenets of Puritan belief. Some sense of this incongruity comes through in his extant sermons, notably *A Discourse on the Present Vileness of the Body* (1732), where Byles lends the traditional Pauline theme of corporeal vanity an extravagant gothic tinge: "This hideous Skull, the frightful Jaw fallen, and the black Teeth naked to the Eye, was it once a thinking Frame, covered with a beauteous Skin? Strange Alteration made by Death!"[58] Byles's sermon emphasizes how the humble human body derives, etymologically as well as physically, "from *Humus*; the moist Ground; the *Clay*; the *low* Earth," and this allows him to develop his fascination with how "Matter is continually changing," as he meditates both on the sinking of the body back into dust and its potential "Transformation" at the Day of Judgment. Accordingly, he advises his congregation "to set a double Value" upon their bodies, acknowledging their "Uncleanness and Corruption" but also how "they are the Members of our Lord JESUS."[59] "Members" is a typical piece of Byles wordplay, signifying both human limbs and also, metaphorically, their membership or fellowship in Christ; the verbal double meaning reflects precisely that idiom of metamorphosis or "double Value" which fires the writer's theological and poetic imagination. In *A Sermon on the Nature and Necessity of Conversion*, also from 1732, Byles similarly expatiates on the "Literal Sense of the Word *Conversion*" as "*turning about*," comparing the sinner who has "his Nature changed" by Christ to the needle of the compass which stops flickering when it points to magnetic North.[60]

The aesthetic corollaries to this discourse of transformation are interestingly illuminated by an essay Byles published in *The American Magazine* in 1745, "Bombastic and Grubstreet Style: A Satire." Perry Miller and Thomas H. Johnson describe this as a theoretical piece that "really ushers in a new era of conscious literary feeling; here is an essay wherein the art of writing is conceived as an end in itself." What is most notable here, they argue, is the relative absence of any moral agenda; for the first time, an American author was producing a "literary essay written solely for entertainment," of the kind that had begun to appear in *The Tatler* thirty years earlier.[61] In this essay, Byles proposes satirically to praise "The Art of writing Incorrectly," and "to entertain the Publick, with a regular Criticism upon Nonsense"; to this end, he delivers a mock encomium to "Extravagance of Imagination," "Folly and Absurdity," and "Disproportion and Extravagance of the Images." Yet, when he avers that this discussion of "Incorrect Writing" is "a Work that I am excellently well qualified for," Byles is not wrong.[62] Indeed, by the kind of double bind familiar to the satirist's art, the author finds himself excoriating those very stylistic foibles that his own work is attracted to and, at some level, complicit with. In Byles's case, a large component of this stylistic "Extravagance" involved his fantastic predilection for punning. (When he died in 1788, Ebenezer Hazard is reported to have remarked: "So the old Doctor has left off punning at last. What must the grave spirits in heaven think on the approach of so ludicrous an one as his?") Byles's congregation at the Hollis Street Church was not impressed by such apparent frivolity, for when they voted in 1766 to dismiss Byles from his pastorate they cited not only his unacceptable Loyalist sympathies but also the fact that he had forfeited their respect by indulging "in a natural vein of low wit and ridiculous punning."[63]

As Avita Ronell has said, the double-sided nature of the pun tends to be "always anally attached in the figurations and metaphorics" that attend it.[64] The two-faced quality of the pun, betokening verbal inversion, can be seen as a correlative to the conceptual inversions associated with the corporeal and political practice of turning things around the other way. This is commensurate with Byles's bizarre forms of epistemological dualism, where the abstract ideals of spirit are conjoined comically with inferior forms of matter. It helps to make sense also of the gross puns Byles perpetrates at the end of his "Elegy Addressed to Governor Belcher on the Death of His Lady," where he puns on the names of himself and the Governor:

> Meantime *my* name to *thine* allied shall stand,
> Still our warm friendship, mutual flames extend;
> The muse shall so survive from age to age,
> And BELCHER'S name protect his *Byles's* page. (79)

Such wordplay can be seen as another style of bathos, a memento of how, as so often in Byles, the aspiring soul is brought low by the material circumstances of natural existence. Here these circumstances are given a specifically fleshly incarnation, as the poet's idealized version of friendship is conflated with burlesque puns on bile and belching. Again, we can see an intellectual association with

Pope, whose important treatise, *Peri Bathous, or The Art of Sinking in Poetry*, was published in 1727. In this work, a knowing travesty of Longinus's work *On the Sublime*, Pope argues that "while a plain and direct road is paved to their ὕψος, or *sublime*; no tract has been yet chalk'd out, to arrive at our βάθος, or *profound*."[65] He goes on provocatively to insist how the "Taste of the *Bathos* is implanted by Nature itself in the soul of man," so that it is the art of demystification and desublimation which is most true to human experience. Pope proceeds to take this line of argument to a comic extreme, eventually arguing extravagantly for bad poetry as more productive of "Tranquility of Mind" than good poetry. Still, as with Byles's essay on bombast, it is not difficult to see the implicit relevance of these aesthetic priorities to Pope's own comic art, where pretensions of various kinds tend to be trumped by the instincts of lower human faculties.[66] Nor is it hard to recognize how such forms of bathos are affiliated ideologically with a form of social and political conservatism. For Pope, as for Byles, the sublime equates with what is unknown, radical, original, while the bathetic drags language and representation back within familiar, comically recognizable, bounds.

This is why eighteenth-century American poets who leaned toward the Tory cause tended to write in a comic and bathetic manner and, like Byles, to cherish Pope as their poetic mentor. Byles himself expresses this idolatry most clearly in "To an Ingenious Young Gentleman, on his Dedicating a Poem to the Author":

> O POPE! thy Fame is spread around the Sky,
> Far as the Waves can flow, far as the Winds can fly!
> Hail! Bard triumphant, fill'd with hallow'd Rage,
> Sent from high Heav'n to grace the happy Age . . .
> 'Tis POPE, my Friend, that guilds our gloomy Night,
> And if I shine 'tis his reflected Light . . .
> POPE'S are the Rules which you, my Friend, receive,
> From him I gather what to you I give. (53–54)

This is also, of course, why Byles and other eighteenth-century poets have found themselves marginalized by the critical canons of American literature. It is not simply that they failed to back the right side during the War of Independence; it is more a question of their acerbic, ironic, and self-deprecating manner remaining outside the privileged circle of American critical orthodoxies, whether Parrington's notion of social democracy, Matthiessen's idealization of transcendental imagination, or Bloom's mystification of romantic selfhood. In his own day, Byles came to be seen as incorrigibly "Old Light" by the "New Light" evangelists, who tended to despise traditional forms of belles lettres as abstruse and elitist, out of kilter with the emerging democratic nature of the country; and subsequent echoes of this conflict between Byles and the forces of Whig sentimentalism have reverberated down the centuries, appearing within the narratives of American literary history in slightly different guises every time.[67] Just as Eliot championed the cause of Pope, though, so Byles is assigned a cameo role in Ezra Pound's Canto 64, where he appears amidst the conflict of the American Revolution talking punningly of "Our grievances red-dressed."[68] Pound represents the Loyalist Byles as mocking the general American hostility to British redcoats, an instance of disloyalty to the American patriot cause which might be said to anticipate Pound's own secession from the national culture of the United States.

Within the new world of the United States itself, however, there was to be no respite for Byles. His taste for philosophical bathos, allied to his style of linguistic punning, came to be seen as profoundly incompatible with the rising glory of literary naturalism in post-Revolutionary America, just as Pope's Catholic duplicities and paradoxes had placed him in an estranged relationship with the Anglican climate of England. Both poets came to be considered reactionary by the societies of their day; both, however, countered this conservatism through a parallel discourse of pun and paradox, which served to train a witty irony back upon their native cultures. Crucially, Pope and Byles shared a comic sensibility, an iconoclastic tendency to puncture pomposity, which placed them in an oblique relation to the civic authorities of their times. Just as the sophisticated sensibility of Pope contrived a structure of duplicity where he could affiliate himself with and disaffiliate himself from English society simultaneously, so Byles reflected the celebrated features of Pope in an effort to reposition the American cultural landscape within a larger sphere of transatlantic influence. Both Pope and Byles promulgated a discourse of bathos, an art of sinking, that would come to appear increasingly antipathetic to the rationalizing radicalism of Enlightenment vision. In the case of Byles, however, his acts of acerbic deflation also incurred specific political consequences, as the emerging forces of national independence worked to expel the Loyalist jester not only from his pastorship but also from American literary history.

Chapter Two
Topsy-Turvy Neoclassicism
The Connecticut Wits

After his death in 1744, Pope's influence lingered longer in America than in Britain. Developments in artistic fashion generally took longer to percolate from London to the provinces, so that for instance Nathaniel Evans (1742–67), a devotee of Pope's work, only became conversant with poets of sensibility like William Collins and Thomas Gray when he visited England toward the end of his career.[1] Phillis Wheatley, who published her *Poems on Various Subjects* in 1773, also cited Pope as her conscious model, and, like the Twickenham poet, she manipulated her style of imitation to carve out for herself a rhetorical persona, an imagined or projected narrative self. It is interesting to note as well that Wheatley was acquainted personally with Mather Byles, who was a member of the Boston committee signing the "Attestation" to the authenticity of her work published as a preface to her *Poems*, and who seems to have influenced her poetic style directly.[2] Wheatley, like Byles, has been chided frequently for apparent cultural conservatism, although there has been much consideration recently of the interplay between tradition and subversion in her poetry—whether she was actually conforming to conventional white views of the world, or whether she surreptitiously pleads for the liberation of black slaves.[3] This is not the place to go over that ground again here. Nevertheless, it is relevant to a reading of the Connecticut Wits to bear in mind, as Charles Scruggs observed in 1981, how a proper appreciation of Wheatley has been hindered by the " 'Romantic' bias [that] has determined her critical reputation," the idea there must somewhere be a "genuine" human soul struggling to free itself from all those shackles of societal artifice.[4]

This is, in fact, a problem which besets any retrospective consideration of eighteenth-century American poetry. For many American readers since the Revolution, the Augustan style itself has appeared to constitute a form of bondage, a surrogate prison from which the native subject must liberate itself. In 1939, for instance, Saunders Redding wrote of how the "tame" and "chilly" aspects of Wheatley's poetry could be traced to "the unmistakable influence of Pope's neo-classicism upon her," an influence he judged wholly malign, adding that her "ready submission to established forms was a weakness of the period." Along the same lines, Evert A. Duyckinck, well known for his involvement with Melville and the nineteenth-century cultural nationalists, described in his 1856 *Cyclopaedia of American Literature* how Wheatley had followed the "formal muse of Pope" to embody "a very respectable echo of the Papal strains." Duyckinck's Pope/Papal pun is revealing, implying how he associated this neoclassical idiom with an Old World style of oppression. His own preference, as he made clear in his essay on Timothy Dwight in the same volume, was for "original invention" rather than mere "imitation or adaptation of different English poets."[5] While the eighteenth century itself tended to distinguish between artifice and artificiality rather than between sincerity and artificiality, the ways in which such conscious artifice might itself be constituted as an "original" category have not always been clear to a post-Romantic American audience.

Wheatley provides an example of an American "papal" poet who might be creatively reimagined, albeit somewhat awkwardly, within a different kind of critical framework. The poetry of Dwight, John Trumbull, and the other Connecticut Wits, however, has generally enjoyed no such saving graces. Joel Barlow, who enjoyed a problematic relationship with the Hartford group before leaving to join the revolutionaries in France in 1788, has generally received more favorable attention, partly because the radical agenda that emerged after his move to Europe has been easier subsequently to reconcile with American democratic ideals. For example, in his "Advice to the Privileged Orders in the Several States of Europe" (1791), Barlow insists, like his friend Thomas Paine, that the "great outlines of morality are extremely simple and easy to be understood."[6] My purpose in this chapter, however, is not to give a full account of the political circumstances informing the Wits' writings, but rather to suggest ways in which their understanding of politics itself becomes textually destabilized by a scabrous idiom of travesty and burlesque, an idiom that makes the whole question of partisan allegiance more difficult to formulate.

As president of Yale and so-called "Pope" of Federalism—a phrase Parrington cited with disapproval—Dwight has most frequently been the object of neglect or derision in twentieth-century literary study. According to Kenneth Silverman, the fact that Dwight's poetry, which began appearing in 1785, is so indebted to the style of Pope demonstrates only the "continued cultural lag in the colonies."[7] Consequently, his epic endeavors, based upon a pastoral idealization of his Connecticut sanctuary, have appeared anything but relevant to the modern

American world; Parrington's view of how there was "no sap of originality in him, no creative energy, but instead the sound of voices long silent" has been echoed many times by subsequent critics.[8] This, though, is a reductive view: in particular, *Greenfield Hill* (1794) can be seen as an interesting renegotiation of pastoral conventions in the service of an American democratic ideology.

Dwight presents pastoral in this poem as an abstract idea, reconceptualizing it within the kind of idealized and radically egalitarian metaphors traditionally embraced by the genre in classical times. Annabel Patterson has written of the ideological conflict within eighteenth-century pastoral between the forces of neo-classical conservatism on the one hand and a poetic idiom more indebted to the rural qualities of Virgilian pastoral on the other, and within this framework *Greenfield Hill* comes closer to the Virgilian mode.[9] Dwight's focus here upon the tranquil, unpretentious homesteads of New England works implicitly to reject the more elaborate rituals of courtly society. By expelling all the hierarchical accretions of English feudal life, the author hopes to introduce into Connecticut a universal economic "competence" resembling that "pure, golden mean" of the original Arcadia:

> Our Sires established, in thy cheerful bounds,
> The noblest institutions, man has seen,
> Since time his reign began. In little farms
> They measur'd all thy realms, to every child
> In equal shares descending; no entail
> The first-born lifting into bloated pomp,
> Tainting with lust, and sloth, and pride, and rage,
> The world around him. (I, 138–45)[10]

The poet cultivates this sense of community by eschewing the more pompous forms of propriety and social elegance so he can emphasize what he takes to be a quintessentially American idiom of fellow feeling and all-inclusive spirit. *Greenfield Hill* is therefore designed to appeal to the sensibility, not just the intellect; by imbuing his local scenery with an "affective dimension," Dwight seeks to consolidate its appeal to the reader's imagination.[11]

Lawrence Buell has written of Dwight as anticipating the conceptualizations of New England in nineteenth-century writing, suggesting that he shares with Thoreau a mode of "lococentrism," a way of transfiguring the emotions associated with particular landscapes into stylized forms of aesthetic practice.[12] Yet to see Dwight as a forerunner of Transcendentalism is to suppress his poetry's satiric qualities, the way it follows Pope in discharging its pedagogical responsibilities through inversion and burlesque. So dedicated is *Greenfield Hill* to the erasure of those decadent aristocratic qualities associated with Europe that it often generates its poetic energy through a scattering of negatives:

> No tyrant riding o'er th'indignant plain;
> A prince, a king, each independent swain;
> No servile thought, no vile submission, known;
> No rent to lords, nor homage to a throne. (VII, 221–24)

Obviously enough, this structure of negative inversion involves Dwight in the kind of metaphysical ironies that Robert Lawson-Peebles has written about in the context of the Revolutionary period, whereby the poet can only reject British royalty by invoking royalist images, by suggesting how in America "each independent swain" becomes his own "prince" or "king."[13] The dialectic in Dwight between the Old World and the New necessarily involves both sides of that equation, and this inevitably exposes his texts to contamination by the very objects and qualities he is attempting to obliterate.

Such ironies manifest themselves most clearly in Dwight's poem, *The Triumph of Infidelity* (1788), a work he chose to publish anonymously. Here the narrative voice of Satan—a curious choice in itself—outlines what the Prince of Darkness considers to be the more positive and promising tendencies of the day: "all-subduing Fashion" (336), ignorant students, the atheism of David Hume, "Jesuitic art" (346), and so on. In this poetic narrative, sardonically dedicated "To Mons. de Voltaire" (329), Dwight, like Byles before him, does not altogether avoid the satirist's traditional bond with the objects under satiric attack. However unintentionally, the representation of good and evil appears to be caught up in a binary opposition of mutual self-definition, with Satan seemingly granted a sinister power to turn the world upside down:

> But soon I bade the floods of vengeance roll,
> Soon rous'd anew my mightiness of soul,
> With arts my own, th'opposer's power withstood,
> And reign'd once more the universal God. (333)

Infidelity is thus represented here as a form of "contagion," as Shirley Samuels describes it, where the transgressive pleasures of sexual or religious heresy are paradoxically highlighted, and therefore enhanced, by the very rhetoric generated to suppress them.[14] Despite Dwight's fervent attempts morally to anchor and direct his poem, it finds itself infiltrated by elements of the social and political confusion that was so widespread at the end of the eighteenth century. Just as Connecticut was finding it increasingly difficult to exist simply as a seat of pastoral exclusivity, so *The Triumph of Infidelity* strays at times from satire into burlesque: from disciplinary correction of moral confusion into a more amorphous acknowledgment of this all-pervasive sense of bouleversement.

This is why Colin Wells's categorization of *The Triumph of Infidelity* as an "American Dunciad," an attack on Charles Chauncy's supposedly foolish doctrine of universal salvation, needs to be qualified by a recognition that the epic poems of Dwight, as well as Pope, tend stylistically to exceed the boundaries of any univocal moral position.[15] The infidelity in this poem can be attributed paradoxically to its anonymous author, Dwight, as well as to the putative object of his satire. Much of the best recent scholarship on the Wits—by William C. Dowling, Christopher Grasso, and others—expertly recovers various social and ideological contexts for these poems, but then seeks to interpret them specifically in terms of this kind of cultural history without also fully acknowledging the burlesque and contradictory elements within these texts, the way their tortuous form frequently compromises their manifest content.[16] From this point of view, the "divided qualities of Dwight's own sensibility," which Peter M. Briggs and other recent critics have commented upon, should be related not just to an intellectual conflict between the poetic embodiment of either romantic or neoclassic attitudes—"progressive visionary" versus champion of conservative "stability"— but, more crucially, understood as an internal fissure within the author's discursive consciousness.[17] Insisting on the material character of light and visual sight, Dwight seeks to convert natural landscapes, through what he called "the three processes of Composition, Abstraction, and Comparison," into resplendent images of America's common destiny.[18] This might be seen as a modernized version of the Puritan conversion narrative: whereas the seventeenth-century New Englanders sought to convert the fallen material world into a hermeneutics of spiritual redemption, Dwight aspires to convert the inchoate landscapes of post-Revolutionary Connecticut into emblems of a new American national identity. But the conjugate dynamics of conversion, as Michael Wigglesworth and the elder Puritans knew, necessarily lays open the possibility of a lapsed state, when matter fails to be translated into spirit, when the corporeal body remains immune to divine transcendence. In attempting allegorically to transmute his environment, Dwight leaves it vulnerable to a kind of negative metamorphosis.

Ironically, though, it is precisely this amorphous quality, or rather the way in which the rational and irrational collide, that gives Dwight's poetry its peculiar resonance. Strewn throughout his verse are dreamscapes where the dangerous allure of anarchy is never far away. In *The Conquest of Canaan* (1785), Joshua's vision of leading his people into a holy war is held back by dreams of guilt associated with a vacant fear of the unknown; in his 1801 satire, "Morpheus," the narrator visits in a dream the "city of Perfectability," only to be confronted with a vision of William Godwin inciting the crowds to hellish disorder. Noting this disruptive strain in his poetry, Peter K. Kafer lamented the fact that "Dwight never persistently and courageously endeavored to explore this latter dimension of himself."[19] This, of course, is to wish Dwight quite a different kind of poet: he was not a Keats or Byron, intent upon cherishing the fabulous or grotesque on its own account. Yet while Dwight's prose is rational and scholarly, his poetry is more riven by the discontinuities of natural experience in the way it incorporates aspects of the emotive and erratic conditions of America in a time of turmoil: "The imagination," wrote Dwight, "is undoubtedly stronger during sleep than when we are awake."[20] While his academic essays were clearly the product of his waking hours, Dwight's poetry is less rigidly consistent in the way it addresses the chimeras of nocturnal vision.

In formal terms, Dwight deliberately set out in *Greenfield Hill*, as he said in his introduction, "to imitate, in the several parts, the manner of as many British poets" (8). Although this general scheme soon fell apart, the first sections of *Greenfield Hill* consciously echo the styles of eighteenth-century British writers—James Thomson, Oliver Goldsmith, and John Dyer—as if to demonstrate Dwight's position on the cusp between British tradition and American independence. Unlike Mather Byles, Dwight did support the patriot cause, though as a staunch Federalist he loathed the Republican movement marshaled by Jefferson and chose to dedicate *Greenfield Hill* to John Adams. For the Federalist party at this time, of course, Alexander Pope remained a great literary hero, with these American conservatives cherishing Pope as an emblem of ethical and social stability. Dowling has written of how Dwight saw his poetry as the moral successor to Pope's Horatian satires, which were themselves an indictment of the financial corruptions in Sir Robert Walpole's England during the early eighteenth century; and from this point of view it is not difficult to see continuities between the reactionary forms of "Country ideology," predicated upon an ideal of classical virtue, on both sides of the Atlantic.[21] Apologists for American independence, such as Dwight, saw themselves as true heirs to a natural order fatally corrupted by the forces of mercantile wealth and urban chicanery. But Dwight's attempt to appropriate Pope as an exemplar of unsullied probity inevitably tended to ignore or suppress the English poet's more sinister, paradoxical aspects. What we find in *Greenfield Hill*, accordingly, is a creative misreading of Pope, a desire to recuperate and hypostatize the English poet's moralizing stances. Dwight suggests that American students might want to trace "Through Pope's clear glass, the bright Maeonian star" (II, 376); and this desire to clean up Pope, to erase the opacity of his worldly themes while reinventing his verse as a transparent medium for the representation of moral issues, is repeated later in *Greenfield Hill*:

> No sickly spot shall soil the page refin'd;
> Lend vice a charm, or taint the artless mind;
> Another Pope inchanting themes rehearse,
> Nor the meek virgin blush to hear the verse;
> Improv'd, and clouded with no courtly stain,
> A whiter page than Addison's remain. (VII, 487–92)

In this way, Dwight makes it clear he wants a plainer Pope, a Pope with the sex and corruption taken out.

Hence there is, as Silverman has suggested, a kind of "pilgrim's progress" mentality at work here, with Dwight somberly imagining "the law of the universe" to involve a necessary conjunction of "Sound taste, sound sense, and sound morals."[22] Consequently, he aligns everything that is decadent and evil with the Old World—slavery, atheism, the feudal system—and then uses his poetry as a form of negative catharsis to disavow such abjection, so as to aspire toward a New World of pastoral sublimity. Though his poetry is engaged with the old infidel world and sometimes imitates its stylistic patterns, Dwight's self-appointed task was to reinvigorate these fallen models so as to make them more fit for American consumption. All too cognizant of the paradoxes of infidelity and heresy, Dwight the Connecticut citizen seeks to regenerate New England landscapes, to convert them anew into scenes of national redemption.

*   *   *

The Dunciad (1743) provides the most obvious example of those features of Pope's poetry that Dwight would have found unacceptable. Indeed, in America generally there was not so much attention paid to the *Dunciad* as to Pope's other works.[23] This did not mean, however, the poem was altogether ignored: Franklin refers to it a couple of times in his *Autobiography*, while John Trumbull also mentioned it in a 1775 letter as a model for *M'Fingal*.[24] On one level, as Linda Kerber remarked, the *Dunciad* might have appeared as a kind of "handbook" for the Federalists, since they shared the apprehension of the Augustans about a degrading "Dulness" spreading across the entire Western world.[25] Yet Pope's most ambitious poem would have been particularly disturbing to American readers not only because of its infamous scatological images, but also because of its paradoxical coupling of good and evil, soul and body, within the same oxymoronic conjunction. The *Dunciad's* scatological impulse works in parallel with this subversion of philosophical dualism and, in the light of Dr. Johnson's complaint about how the *Dunciad* reveals Pope's "unnatural delight" in "ideas physically impure," we can reasonably infer the link between physical "purity" and religious puritanism, both being categories Pope meticulously disavowed.[26] When, for example, Pope says "Dulness is sacred in a sound divine" (II, 352), he is not simply being satirical and suggesting that sound divines should not be dull; instead he is describing how things function in a real rather than ideal world where reason and passion, the rational and the irrational, are always of necessity bound up together.

The Dunciad, then, delineates a world of obdurate materialism, where the gross requirements of the human body refuse to be subsumed within the rarefied air of Cartesian consciousness (as we have seen, Pope openly attacks Descartes in the fourth book of this poem). The peculiar genius of the Dunciad lies in the way it analogically equates apparently respectable and unrespectable activities, suggesting not only on a psychological level how they emanate from similar fields of consciousness, but also how prim neoclassicism and cloacal transgression form part of the same ontological sphere. Again, this is a secularized reworking of Aquinas's Catholic doctrine that good and evil comprise mutually complimentary rather than antithetical forces. In the Dunciad, this gives license to a world where stable categories begin to slide and interpenetrate each other, where the body comes to pervert the mind and vice versa. Hence the parallelism between "morning pray'r, and flagellation" in Book II (270); hence also Book IV's self-reflexive commentary on birching and learning, which is implicitly equated with the agreeable perversions of satire, the paradoxical pleasure of finding a dull-witted world to admonish and chastise. As a poem of inversion, the Dunciad embodies Pope's figure for "Bathos in perfection" as described in Peri Bathous: "as when a Man is set with his Head downward, and his Breech upright, his Degradation is compleat: one End of him is as high as ever, only that End is the wrong one."[27]

The historical contexts framing the production of the Dunciad in the mid-eighteenth century include a burgeoning urban culture, whose grotesque and carnivalesque elements Pope was simultaneously attracted and repelled by, and an equally rapidly expanding culture of print. Pope lampoons this world in his depiction of the quack publishing outfits of London:

> Hence hymning Tyburn's elegiac lines,
> Hence Journals, Medleys, Merc'ries, Magazines:
> Sepulchral Lyres, our holy walls to grace,
> And New-year Odes, and all the Grub-street race. (I, 41–44)

Pope indicts this "Grub-street race" for being enmeshed within a world of fakery, where the secondhand quality of new printing mechanisms necessarily betokens a ceaseless flow of impersonal artifacts, the faceless by-products of a world of urban anonymity.[28] In this respect, it is easier to see how the infamous sewer games of Book II relate to the direction of the poem as a whole: Pope reconceives London as a site of excremental circulation where, through a process of negative alchemy, every object turns to waste matter.

A general tone of confusion and anarchy runs through the *Dunciad*, of course, but Janine Chasseguet-Smirgel has more specifically linked the kind of "anal creation of the world" that is such a peculiar feature of this poem with historical eras of social and political upheaval.[29] In *Creativity and Perversion*, she suggests that such representations of deviance may imply not only mere psychological confusion, but also a wider sense of how the old, familiar conditions of social stability find themselves under threat as traditional relationships with patriarchal authority become increasingly difficult to sustain. The two historical examples she adduces are the fall of the Roman Empire, when "decadence" was widespread, and the French Revolutionary era, when philosophical renegades like Sade were intent on negating traditional hierarchical distinctions, such as those between "parents" and "children," and on creating instead an equal and interchangeable "universe where all differences are abolished." I want to suggest here that the years of turbulence surrounding the American Revolution make up another historical period incorporating, even if in a milder form, what Chasseguet-Smirgel calls "the anal-sadistic desire for muddle and confusion"; I want to suggest as well that a perverse desire to make a mockery of the law by turning it upside down emerges in the work of several late eighteenth-century American poets, notably John Trumbull.[30] Furthermore, we will see how Trumbull and the other Wits were intertextually drawing upon the style of Pope's *Dunciad* to underpin their own topsy-turvy universe, where social rebellion and psychological destabilization went hand in hand.

Trumbull himself was born into a comfortable Connecticut family in 1750, entered Yale at the age of thirteen and stayed there as a tutor into the 1770s. As a young graduate, he published various essays on cultural and political topics in the *Boston Chronicle* and the *Connecticut Journal*, as well as *The Progress of Dulness* (1772), a sequence of short poems satirizing the empty-headed capacities of New England's gilded youth. The first two cantos of *M'Fingal* appeared in 1775, and, after Trumbull had settled as a lawyer in Hartford, two further cantos appeared in the complete version of 1782. Apart from his involvement in *The Anarchiad*, this effectively comprised the sum of Trumbull's literary achievements. He ended his days quietly in Connecticut as a moderately conservative Congregationalist, a friend of John Adams, and an opponent of radical politicians, of Romantic writers (he complained of "the wild unmeaning rants of Coleridge") and of religious enthusiasts for the "New Light." Despite the immense popularity and significance of *M'Fingal* and *The Anarchiad* in the late eighteenth century, Trumbull, like Byles, has been more or less written out of American literary history. Poe in 1849 dismissed *M'Fingal* as no more "than a faint echo from 'Hudibras,'" a "clumsy and imitative work . . . scarcely worth mention," and subsequent critics have tended to take his advice literally.[31]

The Anarchiad, written "in concert" by Trumbull, David Humphreys, Joel Barlow and Lemuel Hopkins, provides the most obvious example of intertextual affiliations between Pope and the Connecticut Wits.[32] Scholars have often argued about who contributed exactly what to the *Anarchiad*, but such disputes ought not to obscure the pleasures of actually reading this convoluted text and appreciating its intellectual form of black humor. The work itself first appeared serially in the *New Haven Gazette* and the *Connecticut Magazine* between October 1786 and September 1787, seeking to exert influence on members of the Connecticut delegation to the Constitutional Convention in Philadelphia. In its heady mixture of poetry and prose commentary, the *Anarchiad* set about attacking factional interests who pursued their own selfish and parochial interests at the expense of broader national concerns. In particular, it indicted the anarchic tendencies of those irresponsible citizens who spent more than they could earn and who, heedless of inflation, favored the printing of paper money in order to discharge their debts.[33]

In formal terms, the ingenious conceit of this mock epic is that it was actually a classical composition recently discovered by "a society of critics and antiquarians" in "folio manuscript" among various "relics of antiquity."[34] (Shades here of Nabokov's *Pale Fire*, perhaps, and of the ludic designs wrought by "clever young men in the colleges," in Parrington's dismissive phrase, who indulged in a manner of wit that American critics have often thought not quite serious enough.)[35] In its first section, the *Anarchiad* openly acknowledges Pope's influence by refracting the *Dunciad* through a prism of pastiche. This is the famous conclusion to Pope's poem:

> Lo! Thy dread Empire, CHAOS! is restor'd;
> Light dies before thy uncreating word;
> Thy hand, great Anarch! lets the curtain fall;
> And Universal Darkness buries All. (IV, 653–56)

And these lines inaugurate *The Anarchiad*:

> In visions fair the scenes of fate unroll,
> And Massachusetts opens on my soul;
> There Chaos, Anarch old, asserts his sway,
> And mobs in myriads blacken all the way . . .
> Thy constitution, Chaos, is restor'd;

Law sinks before thy uncreating word;
Thy hand unbars th'unfathomed gulf of fate,
And deep in darkness 'whelms the new-born state. (6–7)

The American version goes on to remark with a pleasant drollery: "I know not whether it is necessary to remark, in this place . . . that the celebrated English poet, Mr. Pope, has proven himself a noted plagiarist, by copying the preceding ideas, and even the couplets almost entire, into his famous poem called 'The Dunciad' " (7).

The *Anarchiad*, then, is a forgery on two counts: a work of pseudoantiquity, and also a poem that copies from Pope and then tries jokily to allege it is Pope who was the plagiarist. This is particularly ironic in view of the poem's satirical indictment of what it considers to be fake and fraudulent, notably the circulation of paper money, a topic which is addressed in the third section of the poem:

For it will scarcely be denied, in any part of the United States, that paper money, in an unfunded and depreciating condition, is happily calculated to introduce the long ex-pected scenes of misrule, dishonesty, and perdition. (13)

The authors' delight in linguistic inversion is evident again here. Tongue in cheek, they claim paper money is "happily calculated" to bring about misrule, while from their secure vantage point in Connecticut (a state which declined to participate in such a newfangled system) they can witness the agents of corruption accumulating all about them:

Oh, roguery! their being's end and aim,
Fraud, tendry, paper bills, whate'er thy name . . .
And dark injustice, wrapp'd in paper sheets,
Rolls a dread torrent through the wasted streets. (15–16)

The dialogue here is between fraud and chicanery on the one hand and solid currency on the other. Yet the qualities associated with forgery are also, ironically, the categories implicit within the *Anarchiad* itself:

There G — n stands, his head with quibbles fill'd;
His tongue in lies, his hand in forg'ry skill'd. (15)

What forgery is to the realm of currency, the quibble, or pun, is to the realm of language; moreover, there is a comic equation here between these "paper sheets" of false money and the paper sheets of the Connecticut journals where this popular and influential work first appeared. The *Anarchiad*, that is to say, plays knowingly with the idea of fiction and deception. It is quite wrong to misread it as a humorless diatribe against the moral ills linked to an emergent commercial culture, since this poem self-mockingly participates in those very turpitudes it affects to despise.

This is not, of course, to claim the *Anarchiad* secretly approves of paper money; it is rather to acknowledge ways in which the poem is more complex, more multifaceted, than it is usually given credit for. One useful strategy here is for the reader to look less for the obvious moralizing content of the *Anarchiad* and consider more the form in which the text is enunciated. Then it becomes clearer how the poem foregrounds metaphors of sight, the optical instruments of perception, as if to suggest how the substance of what is said depends upon the way any given material is framed. In section 7, for instance, which travesties the old classical ideal of the Olympic Games, a prize is awarded to those who manage to shut their eyes longest to the clear light of day:

Wronghead is the sole conqueror in this game, and is, thereupon, rewarded by the Anarch with a pair of spectacles, which showed every object inverted, and wrapped in a mist of darkness. (35)

"Wronghead," said J. K. Van Dover, is General James Wadsworth, a leading Connecticut anti-Federalist.[36] But more important than this simple identification is to recognize how throughout the *Anarchiad* every character is attempting to appropriate some kind of reflective instrument through which to gain a perspective upon the world. In the poem's final section, the narrative turns to "the famous *Abbé de Pau*, who was then busied in prying with futurity, by the aid of a philosophic telescope, calculated to diminish all objects, according to the squares of the distances":

> There, with sure ken, th'inverted optics show
> All nature lessening to the sage *De Pau* . . .
> His peerless pen shall raise, with magic lore,
> The long-lost pigmies on th'Atlantic shore;
> Make niggard nature's noblest gifts decline
> Th'indicial marks of bodies masculine. (75)

Overtly, the Abbé himself is the object of satire here. The *Anarchiad* ostensibly grounds itself on nature, the plain truth, the solidity of the here and now, empirical categories which the Abbé, with his "philosophic telescope" (75), flamboyantly resists. All the time, however, the *Anarchiad's* own aesthetic effects are being generated through the power of artifice and "inverted optics," as it consciously uses instruments of refraction to deplore the effects of refractive processes. Through a similar kind of double bind, the poem professes to abhor faction, especially factions involved with political pamphleteering, yet in the same ironic breath it conducts its own topical campaigning:

> Your tongues and pens must wake the factious flame!
> And thou, poor Quack, behold thy efforts fail;
> Could one address thy o'erstrain'd wits exhale?
> Wake, scribble, print; arouse thee from thy den,
> And raise conventions with thy blust'ring pen! (10)

These lines are addressed to "Wimble," Judge William Williams; but it is not difficult to see how the *Anarchiad* itself becomes self-reflexively implicated in this critique, since it too is a scribbled and printed document circulated in a particular political cause, that of Federalism.

The representation of prophecy in the *Anarchiad* operates within a similarly duplicitous mode. It is easy enough to mock the Abbé de Pau, and to point out how the *Anarchiad* scorns the radical idealism of millennial vision, as indeed it does:

> And, lo! th'expected scene advances near—
> The promised age, the fiends' millennial year.
> At that famed era, raised by angry fates,
> What countless imps shall throng the new-born States! . . .
> Chimeras sage, with plans commercial fraught,
> Sublime abortions of projecting thought! (68–69)

In his *Enquiry Concerning Human Understanding*, published in 1748, the skeptical David Hume puts prophecies alongside miracles as prime examples of human credulity, adding tersely how it "exceed[s] the capacity of human nature to fore-tell future events."[37] More specifically, the vehement rejection of "visionary" theories of government was a familiar Federalist platform at the end of the eighteenth century: at an Independence Day oration in New Haven in 1798, for instance, Noah Webster cautioned against exchanging "our civil and religious institutions for the wild theories of crazy projectors." To substitute "experiment" for "experience," warned Webster, would be to embark upon a hazardous path which risked unleashing the forces of social and political chaos.[38] Such devaluations of the powers of sublime vision again help to explain why Federalist writers have not been received kindly within the canonical structures of American literature; one could hardly imagine acolytes of Emerson or Whitman finding much to amuse them here.

Yet it is crucial to recognize the *Anarchiad* does not straightforwardly reject the notion of prophecy, but rather travesties it, opting for a form of negative prophecy whereby the mock-epic poem ingeniously puts time in reverse, parodically locating its ultima Thule back in the time of mysterious classical antiquities. The Anarchiad does not simply dispense with the prophetic telescope, but looks through the telescope's wrong end, as it were, so that the focus of this optical instrument is upon the past rather than the future. This fulfils exactly one of Pope's ironic maxims in Peri Bathous, where he said the poet's "Eyes should be like unto the wrong end of a Perspective Glass, by which all the Objects of Nature are lessen'd."[39] Whatever the Anarchiad is, it is not a self-evidently naturalized performance; rather, the poem operates through bizarre forms of parody and pastiche, taking the idea of epic from Pope and others and then, as in the Dunciad, standing the genre on its head. One might go further and suggest that, within this context, epic is to hard currency what mock-epic is to paper currency: the latter categories appear within the Anarchiad as a signifying chain of fakery, whose textual form radically compromises the ethical integrity of that "message" the poem is officially promulgating. As in the Dunciad, the rhetoric of duplicity, the uncertain embroilment of this poetic language within the world of reproduction and circulation it is supposedly satirizing, becomes a central part of the overall texture of this American political poem.

The Anarchiad, then, proceeds through a formal mechanism of confusion, where the verse itself is interrupted by prose interludes, as if pedantically to circumscribe any sublime flights of poetic fancy. In good Federalist fashion, the work comes to imply a continual sense of demystification, the unwrapping of false illusions by a sound common sense that acknowledges the perennial bathos of the human condition, as expressed in book 6:

> But give your toils not o'er—the human soul
> Sinks, by strong instinct, far beneath her goal. (32)

In book 10, the heroic Hesper talks about a "sinking State" (54), overtly referring to the "wild demagogues" (61) with their local, narrow schemes who have threatened to subvert the Federalist ideal of national unity. The tax rebellion led by Daniel Shays of Massachusetts in August 1786 may be the most obvious target here, but this "sinking State" also carries wider connotations of that ontological style of burlesque adumbrated in Pope's Peri Bathous. Just as the efficacy of Pope's satire depends upon the picturesquely negative qualities of the dunces, so the force of the Anarchiad derives paradoxically from the grotesque follies of human behavior, the ways in which Wronghead and Wimble perfectly exemplify a broader Federalist skepticism about the capacity of citizens for rational thought and action. In the Anarchiad, Trumbull and his fellow authors describe a world of inversion where a sinking state becomes the natural state.

In analyzing critical affiliations between Pope and his American followers, one traditional line of thought maintains that American satire of this time was less convincing because it "did not find a controlling center in the ironic perspective cultivated by the Popean literary mind."[40] This was Lewis P. Simpson in 1973, suggesting English satire was more successful because it was ultimately predicated upon a more secure set of intellectual and rational values and could therefore be more effectively scathing toward objects that failed to measure up to those ideals. Peter M. Briggs made a similar kind of case in 1985:

Alexander Pope was able to write satire upon the basis of some notion, real or imagined, of historical and moral order, social coherence, metaphysical balance *betrayed*: satire was a sad record and consequence of the falling away from a coherent and integrated order, civilized in its parts, beautiful and sanctified as a whole. Americans in 1776 or 1789 were much more in the position of discovering and asserting that their culture *had* a true center, a coherence, an order, a teleology—and to such labors a satirist need not apply. By nature conservative and skeptical, satire is best suited to charting known territories and traditional values, not to imagining new ones.[41]

I cite Briggs at length because his valuable essay epitomizes a number of ideological assumptions about this era in American literature that are too often left unexamined. The first assumption is that the British models, Pope and others, were proponents of "historical and moral order." As we have seen, there is a more paradoxical and ambiguous side to Pope's poetic discourse, suggesting it is a mistake to identify the British poet with any unadulterated vision of Augustan order. The second assumption is that American poets in the late eighteenth century were concerned with the invention of some cultural "coherence" or "teleology." But it is important not to impose retrospectively on writers such as Trumbull an ideology of romanticism. Unlike Emerson or Whitman, Trumbull was concerned neither with an "original relation to the universe," nor with that kind of organic relationship to the native country that produced Emerson's later versions of cultural nationalism.[42] Emerson's writings are frequently cited as the literary correlative to the political Declaration of Independence, as if American writers of the 1770s and 1780s had simply failed through their own inadequacies to chronicle the momentous historical changes of that era; in this reading, it took another fifty years before Emerson came along to put American cultural nationalism in its proper perspective. But in fact essays like "The American Scholar" represent Emerson's own fictionalization of the idea of national identity—powerful work, to be sure, and clearly related to the intellectual context of romanticism on both sides of the Atlantic, but not to be made congruent with that earlier quest for political independence, except in the minds of patriots determined to justify American literature and culture through a rhetoric of emancipation.

In his influential discussion of the late eighteenth century as "an age of contradiction," Leon Howard lamented how "American verse" of this era "is full of anticipations of something new which somehow did not quite come off." He attributed this deficiency to internal tensions between "poetry which was often neoclassic in tone and form yet implicitly romantic in its subject matter." For Howard, "great literature" necessarily involved "the reconciliation of many stimuli into one vigorous unity," and so, in his eyes, the tortuous, divided quality of a poet like Trumbull would militate against his status as the exemplar of a new nation, the United States of America. Howard in the 1950s assumed that an "original" poetry was the most fitting expression of American cultural nationalism; yet, a subsequent view of British-American culture in this era as inherently riven and turbulent might conceive a fractious rather than integrated style of poetry as offering more illuminating perspectives on the development of American literature and culture.[43] In *M'Fingal*, his most famous poem, Trumbull is concerned not with freedom but with transgression, not with sublime aspirations of the soul but with the more material business of political representation. Just as Pope's language slides surreptitiously between decorum and subversion, so *M'Fingal* exploits the interplay between epic and mock-epic, convention and parody, to delineate a radically destabilized world whose energy and iconography derive from a perpetual rebellion against established orthodoxies. Early in his career, Foucault asserted that transgression would come to "seem as decisive for our culture, as much a part of its soil, as the experience of contradiction was at an earlier time for dialectical thought"; and, in an equally specific historical sense, it is plausible to argue that the concept of transgression achieves a locus classicus in America at the end of the eighteenth century, where aesthetic pleasure and political self-justification emerge from the paradoxical process of traducing British culture and turning the world upside down.[44]

M'Fingal takes its style of octosyllabic couplets from Samuel Butler's mock-epic poem, *Hudibras* (1680), and its title from James MacPherson's *Fingal*, published in 1762. MacPherson, a Scottish member of Parliament who served as colonial secretary in West Florida between 1764 and 1766, presents the latter poem as the work of Ossian, a Caledonian writer of the third century, with the narrative hero cast as a Scotsman who devotes his life to righting wrongs and defending the oppressed. "Ossian" was in fact purely a product of the imagination of MacPherson, whose fake Gaelic relics of the 1760s appropriately introduce those themes of forgery and the fraudulent status of representation which play a major part in *M'Fingal*. In Trumbull's reworking of this Gaelic legend, Squire M'Fingal appears as a Tory landowner of Scottish extraction who resists the movement for American political independence. Carrying the patriot flag for the other side is the character of Honorius, who, "Inspir'd by freedom's heav'nly charms," seeks to rouse the "sons of glory" to battle against the "proud oppressor" (II, 699).[45] As Trumbull's poem proceeds, however, it comes increasingly to manifest some form of sympathy for the luckless Tory squire, and to associate the War of Independence with a spiral of lawless destruction:

> Thou too, M'Fingal, ere that day,
> Shalt taste the terrors of th'affray.
> See o'er thee hangs in angry skies,
> Where Whiggish constellations rise,
> And while plebeian sighs ascend,
> Their mob-inspiring aspects bend;
> That baleful star, whose horrid hair
> Shakes forth the plagues of down and tar!
> I see the pole, that rears on high
> Its flag terrific thro' the sky;
> The Mob beneath prepar'd t'attack,
> And tar predestin'd for thy back!
> Ah quit, my friend, this dang'rous home,
> Nor wait the darker scenes to come. (IV, 884–98)

Passages like this—some of which were appropriated at the time as propaganda by conservative groups—led Peter M. Briggs to detect in Trumbull "a certain Toryism of the imagination."[46] Similarly, Robert A. Ferguson attributed Trumbull's distancing of himself from the American Revolutionary movement to a conservative theory of order imbibed from his legal training, which would have made him uncomfortable with the whole idea of revolution and would have inclined him, in the best legal manner, toward a "more balanced view."[47]

As with Dwight, however, there is a noticeable discrepancy between the rationalizing mechanisms of Trumbull's prose pieces and the less controlled gyrations of his poetry. In his commencement oration at Yale in 1770, Trumbull chose to advocate "the elegant entertainments of polite Literature" as adding "dignity to our sentiments, delicacy and refinement to our manners" and so helping to polish away "that rugged ferocity . . . which is natural to the uncultivated nations of the world."[48] Such benign sentiments are repeated in the columns he wrote for the *Boston Chronicle* around the same time under the soubriquet of "The Meddler," which impugned the idle young gentlemen more intent upon fencing, gaming and swearing than on improving themselves through education. Trumbull cited Addison as his model in this effort "to lash indecency and immorality, and to convince the world that every extreme on either side of the golden mean is equally vile and ridiculous."[49] In accord with this expression of neoclassical sobriety, Trumbull attacked "the art of Ridicule and Raillery, which consists in putting modest persons to the blush," and specifically condemned the style of

"Double Entendre," which "consists in making words and phrases that are of a doubtful and ambiguous meaning and may be construed to signify obscene ideas." Trumbull concluded censoriously that "no person can be a perfect master of the Double Entendre, while there remains in his mind, the least refinement of thought, or delicacy of sentiment."[50]

The problem, clearly enough, is that in *M'Fingal* and other poems Trumbull does indeed prove himself just such "a perfect master of the Double Entendre." This notion of polite literature supporting a world of republican virtue is contradicted by the dynamics of *M'Fingal*, a poem which does not, in the end, impress us for its judicious or rationalistic qualities. The images that are most striking here revolve around a dynamic of inversion, the circular process whereby M'Fingal and Honorius not only define each other in a political sense but also continually subvert each other's dignity. In *M'Fingal*, nobody, neither loyalist nor patriot, can find solid ground upon which to stand:

> For in this ferment of the stream,
> The dregs have work'd up to the brim,
> And by the rule of topsyturvys,
> The skum stands swelling on the surface.
> You've caus'd your pyramid t'ascend
> And set it in the little end;
> Like Hudibras, your empire's made,
> Whose crupper had o'ertop'd his head;
> You've push'd and turn'd the whole world up-
> Side down and got yourselves a-top. (III, 143–52)

This is M'Fingal speaking, but the narrative tone generally supports this mood of burlesque, in a poem where visions of epic endeavor are mocked by the gross conditions of corporeal and material life. In *M'Fingal*, as in the *Anarchiad*, the whole paraphernalia of prophetic illumination is satirized:

> Nor less avail'd his optic sleight,
> And Scottish gift of second-sight.
> No antient sybil fam'd in rhyme
> Saw deeper in the womb of time;
> No block in old Dodona's grove,
> Could ever more orac'lar prove.
> Nor only saw he all that was,
> But much that never came to pass. (I, 57–64)

The negative syntax of this passage embodies its own kind of "optic sleight," as it appears poetically to conflate M'Fingal's gift of prophecy with that of the "antient sybil." This might be seen as a verbal equivalent of trompe l'oeil, for, by judiciously allowing that no sybil "Saw deeper" than the Scottish squire, the poet leaves open the more skeptical possibility that neither the sybil nor M'Fingal was able to foresee anything at all. Reinforcing this, Trumbull introduces a cutting pun on the meaning of "second-sight": traditionally signifying a sublime power of prophecy, the phrase is reworked ambiguously in this passage to imply the more modest human capacity to reinterpret events retrospectively, to be wise after the fact by second-guessing affairs from a secure vantage point of later time. Thus the author flattens out the ancient idea of prophecy, appropriately recasting it as a form of mock-prophecy in line with the modes of mock-epic inscribed here.

Conventionally, of course, burlesque or comic poetry has not been highly rated within the canons of American literature. Trumbull himself, as we have seen, disparaged the genre as vulgar in his pieces for the *Boston Chronicle*, while Samuel Kettell in 1829 was putting forward a normative romantic point of view when he described burlesque poetry as "but an inferior species of composition," adding how he felt it "to be in some sense a prostitution of poetry, to busy it with the faults and follies of men." Kettell went on, in the most blithe sentimentalist spirit, to claim the "free and chosen haunts of the muse are in the lofty mountains."[51] But in the "lofty mountains" Trumbull's own creative demons were not, and it is interesting to see from the essays he wrote as "The Correspondent" in the *Connecticut Journal* during the 1770s that he was gradually coming round more to the kind of outlook expressed in Pope's *Dunciad*, where folly is not so much a simple antithesis to reason but represents rather the condition of muddled humanity itself. As "The Meddler," Trumbull took a more elitist Addisonian stance, chastising human negligence and vanity; but as "The Correspondent," he inclined more to Pope's perspective, seeing "madness and foolishness" as not to be so easily separated from nobler human ideals:

It hath been universally allowed that one of the highest points of wisdom is to know one's self. I would ask whether this is not an absolute demonstration that wisdom is not only no ingredient of happiness, but the source of innumerable calamities to its possessors? I cannot conceive of a more melancholy circumstance than for a man to look into his own heart and head and view in a just light the vast quantities of vice, madness and foolishness, that like a vast magazine are heaped up in it.[52]

It is this conception of an ontologically divided self that led Trumbull in his "Correspondent" essays to spend more time attacking physicians, metaphysicians, and others who claim some form of "supernatural knowledge," some monopoly on absolute truth.[53] Whereas in the "Meddler" essays it was human venality that was the target of Trumbull's wit, here the focus was more on human pretentiousness. He even delineated an imaginative world upside down, presided over by "Theuth," god of Egypt, whose holy day was said to be 1 April, the anniversary of fools. Under the rule of Theuth, it became "the fashion to despise learning," while, conversely, the "dunce" was "inspired with self-sufficiency."[54] In his final "Correspondent" piece, published in September 1773, Trumbull envisaged how the disciples of Theuth would be "orderly united into a body, and incorporated by the name of the Society for the Propagation of Riot and Slander, and the Discouragement of Arts and Sciences."[55] This exemplifies the same kind of apocalyptic sensibility we find at the end of the *Dunciad*, with its vision of how "Universal Darkness buries All," and it suggests the ways in which Trumbull, like Pope, came to take the genre of burlesque seriously, as a valid intellectual and artistic response to a human world of grand folly. This structure of demystification is, of course, commensurate with Trumbull's opposition to the metaphysical philosophers even within his own Congregational Church, who represented a "New Light" party the poet felt to be too closely associated with the forces of dogmatism. By contrast, Trumbull's own poetic manner was, as he said, designed to set "an example of the use of Ridicule and Humour, to combat the whims of dogmatical Enthusiasts."[56] In this sense, Trumbull reinvents the mode of American burlesque, transposing it from mere satiric raillery into a central component of his poetic vision.[57] In line with these developments, Leon Howard has shown how the revisions and additions Trumbull made to *M'Fingal* between 1775 and 1782 had the effect of shifting the overall tone of the poem from "pointed satire" to "burlesque": whereas the original first canto was designed "as a scalpel for laying bare the tissue of false reasoning that he saw in the Tory arguments," subsequent versions of the poem offered a more systematic exposition of the American Revolution through the aesthetics of "mock epic."[58] Trumbull thus moved from being a partial advocate of American independence to a more impartial witness of human folly.

In *M'Fingal*, "dogmatical Enthusiasts" of every kind are lampooned, every rise is accompanied peremptorily by a fall. The "rule of topsyturvys" ensures that biological necessities displace the aspirations of higher learning; grand flights of political oratory must be suspended when it is "time t'adjourn for dinner" at the end of the first canto, for instance (I, 716). Similarly, the concluding section of the poem features M'Fingal "scorning all the fame of martyr" (IV, 1069) and scurrying off to safety in Boston, while "The Vision" ends up with a deflating disquisition on how abstract ideals of social representation fall flat when confronted by the more customary preference for preservation of self:

> So when wise Noah summon'd greeting
> All animals to gen'ral meeting;

From ev'ry side the members sent
All kinds of beasts to represent;
Each from the flood took care t'embark,
And save his carcase in the ark;
But as it fares in state and church,
Left his constituents in the lurch. (IV, 1085–92)

Implicitly, this in itself involves a Tory principle—self before community—but it is an apposite and comically effective end to this poem whose main thrust is not so much expository, in any philosophical sense, as iconoclastic. M'Fingal does not so much analyze political positions as radically undermine them, a process sanctioned by aggressive invasions and demystifications of abstract sublimity through a contradictory focus upon the corporeal realms of the body.

M'Fingal's strategic absenting of himself at the culmination of this poem epitomizes the way the work is concerned with the hollowing out of representation, political as well as artistic. Both types of representation are predicated upon the idea of something standing for something else: a Congressman represents his constituents, a work of art represents the scene it purports to describe. Trumbull, however, disturbs this balance: by reconstituting the epic as a mock-epic, the author not only undermines the idea of representation within epic forms, but also calls into question the validity of equivalent kinds of representation within the political sphere. Representation in M'Fingal, therefore, involves displacement and absence: just as in that brilliant final simile the delegates to Noah's ark choose to save their own hides, leaving their fellow animals to perish, so throughout this poem the burlesque impetus implies a structural incongruity between accepted theories of political process and the ways these ideas work themselves out in practice. At the end of the second canto, the moderator at the town meeting is forced to conceal himself under the table, only reappearing to adjourn the meeting after everybody has disappeared:

The moderator out of view
Beneath a bench had lain perdue;
Peep'd up his head to view the fray,
Beheld the wranglers run away,
And left alone with solemn face,
Adjourn'd them without time or place. (II, 807–12)

The comedy here lies in the way the moderator pompously insists on clinging to the forms of political protocol, ceremoniously adjourning the meeting even after the need for such a procedure has clearly become redundant. Again, M'Fingal explores the discrepancies between codified principles and inchoate practices, continually transposing one into the other so as comically to highlight these fundamental shifts in perspective.

Just as the prophetic strains of "second-sight" become flattened out into more mundane styles of second-guessing, so abstract political designs are also flattened out into mere simulacra of themselves. As M'Fingal puts it:

> For what's your Congress, or its end?
> A power t'advise and recommend. (III, 157–58)

The conception of a house of Congress is unraveled and revealed in its basic components, as no more than an advisory body. However, the British constitution, which the Scottish squire belligerently defends, finds itself similarly desacralized:

> You scorn the British constitution,
> That constitution, form'd by sages,
> The wonder of all modern ages:
> Which owns no failure in reality,
> Except corruption and venality. (III, 196–200)

The first edition of *M'Fingal* featured illustrations by the miniature painter, Elkanah Tisdale, and a cartoonish element pervades this whole poem, as it does the *Anarchiad* also. It is important to recognize, however, these cartoons do not simply travesty political representation but suggest, more provocatively, how the very idea of political representation itself can be seen as a travesty. Trumbull configures his dramatis personae in two dimensions because of a radical skepticism about what deep or meaningful third dimension might possibly exist within this kind of burlesque scenario, where "corruption and venality" drag everyone and everything down to the same level.

In "The Vision," the final canto of this poem, Trumbull introduces a punning interplay between the "constitution frail" of a political framework and the physical constitution of the human body (IV, 957). No purely abstract mechanism, the American political constitution must, like the people it serves, inevitably be subject to the erratic whims of human nature. This is commensurate with the frequent animal similes throughout this poem: the beasts in Noah's ark, the tarring and feathering whereby M'Fingal is reduced to the appearance of a bird, and so on. In this latter passage, Trumbull specifically provides a footnote to draw the reader's attention to his rejection of Plato's definition of man as "a two-legg'd, unfeather'd creature" (III, 580). Disdaining Plato's dualistic idealism, Trumbull conceives man's cerebral and animal sides to be entirely cognate. Hence *M'Fingal* delineates a world where competing discourses—the soul and the body, Honorius

and M'Fingal, patriot and Loyalist—come to interfere with each other, to challenge each other's premises. Such circuits of perpetual contraposition exemplify
what Chasseguet-Smirgel terms "the anal-sadistic desire for muddle and confusion," whose anarchic impetus links specific representations of physical violence
to disturbances within the broader power structures of an insurrectionary culture.[59] The contorted human body becomes an image of contortion in the body of
the state.

This is the basis of the topsy-turvy aesthetic in *M'Fingal*: the poem's readi-
ness to contradict any given position with another, to be forever turning itself
round the other way. Like Pope in the *Dunciad*, Trumbull's sense of the ontological farce of the human condition manifests itself in scabrous images of aggression,
whose scatological force implies Trumbull's skepticism about all civic issues. In
the third canto, the patriots unceremoniously dangle Squire M'Fingal from the
top of a liberty pole, where he swings "like a keg of ale" (III, 444) and promptly
agrees to say anything at all if they will let him down. The way in which M'Fingal
is so ready to gainsay his own principles in order to save his skin represents
another moment of comic burlesque, of course. Meanwhile, the upended hero is
visited with rude compliments of a more physical nature:

> The deadly spade discharg'd a blow
> Tremendous on his rear below. (III, 421–22)

Later, after the mob has dispersed, the squire finds himself in an even worse
condition:

> The Constable in rueful case
> Lean'd sad and solemn o'er a brace,
> And fast beside him, cheek by jowl,
> Stuck 'Squire M'Fingal 'gainst the pole,
> Glued by the tar t'his rear applied,
> Like barnacle on vessel's side. (III, 615–20)

Nor are M'Fingal's experiences of humiliating reversal confined solely to his
waking hours. In the final canto, he relates a dream vision wherein his fellow
countryman, Malcolm, also finds himself dangling from the gallows:

> And in its noose that wav'ring swang,
> Friend Malcolm hung, or seem'd to hang.
> How changed from him, who bold as lyon,
> Stood Aid-de-Camp to Governor Tryon,
> More rebels vanish once, like witches,
> And saved his life, but dropp'd his breeches. (IV, 69–74)

These images of inversion are not presented haphazardly. They are associated consistently with a principled rejection of idealism, a turning back from high abstractions into the common world of material bathos:

> And better 'twere at their expence,
> T'have drubb'd him into common sense,
> And wak'd by bastings on his rear,
> Th'activity, tho' but of fear. (IV, 639–42)

This burlesque form of aggression, the desire to overthrow one's enemy, was frequently given metaphorical expression during this revolutionary era by imagery of reversal that was tinged with sadistic overtones. In *M'Fingal*, strategic maneuvers in battle are often couched in terms of an invasion or appropriation of another's territory from behind: "Hear bullets whizzing in your rear" (II, 718), "His rear attack'd on Monmouth plain" (IV, 686), "By movements wise made good his rear" (IV, 1068), and so on. Schooled in Pope's style of radical bathos, Trumbull constructs an aesthetics of the rearguard, an idiom of contraction and deflation.

In his analysis of political satire in the American Revolution, Bruce Ingham Granger notes how such scatological patterns offered a condensed means of expression relating to the drive for a more widespread sense of social bouleversement. He quotes from a 1775 example of Revolutionary verse, "The Irishman's Epistle to the Officers and Troops at Boston":

> How brave you went out with muskets all bright,
> And thought to befrighten the folks with the sight;
> But when you got there how they powder'd your pums,
> And all the way home how they pepper'd your bums,
> And is it not, honies, a comical farce,
> To be proud in the face, and be shot in the a——se.[60]

In her essay on caricatures of sexuality during the French Revolution a few years later, Vivian Cameron described the buttocks as a focal point for (erotic and political) desire during that turbulent era. As a site for the humiliation of others, such imagery was frequently exploited metaphorically in political cartoons, while this kind of lewd iconography also became displaced cathectically into characteristic emblems of lust in an age when violent struggles for power formed a significant nexus of social communication. Along the same lines, Lynn Hunt's work on the history of pornography has shown how, until the end of the eighteenth century, the discourse of obscenity was almost always perceived as an adjunct to something else—usually some form of freethinking or heresy, since it was generally thought appropriate to offer a rude depiction of sex in conjunction with equally rude insults to religious or political authorities.[61] Hunt records how politically motivated pornography of this kind reached its zenith in France during the black decade of the 1790s, amid the traumatized conditions of a fractured, post-Revolutionary culture.

Although M'Fingal clearly does not equal the work of these French writers in either political viciousness or sexual explicitness, there is still an element within Trumbull's poem which delights in using a bawdy humor as a fitting counterpoint to the radically destabilized environment being represented here. In M'Fingal, like in the pornography of the French Revolution, a dethroning of political authority can be seen to work in parallel with the savage dissolution of human dignity. We know that Trumbull did indeed compose in his youth a scatological trifle entitled "Poetical Inspiration," which was first published by his biographer, Alexander Cowie, as late as 1936. This piece of juvenilia makes an analogy between "horrid earthquakes" and the "cholic rumbling" of the gods, going on to suggest how the energy of poetic vision itself emerges also from these lower quarters:

> His priest (and in the days we name
> A priest and poet was the same)
> Fixing a sacred three-legg'd stool,
> They call'd a *tripod*, o'er the hole,
> And sitting down in solemn show,
> Drew inspiration from below,
> Which thus received he made the best on,
> And by a *vicevers'* digestion,
> Th'inflation rising from behind,
> It came out verse, which went in wind.[62]

M'Fingal represents, albeit in a much more advanced and elaborate manner, this same principle of vice versa. Compulsively as well as contextually, Trumbull's poetry is driven to portray the world upside down.

In Federalist rhetoric of this era, the idea of "a perversion of taste in composition" was associated frequently with what Richard Alsop in 1807 called "a still greater perversion of principle, in that hideous morality of revolutionary madness, which, priding itself in an emancipation from moral obligation, levelled the boundaries of virtue and vice, while it contemptuously derided the most amiable and sacred feelings of our nature."[63] This has led in a direct line to contemporary discussions of the post-Revolutionary period, which often describe a conflict between the kind of legal and ethical conservatism espoused by

Federalists on the one hand and a Republican emphasis upon natural rights and liberty on the other.[64] Yet the work of Trumbull would seem to circumvent and problematize this binary opposition, for, despite its overtly reactionary qualities, it also delineates with relish a paradoxical landscape of confusion and contradiction where the established world is stood laughingly on its head. Recalling Chasseguet-Smirgel's contention that the iconography of deviance tends to manifest itself most clearly at times of major social and political upheaval, I would argue the peculiar genius of *M'Fingal* emanates from the way it internalizes this principle of contradiction, plays knowingly with the pleasures of transgression. For Trumbull, the power of an object always derives from the pressure of its opposite, and this is why he takes pleasure in yoking together epic and mock-epic, refracting the dark anarchy of war through a low flippancy of style. Such apparent confusion of categories is one of the reasons many American critics have had such a difficult time with Trumbull's work: George F. Sensabaugh, for instance, found in *M'Fingal* merely a "ridiculous" travesty of Milton's "grandeur" in *Paradise Lost*. But, as Ian Jack observed in a famous study of this genre, the purpose of mock-heroic is not simply to ridicule or destroy the heroic impulse, but to play ironically upon the discrepancies between elevated style and reduced substance.[65] This, of course, perfectly anticipates the conclusion of Trumbull's poem, where the concept of political representation—itself a displacement of presence into symbolic abstraction and absence—finds itself travestied, as Noah's animals bail out of the flood, leaving their "constituents in the lurch" (IV, 1092). *M'Fingal* pulls back further and further from the idea of direct aesthetic and political representation until we are left at the end with only a spiral of paradoxical absences. Every stable entity has, like the hero himself, slipped away.

*   *   *

When John Adams wrote to Trumbull in 1785 thanking him for sending a copy of *M'Fingal*, Adams expressed his appreciation of his friend's mock-epic verse, but added how he felt Trumbull should henceforth concern himself with "Poetry of superior kinds" which might "afford full scope for the pathetic and sublime."[66] Such criticism is entirely consistent with the philosophy outlined in Adams's *Dissertation on the Canon and the Feudal Law* (1765), where he declared the great theme of European history had been a struggle between individual freedom and corporate authority, the latter having become insidiously institutionalized by the tyrannical mechanisms of canon and feudal law. For Adams, the advent of American civilization was destined to bring about "illumination of the ignorant, and the emancipation of the slavish part of mankind all over the earth," while American government itself was to be a "plain, simple, intelligible thing, founded in nature and reason, and quite comprehensible by common sense."[67] Here, then, is a point of divergence between the Federalist friends: Adams and Trumbull may have shared political sympathies, but Trumbull's poetry is by no means "plain, simple, intelligible," nor could it ever be unproblematically concerned with the emancipation of the unenlightened. Instead, Trumbull's paradoxes delve back into the more turbulent aspects of the American experience, just as Alexander Pope's poetry holds up a dark mirror to Augustan London.

Nevertheless, Adams' remarks anticipate two centuries of homespun criticism, which has found it difficult to come to terms with the legacy of Pope in eighteenth-century American poetry. It is not so much a question of American followers of Pope entertaining political views that, after the Revolution, came to be seen as unacceptable; this may be true of Mather Byles, but the social opinions of Trumbull were generally unexceptionable. What is more disturbing, from an ideological perspective, is the proclivity of Byles and Trumbull to represent their world through styles of doubleness, filtering the English neoclassical style through a series of American mirrors so their discourse could be seen to cut two different ways at once. In his *Cultural History of the American Revolution*, Kenneth Silverman castigated the "formularism" of American poets in this era who sought to follow English models, and, in a typical nationalist strategy, he attempted to valorize instead those writers and artists who were inventing an "authentically" American style defined by a "Puritan esthetic" of "the 'deep beauty in things as they are' ":

Behind [John Singleton] Copley's fidelity to what his eye saw—a fidelity animating much later American art, including the haphazard visual catalogues of Walt Whitman and the minutely drawn nuts and bolts of Charles Sheeler—behind this fidelity lay a Puritan determination to see the world as God created it, untransformed, without metaphor or imaginative reshaping.[68]

This, however, is precisely the tradition into which Byles and Trumbull do not fit. For them, poetic representation involves a complex business of intertextual inversion, where meaning is created through parody, juggling, turning things upside down. Silverman's antagonism to the idea of poetic imitation is of the same order as John Adams' scorn for European systems of serfdom, and they both imply a self-reliant, "protestant" mode that has long been institutionalized within American thought and culture. But it is important to recognize the conceptual parameters of such assumptions, to observe how closely they are tied in with a specific kind of "Puritan esthetic."

Despite his admiration for the English poet, the "catholic" duplicities of

Pope were always a source of uneasiness for Trumbull. There is a revealing moment in *The Progress of Dulness* when the narrator talks of how certain forms of juvenile "knav'ry" (II, 90) are morally bad but economically productive, since they provide schools with a "copious income" (II, 88):

> Ev'n thus the Pope, long since has made
> Of human crimes a gainful trade. (II, 91–92)

Trumbull is referring here, of course, to the Pope in Rome, with his selling of indulgences; but he could just as easily have been speaking about Alexander Pope, whose satirical poetry secured "a gainful trade" out of human folly. Pope, a Catholic poet of sorts, was ironically continuing the tradition of his religious namesakes, making money out of the inevitable foibles and corruptions of humanity, and Trumbull's own satirical art was wrapped up in the same compromising circuit. This is why the transformational qualities of burlesque humor always appeared to Trumbull in a morally dubious light, something he disapproved of in his more sober prose essays, even though he found himself instinctively drawn toward these transgressive forms in his more compulsive poetic style. Indeed, Trumbull may have found himself attracted to the punning, farcical aspects of Pope's artistic style against his better judgment. It is noticeable how *M'Fingal* makes an association between self-indulgent wordplay and the transubstantive frivolity of Old World Catholicism:

> Aloft a card'nal's hat is spread
> O'er punster Cooper's rev'rend head! (II, 625–26)

And yet such propensity for grotesque "puns and jokes" (IV, 391) is precisely what the mock-epic poet himself cannot avoid. For the Connecticut lawyer, poetry appeared as an aesthetically alluring but ethically uncertain pastime, an arena of duplicity where sober rationality found itself compromised by the ludic mirrors of art. It is this lack of congruence between discursive rationalism and a more multivalent, transgressive style that makes the poetry of the Connecticut Wits so difficult to explicate purely in ideological or political terms.

If reading Byles and Trumbull through what Evert Duyckinck called the "papal" perspective has significant implications for the construction of an American literary canon, the reverse move can also help us comprehend more fully the ambivalent ideological position of Alexander Pope within English literature. Once thought to be an embodiment of what Basil Willey called "cosmic Toryism," Pope is now more likely to be "recuperated" as a covert critic of capitalist enterprises that were emerging in Britain during the eighteenth century. John Barrell and Harriet Guest, for example, have traced in the "Epistle to Bathurst" an implicit critique of mercantile amoralism, together with the structures of commodification and imperial subjugation that accompanied them.[69] While such revisionist readings can be illuminating, they risk attempting to impose upon Pope a moral synthesis which his elusive, multifaceted texts always tend to resist. Pope's genius is to slide between different levels and philosophical positions, to complicate his epic endeavors with mock-epic subtexts. John Bender, writing of eighteenth-century art in general, talks of its capacity to deploy "generic contradiction as a dominant formal strategy," and some sense of this formal interchangeability pervades the poetic worlds of Pope and Trumbull.[70]

Returning the concept of transgression to its literal, etymological meaning—a crossing of boundaries—I would suggest the oxymoronic structures of Pope's aesthetics appear at their most revealing when dislocated from the native customs and political assumptions that have accumulated around them, so they can be read alongside similar kinds of work in a different culture. By comparatively aligning Pope with Trumbull, I am not seeking to "universalize" both writers, to imply the essence of their art transcends time and place. Instead, I am suggesting that the complex, often antagonistic relationship which Mather Byles and Trumbull experienced with their own historical time and place reflects back on the awkward, liminal relationship between Pope's poetry and the conventions of English society. Such awkwardness is too often glossed over or reimagined from a radical point of view as some clearcut form of oppositional hostility. By contrast, a comparative perspective on Pope can allow us to perceive how his art is conformist and subversive both at once, in that ironic, chameleonic, and self-preserving manner Julia Kristeva has associated with the literary style of foreigners and strangers, particularly internal exiles, who enjoy no "natural" sense of affiliation with the world surrounding them.[71]

In their study of transgression, Peter Stallybrass and Allon White define one version of the "grotesque" as "a boundary phenomenon of hybridization or inmixing, in which self and other become enmeshed in an inclusive, heterogeneous, dangerously unstable zone."[72] In this sense, the conditions of Pope's American reception and reproduction describe a boundary, both geographic and metaphorical, that works to defamiliarize his craftily self-contained English persona. To Americanize Pope, in other words, is to expose more fully those aspects of his work that clashed with the norms of Protestant culture, highlighting those paradoxical, burlesque elements with which Dwight was especially uncomfortable, or the obscene, scatological proclivities of *The Dunciad*, by which poets like Trumbull were both attracted and repelled. These overt tensions between Pope and the heritage of American Puritanism suggest, by a process of magnification, the more covert but no less crucial antagonisms between Pope and the Anglican establishment in England. Hence this transatlantic framework effectively reveals within his poetic texts elements of those "dangerously unstable" forces of "hybridization" that make Pope's art so dextrously cosmopolitan and devilishly two-faced.

Chapter Three
From Allegory to Exchange
Richardson and Franklin

At the same time as the Connecticut Wits were drawing upon the hybrid characteristics of Pope to fashion their own epic vision of American independence, philosopher-statesmen like Benjamin Franklin and Thomas Jefferson were constructing narratives that would subsequently come to be understood as representative of the qualities of the new nation. In particular, Franklin's *Autobiography* (begun in 1771, though not published until after the author's death) and Jefferson's *Notes on the State of Virginia* (published privately in 1784–85 and publicly in 1787) have been seen as expressing an emerging nationalist consciousness, a sense of the United States as categorically different from the corrupt old world of Europe. The purpose of this chapter and the next is to interrogate such post-romantic assumptions of American exceptionalism by suggesting the kinship between these exemplars of national identity and those more skeptical, paradoxical attitudes that circulated widely within the North Atlantic cultural Enlightenment. By reading Franklin's *Autobiography* through the perspective of Richardson's epistolary romances, and by reconsidering Jefferson's works in the light of his admiration for writers like Laurence Sterne, we will see how this ambiguous world of seduction and sensibility comes to form an alternative, if latent, strand within the framework of American intellectual life at the time when the nation was declaring independence. Just as the demimonde of Pope provides a destabilizing subtext within the Federalist universe of order and piety, so the profane implications of Richardson and Sterne open up intertextual crevices in Franklin and Jefferson that might not otherwise be visible. In addition, the reconceptualization of these English authors in terms of their reception in America suggests a different dimension to these canonical works: viewed through a transatlantic mirror, the English novel of sensibility finds itself no longer attached so securely to issues of property, patronage, and class.

By an equivalent transatlantic process, the cosmopolitan edges of the eighteenth-century Enlightenment threatened uncomfortably to dislocate the assumptions of an American religious consciousness centered around distinct polarities of good and evil. As Andrew Delbanco has observed, this recognition of evil comprised a traditional element within the New England cultural landscape: seventeenth-century Puritanism resolved terrestrial affairs into an apocalyptic struggle between body and soul, the Indian forests and the city on a hill, darkness and light.[1] Such an emphasis in Christian America upon dualistic typologies, predicated upon the conversion of matter into spirit, helps to explain why the disruptive and skeptical world of the Enlightenment remains, as Giles Gunn puts it, "the absent, or at least the forgotten, integer in the American equation of the relationship between faith and knowledge."[2] Those committed to a separatist rhetoric of salvation were wary of the secular consciousness that seemed to be encroaching across the Atlantic, with its new mechanistic technologies and philosophies. This idiom of fracture and fissure that posed a threat to the self-contained world of America in the eighteenth century developed alongside a dissemination of scientific ideas concerned with optics and the relativism of perspective. In "Conduct of the Understanding," published posthumously in 1706, John Locke uses optical figures to demonstrate what he sees as the empirical basis of knowledge: Locke discusses how "Impressions [are] made on the retina by rays of light," with human understanding being based upon sensory reactions to "material causes."[3] Several of Jonathan Edwards's earliest essays—"Of the Rainbow" and "Colours," in particular—also implicate natural philosophy within metaphors of reflection and refraction, demonstrating the early influence of Isaac Newton's *Opticks* (1704), which established this field as a central concern for Enlightenment thinking.

David Hume similarly develops a thread of optical conceits in *A Treatise of Human Nature* (1739–40), where the "passions of fear and hope" are described through the medium of a prism: "Are not these as plain proofs, that the passions of fear and hope are mixtures of grief and joy, as in optics 'tis a proof, that a colour'd ray of the sun passing thro' a prism, is a composition of two others, when, as you diminish or encrease the quantity of either, you find it prevail proportionably more or less in the composition?"[4] One consequence of this kind of rationalism was to disavow the plausibility and efficacy of spiritual experience; instead, Hume radically externalizes the processes of cognition, denying a priori metanarratives and asserting that knowledge is simply a function of sensory perception and reaction within the terrestrial world. The "minds of men," he says, "are mirrors to one another" (414); significance lies not in men's "souls," but in how their mental processes reciprocally interact. For Hume, therefore, the basis of all knowledge is comparison: "Reason or science is nothing but the comparing of ideas, and the discovery of their relations" (518); and, even more specifically, "All kinds of reasoning consist in nothing but a *comparison*, and a discovery of those relations, either constant or inconstant, which two or more objects bear to each other" (121). By dismissing circular chains of cause and effect, and by disestablishing the "fiction of the imagination" (251) by which we notionally assume the idea of identity—"fiction" is one of his favorite words in the *Treatise*—Hume succeeds in collapsing imaginative unities into divided fragments, what he calls a "double existence internal and external" (255). This "double existence" indicates an ontological dissociation between any material event and its internalization by the human mind; hence Hume constructs what he calls a world of "profound and intense reflection" (268), where there is no necessary correlation between mental projection and external phenomena. Consequently, all categories of understanding can be likened to optical experiments, where the human mind seeks forms of congruence through which to filter the disparate rays of experience.

Hume, then, establishes in the Enlightenment era a philosophy of comparison which was generally understood as antipathetic to interiorized Christian values. This is why his work was seen by many in his own day as dangerously paradoxical: Samuel Johnson dismissed his "pernicious philosophy" as that of a "rat," while Samuel Richardson classed Hume among the "very mischievous writers."[5] Richardson's discomfort with such skepticism was not surprising, given the tone of sentimental moralizing and the nostalgia for religious purity that pervade his own novels. It was this reputation for piety that helped to boost the standing of Richardson in eighteenth-century America: his "popularity as a novelist," records James D. Hart, "was surpassed by no one."[6] *Pamela*, which appeared in England in 1740–41, became the first novel to be published in the American colonies when it was brought out by Benjamin Franklin's printing press in Philadelphia in 1742, and it remained the most widely read of Richardson's novels in the New World, though *Clarissa* (1747–48) and *Sir Charles Grandison* (1753–54) were also well known and much admired. Some of the copies which circulated widely in America were imported directly from Britain; others, particularly the many editions of Richardson's novels published in the new United States toward the end of the eighteenth century, were abridged specifically for the American market. These abridged versions would typically eliminate the complex, convoluted letters that characterize Richardson's epistolary style, opting instead for more straightforward stories of seduction and betrayal related through third-person narration. In this way, says Leonard Tennenhouse, "the abridged Richardson dispenses with all but the most necessary verbal performances in order to concentrate on the conduct of the female body": the focus shifts from literary artifice to moral theme and conduct. This "abridged Richardson," Tennenhouse argues, "was an American phenomenon," profoundly different from the author admired among eighteenth-century English readers, who "much preferred their Richardson unabridged."[7]

Nevertheless, this transatlantic displacement of Richardson did have the effect of illuminating a crucial series of ambiguities within his novels. Despite his mistrust for the paradoxes of Hume, Richardson's own texts were racked from the first by internal tensions between the imperatives of moral virtue and the charms of transgressive sensibility. Richardson himself, the son of a Derbyshire joiner and a devout Calvinist, understood *Pamela* and *Clarissa* as paeans to the ethical probity of the English bourgeoisie in their attempts to resist the licentious assumptions of the post-Restoration aristocracy. The subtitle of *Pamela*, "Virtue Rewarded," indicates the author's stance: he sees his heroine as endowed with unique, meritocratic qualities which will allow her to reap her marital, social and financial rewards. However, as critics have regularly noted ever since *Pamela Censured* appeared in the same year as the original novel's publication, Richardson's overt attempts to cast his story in a stable, pedagogical light are held in check by the narrative's more teasing and provocative aspects. The author, in describing "the endearments between the sexes," has often been thought to advance the cause of illicit passion rather than to suppress it.[8] The representation of romance as transgression in both *Pamela* and *Clarissa* testifies to this discursive strand of division, what John Mullan calls the "fissures" in Richardson's narratives, those "moments at which the instructive component of sentiment was liable to be forgotten."[9] Nor are these moments incidental to the structure of the novels: Michael McKeon has theorized Richardson's texts in terms of an internal dialectic between the genres of romance and realism, leading to a "thread of epistemological reversal . . . continuous with a subversive strain in [the author's] progressive ideology." In this reading, the disjunctions between fantasy and fact— the fantasies of Pamela, as well as those of Mr B—highlight a "turn toward extreme skepticism" that stands as a counterbalance to the tone of "documentary historicity" evoked by the epistolary nature of the novel.[10] In Richardson's narratives, these structural ironies manifest themselves particularly through the manner in which the forms of romance are chronicled circuitously in letters, lengthy inscriptions which involve recollections of events some time after they are said to have occurred. Hence the illusion of immediacy is sacrificed to the thrills of recollection and anticipation, as the relationship between Pamela and Mr. B, for example, works itself out within a framework of textual projection. "I love writing," says Pamela at the beginning of the novel; and, appropriately enough, Mr. B's closet also doubles as his library, thereby suggesting the close associations between books, artifice, and a perverse mode of voyeurism.[11]

What the reader finds in *Pamela*, then, is a series of reversals where the impulse toward historicity is displaced by subjective modes of perception: Raymond Williams, complaining about the attenuated social consciousness in these novels, talked of Richardson's "isolating fanaticism."[12] This helps to account for the book's radical instability in its representation of character, an instability that manifests itself in the blurring of its narrative trajectory through parallel forms of masquerade. The heroine is thus cast as a "sauce-box," a female object of fetishistic desire, while Mr. B is the "gentleman of pleasure and intrigue," spying through a keyhole on Pamela in her dishabille and disguising himself as a maidservant in order to penetrate his victim's defenses.[13] The novel's touches of voyeurism, transvestism, and otherwise aberrant behavior do not, of course, invalidate the text's wider cultural and political implications, its consideration of conflict between different genders and social classes, and so on. What they do suggest, though, is the way in which Richardson, for all his protestations in the book's preface of painting "VICE in its proper colours" and setting "VIRTUE in its own amiable light," effectively inscribes a fictional world of stylistic excess where seemingly antithetical qualities and characters become fatally intermingled.[14] In the chameleonic universe of *Pamela*, everything is in constant danger of sliding into its opposite.[15]

Because of this idiom of excess, we find an uncomfortable feeling among many eighteenth-century savants that Richardson, for all his excellent qualities, should only be approached, as Rhode Island church pastor Enos Hitchcock observed in 1790, "with caution and under the direction of a guide."[16] In his 1782 essay, "Of Novel Reading," English cleric Vicesimus Knox similarly argued that although Richardson's novels were "written with the purest intentions of promoting virtue," nevertheless "in the accomplishment of this purpose scenes are laid open, which it would be fairer to conceal, and sentiments excited, which it would be more advantageous to early virtue not to admit."[17] This has led some English critics, notably Leslie Stephen, to make the patronizing assumption that Richardson was too variegated a writer to be fully appreciated within the provincial world of eighteenth-century America, even though we know that Jonathan Edwards, for example, read his works with pleasure.[18] Nevertheless, it is true that there were concerted efforts in America to allegorize Richardson's texts, to circumscribe their more erratic proclivities within a clear framework of didacticism so that he would appear as "the sublimest teacher of rectitude," as a Philadelphia magazine said in 1800.[19] There is a clear analogy here with Timothy Dwight's efforts around the same time to produce a more sanitized, harmonious version of Pope's epic poetry. Unlike Pope, however, Richardson can be seen as complicit in these attempts to reclassify his works within a framework of moral closure: the novelist became, as Mullan notes, "his own worried reader," always trying to append supplements to his works to ensure they would be understood in the correct spirit.[20] For his third and fourth editions of *Clarissa* in 1751, for instance, he inserted as an appendix a collection of the book's "Moral and Instructive Sentiments," based on maxims gleaned from the novel which a helpful member of the reading public had sent him. Richardson told a friend he had "taken much pains" with this table of moral sentiment, which solemnly cautioned parents against the undue exercise of their authority and warned children not to prefer men of pleasure to men of probity.[21]

So highly did Benjamin Franklin think of this collection of sententiae that he "borrowed" over twenty of them for *Poor Richard's Almanack* of 1752, an act of plagiarism which indicates the value put on Richardson as a moralist in America.[22] It also suggests the continuum between fact and fiction in the eyes of eighteenth-century readers: to understand Richardson solely as a fabricator of imaginative worlds and Franklin as a chronicler of social reality is to misconceive what William B. Warner has called the "hybrid form of writing" at this time, when the novel had not yet assumed the mantle of the exclusively "creative" genre it came to appear in the post-romantic period.[23] For all of their fantastic elements, Richardson would have seen his fictions as a mirror of sober truths, just as Franklin envisaged his *Autobiography* not simply as factual recollection but as a judicious blend of observation and sententiae. In this sense, it would be wrong to see the American refraction of Richardson as simply a misrepresentation of the English Richardson, since the author's own reduction of textual deviation to ethical maxim in his 1751 version of *Clarissa* foreshadows the abridged editions of his works that circulated in America during the late eighteenth century, editions which became the prototype for seduction novels like Susanna Rowson's *Charlotte Temple* (1794) and Hannah Webster Foster's *The Coquette* (1797). In *The Coquette*, Mrs. Richman does indeed describe Eliza Wharton's seducer, Major Sanford, as "a second Lovelace," while Foster's puritanical misprision of *Clarissa* is continued in *The Boarding School* (1798), where one of the characters wonders: "what dreadful effects might the specious manners of a Lovelace have on the inexperienced mind, were they not detected by a just exhibition of his vices?"[24] In the early years of the republic, argues Elizabeth Barnes, the seduction novel offered a fictional paradigm for the establishment of American democracy because it seemed to require the expenditure of sympathy as a necessary investment for the consolidation of familial union, thereby converting fellow feeling for one's victimized compatriots into an emblem of patriotic loyalty to the new nation as a whole.[25] This is why Richardson, as a supposed avatar of the seduction novel, remained so popular in America at the turn of the nineteenth century; it also helps to explain the attempts, both at this time and subsequently, to appropriate his books as models of psychological enlightenment and cultural independence.

The most famous example of such an appropriation came in 1804, when

John Adams claimed that the American people were Clarissa and democracy was the Lovelace leading them to their destruction.[26] But Adams's metaphor is so tortuous and convoluted that it seems significant not so much for its political message but for its indication of the lengths to which American public figures were willing to go in order to requisition Richardson for their own allegorical purposes. Deborah L. Madsen has written of American allegory as typically involving a response to historical crisis, a way of sublimating popular anxieties by reasserting "the authority of some culturally important sacred text" to the imperiled community; and in this sense the attempt of Adams to translate *Clarissa* into an allegorical topos might be seen as a strategy to bind the novel within a rhetoric of exceptionalism, where the prevalence of oppression would serve only to reemphasize the redemptive qualities of American national destiny.[27]

The American Richardson, then, became popularly construed as a guardian of the public conscience. On examining the reception of Richardson's books in the United States, it is clear that matters of class conflict, central to views of Richardson within a British context, have tended to be occluded in favor of readings based more around issues of gender and moral probity.[28] Carroll Smith-Rosenberg has written of how Richardson came to be seen in the early nineteenth century as an advocate for American "Evangelicalism" and "The Cult of True Womanhood," with Pamela and Clarissa perceived as "symbols of woman's powerlessness and her ultimate victimization." Richardson thus became creatively reimagined as a sentimental writer cherishing a vision of family values as a necessary defense against the immoral world of male philandering. (Ironically enough, as Smith-Rosenberg goes on to observe, the family actually plays a relatively minor role in *Pamela*, with the "assertion of individualistic, romantic values" taking the heroine away from what she sees as her ignominious point of origin.[29]) While *Pamela* was thought to anticipate the domestic fictions of Victorian America, *Clarissa*, following the intervention of Adams, has generally been understood more within the realm of national politics: Jay Fliegelman notes how the latter book was "extremely popular" in America during the second half of the eighteenth century, and he reads *Clarissa* as a kind of conversion narrative whereby the heroine's own growth toward maturity runs in parallel with the movement toward American independence. From this perspective, Richardson's text demonstrates the evils of paternal mismanagement (or British tyranny) by describing how Clarissa's avaricious father jeopardizes his daughter's freedom and future happiness by attempting to sell her into an inappropriate marriage. Fliegelman points out that the abridged American editions of *Clarissa* which appeared after 1772 "virtually 'rewrite' the novel in such a way to render it an unadulterated polemic against parental severity"; and he sees this as significantly commensurate with the widespread American interest in the writings of John Locke, dedicated as they were to the prospects of educational reform and cultural emancipation.[30] Cathy N. Davidson, in yet another American allegorization of *Clarissa*, takes the book to be "an apt metaphor for the legal status of the post-revolutionary American girl," who, owing to a "holdover from British law," was still categorized as her father's property.[31]

We know, however, that *Clarissa* was read widely in America in the years between its British appearance in 1747–48 and the first American edition of 1772.[32] This tells us that American readers in the mid-eighteenth century would have been engaging with Richardson's fuller, more complex narrative rather than the shorter, schematic versions which became popular later; indeed, Tennenhouse confirms that the "unabridged, or English, Richardson continued to be available as an imported commodity to American readers throughout the forty-year period when it was not being published in the colonies."[33] This in turn suggests that to resituate *Clarissa* within the framework of the American cultural Enlightenment is to reilluminate some of the more devious and deviant aspects of this multifaceted work. In his preface to *Pamela*, the author states that the capacity of fiction "to divert and entertain" can be balanced by its ability "to inculcate religion and morality"; and it is this transposition of unpredictable behavior into regulated precept which has formed the basis of American allegorizations of Richardson.[34] Yet this process can, of course, work two ways: the conversion of nature into instruction is always threatened, in *Clarissa*, by the dissolution of duty into passion. As in *Pamela*, the mediated nature of desire and the consequent ambiguities of moral freedom are always implicit within this narrative. Lovelace knows he can exploit the side of Clarissa that is twisted and torn, caught between her family duty and Christian morality on the one hand and romantic desire on the other. From this perspective, the English system of gender and class hierarchies becomes a formal tableau or mirror against which Lovelace and Clarissa play out their transgressive romance, as they cross these established boundaries by engaging in the oxymoronic double bind of "resistance . . . so irresistible."[35] In this sense, Richardson's novels do not simply reflect English social hierarchies; rather, they deflect them obliquely into a realm of travesty. As Terry Castle has written, on every level *Clarissa* "subverts the notion of mutually exclusive possibilities and instead—dazzlingly, punningly—merges contraries, fuses opposites."[36]

The crucial point here is a failure of transparency. *Clarissa* can be construed as a paradoxical, doubled-up narrative because of its refusal ultimately to be incarcerated within the logic of sentimental morality or national allegory. Despite the author's own pious propensities, allegorical oppositions between natural independence and patriarchal oppression are confounded by the textual ambiguities of *Clarissa*, where the definition of freedom is surreptitiously turned back against itself. As many recent critics have observed, the form of the English novel in the eighteenth century was inchoate and diverse, compounded from a mixture of middlebrow entertainment and pious moralizing, aristocratic romance and popular journalism; and this heterodox quality would have militated against the pressure for hermeneutic closure that was implicit in any attempt to define Richardson's work allegorically. This swerving away from a plain integrity of meaning was also heightened by the fact that the writing of Richardson, like that of Franklin, emerged from a world in which the multiple impressions of print were coming to supersede the more traditional comforts of an oral culture. In *The Imaginary Puritan*, Tennenhouse and Nancy Armstrong describe how the expansion of "print capitalism" around the beginning of the eighteenth century created an enlarged space for the transnational dissemination of writing, and this, they argue, helped to disturb and displace those localized speech communities that could be overseen more easily by the monarchs of early modern Europe. In their attempt "to think of England as part of a larger nation whose boundaries extended overseas to North America," Armstrong and Tennenhouse suggest how the captivity narratives written in America during the seventeenth century may have served as a model for Richardson's fiction.[37] Mary Rowlandson's account of her imprisonment by Indians during King Philip's War was enormously popular in Britain at the beginning of the eighteenth century, and, without getting into questions of "cultural origins," the more general point here is that eighteenth-century English novels like those of Richardson emanated from a wide variety of cultural sources, so that their "creole" forms cannot be said mimetically to correspond simply with the local conditions of England at this time.[38]

To reconsider Richardson within a transatlantic context, then, is to disentangle him both from his traditional affiliation with English middle-class morality and from his American reincarnation in attenuated, parabolic forms. Critics like Fliegelman and Barnes, responding primarily to the abridged versions of *Pamela* and *Clarissa* that circulated widely around the time of the Revolution, have seen Richardson's novels as foreshadowing the sentimental fictions of the early national period; my suggestion is, however, that if we bear in mind the fuller complexities of Richardson's texts as they were presented in the eighteenth century, then the alignment of these novels with allegories of emerging national consciousness becomes much more problematic. Moreover, these paradoxical aspects of Richardson's art shed an oblique, transnational light on the writings of Franklin, Richardson's first American publisher. By reexamining Franklin through the perspective of the British Richardson, rather than the American Richardson, we may see how Franklin's own narratives incorporate some of the same multifaceted qualities as those of his English contemporary. While associations between Franklin and the development of American culture have been retrospectively institutionalized, both academically and politically, it is important to remember that the United States did not exist, even in an embryonic form, for the first seventy years of Franklin's life. Thus, it would hardly be surprising to find Franklin's elusive refraction of Enlightenment values differing markedly from the consolidation of national standards in the post-Revolutionary period.

*   *   *

Franklin's own engagement with print culture has been well chronicled. Not only was he a printer by trade, like Richardson, but in his *Autobiography* he mentions *Pamela*, along with Defoe's *Robinson Crusoe* and *Moll Flanders* and Bunyan's *Pilgrim's Progress*, as examples of a new professional style of writing, a way of mixing "Narration & Dialogue" so as to give the reader an illusion of being "brought into the Company, and present at the Discourse."[39] Franklin's concern with this new culture of mechanical reproduction can be seen as early as 1729, when, in his first political essay, he undertook "A Modest Inquiry into the Nature and Necessity of a Paper-Currency." Brushing aside the nostalgia for immanent value that was to make the authors of the *Anarchiad* so resistant to this kind of transaction later in the century, Franklin eulogizes the convenience of paper money as "a Medium of Exchange," noting how it increases the efficiency of trade much more than any "immediate Exchange of Commodities" (126). He returned to this theme in another essay on paper currency twelve years later, when he proposed a scheme to gauge its value so as to facilitate the process of transatlantic commerce (288). Marx was subsequently to describe Franklin as one of the first economists "to grasp the true nature of value," to demystify its supposedly natural qualities by reconfiguring it in terms of "the exchange of labour for labour," and in this sense Franklin's theory of commerce is commensurate with his occupation as a printer, because in both cases what would have appeared disconcerting to traditionalists would have been the way he appears to forfeit willingly any investment in authenticity. For Franklin, as a commercial publisher, value emerges through various mechanisms of exchange rather than being inherent within any particular object or dogma.[40] In his "Apology for Printers" (1731), Franklin declares it is in the occupational interest of printers to preserve an impassive neutrality about the multifarious views to which their books and magazines give voice, and some notion of this "vast Unconcernedness as to the right or wrong Opinions contain'd in what they print" (172) manifests itself throughout Franklin's later career.

Meaning, for him, was only ever a provisional operation. This view of paper and print as a medium through which the significance of language fluctuates also appears in his various essays on the distortions of reproductive technologies, such as his amusing account in 1730 of the changes in meaning brought about by printers' errors: "Governor Belcher died elegantly" or "Governor Belcher dined elegantly" (143).

It is this façade of impersonality, Franklin's self-canceling likening of himself to "the Cover of an old Book" (91), which has given rise to many critiques of the American writer from a post-romantic point of view. D. H. Lawrence's comment in 1923 about how the "sharp little man" lacked a "soul" has been reiterated many times in the twentieth century.[41] Mitchell Breitwieser was expressing a similar sense of discomfort when he referred to what he called Franklin's "chilling blankness"; Leslie Fiedler described Franklin as an equivalent to Richardson's Pamela in the way both shrewdly manipulate circumstances to achieve their ultimate goals; Jay Fliegelman compared Franklin to the villainous Lovelace because of their shared skill in problematizing the apparently natural order of cause and effect.[42] Just as Richardson's narratives veer away from their centers of ethical stability toward a darker world of chameleonic cynicism, so, in the eyes of these critics, an image of Franklin the chess player is never far from the surface of his writings. Like Pamela and Lovelace, Franklin's personae balance an appearance of submission to the forces of cultural conformity with a more astute appreciation of ways in which the conditions of society might be reorganized to their own advantage: "life," declares Franklin in 1779, "is a kind of Chess, in which we have often points to gain, & Competitors or Adversaries to contend with" (928). This enigmatic image of the chess player exemplifies the duplicitous aspect of Franklin which led American Loyalists like Peter Oliver to deplore "the Mischiefs which he plunged Society into, by the Perversion of his Genius." For Oliver, a native of Boston who migrated to England in 1776, the colonies were engaged in an "unnatural Rebellion," with Franklin cast as a heretic skilled in the black arts of subversion from within: "The Doctor himself was what is called a Printers Devil, but, by a Climax in Reputation, he reversed the Phrase, & taught us to read it backward, as Witches do the Lords Prayer."[43] To Oliver's mind, Franklin's uncanny ability to mimic established cultural forms while emptying out their positive content betokened a crime against nature, the dangerous redescription of morality as aesthetics and law as convention. Franklin himself once described his friend Joseph Priestley, the British scientist who fled to Pennsylvania, as an "honest heretic," and that sense of virtue existing alongside a spirit of blasphemy or insurrection is characteristic of Franklin's iconoclastic temper.[44]

The extent to which Franklin consciously manipulated this transatlantic print culture to fashion alternative personae has recently been the subject of considerable critical debate. Michael Warner believes he was exploiting the medium of letters to invent a new kind of identity linked to the improvisatory quality of role play, an identity grounded upon the "principle of negativity" that was closely associated with the impersonal "ideology of print" within the emerging republic.[45] Grantland S. Rice, by contrast, refers to the "anxiety of objectification" lurking in Franklin's accounts of this marginalization of individual integrity. Incidents recorded in the *Autobiography*, such as the way James Ralph fraudulently assumes Franklin's own name, suggest to Rice a latent apprehension about what was later to be called "reification," the manner in which an increasingly complex capitalist culture seemed to pose a threat to that basis of self-control and personal responsibility upon which Franklin's own quest for advancement was predicated.[46] Christopher Looby chooses to locate Franklin even more firmly within an imaginary American speech community, emphasizing how he identifies himself with a tradition developed by Cotton Mather of conflating "individual experience and national destiny in a celebration of representative American selfhood." Hence the fundamental tension in the *Autobiography*, argues Looby, revolves around the way Franklin's "self-identity" in narrative speech encounters "the historical rupture of the Revolution," thereby introducing into this text various divisions and interruptions which the author attempts vainly to gloss over. It is, he says, no coincidence that the war with Great Britain should be referred to only indirectly in the *Autobiography*, because Franklin was "quasi-somatically" committed to a sense of colloquial continuity between himself and his world, a continuity that the legal rhetoric of independence threatened to alienate and destroy.[47]

I think it is arguable that Franklin's texts are structured in a more sophisticated way than this. If the author is interpreted within a transnational framework of Enlightenment literature and philosophy, rather than understood merely in terms of the fluctuations of American national politics, then the idiom of exchange within his writings becomes easier to elucidate. Just as Richardson's narratives are organized around an axis of paradox and self-contradiction, so Franklin's writings expertly deploy language in order to switch positions, to introduce continual changes in perspective. In this way, any given object is transposed into a bifurcated image through the medium of the author's bifocal lenses, a stylistic counterpart to those ingenious spectacles Franklin devised to remedy his own distorted eyesight.[48] We see this most obviously in the satirical pieces, where Franklin's reactive genius is at its most apparent. His writing is particularly compelling when it is reconstructing rhetoric as a secondary reflection of established phenomena, recasting the Lord's Prayer or the Book of Job into alternative versions of themselves that hover somewhere between modernization and parody. In this satirical mode, Franklin takes delight in examining familiar issues and dilemmas through, as it were, the wrong end of a telescope: in "Rules by Which a Great Empire May Be Reduced to a Small One" (1773), for example, he ludically lays down the procedures Britain should follow—high taxes, misadministration—in order to be sure of ridding itself of the American colonies.

In *The Rhetoric of Fiction*, Wayne C. Booth distinguishes between Daniel Defoe's "masterful" style of eighteenth-century satire, based around "dramatic, realistic impersonation," and Jonathan Swift's more manic writings, such as "A Modest Proposal" (1729), whose power derives from "its very willingness to sacrifice consistency to satiric force."[49] When Swift extols the economic virtues of cannibalism as a solution to Irish poverty and famine, his mordant humor engenders an absurd view of the world that cannot safely be rationalized or contained within the framework of a political manifesto. This sense of a disjunction between political authorship and textual excess is what we find in Franklin's satires of the 1770s as well. Just as the reader of "A Modest Proposal" can never quite make out where Swift stands in relation to his farcical proposition, so "Rules by Which a Great Empire May Be Reduced to a Small One" creates a crazy internal logic of its own, as if Franklin, like the master scientist he was, were fascinated by this experiment of running everything backward, seeing how the political system might work if put into reverse. This is more than the satirist's customary reliance upon, and therefore surreptitious attachment to, the object satirized; it also indicates Franklin's propensity to create alternative worlds that mirror each other for the purposes of destabilizing dogmatic conceptions of philosophical truth or political certainty. The pedagogical directive of pure satire thus finds itself compromised by the anonymous measures of ventriloquism, whereby Franklin takes delight in playing with alternative voices and working ludically through their perspectives. The political force of his satires relies less upon any thematic impulse or ethical coherence than upon this process of formal alterity, the ability dangerously to disturb existing points of view.

This pattern is exemplified again in "An Edict by the King of Prussia," also first published in 1773. Here Franklin demystifies the English claim to America by describing how, according to the same territorial logic, London should still be groaning under the yoke of Prussian King Frederick, since Britain itself was first colonized by "German Settlements" (699). Again, the author uses his sophisticated language to compel his readers to change positions, to look at the question of American independence from quite a different point of view; he thus holds up a glass to the British claim and reveals, through this bizarre reflection, how it might be turned back upon itself. In a letter to his son just after "An Edict" was published, Franklin recounts with glee how various guests of Lord Le Despencer for a few minutes "imagined it a real edict," and were cursing the King of Prussia's "impudence" (887). Indeed, the piece derives its satirical edge precisely from this sense of plausibility; it does not simply inveigh against King George III, but compels the reader to refigure him from another angle of vision. In this period immediately prior to open hostilities breaking out between Britain and America, Franklin concocts as many mock treatises as "serious" ones, as if his skill in formally switching positions were a correlative to that more general mood of turbulence and bouleversement within the North Atlantic community. "A Method of Humbling Rebellious American Vassals" and "An Act for the More Effectual Keeping of the Colonies Dependent" both date from 1774, while a few years earlier, in 1768, we see Franklin fabricating another of these ingenious political reversals when he speculates on how a future British king might choose to live in Ireland, with the Irish parliament consequently assuming the right to tax the people of England. His method is, as he puts it, to "illustrate this matter by a comparison" (617), to throw the situation of America into relief by aligning it with some theoretically possible but incongruous alternative.

In this light, Franklin's texts might best be thought of as mediating between different positions and possibilities. The *Autobiography* mentions the establishment of a Junto Club in Philadelphia, a debating society whose members were obliged to eschew "all Expressions of Positiveness in Opinion" (1361), and many of Franklin's own narratives preserve something of this spirit of elusiveness. One of the key debates in America toward the end of the eighteenth century was how the republican ethic of sobriety and communal responsibility should relate to the liberal demand for freedom in thought and trade, and the *Autobiography* skillfully negotiates a passage between these competing principles in that it might be seen as endorsing either of them.[50] The book is offered ostensibly as a manual for moral self-improvement in the manner of Cotton Mather, and, as Breitwieser has said, it exploits the "trappings of Christian goodness: denial of impulse in the interest of a detached calculation and fidelity to distant ends."[51] At the same time, Franklin also places himself at one remove from this traditional kind of Puritan idealism, as he relates the story of what he calls his "bold and arduous Project of arriving at moral Perfection" (1383): he draws up a list of "moral Virtues" (1384) which he plans to acquire "one of them at a time" (1385), taking care to ensure "chastity" and "humility" appear at the bottom of this list and will, consequently, be the last of these personal mountains to be climbed. With "humility," indeed, Franklin admits he "cannot boast of much Success in acquiring the *Reality* of this Virtue; but I had a good deal with regard to the *Appearance* of it" (1393). The moral idea here has been turned on its head, not so much by the hero's failure to be humble as by his charmingly insouciant acknowledgment of his own duplicity. He strikes a similar note when talking about rolling his wheelbarrow through the streets of Philadelphia, so as to be "esteem'd an industrious thriving young Man" (1369) rather than a rich entrepreneur prone to "lampooning" the dull-wittedness of the natives (1335); again, the ingenuous tone emerges paradoxically from an admission of disingenuousness.

This deflection of propriety into gamesmanship owes much to the emerging ideology of capitalism, based around the manipulation of appearances to secure good credit: Franklin writes in a 1748 essay of how the sound of a hammer heard at five in the morning will make a creditor "easy Six Months longer" (321).[52] But what is most interesting in the *Autobiography* is the way Franklin openly flaunts these renegotiations of his self-image, foregrounding a style of conscious artifice that has something in common with the vast number of visual portraits of himself he arranged to have produced during his own lifetime.[53] Rather than simply chronicling the life of one capitalist entrepreneur, Franklin takes delight in iconoclastically playing off his chameleonic proclivities against the more sober assumptions of Puritan America. This idiom owes something to Hume's sacrilegious view of personal identity as a fiction. In his *Treatise of Human Nature*, Hume argues that the "identity, which we ascribe to the mind of man, is only a fictitious one" (306), bound up with the habitual nostalgia for assimilation and coherence within human memory; and an equivalent sense of selfhood as contingent, recognizable more on a popular than intellectual level, manifests itself in Franklin's *Autobiography* as well. There are innumerable instances in this book of him self-consciously politicizing his own image, coolly transforming its exterior prospect into a model worthy of imitation. Since the narrative explicitly acknowledges these anomalies, the reader is confronted not so much with any Machiavellian strategy but rather with an indication of how the author was concerned to harness the new technologies of the eighteenth century in order to transliterate himself into a man made out of words.

In the *Autobiography*, then, Franklin is more concerned with representations of the self than with any humanist center of gravity or Christian "soul." He writes of how the manner of his printing associate, Keimer, "was to Compose . . . in the Types directly out of his Head; so there being no Copy, but one Pair of Cases" (1331); and here the author is punningly transforming the Puritan "Types" of scripture into these more secular types of the modern printing press. "Copy" and "Correspondencies" are other words in this text that reverberate ironically with a lapsed spiritual significance; the old correspondences between earth and heaven find themselves superseded by new epistolary conventions and communication networks that have developed within this first age of mechanical reproduction.

Although the *Autobiography* itself did not appear in print until after Franklin's death, one of its central, recurring patterns involves the interchange between proximity and distance, between the memorializing accent of an affective, speaking subject and a more impersonal tone signified by the categorization of his false moves in life through the impassive printing term, "Erratum."

The extent to which the *Autobiography* is consciously structured around a pattern of deceit and double-dealing has been another of the controversies in Franklin criticism over recent years. Cynthia S. Jordan, for instance, reads it as an "artful" text, "a surface narrative whose continued existence depended upon the repeated suppression of dissident voices and dissident points of view." Jordan's argument is that Franklin manipulates his rhetoric so as to underline his own political and patriarchal authority, to consolidate his status as a Founding Father. By contrast, Douglas Anderson, who sees Franklin more directly as an exemplar of civic virtue, finds in the *Autobiography* a "language of the moral sublime" predicated upon "the vital intersection between private piety and public works that guided his entire life."[54] It is possible, however, that this issue has been framed in a misleading way. For Franklin, morality involved not the dogma of singular assertion but the process of transposition and exchange; consequently, the categories of morality and duplicity should not be seen as mutually antipathetic but as mutually intertwined. While Jordan is right to identify what she calls a "second story" in the *Autobiography*, this counternarrative is organized not so much around "transformation and concealment," but rather a kind of pseudo-concealment, where ironic anomalies are slyly acknowledged rather than repressed.[55] Franklin tended to revel in a conceptual interplay between contraries since his response to his eighteenth-century environment involved the projection of what might be called an ontological duality. His perception of reaction and comparison as the only valid methods of knowledge brought him to a recognition of paradox as the appropriate tropological mode for a world in which nothing lacked its polar opposite: only "the Fool," he wrote in 1735, "the self-sufficient Man, who proudly arrogates all Knowledge and Science to himself, rageth at Contradiction" (253).

This style of contradiction works its way through Franklin's satirical, political and philosophical writings. In scientific terms, the two dominant methodologies of this Enlightenment era were hypothesis and induction: the idea of a proposition through which particular phenomena might be tested and verified, along lines outlined by Descartes and Leibniz, as opposed to the more empirical approach favored by Isaac Newton, which preferred cautious experiment to abstract speculation.[56] It is easy enough to see why the inventor of the lightning rod would admire the work of Newton, whose fame he acknowledges in the

Autobiography; but it is also important to recognize how Franklin's text itself derives much of its paradoxical character from crossing hypothesis with induction, setting out a series of propositions—the author's "Enumeration of the moral Virtues," to take the most obvious example (1384)—before recording how time and contingency inevitably undermine such high-flown schemes.[57] Nevertheless, it is within this interplay between theory and practice that Franklin's genius emerges. His capacity for self-contradiction does not seem like a regrettable lapse into incoherence, as Looby believed, but appears rather as the discursive correlative to an increasingly multifaceted world, in which the only way never to be wrong was to avoid making the mistake of committing oneself to any particular position. Accordingly, to define Franklin in terms of an ideology of exchange is not just to describe his texts as saturated with commercial values, but also to observe how this exchange principle is woven into the formal fabric of his writings. Just as commodities change places in the marketplaces of Philadelphia and London, so hypothesis and induction, print culture and oral tradition, Britain and America all change places within the circumference of the North Atlantic Enlightenment. These commercial circuits of exchange can thus be seen to work in parallel with a comparative idiom, since both depend for their efficient operation upon an intersection between two opposing forces, a process of mutual reciprocation where one side of the equation only makes sense in terms of the other.

One early work of Franklin's that expresses this paradoxical condition within a raw philosophical context is *A Dissertation on Liberty and Necessity, Pleasure and Pain* (1725). Here Franklin maintains that individual states can have no meaning in themselves, since their significance emerges only through the process of comparison: "Are not the Pleasures of the Spring made such by the Disagreeableness of the Winter?" (68). The consequence of this chain reaction, he argues, is that "no Condition of Life or Being is in itself better or preferable to another: The Monarch is not more happy than the Slave, nor the Beggar more miserable than Croesus" (66). Pain and pleasure merely pursue each other in an equal and opposite reaction, a push/pull mechanism where "The *Pain* of Labour and Fatigue causes the *Pleasure* of Rest, equal to that *Pain*" (65), and so on. Thus, morality is extracted from "this great machine" of the universe (61): since "*Pain* naturally and infallibly produces a *Pleasure* in proportion to it" (66), the idea of pleasure being in some sense associated with virtue and pain with punishment is altogether undermined. Abrogating the self-deluding tendency "to exalt our Species above the rest of the Creation" (71), Franklin rewrites theology as physics, attempting "to prove the doctrine of Fate," as he wrote to Benjamin Vaughan, "from the supposed attributes of God" (1016). Again, Franklin's idiom is based around a reactive formula, taking the forms of Puritan orthodoxy and blasphemously emptying out their substantial content. In his *Autobiography*, Franklin described the printing of this pamphlet as an "Erratum," since he was laying himself open to the charge of harbouring "abominable," atheistic views (1346); but something of this paradoxical mentality still lingers, albeit in a much less overt fashion, within many of the author's subsequent writings. His conception in the *Dissertation* of the universe as organized according to a system of checks and balances, for instance, anticipates his investigations into the "global balance of Attraction and Repulsion" within electric currents a quarter of a century later.[58]

Franklin, then, chronicles a world organized around the principle of contradiction. Just as local concerns for property and propriety in Richardson's novels are compromised by the paradoxes of excess, so Franklin's *Autobiography*, for all of its American bravado, maintains significant links with a self-consciously intellectual tradition of clandestine writing. Charles Sanford, J. A. Leo Lemay and many others have seen Franklin's story as paradigmatic of the American dream, with its "rags-to-riches" fable of individual success, while Kenneth Silverman, in reading the *Autobiography* as a "quiet book, written in a neoclassical version of the Puritan plain style," also risks equating Franklin's work with some essentialized notion of national specificity.[59] Yet, the first two parts of this memoir were written in Europe—the first in England in 1771, the second in France in 1784—and this supports the point made by Rousseau, in his *Confessions*, that exile is the ideal condition for authorship. Rousseau argued that a writer can be most useful to his country by not being contained within its bounds, and Franklin here seems to maintain a fine balance between enthusiasm for the values of American society and an ironic detachment from them.[60] In a letter of 1768, Franklin described himself as suspected "in England, of being too much an American, and in America of being too much an Englishman" (840); and this recognition in himself of a transnational, double-edged persona works its way implicitly into his memoirs.

It is this swerve away from the narrower outlines of national allegory which links the *Autobiography* with Enlightenment traditions. Roseanne Runte describes how Jean La Fontaine was the forerunner of many Enlightenment writers who would cover their works with a decorous stylistic veil, while at the same time teasingly inviting the reader to "undress" the text through a process of uncovering the more improper implications buried within. Tracing this "cerebral eroticism" through eighteenth-century French literature, she observes how this libertine style involves an "absence of the explicit, a conscious emphasis on illusion and the evocation of the reader's imagination" by way of a "poetics of periphrasis" that might involve an image of the veil, ellipses, euphemisms, or other substitutions. Through these strategies, says Runte, the "reader becomes more than a simple voyeur"; he or she becomes also "an active participant in the libertine creation," supplying the details the author has left ostentatiously absent.[61] Bearing in mind how libertinism in its original definition involved the radical explorations of free thought rather than just the licentious nature of sexual behavior, we can see how Franklin's *Autobiography* provides an oblique instance of this libertine method applied to questions of intellectual (as well as erotic) practice. In keeping with this style of gamesmanship, the narrative can be read on several different levels: a more straightforward moral interpretation is readily available, but readers also find themselves actively challenged to recognize those paradoxes and contradictions in which the author revels.

Franklin's sly attitude toward Christian conventions also comes through in the various kinds of banter Franklin enjoyed with the infamous skeptic, David Hume. In a letter of October 1771, Franklin records a stay with Hume in Edinburgh: "Thro' Storms and Floods I arrived here on Saturday night, late, and was lodg'd miserably at an Inn: But that excellent Christian David Hume, agreeable to the Precepts of the Gospel, has *received the Stranger*, and I now live with him at his House in the new Town most happily."[62] In another letter some three weeks later, Franklin refers to Hume as "the good Samaritan"; while, three months after this, Hume returned the compliment by writing to Franklin: "I was very glad to hear of your safe Arrival in London, after being expos'd to as many Perils, as St. Paul, by Land and by Water." That Franklin should have been calling a man constantly in trouble with the religious authorities in Scotland an "excellent Christian" and a "good Samaritan" suggests a comical dimension, while Hume's likening of Franklin to St. Paul indicates a similar kind of whimsical, donnish humor.[63] These are the knowing jests of two Enlightenment philosophes, sporting with a paradoxical situation where they were constantly being obliged to assume conventional roles for the benefit of society. In his *Treatise of Human Nature*, Hume quotes Cardinal de Retz on how "it more easily excuses a person acting than in talking contrary to the decorum of his profession and character" (203), and both Hume and Franklin assume this duplicitous stance where it is acceptable to act, but not to talk, transgressively. This position implies, of course, the more elitist aspects of Enlightenment philosophy, the idea that libertine thought should be confined to the privileged few, while quietist conformity suffices for the unlettered masses.

This mode of self-contradiction is not incidental to Franklin's works, but forms the basis of his achievements. It also serves as the cultural framework for those debates about abolition which were taking on increasing political significance toward the end of the eighteenth century. In "A Conversation on Slavery," published in 1770, he turns the slavery debate on its head by asserting it was England that "began the Slave Trade" since "her Merchants of London, Bristol, Liverpool, and Glasgow, send their Ships to Africa for the purpose of purchasing

Slaves." He also problematizes the abstract category of slavery itself by placing it alongside the actual situation of British workers:

Your working Poor are not indeed absolute Slaves; but there seems something a little like Slavery, where the laws oblige them to work for their Masters so many Hours at such a Rate, and leave them no Liberty to demand or bargain for more, but imprison them in a Workhouse if they refuse to work on such Terms, and even imprison a humane Master if he thinks fit to pay them better; at the same Time confining the poor ingenious Artificer to this Island, and forbidding him to go abroad, though offered better Wages in foreign Countries. (648)

Franklin refers here to the fact that workers in the woolen and other trades were forbidden to emigrate. He extends his critique of British arrangements to the Scottish mining industry, where workers were bought and sold with their colliery and could no more quit the workplace than American slaves could their planta-tions; along the same lines, he indicts practices in the British army and navy, where unwilling conscripts were often pressed into service. Franklin's method here is similar to the one he employs in more famous pieces such as "An Edict by the King of Prussia," where he undermines British claims to America by im-plicitly aligning them with Prussia's ancient rights over Britain. Again, Franklin's technique involves an Enlightenment interplay of "mirrors within mirrors," as Robert Darnton described the figurative pattern of clandestine writing in pre-Revolutionary France.[64] Through a process of comparative decentering and para-doxical exchange, he reilluminates the American scene by playing it off against British assumptions, thereby highlighting unexpected areas of congruence and crossover.

   In the eighteenth century, the Quakers, who controlled Philadelphia, held slavery to be a sin, a state contrary to both nature and Scripture. Indeed, accord-ing to David Brion Davis, toward the end of this century the protest against slavery was increasingly seen as a test of Christian sincerity, with the Scottish philosopher James Beattie regarding a defense of this nefarious institution as one of the negative consequences of religious skepticism.[65] This, of course, represents precisely the kind of pressure toward social conformity with which Franklin would have been uncomfortable. His ironic temper could never entirely ac-quiesce in the civic norms of Philadelphia, and in this respect it is not surprising to find that he "invested in slave ships, sold advertisements in his newspaper for slaves to be sold or auctioned, and actually owned slaves when he was elected president of the Pennsylvania Abolition Society."[66] But, as Davis observes, Frank-lin became more engaged with slavery as a moral concern later in his life, after his transatlantic experiences had helped to open up different ways of looking at the problem. Hume, though no abolitionist, regarded slavery as an economic aberration which impeded the development of free trade, while French philosophes like Rousseau and the atheistic Diderot opposed the practice according to their lights of secular humanism. In a satirical piece published in the *Federal Gazette* shortly before he died, Franklin applied to the question of abolition those same reflexive mirrors with which he had undermined British claims to America a couple of decades earlier. By transposing arguments for the preservation of slavery into the fictional mouth of "Sidi Mehemet Ibrahim, a member of the Divan of Algiers," Franklin lampoons the Southern case, not by directly opposing it, but by turning it into a grotesque caricature of itself. Rather than relying on religious authority to counter the pro-slavery lobby, Franklin mocks the Algerian "sacred Book," the "Alcoran," with its supposedly "clear Proofs" of God's position on slavery (1160). It is the kind of piece more characteristic of Voltaire or Diderot than of a Philadelphia Quaker, and it suggests how various aspects of Enlightenment skepticism worked their way into the domain of American politics.

In this light, the American philosopher's flings with Parisian courtesans, his fantasies about wife-swapping in "The Elysian Fields" (1780), his "Letter of Advice to a Young Man on Choosing a Mistress" (1745)—all represent a form of erotic masquerade that was an exact counterpart to the author's intellectual masquerades, his cerebral deviations from the more staid orthodoxies of eighteenth-century American life. By situating himself on a fine line between the orthodox and the heterodox, Franklin carefully cultivated a style of transgressive duality, a shuttling between the law and its infraction; he did not attempt, like the antinomian Roger Williams before him or the transcendentalist Thoreau afterward, to upend the law entirely. Franklin's use of comical puns in a number of his more offbeat works, like "The Speech of Miss Polly Baker" (1747), represents another perfect image of the author's propensity to preserve a formal front while simultaneously taking pleasure in turning words around to find their less respectable side.[67] He delighted in sporting with the forbidden, in devising a chameleonic manner that allowed him both to preserve his reputation within American society and also to participate in the cosmopolitan quest for universal knowledge. Joseph Fichtelberg has argued that the inherently duplicitous status of writing appears to pose a threat to Franklin's concerns for social order and moral self-control, but this is perhaps to typecast Franklin as a republican statesman rather than recognizing him as the sophisticated satirist that he also was.[68] For Franklin the ironies and paradoxes of writing were crucial to his political vision, not ancillary to it.

To read Franklin alongside Richardson, then, is to highlight within their works those elements of textual excess which fail to conform to the conventional demands of national allegory. Franklin has been described by Sacvan Bercovitch as an exemplar of "auto-American-biography," just as Richardson was hailed by Ian Watt in 1957 as a forerunner of the English middle-class novel, grounded in literary realism, bourgeois commodification, and social propriety.[69] Indeed, one of the anomalous aspects about the reception of Richardson in Britain is that his novels have tended to be read, as it were, backward: they have often been approached retrospectively, as if anticipating the Victorian novel of money and manners, rather than being seen as part of the Enlightenment world of reflection and refraction. Despite the challenges in more recent times to Watt's nationalist thesis on the "rise" of the English novel, his understanding of eighteenth-century fiction in terms of a theory of "formal realism" has remained very influential.[70] Consequently, to read Richardson alongside Franklin is to reilluminate some of the self-consciously allegorical and therefore metafictional aspects of Richardson's fiction, the way in which, like the American politician, he sought to convert the haphazard crosscurrents of experience into emblematic categories of virtue.

In both Richardson and Franklin, however, we find this impulse toward civic and religious orthodoxy crossed with the more inchoate aspects of desire. In the case of Richardson, this paradoxical structure turns his fictions into putative allegories that are always unpicking their own allegorical status, inviting the pedagogical interpretation but ultimately frustrating it. In the narratives of Franklin, similarly, we find moves toward ethical consistency and interpretative closure undermined not so much by the political uncertainties of the author, nor by the historical discontinuities of his era, but rather by his own intellectual preference for devising a complex, multifaceted style which could be effective on many different levels. One of his first authorial pseudonyms was "Old Master Janus," an identity he assumed in 1723 as publisher of the *New England Courant*, and something of this inclination to see "two ways at once" stayed with him throughout his literary and intellectual career.[71] In this sense, the textual productions of both Franklin and Richardson institutionalize transgressive styles of duality as they circulate according to Enlightenment principles of transnational comparison and formal exchange.

Chapter Four

The Culture of Sensibility

Jefferson, Sterne, and Burke

To say Jefferson is a figure of the Enlightenment is to emphasize his intellectual affiliation with the skeptical, scientific, and empirical temper of the eighteenth century. Like Locke, Jefferson rejected any idealist notion of innate ideas. He found Plato nonsensical, disliked the emerging Romantic poets— Wordsworth, Coleridge, Byron—and was worlds away from the transcendental rhetoric of Lincoln and Whitman that governed the Civil War era. The materialist impulses of this age of Enlightenment have often been a source of unease for later American intellectuals more at home in a tradition of liberal reformism, and, as May noted, Jefferson in particular has been retrospectively "moved out of the eighteenth century and forced into conformity with the needs of Jacksonian Democracy, Wilsonian Progressivism, the New Deal" and other aspects of a politically idealist agenda.[1] To consider Jefferson within a very different British-American context is not to recuperate him as a closet conservative but rather to emphasize how his radical perspectives emerged through dialogues with Laurence Sterne, Edmund Burke, and other British writers who were influenced by Enlightenment sensibilities. Although it might seem strange given his lifelong anglophobia, there is an important sense in which Jefferson's systems of thought can be seen as interwoven with various aspects of British culture.[2]

As Merrill D. Peterson observed long ago, Jefferson's image in the American mind seems to maintain a chameleonic capacity to mold itself to the requirements of widely divergent political interests, all of which have been keen to requisition America's third president as their honorary forefather.[3] Such versatility does of course say something about the complexity of Jefferson's philosophical outlook, his willing encompassing of ambiguities and contradictions, as well as his diplomatic propensity to accommodate diverse points of view. But the subsequent mythic dimensions surrounding Jefferson's persona have been so powerful that it is easy to lose sight of how controversial he was in his own time because of what was seen as his radical departure from Christian traditions. Jefferson was accused of atheistic and Jacobin sympathies by political opponents like Alexander Hamilton, Timothy Dwight, and Jedediah Morse, and, despite the partisan nature of these charges, it would be true to say that he was working within a sophisticated intellectual framework of neoclassical learning where the allure of paganism was never far away. Deploring Calvin, Jefferson was attracted instead to ideas of the Stoics and Epicureans; Epicurus, in particular, he considered a much maligned character, whose popular reputation for empty hedonism unfairly obscured the moral foundations of his classical materialism.[4] Jefferson's engagement with Roman architecture, evident from his house at Monticello as well as his plans for the State Capitol of Virginia at Richmond, similarly derived in part from his contempt for a "Gothic" style that he associated with the old Christian superstitions of medieval Europe. In a letter of 1801, Jefferson echoed Diderot in scorning "Christian philosophy" as the "most perverted system that ever shone on man"; again like Diderot, he specifically deplored the "ignorance" of "priestcraft" as well as the "mystery and *charlatanerie*" of Catholicism.[5]

The question of atheism itself, however, was one Jefferson deemed insignificant precisely because he saw it as a metaphysical problem. Atheism, he wrote to John Adams in 1816, was a phenomenon of Catholic countries, inculcated as they were with devotional paraphernalia, while "the infidelity of the Protestant generally took the form of Theism."[6] It is true that, especially later in his life, Jefferson took a more quietist approach toward Christian doctrines: the influence of Joseph Priestley in the 1790s helped steer Jefferson toward a vague Unitarianism, while in 1813, when writing to the more conservative Adams, he struck a typical note of compromise by describing Christ's teaching as "the most sublime and benevolent code of morals which has ever been offered to man."[7] Even toward the end of his life, though, Jefferson was insistent that the University of Virginia, in whose planning he was heavily involved, should not only disavow any particular religious affiliation but should avoid the teaching of theology altogether.[8]

Jefferson, then, is a notoriously difficult character to categorize because his more conventional, diplomatic aspects ran alongside some peculiarly iconoclastic proclivities. In this sense, the dialogue played out between "head" and "heart" in Jefferson's famous letter to Maria Cosway (866–77), written in Paris on 12 October 1786, expresses a wider truth about his divided self: Jefferson's life and work embrace unresolved dialogues between the classical libertine and the American republican, between the Old World and the New. It would not, in fact, be going too far to suggest that Jefferson's was a dialogical imagination, in the

Bakhtinian sense of liking to formulate ideas in terms of unresolved contraries. This is why his epistolary dialogues with John Adams after 1812 are so evocative, because they show Jefferson taking pleasure in playing his own theories off against competing views, with any given position necessarily involving some fusion of opposites, what he describes in one letter as "a just equilibrium of the passions."[9] Jefferson's divided sensibility might be seen as a particularly apt mirror of the social and political situation in post-Revolutionary America, when, as Gordon Wood has shown, tensions and confusions of various kinds permeated the cultural landscape, so that often "opposing monarchical and republican strains of thinking existed simultaneously . . . within the minds of individuals."[10]

Such a Janus-faced condition is hardly surprising, of course. Any revolutionary transformation brings with it baggage accumulated from the past, as Sade recognized sardonically in 1795 when he urged upon his compatriots the need of an insurrectionary "encore," of producing "yet another effort" if they would become republicans.[11] The point remains, however, that Jefferson's understanding of what he saw as America's new pastoral identity, predicated upon the exceptional qualities of the western land, involved a conscious mediation between conflicting points of view. This is the "syntax of the middle landscape," as Leo Marx famously described it, involving a "dialectical" field of antitheses bringing together agrarian ideals and industrial progress, the sanctuary of rural America and the demands of international politics. This, observed Marx, is why Jefferson's thought "does not lend itself to ordinary standards of consistency": he uses the artifice of pastoral to translate "the doubleness of his outlook" into a metaphoric unity, while never entirely sublimating the "inconsistency" that remained "a source of his political strength."[12]

This conception of the author as a reflector or mediator rather than originator is characteristic of the traditions of Enlightenment writing to which Jefferson was indebted. In putting together his *Encyclopaedia*, for example, Diderot envisaged editing as an "imperial act," a task of synthesizing and creating order by regulating heterogeneous ideas within one all-encompassing whole, and Jefferson's own works follow a similar pattern of deliberately interweaving disparate strands. Rather than seeing tradition and innovation as mutually incompatible forces, he sought to reconcile them, appropriating what was useful from the past or from European thought and redirecting it toward his own ends: since "we cannot make events," he wrote, "our business is to improve them."[13] Jefferson impounded a public copy of the *Encyclopaedia* in June 1781, while he was writing *Notes on the State of Virginia*, and his own work shares some of Diderot's capacity to mix public-spiritedness with a tone of recusancy.[14]

It is within this architecture of paradox that Jefferson's implicit engagement with the more materialistic emphasis of French Enlightenment philosophy should be situated. He served in Paris as American ambassador in the turbulent period between 1784 and 1789, and he was very active in intellectual circles at this time, counting among his close friends the Marquis de Chastellux (who visited Monticello in 1781), the Duc de la Rochefoucauld (who stayed there for a week in 1796), and the Marquis de Condorcet. He was also on familiar terms with Diderot and d'Alembert, and even became well disposed toward a figure like Friedrich Melchior Grimm—"the pleasantest and most conversible member of the diplomatic corps," enthused Jefferson.[15] By contrast, Grimm was singled out by Rousseau in his *Confessions* as a particularly otiose member of what he termed pejoratively the "coterie holbachique," a group gathered around the Baron d'Holbach which was disliked by Rousseau for its combination of expensive urban manners, aristocratic social assumptions, and elitist variations of atheism.[16] In *Système de la Nature* (1770), d'Holbach proposed an inverted theology whereby the world was said to be governed solely by the machinations of nature through a mode of materialist determinism from which all divine purpose has been expelled. D'Holbach's system comprised a closed loop, wherein matter was said to circulate indefinitely: "A great variety of matter, combined in an infinity of forms, receives and communicates, incessantly, a variety of motions. The different properties of this matter . . . constitute for us, the essence of beings . . . of which the sum total makes what we call, Nature."[17] This scientific idiom led d'Holbach to reject both the sublimity and the sense of misanthropic alienation which he associated with the metaphysical nostalgia of Pascal, writing a hundred years earlier. Instead, d'Holbach chose to emphasize self-love, pleasure and sociability: "Social life is a religious act," he wrote, since "no one can be happy alone."[18]

It is not difficult to see how this demystified version of secular happiness fits comfortably with certain Enlightenment ideals. Between 1760 and 1780, indeed, d'Holbach's salon played host to many of the key intellectual figures of this era: Hume, Franklin, Sterne, Gibbon, Priestley, and others. Robert Darnton has demonstrated the popularity in pre-Revolutionary Paris of a libertine literature, "philosophy under the cloak," which brought together pornography and atheism in its savage attacks on the old regime, and d'Holbach was a key figure within that profane milieu.[19] Joseph J. Ellis, along with some of Jefferson's other biographers, has expressed surprise about the "extremely radical" nature of his sympathy for the idea of violent insurrection, which even led him implicitly to support the Reign of Terror in France during the early 1790s; but the extent to which Jefferson was permanently marked by revolutionary principles during his spell in France should not be underestimated. Yet Darnton also records how, despite the increased emphasis by the 1770s on the possibilities of knowledge for all rather than just for an enlightened few, many of these French philosophes still stuck to an older, aristocratic pattern whereby intellectual freedom for the privileged classes was balanced by a quiescent religious faith for all the rest.[20] Chastellux, who admired the newly independent United States, nevertheless cautioned against any general extension of democratic principles: "It is up to the sages to govern," he wrote, "and up to the stupid to obey."[21] Addressing himself more specifically to the situation of his American friend, Chastellux observed how Jefferson had been obliged to isolate himself from "his fellow citizens," who were, said the marquis, "not yet in a condition either to bear light, or to suffer contradiction."[22] Within this context, radical skepticism became an outlook reserved for the learned elite, the philosopher kings, with the fortunes of the masses depending upon the extent to which ruling classes might be educated into the enlightened cause of secular reform.

It is clear, of course, that Jefferson himself did not take such a pessimistic view of democracy, but it is also true that in a less outspoken way he shared some of Chastellux's reservations about the consequences of popular government. In his contempt for those Christian zealots who attempted to force sectarian legislation through the Virginia legislature, and in his more general dislike of the evangelical revival at the beginning of the nineteenth century, we see the American leader balancing off his professed public sympathies against a more Holbachian sense that he, the enlightened aristocrat, knows what is right. From this perspective, the standard line of how the "bold, unabashed scientific materialism" of eighteenth-century France cut little ice in Christian America needs to be modified through some recognition of how civic conformity could exist alongside intellectual agnosticism.[23] Over the years, various binary oppositions have been proposed to explain the flux and conflux of interests in early American history: Perry Miller discussed the clash between piety and intellect in seventeenth-century New England, Alan Heimert the oscillation between evangelicals and rationalists in the eighteenth-century colonies, with much subsequent debate focusing upon where this balance actually lay in any given situation.[24] Less attention has been paid, however, to the possibility of double identities, to the kinds of duplicity that were endemic to intellectual life during the Enlightenment. Diderot, like Jefferson, was partial to the literary form of dialogue as expressing ways in which mythic forms of identity might be splintered into their constituent components, as we see most obviously in the interchange between "Lui" and "Moi" in *Rameau's Nephew*; d'Alembert, similarly, wrote that intellectuals should give only their external selves to existing social arrangements, thereby tactfully sidestepping any direct confrontation with popular social prejudices. Another influence here would have been Montesquieu, a favorite author of Jefferson's, whose "Dissertation sur la politique des romains dans la religion" (1716) discusses how the lawgivers in classical Rome were intent upon "instilling the fear of the gods" in the people, so they could use "this fear to allow them to govern as they pleased."[25] Lurking behind this mode of behavior was the time-honored maxim of the Stoics: external conformity, internal freedom.[26]

All of these arrangements imply some form of disjunction between social orthodoxy and philosophical heterodoxy, between conventions of the public sphere and their infraction within a more private realm. This is not to suggest Jefferson was secretly a devotee of d'Holbach; in fact, he was generally less sympathetic to the more doctrinaire aspects of d'Holbach and la Mettrie, whose systematic materialism was in effect a reversed form of Scholastic theology, preferring instead the more pragmatic approach of French "ideologues" like Condorcet, Condillac, and Destutt de Tracy. Destutt de Tracy's *Elémens d'Idéologie*, finally published in 1815 but which Jefferson read in manuscript form, was concerned to apply the traditions of Lockean sensationalism to specific questions of politics, economics, and moral education. So impressed was Jefferson by this work that he conducted a long correspondence with de Tracy between 1802 and 1824 and was instrumental in having the Frenchman elected to the American Philosophical Society.[27] The general point is simply to emphasize how Jefferson had one foot in each camp: he was both an American statesman and an Enlightenment philosopher, both a popular leader and a materialist skeptic. Far from seeing any incompatibility between these roles, Jefferson was quite content to embody the contradictions within his own person because, like the Roman statesmen he so much admired, he made a categorical distinction between public responsibilities and private values. While it is true, as Gordon Wood and other historians have argued, that the American appropriation of republican values at this time added a "moral dimension" to the country's quarrel with Great Britain, it would be wrong simply to equate such moral dimensions with forms of ethical transparency.[28] Though he indicted Britain for corruption in its public life, Jefferson did not extrapolate from this critique any compulsion toward an ideal of consistent virtue, Christian or otherwise. While acknowledging the force of what Bruce Burgett has called the "logic of republican self-abstraction," the mode of systematic impersonality that guaranteed his authority to speak and act within the public sphere, Jefferson no more chose to alienate his intellectual and physiological faculties on this point of principle than did the pagan politicians of two thousand years earlier.[29] Jefferson was, in this sense, a pagan republican, not a Christian republican.

This is why the typical nineteenth-century criticism of Jefferson as a fraud or hypocrite, a man unable to reconcile his inner and outer selves, can be seen as inappropriate within the political context of the late eighteenth century.[30] Recent historiography of the early national period has often posited an antithesis between staunch republican virtue on the one hand and an ideal of liberal individualism on the other, associating the former with moral integrity and the latter with a division of society into public and private spheres. But this is retrospectively to conflate the American Enlightenment with a spirit of Christian virtue, implying a model of republicanism more indebted to the Puritan legacy described by Miller and other early American historians rather than to the skeptical traditions of classical learning that were prevalent at this time. Jefferson was no Puritan, though, and for him what he "believed" in his private capacity was an issue with no bearing upon his status in public life. His personal thoughts on the practices of slavery or the feasibility of a Christian God would have relatively little effect on his attitude toward such matters within the social sphere, where Jefferson approached the art of politics with all the performative skills of an actor on a stage.[31] He was always committed to a view of public office in accord with what he called "the Roman principle" and, like many other American leaders of this time, was a particular admirer of Cicero, who had, in Jefferson's view, managed judiciously to balance his more reclusive scholarly interests with a high-minded sense of public duty.[32]

*   *   *

Like Cicero, then, Jefferson was highly conscious of acting in public, of putting on a public act. As a good republican, he did not equate such duplicity with mere deceit, but with the contextual modification of mores to suit different social and political circumstances. One instance of this chameleonic capacity manifests itself in his 1785 suggestion that the identification of national identity with a specific country of origin or assimilation should be superseded by a more flexible law of international exchange. This, explained Jefferson to John Adams, would involve a process of "mutual adoption by each of the citizens or subjects of the other, insomuch that while those of the one are traveling or sojourning with the other, they shall be considered in every intent and purpose as members of the nation, where they are, entitled to all the protections, rights and advantages of its native members."[33] In this formula, Jefferson would become a French citizen while in Paris, while Chastellux would be American for the duration of his trip to Monticello. While this underlines the Virginian's cosmopolitan inclinations, it also emphasizes even more his metamorphic tendencies, his intellectual predilection for assuming radically different identities in different situations.

This is where Jefferson's encyclopedic rationalism becomes crossed with more emotive faculties, where sense merges into sensibility. The expression of empathy with particular environments that we find in his political philosophy seems to owe less to any administrative logic than to the kind of sensibility expressed in works by Laurence Sterne. In *A Sentimental Journey*, published by Sterne in 1768, the author's persona, Mr. Yorick, experiences similar moods of transitory emotional affiliation on his travels through France and Italy. Dumas Malone recounts a story of how Jefferson, passing through Calais in 1786, paid a small gratuity to someone he described as the successor to Sterne's monk in *A Sentimental Journey*, while one year later Jefferson declared explicitly: "The writings of Sterne particularly form the best course of morality that ever was written."[34]

Given the writer's somewhat *louche* reputation, the immense popularity of Sterne's work in America toward the end of the eighteenth century tends to militate against the received image of the country at this time as a bastion of provincial decency. Seven editions of *A Sentimental Journey* were printed in America between 1768 and 1795, while in 1774 Sterne became the first novelist to have a collected edition of his complete works published in the New World.[35] Jefferson himself purchased all of Sterne's books as early as the 1760s, and while in France during the 1780s he even bought extra pocket-size editions so as never to be without the English cleric's coy wisdom.[36] American supporters of Sterne tended to emphasize his capacity for fellow feeling. In William Hill Brown's *The Power of Sympathy* (1789), the character of Worthy vigorously defends, in "Shandean tone," Sterne's novels from the charge by "antisentimentalists" that they are "out of date."[37] Other readers, however, took exception to what Samuel Miller in 1803 called Sterne's "system of libertinism." One frequent complaint was that by "indulging his darling sensibility," as the *Massachusetts Magazine* put it in 1794, Sterne was helping, even if unwittingly, "to seduce others into trouble and disgrace, by their sentimental pursuits." In 1802, the *New England Quarterly* was even more censorious about ways in which Sterne's representation of agape could have negative consequences: "I suppose few writers have done more injury to morals than Sterne," it complained. "By blending sentiments of benevolence and delicacy with immorality and looseness, he induces some people to think that debauchery may be innocent, and adultery meritorious."[38] It is appropriate that Sterne should have been a visitor to d'Holbach's salon, because this structure of equivocation might be construed as another version of "philosophy under the cloak." According to the *New England Quarterly*, at least, Sterne's façade of Christian charity belied a less respectable interest in sexual transgression, while John Trumbull (himself no stranger to verbal innuendo, as we have seen) associated Sterne with one of the most notorious literary rakes, when he joked in *The*

Progress of Dulness about "double meanings, neat and handy, / From Rochester and *Tristram Shandy*" (60). It was this issue of duplicity and concealment by which American moralists of the time felt most threatened: one of the characters in Foster's *The Boarding School* complains of how in Sterne's books "the noxious insinuations of licentious wit are concealed under the artful blandishments of sympathetic sensibility." More recent critics have echoed this recognition of something prurient or clandestine in Sterne's writing: "the suggestiveness of his texts," wrote John Mullan in 1988, involves "not just their bawdy, but the half-concealment of that bawdy."[39]

Since we know that Jefferson was enamored of Sterne's work, it would seem likely that he admired the many different sides of Sterne's achievement: not only the sentimental moralist and cosmopolitan traveler, but also the indecent jester and metafictional sophist. In the light of Jefferson's disdain for Britain, particularly in his later life, it is not surprising to find the Yorkshire clergyman also enjoying a fractious, awkward relationship with conventional British culture. Sterne was praised by another English renegade, Thomas Paine, for being free of the usual prejudices harbored by his countrymen toward France, while Dr. Johnson's 1765 judgement on *Tristram Shandy*—"not English, sir"—carried right through to his twentieth-century compatriots like F. R. Leavis, who found Sterne's whole ambience disconcertingly amoral.[40] John Wesley, writing in 1772, similarly suggested that the very word "sentimental" implied a "queer" tone that was "not English." Indeed, looking at Sterne within a transnational framework we can see how he deliberately appropriates the landscape of France to smuggle a subversive cult of sensibility into English culture, just as Jefferson exploited his years in Paris to gain another perspective on his own American heritage.[41] In the late eighteenth century, the idea of "sentiment" designated primarily a moral reflection or rational opinion; by contrast, sensibility—or sentimentality, as Wesley objected to it—involved a faculty of feeling and refined emotion which could manifest itself in a quickness to display compassion, but which was also associated with crying, swooning, and other indices of corporeal excess. "I have torn my whole frame into pieces by my feelings," wrote Sterne plaintively in 1767: "I have long been a sentimental being." Hence, when John Adams's daughter described Jefferson as "a man of great sensibility," she was not necessarily—and certainly not in her father's eyes—paying him a compliment.[42]

Sterne's most overtly didactic work is *The Sermons of Mr. Yorick*, first published in 1760. This was the only contemporary work under the category of "religion" that Jefferson recommended in 1771, when Robert Skipwith asked him to produce a list of books suitable for the "common reader" (744). Yorick's first sermon is entitled "Inquiry After Happiness," where the author, true to his sentimental principles, attempts to elevate the quest for happiness into a philosophical virtue:

The great pursuit of man is after happiness: it is the first and strongest desire in his nature;—in every stage of his life, he searches for it, as for hid treasure;—courts it under a thousand different shapes,—and though perpetually disappointed,—still persists—runs after and enquires for it afresh—asks every passenger who comes in his way, *Who will shew him any good?*—who will assist him in the attainment of it, or direct him to the discovery of this great end of all his wishes?[43]

Concerning Jefferson's famous statement in the Declaration of Independence about man's right to "the pursuit of happiness," the general assumption has been that he is talking either about a public conception of happiness, incorporating republican virtue, or a more private sense of individualism influenced by Locke, or some combination of these factors.[44] But Sterne's sentimental account of the "pursuit . . . after happiness," which may significantly have affected Jefferson's rhetoric, involves neither a traditional pursuit of property nor a liberal pursuit of freedom but rather an impulse of sensibility that manifests itself through emotional affiliations with, and aesthetic recreations of, particular objects within "nature." Pauline Maier, who sees the Declaration of Independence as a derivative political document and who is generally skeptical about the extent of Jefferson's engagement with abstract ideas, observes that references to happiness were quite commonplace in American political writings of this time and that they usually designated no more than an idea of safety or security.[45] There may be some truth in this, but if we consider Jefferson's preferred literary models as well as his philosophical sources we can see how his notion of happiness, like Sterne's, embraced the body and the heart as well as the mind. In this sense, local attachments and the conditions of corporeal desire were to make up, by definition, a crucial part of Jefferson's Enlightenment persona.

Critics who analyze Jefferson's relationship with Sterne, most notably Garry Wills, tend to focus on the belief expressed by both writers in the moral guidance of the heart, such as we see in *A Sentimental Journey* and *The Sermons of Mr. Yorick*. While this is clearly important, it does not do sufficient justice to the complex literary qualities of Sterne, who is renowned for his tricksy formal experiments as much as for the qualities of his Christian virtue. According to Wills, this kind of humor manifests itself in Jefferson's writings only through the rather labored drolleries of his letters.[46] It is arguable, though, that there is a more structured sense of irony throughout Jefferson's work, which, like that of Sterne, was motivated not so much by the heart alone but by that tortuous, paradoxical place where head and heart intertwine. In this respect, the ramifications of Jefferson's interest in the twists and turns of *Tristram Shandy* are particularly illuminating. Sterne's longest novel, originally published in nine volumes between 1759 and 1767, was very popular in Virginia and it became one of Jefferson's most cherished books. More deliberately self-referential than Sterne's other writings, *Tristram Shandy* plays with ideas of the materiality of the text so as to highlight its own incorporation within a culture of print where all representations must necessarily appear as secondary, mediated phenomena. Sterne conceives this loss of natural presence in terms of optical images: describing a "fine transparent body of clear glass," he writes of how "the rays of light, in passing through . . . become so monstrously refracted, or return reflected from their surfaces in such transverse lines to the eye, that a man cannot be seen through."[47] This passage works as a microcosm of *Tristram Shandy* itself, since Sterne understands his text to be a focal point where contradictions between nature and art, the sublime and the ironic, are ingeniously brought together. As the novel puts it: "the machinery of my work is of a species by itself; two contrary motions are introduced into it, and reconciled, which were thought to be at variance with each other."[48] Hence *Tristram Shandy* accommodates what Jonathan Lamb has described as a "double principle," where the work of fiction mediates between abstract forms of idealism and the contingent world of matter. The "comic incongruity" of Sterne's narrative thus involves a process of transition between what Lamb calls the "tautological sublime," where everything is said to resemble itself, and that discordant sense of deviation evoked when random accident is played off against the ghostly shadow of symmetrical design.[49]

Consequently, *Tristram Shandy* is a self-reflexive work in the purest sense of that term, a text that relentlessly interrogates the ontological status of its own existence. Its most characteristic scenes revolve around deliberate disjunctions, the translation of one epistemological form into another. Representing death by a blank page, for instance, might be understood as a kind of visual pun which reconfigures a metaphorical vacancy as a literal one, thereby defamiliarizing the linguistic conventions with which death is customarily enshrouded. Similarly, Tristram's attack on plagiarism at the beginning of the fifth volume is itself plagiarized from Burton's *Anatomy of Melancholy*, raising imponderable questions about how we understand notions of originality and replication. Despite Sterne's own maverick qualities, this idiom of radical ambiguity is not uncharacteristic of the intellectual climate in which he was writing. As James Rodgers has observed, *Tristram Shandy* draws upon late Enlightenment understandings of sensibility in the way it depicts the mind and body as interwoven, so that any given concept necessarily slides away from a single point of reference to reformulate itself within a redoubled, paronomastic format.[50] Thus the breaches in Uncle Toby's lines of defense during his wargames pun on his sartorial breeches, while his impotence is seen to involve mental as well as physical problems. Indeed, many of the sensations typically experienced by Sterne's characters—blushing, crying, erections—testify to points of intersection between mind and body, with the ridiculous human frame dubbed, like *Tristram Shandy* itself, as the odd medium for incorporating "contrary motions" which seem to vary wildly in their provenance.

There are many ways in which the willful duplicities of *Tristram Shandy* work their way into the body of Jefferson's writing.[51] Sterne's play on "contrary motions," for instance, might interestingly be juxtaposed with Jefferson's celebrated description of his estate at Monticello in a letter of 1806. Talking of the "advantageous arrangement" of the grounds, "which I destine to improve in the style of the English gardens," he says the "subject is so unique and at the same time refractory, that to make a disposition analogous to its character would require much more of the genius of the landscape painter and gardener than I pretend to" (1167). Both "unique" and "refractory": this Sternean admission of paradoxical contraries implies Jefferson's position on a cusp between American originality and European tradition. What appears at first sight "unique" or natural is also, in fact, a secondary refraction of aesthetic traditions. Similarly, the reference here to England—"Thither without doubt we are to go for models in this art" (1168)—may refer to the aesthetic mode of Picturesque, which was being developed in England during the 1790s, and which followed writers of sensibility like Sterne by attempting to incorporate irregularity, contradiction, and sometimes deceptive forms of partial concealment into its field of vision.[52] In this letter to William Hamilton, Jefferson talks artfully of "thickets so disposed as to serve as vistas, with the advantage of shifting the scenes as you advance on your way" (1169).

By the same token, various passages in *Notes on the State of Virginia* suggest the kind of play with optics and reflection that we find in Sterne's novel. Partly because Jefferson was responding to the negative opinions of America expressed at this time by the Count de Buffon, his narrative is framed by what he himself calls a "comparative View" (172), whereby local phenomena are perceived and valued in terms of their relation to the Old World: he enumerates, for instance, "18 quadrupeds peculiar to Europe; more than four times as many, to wit 74, peculiar to America" (179–80). In keeping with this style of refraction, Jefferson focuses on how the external landscape of Virginia appears to modify itself in accordance with the faculty of human sight. In a reversal that Sterne would have been proud of, the actual direction of the road is balanced off in Jefferson's description against its appearance in the mind's eye: "Here the eye ultimately composes itself," he writes, "and that way too the road happens actually to lead"

(143). In Query VII, he elaborates on this theme of optical illusion in his discussion of what the "seamen call . . . *looming*," whose "principal effect is to make distant objects appear larger, in opposition to the general law of vision, by which they are diminished" (207). This can be differentiated from the romantic idiom that was to become popular a few years later because what interests Jefferson is not so much the new idea itself, but rather the point of intersection or reversal, that cusp where a conventional image suffers the indignity of being usurped:

There is a solitary mountain about 40 miles off, in the South, whose natural shape, as presented to view there, is a regular cone; but, by the effect of looming, it sometimes subdivides almost totally to the horizon; sometimes it rises more acute, and more elevated; sometimes it is hemispherical; and sometimes its sides are perpendicular, its top flat, and as broad as its base. In short it assumes at times the most whimsical shapes, and all these perhaps successively in the same morning. (207–8)

Like *Tristram Shandy*, the landscape of Jefferson's narrative fluctuates wildly according to the viewpoint of its observer, taking on chameleonic aspects, "whimsical shapes." While Jefferson's account of the flora and fauna of his native Virginia country started out as a sober scientific exercise, based upon the method of natural history expounded by Linnaeus in *Systema Naturae*, it is easy enough to see how the basis of this empirical investigation becomes radically problematized. As Susan Manning has observed, the structure of bricolage in *Notes on Virginia* implies, paradoxically, a mode of incompleteness, a failure to impose that finality and closure toward which the author's encyclopedic lists seem constantly to strain.[53]

More casual references to Sterne recur throughout Jefferson's life, particularly in relation to his associations with women. He cited a scene full of sexual double entendres from *A Sentimental Journey* in a 1788 letter to Angelica Schuyler Church, with whom he enjoyed a flirtatious friendship in Paris.[54] In the same year, he favored Maria Cosway with some phallic innuendo about "the promontory of noses," taken from *Tristram Shandy*: "Had I written to you from [Strasbourg]," he declares, "it would have been a continuation of Sterne upon noses" (921–22). From this perspective, the probability of a long-term, clandestine relationship between Jefferson and his black slave, Sally Hemings, does not seem so bizarre or anomalous as was once generally imagined. Annette Gordon-Reed has shown that circumstantial evidence for an affair is very strong, particularly with regard to the consistent pattern whereby Jefferson, despite his frequent absences on business, was always in close proximity to Hemings just before she became pregnant. As Gordon-Reed says, the main obstacle to a general recognition of this relationship is an unwillingness on the part of Jefferson's white biographers to acknowledge that he might have been so inconsistent in his general standards of conduct.[55] But, in the light of his devotion to Sterne, we can see how a willingness to embrace contradictions was part of Jefferson's intellectual makeup. As a philosopher of sensibility, he took pleasure in situations where the abstractions of the mind would fluctuate according to the natural demands of the body, where the material body equally found itself modulated by fancies of the mind. We see this "double principle" in his major works, like *Notes on the State of Virginia*, as well as in other aspects of his private life. Just as Sterne's sexual badinage is reproduced frequently in Jefferson's letters, so the English author's reputation for furtive concealment also found its way into the American statesman's repertoire.

This culture of sensibility indicates Jefferson's affiliations with the more somber aspects of the Enlightenment as they developed toward the end of the eighteenth century. Fliegelman draws a contrast between the American philosopher's utopianism and "the darker implications of sensationalism" evident elsewhere at this time, pointing to Jefferson's fascination with "the pure forms both of nature and of neoclassical architecture" as evidence of his environmentalist idealism and his belief in the regenerative possibilities of the new world.[56] While this is not wrong, it is not the whole story. Attracted to an aesthetics of balance and symmetry, Jefferson also found himself drawn compulsively toward the decomposition of this human architecture, its dissolution within the larger erosions of time.[57] Again, this juxtaposition of fragile artifice and death is very characteristic of Sterne; it is characteristic also of Edward Gibbon, the first volume of whose *Decline and Fall of the Roman Empire* was published, ironically enough, in 1776. Like Sterne and Jefferson, the English historian was aesthetically enthralled not only by the grandeur that was Rome but also by the picturesque collapse of these monuments into classical ruins. It is the precariousness of this balancing act between sense and sensibility that the end of the eighteenth century found so philosophically and affectively compelling. Jefferson came to intellectual maturity within an Age of Sensibility in which representation appeared inexorably bound up with styles of paradox.

In its sardonic conjunction of reason and absurdity, imperial idealism and base corruption, the work of Gibbon involves the same style of antithesis that we find in Jefferson's writing. With the utmost Enlightenment politesse, Gibbon chronicles mournfully "the crimes, follies, and misfortunes" of Roman history, establishing throughout his text a linguistic and thematic structure of bathos, where every good hope or decent intention ends up in rack and ruin, confounded by the innate greed and stupidity of mankind.[58] All is vanity: Gibbon takes an almost satirical pleasure in his incongruous conjunction of Augustan understatement with these wrecks of human ambition across such a vast expanse of space and time. His mode of romantic irony is similar to the style we find in Sterne's novels, and it betokens that same late eighteenth-century sense of contraries colliding, of rationalist epistemologies pushing inexorably toward, and beyond, their own limitations. Robert A. Ferguson observes how Jefferson, like Gibbon, is ironically aware of the growth, maturity and decay of nations as a predetermined cyclic process: in *Notes on the State of Virginia*, for instance, Jefferson mentions the necessity for fixing legal rights "while our rules are honest, and ourselves united," because soon enough, he says, America will inevitably be going "down hill."[59] The narratives of both Jefferson and Gibbon evoke a conception of natural law that owes more to the fatalistic cycles of classical materialism than to the millennial teleologies advocated by proponents of "higher law" in the nineteenth century.

Another dominant metaphor of this Enlightenment era involved the emergence of light from darkness, with this image of light, particularly in America, indicating both rational illumination and revivalist effulgence.[60] Toward the end of the Enlightenment, however, the ambiguities of improvement and degeneration were also frequently expressed through metaphors of deviation and refraction, the transference of light into another medium. In this sense, the first word in the title of Edmund Burke's *Reflections on the Revolution in France* (1790) is by no means coincidental. Early in this disquisition, Burke develops his favorite theory about how no abstract idea or event can possibly enjoy any essential autonomy free from the necessary corruptions and "reflections" bound up with terrestrial existence:

These metaphysic rights entering into common life, like rays of light which pierce into a dense medium, are, by the laws of nature, refracted from their straight line. Indeed in the gross and complicated mass of human passions and concerns, the primitive rights of men undergo such a variety of refractions and reflections, that it becomes absurd to talk of them as if they continued in the simplicity of their original direction.

Scornful of both "metaphysical abstraction" and transcendental prophecy, Burke denies that questions of freedom can be considered in isolation from the specific historical and political circumstances surrounding them.[61]

The posthumous characterization of Burke, like that of Jefferson, has fluctuated enormously. Usually considered a liberal throughout the nineteenth century because of his failure to locate fundamental value within the established social order, Burke today is more often regarded as a conservative because of his pragmatic skepticism toward radical ideals. Yet there is an elusiveness in Burke, a double-edged quality, which is typical of the late Enlightenment sensibility, and it is this kind of ambivalence that links him with Jefferson. The irritated Thomas

Paine complained in 1791 about "the paradoxical genius of Mr Burke," whose "arguments" seemed to consist of "paradoxical rhapsodies" that continually recede before the reader's eyes just as he thinks he is reaching the heart of the matter; but this famous antagonism between Burke and Paine is an instructive one, for Paine's own ethical imperatives involve qualities the paradoxical styles of Burke and Jefferson deliberately lack.[62] For Paine, revolutionary affairs are susceptible of resolution into the most clear-cut ethical choices. Speaking about the French Revolution in *The Rights of Man*, for instance, he declares boldly: "The event was to be freedom or slavery." Paine thus favors "a heart feeling as it ought," "soul-animating sentiments," and a clear-cut commitment to good rather than evil, "principles" rather than "duplicity."[63] In his eyes, any form of mediation—government, religious institutions, language itself—should be seen as inherently jesuitical and perverse, since it has the effect of deflecting primary natural rights into corrupt secondary phenomena. For Burke, on the other hand, no object ever manifests itself as entirely straight or natural. Everything is refracted or reflected, destabilized by being defined in terms of its contrary. It is, says Burke, the idea of emancipation that introduces the idea of slavery; as a metaphysical abstraction, a metanarrative, the concept of liberty in itself signifies very little. "Abstract liberty," he declares in a speech of 1775, "like other mere abstractions, is not to be found. Liberty inheres in some sensible object."[64]

Recent work on Burke has underlined the unresolved contradictions in his work, the way in which *Reflections* seeks both to "deflate the revolutionary sublime" and also to "maintain the sublimity and beauty of the institutions (such as the British constitution)" which Burke wishes to exempt from rational inquiry. In this way, argues Tom Furniss, Burke and Paine have more in common than at first appears, since both are attempting to ground their political rhetoric in the laws of nature, while striving to eliminate negative ideas from their own discourses by locating them in the text of the other.[65] There remains here, perhaps, a difference of stylistic emphasis which should not entirely be occluded: Burke's sometimes "manic" and "schizoid" willingness to entertain contradictions is different in kind from the appearance of logic and lucidity that governs the commonsensical world of Paine. Nevertheless, within this debate between Burke and Paine, argues Furniss, "England and France seem less opposites than mutually constitutive—or mutually subversive—models for each other, each potentially repairing and impairing the other's 'national character.'"[66] A very similar case might be made about the intellectual relationship between Burke and Jefferson within the context of American independence. Both political philosophers, despite their nostalgic attraction to the sublime, recognize ways in which such subliminal categories turn back reflexively upon themselves, so that principles of individual freedom and constitutional liberty can appear only as a relative rather than an absolute construction.

This led both Burke and Jefferson to a position where political judgement came to seem very much like aesthetic discrimination: not so much a question of positive truths, but of affective, experiential choices. In his speech of 1775 advocating conciliation with the American colonies, Burke described the kind of hypostatization of freedom common in the New World as a by-product of the colonists' religious affiliations: "The people," he said, "are Protestants, and of that kind which is the most adverse to all implicit submission of mind and opinion."[67] As an Irishman living in England, the son of a Catholic mother and Protestant father, Burke would have known something about cultural relativism and hybridity, and he also recognized how what appear to be disinterested or objective philosophical principles are actually rationalizations of some subjective, culturally determined prejudice or passion. This consciousness links Burke with cynics of the Enlightenment like Hume or Sade, who were also concerned with the limits and limitations of human reason. In its meditation upon the residual (if irrational) power of old authorities, a power that necessarily compromises any move toward radical change, Burke's *Reflections on the Revolution* anticipates by five years Sade's *Philosophie dans le Boudoir*, a work that more nihilistically adumbrates a similar theme. "In that general territory [of France] itself," says Burke, "as in the old name of provinces, the citizens are interested from old prejudices and unreasoned habits, and not on account of the geometric properties of its figure."[68]

In this respect, Burke, like Sade, aestheticizes politics: he recognizes how social life is organized emotively and intuitively rather than positivistically. Indeed, as Garry Wills pointed out, Burke's 1756 essay "On the Sublime and Beautiful" (which Jefferson owned) reveals marked similarities with later Sadeian treatises.[69] This emerges most obviously in Burke's continual subversion of rationality, and in his description of blackness, terror, and pain—including "the real misfortunes and pains of others"—as sources of delight and the sublime.[70] In addition, Burke, like Jefferson, assiduously eradicates any metaphysical or neo-platonic component from the realm of aesthetics, focusing instead on human art as a secular and material affair. "On the Sublime" includes many optical metaphors, as if to stress how ideas of the beautiful or transcendent have no substance except insofar as they become transmitted into people's minds. The sense of awe, fear or frenzy can thus be traced back to an empirical cause: writing of color, for instance, Burke notes how when a blue or red ray "passes without . . . opposition through the glass or liquor, when the glass or liquor are quite transparent, the light is something softened in the passage, which makes it more agreeable even as light." As a result, the dimension of color "has such an effect on the eye, as smooth opaque bodies have on the eye and touch."[71] Aesthetic properties are said accordingly to reside at the level of sensory perception; art is connected not with idealist abstractions but with particular, recognizable effects within the physical world.

For Burke, the corollary of this process of desublimation is that the idea of freedom also has no substance except within the human imagination. Since liberties "vary with times and circumstances," "admit of infinite modifications" and "cannot be settled upon any abstract rule," he chooses to disparage the mystification and mythologization of slavery, especially the way the French Revolutionaries attempted to represent themselves "as a gang of Maroon slaves, suddenly broke loose from the house of bondage."[72] Similarly, Burke's attitude toward slavery in his 1775 speech on reconciliation with America is pragmatic and dismissive: it is, he says, "a weed that grows in every soil," familiar enough from other countries such as Spain and Prussia, not something to be unduly troubled by. Like Jefferson, Burke remains cautious about the idea of emancipation: "Slaves are often much attached to their masters," he claims. "A general wild offer of liberty would not always be accepted. History furnishes few instances of it. It is sometimes as hard to persuade slaves to be free as it is to compel freemen to be slaves."[73] The antithesis in that last sentence is an excellent example of what Paine called the "paradoxical genius" that structures Burke's discourse, his proclivity for standing ideas on their head by reconceiving them in terms of their contrary.[74] Within the turbulent social and cultural world of the late Enlightenment, Burke embodies what Isaac Kramnick called a "deeply divided self," a self that was both fascinated and repelled by the capacity of French Jacobins to "pervert the moral sense."[75] His conception of the French Revolution as a world turned upside down manifests itself, as Kramnick noted, in a series of scatological images, the vigorous repression of which parallels, and perhaps partly motivates, the impetus toward political conservatism in his later writings.

Simply to equate Jefferson's views on slavery with those of Burke would, of course, be an exaggeration. Jefferson, a revolutionary and a radical idealist of a particular sort, could never be happy to rest within the limitations of the status quo. In his *Autobiography*, Jefferson writes of the *Reflections on the Revolution* as "gaudily painted . . . with some smartness of fancy, but no sound sense" (92). Yet it is, perhaps, also misleading to follow Conor Cruise O'Brien's line that Jefferson's dedication to that "holy cause of Liberty" exemplified by the French Revolution led him to spurn Burke's *Reflections* as merely corrupt or "satanic."[76] While Jefferson was certainly struck by the boldness and iconoclasm of French radical thinkers, as we have seen, his own theoretical style is somewhat more ambivalent, being caught, as it were, somewhere between Burke and Thomas Paine. If he did not altogether share the American South's affection for Burke's more conservative tendencies, neither did he go along entirely with the more radical, foundational rhetoric of Paine, whose attempt to reify original liberty was something he found intellectually disingenuous: "By the 1780s," as Ludmilla Jordanova writes, "the idea that the natural world contained unambiguous ethical prescriptions was coming to seem naïve."[77] As a connoisseur of sensibility, Jefferson preferred to circumvent rigid dualisms by seeking points of intersection, bridges, between mind and body, past and present. This is one of the reasons the "Natural bridge," as described in *Notes on the State of Virginia*, is such an evocative image in Jefferson's eyes: it offers a literal correlative to that process of linking opposites which he conceived to be inherent within human society (148). Again, Jefferson's involvement in these theoretical areas would have been stimulated by his years in Paris, when he became personally friendly with Pierre-Georges Cabanis, whose work on physiology he much admired. For Cabanis, sensibility lay at the heart of all things, including human intelligence; the seat of intelligence, he explained, was the brain, itself directed by a nervous system through which all the organs and muscles were connected, thereby providing a physical basis for sympathy. Cabanis' major work, *Rapports du physique et du moral de l'homme*, was not published in Paris until 1802, but Jefferson had the two volumes sent to him in Washington, and he warmly recommended the treatise to his friends.[78] All this suggests the extent to which the American statesman continued to be influenced by the profane materialism he encountered in Paris during the 1780s, and it suggests as well how, like Burke, he understood abstract conceptions to be ironically interlaced with cathectic desires.

As Pauline Maier has observed, it has been common retrospectively to conceive the advent of American independence in a religious light, envisioning it as the natural culmination to New World myths of pastoralism and exodus.[79] Conversely, in a letter to Jefferson on 3 July 1813, John Adams expressed his surprise and regret that "a Tory History of the rise and progress of the Revolution" had never appeared.[80] Although, of course, such a work would have been encumbered with all kinds of ideological freight of its own, it might have helped to counterbalance some of the more romanticized accounts of this revolutionary era that have emerged since the nineteenth century. It might also have helped shed some light upon the vexed question of how the Founding Fathers understood the issue of slavery. It has become standard practice, particularly among contemporary scholars who emphasize America's cultural and racial diversity, to criticize politicians of the late eighteenth century for their blindness to the constitutional implications of slavery, particularly in the South.[81] In fact, though, like other American intellectuals of his time, Jefferson was not unduly concerned about the anomalous position of slavery because he saw it as something that would be erased by the passing of time. To Enlightenment sages, it appeared rather as an irksome, primitive residue from ages past, rather like Christianity itself. In 1786, Jefferson's friend and admirer, the Marquis de Condorcet, published his prize-winning essay "The Influence of the American Revolution on Europe," in which he specifically equated the political emergence of the United States with the beneficent dissemination of Enlightenment values, going on to assure his readers that any "particular errors" still lingering in the American system would ultimately be put right by the inevitable progress of Enlightenment understanding: "even though one may justifiably censure Americans for some things, it is only for certain particular errors or for long-standing practices which they have not yet been able to correct. If they pursue consistently their present course they will eventually set right all these faults . . . Let men be enlightened, and soon you will see good arise spontaneously from the common will.[82]

Without moving into a full-scale consideration of Jefferson's views on slavery, which is outside the scope of this project, I would suggest that the manifest contradictions in his attitude to this issue can more easily be understood in terms of a cultural framework of sensibility. Progressivist historians have noted with dismay how Jefferson, like many other leaders of the early Republic, was a keen slaveowner, making sure all runaways were flogged mercilessly and being far from generous in his attitudes toward manumission.[83] In *Notes on the State of Virginia*, Jefferson also indulges in some supposedly scientific theories about "the real distinctions which nature has made" between black and white people (264), assuring his audience that the "very strong and disagreeable odor" emitted by black people can rationally be traced to the way they "secrete less by the kidnies, and more by the glands of the skin" (265). At the same time, though, Jefferson inveighs against the "infamous practice" of slavery, which he calls a "blot in our country" (214). Eventually, he says, he hopes for "a total emancipation" (289), and in his *Autobiography* he recalls with pride his successful introduction of a bill to the Virginia legislature in 1778 outlawing the importation of slaves (34). Yet, as Markman Ellis has shown, the politics of sensibility tended to resist the equation of political judgement with moral absolutes by making them both analogous to questions of aesthetic taste. Whereas the politics of romanticism have been thoroughly unpacked in recent years—links between Wordsworth and the French Revolution have frequently been examined, for instance—the politics of sensibility remain much more obscure as a category. John Mullan, for example, has suggested there was "no social space for sensibility" except for "illness"; for Mullan, sensibility by its very nature implies retreat into a private consciousness. But we could infer, from Jefferson's praise of Sterne's writings as "the best course of morality that ever was written" (902), that works of fiction were seen in the late eighteenth century as potentially exercising a significant influence on the wider world. Indeed, Hugh Blair wrote in 1762 that novels demanded "particular attention" because they were likely to have a considerable effect "both on the morals, and taste of a nation."[84]

In this respect, Sterne's attitude to slavery is instructive because it was very similar to Jefferson's. As we see from his letters to Ignatius Sancho, a black polymath living in London, Sterne did oppose slavery on principle, but his sense of outrage was always sliding off into what he thought of as the more human, humorous aspects of any given situation:

There is a strange coincidence, Sancho, in the little events (as well as in the great ones) of this world: for I had been writing a tender tale of the sorrows of a friendless poor negro-girl, and my eyes had scarse done smarting, When your Letter of recommendation in behalf of so many of her bretheren and sisters came to me—but why, *her bretheren?*—or yours? Sancho,—any more than mine: it is by the finest tints, and most insensible gradations, that nature descends from the fairest face about St. James's, to the sootyest complexion in Africa.[85]

That was Sterne in 1766. We can see how he prefers to reimagine racial conflict in picturesque terms ("a tender tale of the sorrows of a friendless poor negro-girl"). We see as well that he favors here a benign universalism, where the race of the "negro-girl" should be irrelevant, since, according to sentimentalist doctrine, the white Sterne should be no less part of the negro-girl's "bretheren" than the black Sancho. Also apparent is Sterne's implicit conservatism, in the way he reproduces intact the idea of social hierarchy that "descends" from St. James's Park, in London, to the "sootyest" parts of Africa. The writer of sensibility can only intervene within this traditional design to the extent of recognizing "the finest tints, and most insensible gradations." This is an aesthetics of discrimination, which flourishes precisely because of its political impotence.

As Ellis observes, such redescriptions of slavery within an aesthetic format lead Sterne eventually to "a deeply reactionary and perhaps quietist position."[86] In *Tristram Shandy*, again, the author attempts not so much to repel violence as to aestheticize it, to render it harmless by containing it within ludic parameters, as when Corporal Trim and Uncle Toby come across "a poor negro girl, with a bunch of white feathers slightly tied to the end of a long cane, flapping away flies—not killing them":

—'Tis a pretty picture! Said my uncle Toby—she had suffered persecution, Trim, and had learnt mercy . . . 'tis the fortune of war which has put the whip into our hands now—where it may be hereafter, heaven knows!—but be it where it will, the brave, Trim! will not use it unkindly.
—God forbid, said the corporal.[87]

Despite its characteristic air of benevolence, this representation of slavery anticipates the Sadeian model in its aestheticization of violence, its conception of
power as a commodity to be exchanged, and its assumption of human sensibility
as the necessary counterbalance to this cycle of domination. Sterne, like Sade,
writes out of a culture of materialism within which the inevitable circulation of
power exchanges is tempered only by the capacity of the human sensibility
ironically to reflect upon them. In discussing how sensibility developed as a
"public emotion" toward the end of the eighteenth century, Julie Ellison emphasizes how it became bound up precisely with "narratives of inequality," manifest-
ing itself as a "practice of mobile connection," a "transaction" between individuals
at opposite ends of a particular power spectrum.[88] Sensibility, in other words,
came to imply a process of exchange, rather than serving merely to exemplify a
certain type of sensitive character. This is just how it is represented in Sterne's
writing, which thematizes both distance and incompatibility, the projection of
sympathy over a geographical, psychological, or racial divide which can never be
eliminated.

Jefferson himself read Sancho's letters, which were published in London
in 1782. In *Notes on the State of Virginia*, he comments patronizingly on how
Sancho's writings "do more honour to the heart than the head," adding that "His
subjects should often have led him to a process of sober reasoning: yet we find
him always substituting sentiment for demonstration" (267). On the face of it,
this indicates Jefferson's predilection for "the vigor of simple dichotomy," as
Winthrop D. Jordan put it; but, as always with Jefferson, one side of the equation
begins to interfere with and to destabilize the other.[89] His preference is not for
binary opposition, but for syntactical balance. When he writes of how Sancho's
"style is easy and familiar, except when he affects a Shandean fabrication of
words" (267), he is playing one half of this description off against its corollary,
thereby making each part essential to the other's meaning. Jefferson's rhetoric is
therefore self-reflexive on a microcosmic as well as a macrocosmic scale. Just as
Sterne's characters ride their own hobbyhorses, invent their own self-enclosed
universe, so Jefferson toyed with a succession of aestheticized model villages—
Monticello, his encyclopedic Virginia, the vision of America separated from Europe by an "ocean of fire" (1044)—all of whose circumferences would remain
immune from rupture by the forces of categorical difference.

This is not, of course, to suggest Jefferson always remained closeted in some
imaginary world, or to deny his manifest political ability to respond to changing
events as they unfolded. But, in line with this ideology of sensibility, his policies
kept gravitating toward the position of "amelioration" that Markman Ellis has
argued was characteristic of sentimental writers. Being neither decidedly for or

against slavery, the sentimentalists were most concerned instead for the mitigation of its harshest conditions: "Sentimental writers," suggests Ellis, "found it difficult to cross certain limits in their portrayal of the victims of social and economic change without endangering the entire system of values by which their world was ordered, and this they were disinclined to do."[90] The latter description fits Jefferson almost exactly, and his increasing tendency after the move to Paris in 1784 to procrastinate on the issue of abolition suggests his willing embrace of the radical ambiguity characteristic of a politics of sensibility. Of course, Jefferson was almost inevitably drawn toward the praxis of compromise by the experiences of his presidential administrations after 1801, but even after leaving the White House he tended to embrace contradiction rather than confrontation. As late as 1819, when the Missouri question reintroduced the dilemma of whether or not individual states had the right to legislate for slavery, Jefferson clung to the theoretical legacy of sensibility as he argued that American expansion westward would slowly dissolve conflicts on the abolition issue and would ultimately lead to the disappearance of slavery itself.[91] This represents the principle of amelioration on a grand scale, both in its gradualism and in its idea that sharp conflict is unnecessary.

One of the most familiar lines about Jefferson's approach to slavery is that it demonstrates what John P. Diggins called "the pathos of the Enlightenment," its apparent inability to reconcile the doctrines of equality and natural rights. Diggins himself, following the work of Winthrop D. Jordan, attributed this failure to a form of psychopathology, Jefferson's unconscious attraction to, and repulsion from, various aspects of black culture. Yet this view seeks simply to erase contradictions by its assumption that Jefferson should have been operating within the kind of organic logic, the rhetoric of integrity and integral wholeness, that was intellectually much more characteristic of the mid-nineteenth century than the late eighteenth. Uncomfortable with the paradoxical preconceptions of the Enlightenment, Diggins could only look forward to Lincoln as the agent of a higher law, the savior through whose agency spiritual belief and political reality would become reconciled: "It was," he declared, "Lincoln who tried to liberate American attitudes from the naturalistic heritage of the Enlightenment by explaining equality as a moral imperative rather than as a scientific postulate, an ideal to be pursued rather than a fact to be assumed."[92] I highlight this argument only because it exemplifies the way Jefferson has frequently been misrepresented by scholars approaching his era from a post-romantic viewpoint, and, in some cases, refusing to acknowledge the theoretical conception of an American Enlightenment at all. This is not, of course, ultimately to disagree with the political direction of the argument Diggins or Jordan is making, merely to suggest that, within the complex, transnational world of this cultural enlightenment, Jefferson, like Sterne, approached the epistemological structure of self-contradiction as something to work with rather than against.

Hence we can see how the patriarchal designs of the American Founding Fathers are shadowed, like those of the French Revolution, by the kind of violent paradoxes, an intermingling of creation and destruction, endemic to this particular historical era. The culture of the American Revolution was, in this sense, closer in many ways to that of the French Revolution than it liked to imagine. David Morris has suggested that Anglo-American critics—unlike their French counterparts—have never felt compelled to confront the significance of this kind of Sadeian materialism within their national literature and culture. In particular, the traditionally optative mood of American romanticism would appear to be at the opposite pole to Sade's savage demystification of affairs of the "spirit," just as Hobbes and Machiavelli, two earlier Old World materialists, were demonized by the Puritans in seventeenth-century America. By his move to abolish the soul and cancel the sublime, Sade instituted a mode of writing based upon the "experience of limits," as Philippe Sollers put it, where the guise of freedom can manifest itself only through the circular mode of transgression, a style of reversal which suspends a particular prohibition without altogether suppressing it.[93] American visionaries at the beginning of the nineteenth century sought to transcend Europe, to rise above the paradoxical equation that would define their new beginning only in terms of an infraction against the laws of Europe. Just as in the Sadeian impulse all spirit can be seen as ironically conjoined with matter, however, so the illuminations of the American Enlightenment appear as "reflections," in Burke's sense, of materials from other sources.

Such philosophical materialism did not, of course, necessarily compromise the political agenda of the new American nation. We know, for instance, that d'Holbach's *System of Nature* was the major intellectual influence upon Sade's writing, yet when Jefferson read d'Holbach he tended to ignore these more nihilistic elements, preferring instead to see d'Holbach as a prime example of how morality might reasonably be divorced from Christian codes of conduct. "Diderot, D'Alembert, D'Holbach, Condorcet, are known to have been among the most virtuous of men," he wrote in 1814: "Their virtue, then, must have had some other foundation than the love of God" (1336).[94] I am not, then, trying simply to equate Jefferson's viewpoint with that of d'Holbach, but rather to suggest how their writings represent different responses to similar historical and intellectual situations. Nevertheless, this is the transnational milieu from which Jefferson's intellectual project emerged, and his intertextual relationship with these philosophes serves to problematize his affiliation with what Malcolm Kelsall has called the "iconography of Romanticism."[95] It also, more generally, challenges his incorporation within the charmed circle of American exceptionalism, whose mystique has traditionally revolved around a putatively spiritual autonomy granted to ideas of national "liberty." Though he subsequently liked to portray himself as an avatar of the new nation, Jefferson was, like Sterne, a philosopher of sensibility indebted to a late Enlightenment culture of profanity and contradiction. Republicanism and liberalism, as they were constituted in America during the late eighteenth century, were both framed by this culture of sensibility, with the moral dimension of republicanism involving a pagan rather than a Christian virtue. Consequently, Jefferson's reinvention of the Roman republican idiom involved not a perfect ethical consistency or Puritan steadfastness, but rather a chameleonic capacity to adapt his manner to many different situations. Within a material world charged with the fluctuating substance of sensibility, as Jefferson, Sterne and Burke all recognized, the idea of freedom appeared as an elusive phenomenon, a relative and doubled-up conception rather than an absolute or integral category.

Chapter Five

"Another World Must Be Unfurled"

Jane Austen and America

It is not a truth universally acknowledged that Jane Austen's most celebrated novels, with their polite representations of English life, were written at a time when Britain was at war with the United States. Tension between the two nations had been rumbling on since the American War of Independence in the 1780s, and conflict broke out again in earnest in June 1812, one year after the publication of *Sense and Sensibility* and one year before the appearance of *Pride and Prejudice*. *Mansfield Park* came out in 1814, at the height of these transatlantic hostilities, which were officially concluded in December of that year by the Treaty of Ghent. The purpose of this chapter is to consider how Austen's texts refract the turbulence of British relations with America in the early nineteenth century and how the problematic status of familial and pedagogical authority in her narratives can be related to the insurrectionary temper abroad in the English-speaking world of this time.

The apparent invisibility of the American Revolution in the annals of English literature is something of a curiosity, but, as I suggested in the introduction, one reason for the impact and aftermath of this event remaining largely obscure is that it was a war the English lost. By contrast, there have been many considerations of how the development of Anglo-Saxon Romanticism in the early nineteenth century ran in parallel with the Napoleonic wars, where, of course, the country's military forces emerged triumphant. The common denominator in British politics and literature of this period was a growth in the idea of patriotism and an increasingly idealized notion of the national soil, qualities which informed the representation of nature in Wordsworth's poetry as much as the popular response to Wellington's exploits. It was at this time, says David Simpson, that characterizations of a "national personality" were promoted in Britain, partly in an attempt to forestall the threat of radical revolutions; as a race, the British were held to cherish common sense and solid particulars rather than those abstract generalizations deemed to be more typical of the French. By 1816, Coleridge was rejecting the whole notion of reason as excessively abstruse and theoretical, preferring instead to luxuriate in an "organic" poetic consciousness that worked in comfortably with his view of the organic state of British cultural tradition.[1]

In this sense, the British declaration of war against France in February 1793 can be seen to have unified and galvanized a nation that had been disturbed during the previous twenty years by conflicts with American opponents whom it had been less easy to demonize. The American War of Independence, argues Linda Colley, was in fact a civil war, not only because both sides had much in common, but also because each side was split within itself. Many people in Britain preserved strong family links with emigrants to America, just as most Americans up until the mid—1770s prided themselves on being loyal subjects of the king.[2] After the Declaration of Independence, however, the idea of America came to be generally associated in Britain with an idea of insubordination, an insidious resistance to authority. Thomas Paine, whose pamphlets circulated in huge numbers among English workers, was a crucial figure in promoting America within these circles as a beacon of liberty, an example of how agreeably society might function without the malign powers of hereditary monarchy or aristocracy. The extent to which William Pitt's government was perturbed by the general dissemination of antiestablishment ideas at this time can be gauged from their determination to prosecute Paine at the Guildhall show trial in 1792, where he was convicted in his absence for the "seditious libels" contained in *The Rights of Man*.[3]

Paine's Quaker iconoclasm can be seen as a bridge between lower-class discontent in Britain and what Isaac Kramnick has called the "bourgeois radicalism" of this era.[4] This more intellectual style of dissent, which took its liberal ideas from Locke and its emphasis upon individual freedom of spirit from the Nonconformist churches, protested particularly against the institutionalized religious discrimination which prohibited non-Anglicans from holding public office. These radical "Commonwealthmen" looked back consciously to the Civil War of the 1640s, seeking there a justification not only for greater religious tolerance but also for other kinds of freedom: for instance, the Society for Constitutional Information, a political association with which many of them were associated, campaigned actively for the unhindered circulation of knowledge.[5] By the early nineteenth century, the radical focus in Britain had moved more toward the issue of equality, but in the late eighteenth century it was still concerned primarily with questions of liberty. Within that framework, America, not France, appeared as Britain's alter ego, the kind of society it might be, but wasn't. Consequently, many British intellectuals in the 1790s remained sympathetic to the American cause:

the prominent scientist and Unitarian clergyman, Joseph Priestley, emigrated from Birmingham to Pennsylvania in 1794, while in the same year the younger Coleridge planned with Robert Southey to establish a utopian community in America, an idea that in the end came to nothing. James Chandler, echoing the title of a pamphlet by Charles Ingersoll in 1824, speaks of "the influence of America on the mind" around this time, and it is clear that the New World manifested itself within the consciousness of British writers at the turn of the nineteenth century more as an abstract conception than a material place.[6] Just as Paine declared his native "country" to be "where liberty is not," so British radicals projected an image of America as an externalization of their own ideologies of emancipation, a utopian image of alterity and virtual fulfillment.[7]

This reflexive understanding of America circulated on both sides of the Atlantic. One of its clearest manifestations is in the writings of a native of New Jersey, Gilbert Imlay, who left America for Europe in 1786 and subsequently formed a close friendship with Mary Wollstonecraft, with whom he had a daughter in 1794. Through Wollstonecraft, Imlay's work became influential in British radical circles, and in *A Topographical Description of the Western Territory of North America* (1792) he lays out his vision of the American West as a vista relatively untouched by corrupt European values. In *The Emigrants*, a novel published in 1793, he specifically invokes the metaphor of a mirror to describe how America holds up a glass to the British tradition of civic freedom: "it is perhaps time to place a mirror to their view, that they may behold the decay of those features, which once were so lovely."[8] This novel is suffused with images of reflection, whereby light is seen to be refracted from its natural source and to become, through "the element in which we live, deviable." The idea of perversion, similarly, comprises a significant thread within Imlay's text, and again it signifies a deviation or displacement, a swerve away from original virtue: "Every thing has been perverted," laments the narrator, "and while the tyranny of custom has substituted duplicity for candour, the crude sentiments of cunning have destroyed that genuine felicity which flows from the genial currents of the human heart."[9] What is interesting here is how Imlay's trope of perversion implies a clash within his text between very different constructions of "nature." Whereas nature in the conservative or Burkeian version involved organic continuity and traditional hierarchy, nature in the radical or dissenting interpretation was based around the doctrine of natural human rights. Imlay, as a close associate of Wollstonecraft, clearly favored the latter view; just as she advocated divorce as a natural right for woman, so he advocates emigration—itself a kind of volitional "divorce" from one's native heritage—as a natural right for all mankind.

Sharp conflicts between Britain and America over competing interpretations of natural rights continued well into the nineteenth century. Indeed, the renewal of hostilities in the War of 1812 came about partly because of this kind of dispute. One of the chief complaints of the Americans was that the British fleet were insisting upon a right to search their merchant ships in order to track down "British" men who could be impressed into the Royal Navy. Underlying this quarrel were two distinct conceptions of national identity: for the Americans, citizenship was an affiliation which could be chosen and bestowed voluntarily, so that in their eyes British sailors had every right to renounce their fatherland and join the well-paid American ranks; but for the British, then as now, no subject of the king could ever "alienate his duty." In the eyes of the British government, citizenship embodied a native, not an elective, affinity. Indeed, as Patrick C. T. White has noted, the controversy over impressment "was difficult to resolve because it touched deeply the sovereignty of both nations," including their respective understandings of the equation between the natural and the national.[10] The practice of impressment was discontinued after the Treaty of Ghent in 1814, even though it was not addressed directly in the peace agreement, and the way in which the issue was silently dropped shows Britain reluctantly coming to terms with the idea of America as a separate country in this post-Revolutionary era. While the 1812 conflict revolved mainly around arguments over trade, it did help to unite America against the specter of British domination—it was popularly referred to in the United States as the "Second War of American Independence"— and this in turn helped to emphasize to the British how the world of North America was finally spinning out of their control.[11]

In this sense, the sudden emergence of the United States at the beginning of the nineteenth century not only gave Britain a new political rival, but also provided a disturbing alternative vision of how nature and society might be organized. There were many English writers at this time whose perspectives were informed to some degree by transatlantic horizons, prominent among them William Cobbett. Cobbett was stationed during the Revolutionary War in New Brunswick, from where he came to admire American society, thinking "that men enjoyed here a greater degree of liberty than in England"; accordingly, he returned to the fledgling United States in 1792 as a follower of Paine and an advocate of the rights of man.[12] Soon, however, he became irritated with the anti-British sentiment widespread in the 1790s, and, as "Peter Porcupine," he published from Philadelphia *Porcupine's Gazette*, which attacked what it proclaimed to be the complacent nature of American republican ideals. Cobbett sought to expose hypocritical proclamations of freedom by juxtaposing them with advertisements offering slaves for sale; he also savaged what he saw as the literary and political pretensions of writers inspired by the American national cause.[13] The enormous popularity of *Porcupine's Gazette* during this decade as "the voice of British Loyalism in America" suggests that Cobbett was not alone in these opinions, but his intemperate handling of local politicians and institutions caused him to be convicted of criminal libel in 1799, after which he returned to England.[14] Here, though, he found himself equally uncomfortable amidst the growing commercialization of his native country and the financial exploitation of traditional rural communities which he remembered nostalgically from his youth. He consequently realigned himself with the radical reformers, backing the United States in the War of 1812, when he asserted that Britain's belligerent policy was motivated less by competition with an imperial rival than by the desire to destroy the American source of inspiration for the British reform movement. In 1817, Cobbett crossed the Atlantic again to reside temporarily in Long Island, publishing an account of this sojourn, *A Year's Residence in the United States of America*, two years later.

While Cobbett has often been accused of extraordinary inconsistencies in his attitude toward America, there is actually a paradoxical consistency throughout his career in the way he plays Britain and America off against each other so as to highlight what he sees as the limits and limitations of both.[15] Cobbett was one of the first in Britain to recognize that the American Revolution was an epochal event, and his concern is always with ways in which the Old World and the New might relate to, and mutually influence, each other.[16] In Philadelphia he reacted against the embryonic version of American exceptionalism promulgated by early republicans, who self-righteously pursued a separatist agenda of simply sloughing off corrupt European customs, just as later on he had no patience with the English landed gentry who failed to countenance the social and political lessons of the wars with America. Cobbett was always concerned primarily with how American values might reflect back upon British culture, and in *A Year's Residence* he deliberately plays off his Long Island environment against the benighted condition of England. Americans, says Cobbett, enjoy a better climate, cheaper prices, fewer taxes, and less interference from the dreaded "boroughmongers." He also comments on how the absence of a traditional class system helps to ensure laborers in America are civil rather than surly, never rude but, equally, never cringing: "This, too, arises from the free institution of government. A man has a voice because he is a man, and not because he is the possessor of money. And shall I never see our English labourers in this happy state?"[17] As that last sentence indicates, Cobbett always seeks to use America so as to reflect back upon his native situation; he speaks in the book's preface about being "bound to England for life" and of his "anxious desire to assist in the restoration of her freedom and happiness," a project he hoped to advance by ceremonially carrying with him across the Atlantic the bones of Thomas Paine on his return to England in 1819.[18] Many of his subsequent projects, including the campaign for parliamentary reform and the observations on England in *Rural Rides* (1830), are informed at some level by his internalization of these American experiences. In *Rural Rides*, for example, he suggests that the introduction of American apple trees "would be a great improvement" within the English countryside, showing a taste for horticultural hybridity that also implies his aspiration to integrate an American spirit into the English landscape more generally. Again, when visiting Tutbury, in Gloucestershire, he sympathizes with a poor man accused of stealing cabbages by remarking upon the very different attitudes toward neighborliness in America: "it is impossible for me to behold such a scene, without calling to mind the practice in the *United States of America*, where if a man were even *to talk* of prosecuting another (especially if that other were *poor*, or *old*) for taking from *the land*, or from *the trees*, any part of a growing crop, *for his own personal and immediate use* . . . such *talker* would be held in *universal abhorrence*."[19]

There has, of course, been little direct consideration of the American Revolution itself within conventional narratives of English literature. Various conservative versifiers in Britain during the late eighteenth century approached the conflict in a simplistically authoritarian manner: thus, in "The Rights of Sovereignty Asserted" (1777), Thomas Warwick punningly attributes the current state of "civil gore" to the "unfilial hand" of the American "Monster," and goes on loyally to assert that the British forces will emerge triumphant.[20] More radical sympathies were expressed in William Blake's long poem, *America: A Prophecy* (1793), which mythically envisions the Revolution as both creative and destructive, with the "fierce flames" of Orc destroying the "bolts and hinges" of Albion's "law-built heaven." Rebellious Orc aspires to evade the "mental chains" of "the thirteen Governors that England sent"; but "Albions Angel" responds by vengefully casting red Orc in the role of satanist:

> Blasphemous Demon, Antichrist, hater of Dignities
> Lover of wild rebellion, and transgressor of God's Law.[21]

Early in the nineteenth century, this metaphorical notion of Albion and Orc, Britain and America, forming disorienting mirror images of each other became a more common idea within the Romantic field of vision. For instance, in canto 14 of *Don Juan*, published in 1823, Byron represents America figuratively in terms of alterity and exchange:

> How oft would vice and virtue places change!
> The new world would be nothing to the old,
> If some Columbus of the moral seas
> Would show mankind their soul's antipodes.

Byron's image of a new Columbus redescribing the map of the globe is commensurate with the style of inversion that runs through *Don Juan*, where orthodox genres and morals are stood on their head, as the poem self-consciously "Turns what was once romantic to burlesque."[22]

Such imaginative projections of America in terms of a reversal of British traditions reinforce J. G. A. Pocock's point about how the wars with America created a lasting fissure within the body politic of Great Britain, with the "American Revolution" being "a British revolution before it became something else."[23] The intellectual and military threat from France at this time was relatively easy for Britain to deal with, since France, with its radically different language and culture, its alleged infatuation with sophistry and system, could be smothered by a "common-sense" reaction underlining the native genius of free-born Englishmen.[24] America, from this transatlantic perspective, represented a more disconcerting and uncomfortable prospect: as in Imlay's tropes of mirroring and perversion, it embodied the same, yet other. Cultural theorist Jonathan Dollimore has traced the connotations of "perversion" back through its various theological etymologies, concluding that the most sinister manifestations of this phenomenon occur when the "perverse dynamic" is concerned to transgress, invert, and displace "the true and authentic" from within, thereby constituting a discourse that is "at once utterly alien to what it threatens, and yet, mysteriously inherent within it."[25] To extend this logic into a social and historical realm would be to suggest that in the late eighteenth and early nineteenth centuries Britain and America came to be positioned as heretical alternatives to each other, uneasy mirrors wherein the assumptions of each culture were both reflected and refracted. There was enough of a shared heritage within this Anglo-Atlantic world for the discordances and discontinuities to appear especially threatening to both parties.[26]

This is why British writers like Edmund Burke found the most appropriate way metaphorically to describe the conflict with America was not as a revolution but as a "Civil War"—a phrase he used in a 1777 letter on American affairs to his constituents in Bristol.[27] In 1800, Poet Laureate Henry James Pye, who had been a Tory member of parliament during the 1780s, picked up on this theme of internal strife by incorporating the metaphor of patricide into his rueful retrospect on the war with America. Pye sought to combine his political and artistic functions in excoriating those Whig opposition parties which had encouraged the seditious and ungrateful Americans, who

> Rear'd, like the pelican, with parent blood,
> Turn their wild vengeance 'gainst Britannia's heart,
> And aim with fatal rage, the parricidal dart.

Such a matrix of interfamilial conflict was much in evidence within British discourse of this era.[28] Its symptomatic significance should be understood in broadly cultural rather than political or economic terms: that is to say, while the loss of rebellious scions may not have seriously threatened the British system of government itself, nevertheless the sharp challenge to patriarchal authority which this conflict represented led British writers in the nineteenth century to reimagine "family values" in noticeably different ways. Linda Colley has argued that "the humiliation of defeat at the hands of a former colony was profound for a ruling élite possessed of strict notions of hierarchy and massive pride," so that "a sense of embattled identity" became widespread over the next generation, as the British rulers sought urgently "to shore up the fabric of the state." Attributing their unexpected reverse to an excessive leniency toward the colonies, the British government introduced a series of measures to strengthen their apparatus of centralized control over India, Canada, and Ireland, so as to impress upon their (willing or unwilling) subjects the virtues of monarchy, empire, and "strong, stable government."[29]

In the aftermath of the American Revolution, then, fragmentation and reconstruction of the body politic took place in Britain as well as North America. It is, of course, a commonplace to note how the political world of the United States in the 1790s was haunted by division and confusion, with the Federalists remaining more sympathetic to traditional versions of hierarchical authority than the Anglophobic Republicans.[30] In his *Eighteenth Brumaire of Louis Bonaparte* (1852), Marx looked back at this revolutionary era of the late eighteenth century as an occasion for the renewal of spirit, a rare opportunity for the dispossessed to aspire toward an ideal of pure liberation through the rejection of dead traditions. Yet Marx also spends a good part of this essay describing the forces that tend to circumscribe such radical ambitions, the ways in which quests for freedom find themselves haunted by ghosts from an unwillingly inherited past. As he puts it: "the beginner who has learned a new language always retranslates it into his mother tongue: he can only be said to have appropriated the spirit of the new language and to be able to express himself in it freely when he can manipulate it without reference to the old, and when he forgets his original language while using the new one." In this way, as Marx famously went on to say, the "tradition of the dead generations weighs like a nightmare on the minds of the living."[31] These Gothic specters in the *Eighteenth Brumaire* echo the intuitions of Sade at the time of the French Revolution, who was also concerned to unpack the grotesque paradoxes lurking on the margins of this rationalist enterprise. The crucial point about Sade's writings within this context is how they appear poised on the cusp between virtue and self-interest, between idealism and corruption; his philosophy paradoxically dissolves didactic imperatives into libidinal drives, thereby redefining ethical positions as aesthetic desires. In this sense, as Philippe Roger puts it, "Sade holds up the bloody mirror to the French Revolution," reflecting its violence, but inverting its moral perspectives.[32]

Such paradoxes were no less pertinent to the climate of the American Revolution than to the French Revolution. John Quincy Adams, who in 1800 had found it imperative to "rescue" the American Revolution "from the disgraceful imputation of having proceeded from the same principles as that of France," was by 1837 claiming the "highest transcendent glory of the American Revolution" to be the way "it connected, in one indissoluble bond, the principles of civil government with the principles of Christianity."[33] This, though, is a typical nineteenth-century piece of revisionism, which attempts to gloss over the disorder of the late eighteenth century by assimilating it within the "transcendent" consciousness more characteristic of Victorian America. Indeed, in the very urgency of these attempts by Adams to dissociate his compatriots from the bloody affair of the French Revolution, we may detect a hint of insecurity about the purity of their own insurrectionary actions. There lurks an uneasy sense here of how the American Revolution, like all revolutions, was shadowed by the discourses of blasphemy, transgression, and perversion. This was certainly how it appeared to the conservatives in England, in whose eyes the natural order had been usurped and overturned.

One implication of this transatlantic division between Britain and America was to relativize the power structure of each country, to suggest how its system of authority might be construed as an arbitrary and performative rather than integrated or naturalized phenomenon. Cathy N. Davidson has noted how many early American novels are concerned in some way with the theme of education, and the same thing is true of English writing during this post-revolutionary period, as we shall see in the works of Jane Austen.[34] What I would suggest, however, is that this style of pedagogy does not always involve education in the substantive, ethical sense but rather education as a ritualistic exercise, a mask of authority. It is the form, rather than the content, of education which is at stake here. Both British and American writers of this time are impelled to seek, and to negotiate with, emblems of power, structures that appear to promise social legitimation and thus to reinforce an insecure cultural identity. Consequently, the novel of education frequently involves a forced process of internalization, where characters become initiated into a psychological acceptance of authorities that may to them initially seem specious. It is the status of such authorities that novels of education turn upon, since, within this turbulent and relativistic world of revolutionary uprisings, authority is always in danger of finding itself demystified and exposed to the indignities of irony. Hence, the nostalgic search for validating mechanisms of power swerves away into a more affective relationship with authority; in typically Sadeian fashion, authority turns into an aesthetic rather than ethical imperative. In the case of British and American writers in the two generations after the War of Independence, it is the hybrid interplay between different transatlantic perspectives that threatens to cut the art of governance adrift from its traditional juristic moorings. This process of mutual mirroring and intertwining serves radically to destabilize authority, casting a disorienting shadow over British and American attempts to map out their territory, to circumscribe the boundaries of their national jurisdictions.

*   *   *

Critical associations between Jane Austen and a historical context of any kind are of relatively recent vintage. The English conservative approach, which for a long time successfully appropriated the writer as one of their own, found in her novels an agreeable retreat from the modern world. Deirdre Lynch has written of how, between the world wars, hagiographies of Austen formed part of an ideological mission to repackage "Englishness" by shifting national identity away from Victorian imperialism toward a more inward-looking, domestic agenda, based upon the supposed stability of rural life and the maintenance of naturalized class hierarchies.[35] Even in the middle of the twentieth century, her editor, R. W. Chapman, was still insisting Austen's novels had nothing to say about history.[36] That view of her fiction as an escapist idyll has been challenged more recently by well-known critics like Marilyn Butler and Raymond Williams, even though the contextual frameworks they chose to introduce were quite different, Butler stressing Austen's reactionary outlook and her rejection of fashionable Jacobin ideologies, Williams concentrating on the social and economic determinants brought to light in microscopic detail within her fiction, along with all the class issues negotiated therein.[37] Nevertheless, there still remains considerable resistance to such demystifications of Austen's texts in Britain, where any theoretical attempt to disentangle the various aesthetic paradoxes within her work is frequently alleged to spoil the unadulterated pleasure of appreciating her masterpieces.

The furor that followed upon American critic Terry Castle's suggestion in the *London Review of Books* that Jane Austen may have "acted out unconscious narcissistic or homoerotic imperatives" in the company of her sister, Cassandra, exemplifies the protectiveness felt by the British cultural establishment toward their cherished icon. Castle's line of argument was not that Austen could be considered a lesbian in the modern sense, but that the closeness of her relationship with Cassandra implied "unconscious homoerotic dimensions" which are reflected in her writings, notably in the way she comments in detail on women's bodies and clothing while allowing the figures of men to remain relatively blank.[38] Among the predictable cries of outrage, the most thoughtful response came from Claudia Johnson, another American critic, who pointed out how there have been "two contending traditions of Austenian reception" since the mid-nineteenth century, one British, the other American. The British critical heritage is essentially "elegiac," situating Austen in a pastoral world before the onset of social and psychological modernism; the American tradition, by contrast, tends to be "anti-normative," probing beneath the decorous surfaces of Austen's fictions so as to elucidate some of their implicit lacunae and disjunctions.[39] The intractability of this debate reveals something significant about the relationship between British and American intellectual traditions: if American analysis tends sometimes toward the extravagant or abstruse, the empiricism and, at times, insularity of British critical consciousness makes it frequently hostile to American versions of alterity. This has led to an odd kind of schism in the interpretation of Austen, where iconoclastic transatlantic readings are frequently accused of distorting the moral and artistic sanctity of the British author.

In a famous feminist argument from 1979, for example, American scholars Sandra M. Gilbert and Susan Gubar described what they saw as Austen's "discomfort with her cultural inheritance," especially "the culturally induced idiocy and impotence that domestic confinement and female socialization seem to breed."[40] Gilbert and Gubar argue that the author's covert dissatisfactions with her social milieu manifest themselves in the way her heroines tend to operate by a mode of "double-talk," whose conventional finesse belies a sardonic recognition of ways in which these conversations actually signify something like the opposite of what they appear. Gilbert and Gubar take as their point of departure the long-established recognition of Austen's ironic style, seen for example in the first sentence of *Pride and Prejudice* (1813)—"It is a truth universally acknowledged, that a single man in possession of a good fortune must be in want of a wife"— where the comic point lies in the reader's recognition of how this is, in fact, very far from "a truth universally acknowledged." From this basis of linguistic irony and reversal, Gilbert and Gubar move on to talk more widely about the "self-division" in Austen's fiction, where the embryonic feminist consciousness can only fight subversively, if intermittently, against the stultifying forces of social conformity.[41] Five years later, Mary Poovey developed from this a wider thesis about ideological contradictions in Austen's works, arguing that the "complex relationship between a woman's desires and the imperatives of propriety" tends to produce expressions of indirection or "doubling," through which these conventional narratives would veer off into "the tonal uncertainties of parody."[42]

More recently still, other American critics like D. A. Miller, Eve Kosofsky

Sedgwick, and Joseph Litvak have engaged with "queer" theory to write about the ambivalent crosscurrents between ideology and desire in Austen's fiction. Both Miller and Sedgwick have been alert to darker subtexts that seem on occasions to cut across the polite facades of Austen's cultural world. Miller contrasts an explicit "ideology . . . of settlement" in Austen's world, involving marriage, stability, and a moral vision where the designs of characters appear transparent to each other, with a more irregular aesthetic delight in "unsettled states of deferral and ambiguity."[43] Such teasing denials of closure, he argues, are predicated upon the desire for what is excessive or transgressive, a desire Austen's fiction simultaneously admits and disavows, as, for example, with the equivocal representation of the urbane and immodest Crawfords who disturb the serenity of provincial life in *Mansfield Park* (1814). Sedgwick, who more brazenly chastises "Austen criticism" for "its timidity and banality," chooses to focus upon Marianne Dashwood's propensity for "autoeroticism" in *Sense and Sensibility* (1811), examining how the scene when Marianne is writing to Willoughby from the privacy of her bedroom encompasses more uncomfortable psychological and erotic undercurrents than conventional critics of the novel have liked to acknowledge.[44] Litvak, meanwhile, discovers in Austen's novels a world of "perverse privilege," a site of sophistication and pleasure which he associates with the oppositional consciousness of gay politics. For Litvak, the mood of luxury and excess projected by Austen's verbal mastery betokens an implicit resistance to the coercive claims of "normality," and so he perceives a contradiction between the author's inclination toward stylistic deviance and the "heterosexist teleology" that underwrites her "master plot."[45]

All these American revisionist readings express a sense of dissatisfaction with the explicit directions of Austen's work. Gilbert and Gubar, Miller and Sedgwick each probe to recover instead a more challenging, disquieting mentality that seems to lurk around the margins of her fictions. Litvak, similarly, defamiliarizes Austen's representation of social customs, reinterpreting these rituals of privilege, which to many English eyes have seemed entirely natural, as scenes of a mordant, iconoclastic wit. In general, American critics have been remarkably perceptive in alerting readers to these elements of disturbance and paradox in Austen's narratives, and they have certainly provided a necessary counterbalance to readings from English traditionalists. Still, such American interpretations would seem to run up against the critical problem of tautology: do readers like Gilbert and Gubar simply see mirrored in Austen what they themselves want to find, a cultural schizophrenia between female autonomy and "feminine gentility" that speaks more plausibly to the conditions of late twentieth-century American feminism than early nineteenth-century life in rural England?[46] Admittedly, all interpretations must be tautological to some extent, since they can never achieve independence from the vantage point of their observer. But the issue of tautology is made more obvious here by the way these responses seem to correlate so clearly with that moral disapprobation of Austen voiced by nineteenth-century American intellectuals. In 1861, for instance, Emerson deplored Austen's novels as "vulgar in tone, sterile in artistic invention, imprisoned in the wretched conventions of English society"; a few years later, Henry James damned with faint praise the "light felicity" of Austen's work, lamenting how popular magazines had woven sentimental legends around "their 'dear,' our dear, everybody's dear, Jane."[47] The point here is that American critics have tended to perceive the literal world presented by Austen as not serious enough, not sufficiently concerned (overtly, at least) with scrutinizing the assumptions of what appears to them an ethically bankrupt and claustrophobic society. Hence the frequent drive to deconstruct or allegorize her work, to expose its alleged contradictions, or to project a tone of didactic purpose through the mechanism of characters who come figuratively to embody particular forms of virtue or vice.

In a 1968 essay entitled "The 'Irresponsibility' of Jane Austen," Oxford critic John Bayley took issue with these more abstract and distant conceptualizations of Austen's world. Bayley preferred to stress instead the "plastic" qualities of her characters, their freedom to interact with each other in a fully realized society, a freedom he recognized as "a peculiar kind of liberation from morality." Rather than being burdened with heavy allegorical duties, Bayley argued, Austen's characters are empowered by the author's "creative joy," a joy that permits them to live inside these communities without becoming forced to act out morality plays about the justness or unjustness of their situation.[48] Reacting against the ethical imperatives of New York intellectuals like Lionel Trilling, who had called Emma Woodhouse "a dreadful snob," Bayley attributed the idiosyncratic genius of Austen's novels to their being "so like life," and he went on: "Although some of the most perceptive discussion of Jane Austen's world has come from America, it may be that the American mind does have difficulty in taking for granted the reality of Jane Austen's social units. Nothing in America is quite real in this way—perhaps because there is always an *alternative* to it.[49]

The ideological implications of Bayley's quietist position are obvious enough, and I do not wish to belabor that point here. At the same time, Bayley's treatment of Austen in terms of an aesthetic excess, a ludic "irresponsibility" that evades the stricter patterns of allegory, interestingly anticipates the more overtly theoretical direction of D. A. Miller's 1981 post-structuralist reading, where Miller describes the "fascinated delight with unsettled states of deferral and ambiguity" that permeates Austen's novels, despite their simultaneous commitment to an ideology of "settlement" and moral closure: "The work of closure," writes Miller, "would seem to consist in an ideologically inspired *passage* between two orders of discourse, two separable textual styles. One of them (polyvalent, flirtatious, quintessentially poetic) keeps meaning and desire in a state of suspense; the other (univocal, earnest, basically cognitive) fixes meaning and lodges desire in a safe haven."[50] It is, then, this "passage" between morality and aesthetics, between sense and sensibility, that constitutes the perverse "irresponsibility" of Austen's fiction. To reformulate Bayley's argument, it is not the pure freedom of Austen's characters that guarantees their authenticity so much as their perpetual transgression against the various categories that are trying to box them in. Too many critics, struggling to get some firm handle on Austen's elusive world, have opted to find her texts finally "conservative" or "subversive." But in fact they are neither, for their brilliance lies in the way Austen exploits each side of the equation to ironize the other, thereby describing a world of parallel narratives where nothing is ever quite what it seems, or all that it seems.

This self-perpetuating oscillation between the law and its infraction indicates the way in which her novels are motivated by the dualistic pattern of transgression. In this way, Austen's fictions, like those of Sade, structurally require the motivations of laws against which they can transgress. In *Northanger Abbey* (1818), this transgression manifests itself in the interplay between Gothicism and realism, the thrills of aesthetic terror through which the placid domestic life of Catherine Morland is disturbed. In *Sense and Sensibility*, it appears in the interaction between the rationalist mind of Elinor and the more irrationalist sensations of Marianne Dashwood. In *Mansfield Park*, it emerges in the way the Crawfords' fast style of urban manners is played off against the Christian, evangelical virtues of Edmund Bertram and Fanny Price. Mary Crawford's famous linguistic dexterity with "*Rears*, and *Vices*," where the meaning slides between naval admirals and sexual deviance, comprises the most obvious example of the double movement between parallel narratives in this novel. "'Now, do not be suspecting me of a pun, I entreat,'" declares Mary, ironically of course implying just the opposite; whereupon, so we are told, Edmund "felt grave."[51]

The specific link I want to make here is between this pattern of perverse, parallel narratives and an aesthetic reconstruction of authority than can be related to the historical circumstances of this post-Revolutionary era. Park Honan has demonstrated the likely extent of Austen's knowledge of American affairs in the late eighteenth century, information she would have acquired partly through her geographical proximity to the naval base at Portsmouth—a center of operations during the American War of Independence—partly through her own relatives' service in the navy, partly through the extensive reporting of the war in the Winchester-based *Hampshire Chronicle*, and partly through a more general concern with the way certain British "Whigs had weakened the national resolve by sympathizing with American political ideals." This last issue was addressed by Austen's brothers, James and Henry, in a 1789 piece on the American war in their Oxford journal, *The Loiterer*.[52] Austen's awareness of the war is emphasized by a specific reference in her own juvenilia, in the story "A Collection of Letters," where Miss Jane tells of the death of her "dear Captain Dashwood," who fell "while fighting for his Country in America."[53] We know, moreover, that Austen's father was a "principal trustee" of a valuable plantation in Antigua, a fact which brings to mind Edward Said's well-known analysis of *Mansfield Park*, where he describes how the familial authority which Sir Thomas Bertram exercises in the domestic sphere was underwritten by a system of slave labor maintained in West Indian sugar plantations until the 1830s.[54] Sir Thomas's little empire at Mansfield Park would not have been possible without his stake in the larger colonial empire, and, as Moira Ferguson has observed, the word "plantation" is used frequently in this novel to denote Sir Thomas's property on either side of the Atlantic.[55]

The crucial point to emphasize in this regard is how the Bertrams' transatlantic business is not contrasted with the serenity of their country seat at Mansfield, but rather seen as analogous to it. We know that Austen herself was an admirer of contemporary antislavery campaigners, notably Thomas Clarkson, and that her novel, whose time frame spans a period from 1810 to 1813, was published only seven years after the successful passage of the Abolition Bill by the British Parliament in 1807.[56] While Katie Trumpener may be right to suggest that Sir Thomas Bertram seems more aware of slavery as a political issue after his return from Antigua—he is even willing to discuss it with Fanny at the dinner table—it would also be true to say that Sir Thomas's manners are so attached to the old patriarchal ways that he cannot recognize the dramatic irony whereby a charge of oppression might also be applicable to his own domestic situation.[57] Austen, however, disconcertingly expands the circumference of her narrative, juxtaposing the much-vaunted "harmony" of Mansfield Park (139) with the sense of "noise, disorder, and impropriety" (381) shadowing both Fanny's family home in Portsmouth and the unseen world of the Caribbean; and, through this formal structure of dislocation and parallelism, she implies how these different geographical locations contribute to the formation of each other's cultural meaning. Austen had probably read *Caleb Williams*—she refers to William Godwin in a letter of 1801—and in that novel Squire Falkland is also described as owning a "very valuable plantation in the West Indies," as if to emphasize how these oppressive systems of North Atlantic commerce were a familiar instrument within the English gentry's armory around this time.[58] There is a similar reference in

Emma (1816), where Jane Fairfax compares the American slave trade to the exploitation and exchange of governesses in England: "'the sale—not quite of human flesh—but of human intellect.'"[59] Again, Austen here represents American practices as a brutal literalization and magnification of parallel customs that operate in a more genteel, understated way in England.

In one of the poems she composed just a few days before her death in 1817, Austen likened the spirit of her niece, Anna Lefroy, to the undomesticated landscape of the American West:

> In measured verse I'll now rehearse
>   The charms of lovely Anna:
> And, first, her mind is unconfined
>   Like any vast savannah.
>
> Ontario's lake may fitly speak
>   Her fancy's ample bound:
> Its circuit may, on strict survey
>   Five hundred miles be found.
>
> Her wit descends on foes and friends
>   Like famed Niagara's Fall,
> And travellers gaze in wild amaze
>   And listen, one and all.
>
> Her judgment sound, thick, black, profound,
>   Like transatlantic groves,
> Dispenses aid, and friendly shade
>   To all that in it roves.
>
> If thus her mind to be defined
>   America exhausts,
> And all that's grand in that great land
>   In similes it costs—
>
> Oh how can I her person try
>   To image and portray?
> How paint the face, the form how trace
>   In which those virtues lay?
>
> Another world must be unfurled,
>   Another language known,
> Ere tongue or sound can publish round
>   Her charms of flesh and bone.

Clearly this is a light and occasional poem, and many of its angles on America would have derived from standard accounts of the New World environment that were familiar enough to British readers from Oliver Goldsmith's "The Traveller" and other sources.[60] Nevertheless, what is particularly interesting here is the way Austen oxymoronically plays off her own "measured verse" against the "unconfined" mind of Anna, figuratively represented in this work by the "vast" world of America. All through the poem, we see her delight in stylistic and metaphorical contradiction: in the second stanza, the conservative connotations of "fitly" and "strict" are juxtaposed with the "ample bound" of Lake Ontario's circumference; in stanza three, her subject's "wit," normally considered a polite and genteel commodity, becomes a thing of "wild amaze," to be compared only with Niagara Falls. The suggestion of this poem, that even the "similes" of America are insufficient to describe the original qualities of her niece's mind, indicates ways in which Austen understood the "transatlantic" dimension represented here to stand as a corrective to the customary standards of British society. As she puts it in the last stanza, "Another world must be unfurled" in order to assist with this process of representation. Once again, the image of America serves to illuminate and externalize what in Britain remains latent and suppressed.

Within the more established landscapes of Austen's fiction, the shadow of America similarly comes to hint at a mode of estrangement, a mirror of alterity, that threatens to redefine the weighty tradition of English patriarchy as merely a performative structure. At one point in *Mansfield Park*, Tom Bertram remarks to Dr. Grant on what a " 'strange business this in America' " (145), probably referring to the American declaration of war against Great Britain in June 1812. This draws our attention to the fact that Mansfield Park was written at precisely the time Britain and America were once again engaged in military conflict; the novel, published in the same year as the Treaty of Ghent was concluded, emerged from a political context in which British authority was being belligerently challenged. Austen displaces such historical contumacy into one of the most comically effective scenes in her novel, when Sir Thomas, returning unexpectedly from Antigua to find his house caught up in amateur theatricals, opens the door of his billiard room to find himself "on the stage of a theatre," an occasion which the narrative describes dryly as the paterfamilias's "first appearance on any stage" (198). John Bayley would see this as a moment of delicious, irresponsible anarchy, and so indeed it is; but the anarchy depends specifically upon transgression against established social conventions, a point not lost upon Sir Thomas himself, who is said to be full of "anger on finding himself thus bewildered in his own house, making part of a ridiculous exhibition in the midst of theatrical nonsense" (199). One reason Sir Thomas Bertram is so furious is that his authority appears to have been subverted; it is not just the misuse of the billiard room in itself that is so threatening, but the way in which he has found himself "framed" within an aesthetic artifice, his power of "government" (211) suddenly transposed into a dramatic performance. Recent work on both the French and American Revolutions has shown how an emphasis on "specularity" and theatricalization became a tool of insurrection, as the radical leaders skillfully choreographed pageants or produced other kinds of indecorous art in order to dramatize the follies of the old regime; and something of that demystifying impulse to represent power as performance also pervades *Mansfield Park*.[61]

Sir Thomas, of course, promptly ensures "the destruction of every theatrical preparation at Mansfield" (209) and reestablishes himself as "master of the house" (206), at the center of his family hearth. Yet this attempt to restore a reactionary tone of hierarchical sobriety has been fatally compromised by those ludic, ironic elements that lurk around the margins of Austen's texts, rendering their narratives contingent, paradoxical, and seemingly reversible. Homi K. Bhabha has commented on what he calls "Sade's scandalous theatricalization of language," its tendency to disrupt those established customs associated with more prosaic modes of representation by dramatizing philosophical positions so as to make them appear mere externalizations of subjective desire; and it is a similar fear that his authority might be exposed as a mere artifice, a mask or projection, that provokes Sir Thomas Bertram's violent attempt to erase every trace of theatrical artifice from Mansfield Park.[62] Sir Thomas, we are told, intends "to wipe away every outward memento of what had been, even to the destruction of every unbound copy of 'Lovers' Vows' in the house, for he was burning all that met his eye" (206). For the English aristocracy, according to Linda Colley, the most "immediate way in which defeat in America proved devastating was that it called into question the competence of the British governing élite," subjecting their authority, which had previously been more or less unquestioned, to more uncomfortable kinds of scrutiny.[63] The exercise of power, once opaque and diffuse, becomes increasingly transparent and self-manifesting. In this light, it is not surprising Sir Thomas would feel so disconcerted by the prospect of finding his gubernatorial capacities metamorphosed into the form of a charade.

Sir Thomas's efforts to restore a naturalized authority after his return to Mansfield Park turn out to be less than entirely successful. The father figure can never quite detach himself from the trappings of his stage role; indeed, as Litvak notes, a "subtler and more comprehensive theatricality . . . persists long after Sir Thomas has reclaimed his study."[64] This more subtle atmosphere of theatricality emerges through the narrator's stylistic parallelisms, the double-edged discourse that ensures Sir Thomas's paternalistic directives come to be revealed in a wry, defamiliarized light. Claudia Johnson has written of how the patriarch's treatment of Fanny Price after her rejection of Henry Crawford's proposal of marriage brings to mind his professional occupation as a slaveowner, since he manifests a violent hostility toward any notion that Fanny should be free to choose her partner for herself. Blaming her reluctance on "that independence of spirit, which prevails so much in modern days," Sir Thomas chastises Fanny as "wilful and perverse" (318); again, as with the amateur dramatics, it is not this particular event which infuriates Sir Thomas so much as what it implies about the larger patterns of what he would see as creeping anarchy within the social world. Slightly earlier, Sir Thomas had cut short Fanny's participation at the ball "by advising her to go immediately to bed. 'Advise' was his word," continues Austen's narrator sardonically, "but it was the advice of absolute power" (285). Johnson suggests this kind of irony testifies to the way *Mansfield Park* engages in a "bitter parody of conservative fiction," but that is not the dominant impression a reader takes from this novel.[65] Authority here is not so much parodied but demystified. Austen's texts privilege neither conservatism nor radicalism, but play these styles off against each other through a system of parallel narratives, narratives which modulate between conventionalism and irony, decorum and transgression.

In this respect, the formal parallelism of Austen's narratives can be related to the fissuring effect of the American Revolution, the "Civil War" as Burke called it, since in both cases it is a structural fracturing and fragmentation from within that appears to threaten the viability of a naturalized order. By contrast, the Jacobin theories associated with the French Revolution—those of Rousseau, Wollstonecraft, Godwin, and so on—remained relatively untroubling to Austen. As Marilyn Butler has shown, her narratives display little compunction in dialectically expelling conceptions or characters linked explicitly to the "radical inheritance" of "sentimentalism": the elopement of Lydia and Wickham in *Pride and Prejudice* is treated dismissively within the framework of that novel, for example.[66] Much more disturbing and problematic is the status of authority in general: her narratives may give short shrift to the open defiance or subversion of established order, but they are far more ambiguous when it comes to the perversion of authority, that more duplicitous situation where the legitimacy of government can neither be wholly invalidated nor simply taken for granted. Pierre Klossowski has described how Sade's texts refract a similar aestheticization of authority within the context of revolutionary France: "The libertine great lord . . . is on the eve of the Revolution a master who knows he is the legal wielder of power but who also knows that he can lose it at any moment and that he is already virtually a slave . . . in his own eyes he no longer has an uncontested authority, but still has the instincts of such authority."[67] Though of course they are not libertines in the same way, Austen's wealthy landowners—Sir Thomas Bertram, Darcy, Knightley— possess exactly this combination of authority and insecurity. Their manners and instincts are attached to the past, but their minds are forced to recognize the changing circumstances of the present. What the French Revolution was to Sade, the American Revolution was to Austen: a civil war, an internecine uprising, that served to problematize and subtly undermine the nature of authority from within. The double structure of Austen's parallel narratives can be seen as analogous, both formally and historically, to the internal divisions of this British civil war, which involved an uprising against the constraints of familial government.

Nevertheless, such styles of transgression which involve a disestablishment of "natural" authority also prove to be the discursive basis for Austen's versions of romance. Her novels recapitulate the issues of power and subjugation in formal terms, structurally displacing them from a political to an aesthetic and psychological level. While this kind of power play is comically visible within the "light, and bright, and sparkling" world of *Pride and Prejudice*, Austen's most profound exploration of the psychology of authority occurs in *Emma* (1816), which raises uncomfortable questions about circumferences of dominion in the public as well as the private sphere.[68] The dynamics of the relationship between George Knightley and Emma Woodhouse are not dissimilar to those of the romance between Darcy and Elizabeth: Emma enjoys the power of interference and manipulation, a transgressive trait that Knightley also takes pleasure in, since he, true to his vocation as a magistrate, can then correct her when she errs.[69] Emma's very first words to Knightley in the book are spoken "playfully" (41), and she reassures her father about how "Mr. Knightley loves to find fault with me," though she says it is only "in a joke—it is all a joke"(42). Later, Knightley insists on the natural advantage of his being sixteen years her senior, so he can restrain her "sauciness" (121) with his tutelary authority. Toward the end of the narrative, Emma admits she has often been "negligent or perverse," and she thanks Knightley for trying to "improve" her (404). After their engagement, Emma says she can never call him anything but "Mr. Knightley," whereupon George solemnly avows that he has been in love with her "saucy looks" since she was thirteen (445). It is true, as Trilling said, that for Austen love tends to be linked closely with pedagogy, but in *Emma*, as in *Pride and Prejudice*, this pedagogy is eroticized rather than moralized, with authority becoming an aesthetic rather than an innocent or didactic phenomenon.[70] Hence, the relationship between Knightley and Emma involves structures of authority and desire than run in parallel with, but cannot simply be reduced to or explained in terms of, the traditional British class system. To put this another way: the patriarchal and hierarchical framework informing *Emma* provides the impetus for the various power plays in the novel, but Austen's characterizations then swerve away into an alternate psychological zone of their own, where power finds itself refracted through a glass darkly rather than being expressed in a self-evident, social light.

This is why throughout *Emma* the ironic narrative works to problematize the clarity of its apparently classical representations. We are told, for instance, that Knightley's residence, Donwell Abbey, "was just what it ought to be, and it looked what it was" (353); and some residual sense of this ideal of transparency—the ideology of "settlement," as D. A. Miller terms it—still lingers in the novel.[71] But *Emma* is also a text of disguise, deceit, and deferral, attributes which appear, most obviously, in connection with the concealed romance between Jane Fairfax and Frank Churchill. Frank's false surname—he had decided to "assume the name of Churchill" (48)—anticipates a sequence of riddles where the inhabitants of Highbury are forced to try to decipher handwriting on letters and to unravel the significance attached to verbal games of acrostics, in situations where Frank is communicating secretly with Jane. Frank, of course, is a master of masks and artifice: when he goes across the room to speak with his fiancée, he places himself strategically between Jane and Emma so the latter will not be able to "distinguish" Jane's reaction (231). Knightley, who smells a rat early on, abhors this "Disingenuousness and double-dealing" that "seemed to meet him at every turn" (344); he complains to Emma of how "Mystery" and "Finesse . . . pervert the understanding" (430); and he expresses his decided preference for "plain, unaffected, gentleman-like English" (432). But the construction of the novel, through its pattern of parallel narratives, denies Knightley such an unequivocal resolution. In the "confusion" at dusk after the acrostics game, Knightley detects between Frank and Jane "certain expressive looks, which I did not believe meant to be public" (345–46). This is why W. J. Harvey acutely observed of *Emma* that the "written novel contains its unwritten twin whose shape is known only by the shadow it casts": the novel's world of polite conversation runs in parallel with a more sinister underworld of jealousy, passion and resentment.[72]

What Harvey did not go on fully to acknowledge is how the liaison of Knightley and Emma also participates in this secretive subtext. Despite his agenda of gentlemanly plain dealing, Knightley is, as Harvey recognized, "not entirely lucid to himself about his dislike of Frank Churchill." Knightley believes he disapproves of Frank purely on moral grounds, whereas, as we are told toward the end of the book: "He had been in love with Emma, and jealous of Frank Churchill, from about the same period, one sentiment having probably enlightened him as to the other" (419). (Note how the stylistic parallelisms here, the clauses balanced off against each other through formal paradoxes and reversals, mirror the mutually self-reflecting narratives that Austen inscribes.) But Harvey, like so many other critics, also went on to talk about the "perversion of imagination" as "Emma's most radical failure," a "lesson hammered home" by the various humiliating "punishments" inflicted on her throughout the narrative.[73] Eve Kosofsky Sedgwick has written of how a "lot of Austen criticism sounds hilariously like the leering school-prospectuses or governess-manifestoes brandished like so many birch rods in Victorian sadomasochistic pornography"; and though Sedgwick makes her suggestion with a typically hyperbolic flourish, it is hard not to agree with her assessment that because of these moral presuppositions "the sense of an alternative, passionate sexual ecology" in Austen's work has not been touched upon in most critical readings.[74] Emma Woodhouse, like Elizabeth Bennet, works her way toward a successful marriage because of her "perversion of imagination," not in spite of it. Rather than austerely disapproving of Emma for her deficient sense of ethical purpose, "Mr. Knightley" takes delight in his young charge's insouciance, just as she herself is attracted to his paternalistic manners. It is significant, of course, that after their marriage Knightley has to move into Hartfield because Emma will not abandon her father. In that sense, Knightley appears only too obviously for Emma as a surrogate father figure, an eroticized version of the immovable Mr. Woodhouse, a fixed point of reference to which the wayward heroine can return.

Austen's texts, then, refract ethical issues into aesthetic styles. This is why to interpret Austen through a framework of moral preconceptions of whatever kind is to risk missing the crucial element of disturbance within her work, the way her texts carve out for themselves psychological recesses behind the masks of social conformity.[75] To speak of a civil war in Austen's narratives is not just to indicate internal division, but also to suggest how such divisions are themselves masked by a form of civility which is sometimes misconstrued as a more straightforward impulse toward epistemological closure. In a recent rereading of *Emma*, Nicola J. Watson acknowledges "perversions of proper application" of language in the various conundrums and riddles scattered throughout the book, but then she asserts, in traditional British style, that "Austen's didactic programme" is ultimately "to ensure a world of near-perfect, institutionalized intelligibility."[76] But more useful for understanding the peculiar kind of cerebral eroticism that permeates *Emma* is Maurice Blanchot's remark about how Sade's texts intermingle neoclassical "clarity" with an "obscurity, which troubles and complicates our reading, renders it internally violent."[77] This is precisely what we find in Austen's work, where the drive for enlightenment and elucidation is held in check by irregularities and deviations which ultimately provide the most powerful motivation for the libidinal drive of the fictional characters as well as for the hermeneutic drive of the narrative.

Austen's fictions, then, revolve crucially around questions of authority: the violent impulses of authoritarianism, the power of control associated with authorship. As R. F. Brissenden has argued, such issues manifest themselves most clearly in her juvenilia, where Austen's contextual links with Sade become more apparent.[78] *Love and Friendship*, which was written in 1790—one year before *Justine*—exposes the weakness of sensibility and the fundamental selfishness of human behavior, while the letters "From A Young Lady," written in 1791 or 1792, extol crime and murder as panaceas for disappointment in love. Again, the fragment entitled "Henry and Eliza: A Novel," drafted at the end of the 1780s, has an odd opening sentence that implies the more atavistic aspects of domination and submission lurking beneath the surface of the civilized social order: "As Sir George and Lady Harcourt were superintending the Labours of their Haymakers, rewarding the industry of some by smiles of approbation, and punishing the idleness of others, by a cudgel."[79] This bizarre beginning has been analyzed perceptively by Claudia Johnson:

Who would dare imagine Knightley, Darcy, or Mr. Bennet beating their negligent farmers? The shock here derives not from simple incongruity—i.e., a belief that such people do not do such things. It derives rather from an unexpected disclosure—i.e., a discovery that such people may indeed beat their farmers, but that certain novelistic forms do not permit us to imagine, much less to represent, realities of this sort. . . . The central enterprise of the juvenilia . . . is demystification: making customary forms subject to doubt by flaunting their conventionality.[80]

Johnson's reading is excellent, but I would demur from her on one point. It is not a question of whether or not the landed gentry actually attack their farmers with cudgels but, more importantly, the symbolic aspects of domination that such an image represents. Austen thus satirically exposes a darker desire for mastery that runs in parallel with the more established conception of social hierarchy, a desire normally smothered by all the accouterments of morality and gentility that make up the civilized English world. It is noticeable in "Henry and Eliza" that Sir George Harcourt is said to have returned quite recently from the New World— "when you sailed for America," complains his wife, "you left me breeding"—and, as in *Mansfield Park*, this transatlantic dimension serves to make explicit those forces of oppression that remain latent within the home country.[81]

It is this dialectic between subjective and objective definitions of authority, the pleasures of self-gratification against the burdens of social responsibility, that provides some of the central tensions in Austen's major novels. Such a recognition of the limitations of subjective consciousness and of the problematical affiliation between private desire and public power can be traced right back to her "History of England," written in 1791. Here the sixteen-year-old author plays around with the representation of chronological sequence, beheading monarchs at an alarming rate and turning the idea of history itself into a form of subjectivist farce. In the subtitle to her work, Austen describes it as written by "a Partial, Prejudiced, and Ignorant Historian"; yet the tone here is not merely one of polite self-deprecation, for the purpose of this metahistorical comedy is to scrutinize skeptically the rational sequences of cause and effect through which narratives of history seek to reconstruct the past.[82] "Just as history is about the exercise of power," observes Christopher Kent in an essay on Austen's juvenilia, "so history writing is the exercise of power"; the author insouciantly introduces her own private friends and relatives into this narrative, thereby annihilating the more customary processes of historical cause and effect.[83] Instead, she substitutes what Ellen E. Martin has called a series of textual "fetishes"—trivial, irregular details— which effectively undermine any basis for linear sequence and so expose the idea of rational order as a chimera. Austen's sense of history here, again like that of Sade, involves "a flat repetition of the same, deprived of any significance or dramatic interest," as ideas of Enlightenment rationalism and progression fall back into cycles of compulsive irrationalism and absurdity.[84] As an experienced novelist, Austen is not so self-indulgent as this, of course; in her longer works, the vengeful impulses of the self are balanced more firmly against the responsibilities and disappointments of society. As Brigid Brophy noted in a fine essay, Austen's mature writing seems to punish her own desire for infantile mastery, playing off the delights of fantasy against the more complex, inconsistent world of adult consciousness.[85] Nevertheless, traces of this aggressive, iconoclastic wit always remain. "The History of England" reveals notions of national identity and tradi- tion to be arbitrary, subjective constructions; similarly, Mansfield Park and Emma are shadowed by parallel narratives that never cease to imply how the social customs on display here remain provisional fictions, contingencies of value.

In this way, Austen critiques the various forms of idealism that were becom- ing associated with national identity around the turn of the nineteenth century. Austen's "History of England" dissociates linear chronology from any imma- nent teleology or meaning by transferring history into the realm of burlesque, an idiom that becomes suppressed, though never entirely muted, in her subse- quent, more famous works. In these later narratives, we witness a series of dis- placements, both geographical and gubernatorial, as the turbulence of this post- Revolutionary era works its way surreptitiously into the interstices of her fiction. Her novels recapitulate Anglo-American battles around questions of political domination and representation in formal ways, investigating the problems of who should control who, and why. I would also suggest it has tended to be the subsequent American tradition in Austen criticism, as Johnson defines it, that has highlighted these more destabilizing elements in her writings, unfurling that alternative transatlantic perspective which Austen herself adumbrated in her poem for Anna Lefroy. Just as the French Revolution (or civil war) liberated Sade's divided imagination, underwriting his rationalistic scorn for emblems of tyranny to which he was still affectively attached, so the American Revolution, the British civil war, provokes in Austen a split allegiance, as her narratives ironically disestablish powers with which her characters retain instinctive and emotional affinities. In the "war of ideas" with Jacobin France, Austen's novels may indeed, as Marilyn Butler argues, be seen dialectically to reject that alien style of radicalism; but it is equally important to consider her texts in the light of an interplay with America, Britain's own shadow self, the offspring that had recently revoked its allegiance to natural, familial authority. In relation to such consanguinity, Austen's family romances may come to seem more equivocal than they appear at first sight.

Chapter Six

Burlesques of Civility

Washington Irving

The narratives of Washington Irving, like those of Jane Austen, appear in a different light if they are understood as reflecting the suppressed trauma of internecine conflict in the first generation after the American Revolution. To rotate Irving's work through this particular axis is to elucidate unsettling new angles on a body of writing which, again like Austen's, has too often been ethically domesticated, especially by critics drawing their assumptions from the values associated with national literary traditions constructed later in the nineteenth century. Melville, inspired in his early days with the energy of the "Young America" movement, quickly wrote off Irving's literary persona, Geoffrey Crayon, as an almost plagiaristic extrapolation from the work of Oliver Goldsmith, while Emerson similarly upbraided Irving for lacking "nerve and dagger."[1] Irving's tentative, self-deprecating fictions did not find favor with American intellectuals of the generation after his own, a generation whose agenda involved more boisterous or visionary forms of self-reliance. What I want to argue in this chapter, however, is that Irving's writing works itself out through an elaborate stylistics of burlesque, through which assumptions of authorial integrity and national identity are deliberately deflated and parodically renegotiated. Irving is perhaps the best example of an American author whose stature is diminished by any forced affiliation with agendas of literary nationalism, but whose subtleties can be appreciated more readily once he is situated within a transnational context.

In *The Sketch Book* (1819–20), the narrative voice of Geoffrey Crayon tends to avoid any direct representation of the American landscape. Such portrayals of nature, as Homi K. Bhabha says, often manifest themselves as a kind of "inscape of national identity," a way of externalizing and giving artistic expression to the politics of nationalism.[2] Instead, Crayon prefers an evasive style of "playfulness," as Jane D. Eberwein describes it, being intent upon manipulating "transatlantic comparisons" in a "genial but frequently double-tongued voice."[3] Discussing the pastime of angling, for example, Crayon talks of how his party's "first essay was along a mountain brook, among the highlands of the Hudson, a most unfortunate place for the execution of those piscatory tactics which had been invented along the velvet margins of quiet English rivulets."[4] No attempt is made here to encompass stylistically the "highlands of the Hudson," except through a process of comic deflation and negation; the Hudson turns out not to be an appropriate milieu in which to practice those civilized arts of English fishing, arts which the overblown phrase "piscatory tactics" slyly lampoons. Such secondhand reflections of American life through the lens of European customs would not, however, have endeared Irving to the likes of Melville or Emerson. It is true that Irving avoids here any simple sycophancy to English traditions, but more disturbing for American cultural nationalists would have been the author's implicit denial that any representation of the "natural" could exist outside this framework of intertextual reflection, comparison, and inversion which the prismatic style of *The Sketch Book* delineates.

Similarly, though for different reasons, the elaborately wrought style of Irving's bifurcated narratives has often been underestimated by twentieth-century readers accustomed to the self-promoting complexities of modernism. In recent times, Irving's work has frequently been consigned too easily to categories of the sentimental or the picturesque. Donald Ringe, for example, argues that the central function of Irving's grotesque narratives is to expose the purely mental basis of the Gothic experience and thus to return readers to "the reality of the world perceived through reason—the world of common sense and prosaic daylight." Hawthorne, of course, was read in this kind of way for years, as a social realist whose paraphernalia of Gothicism lent a charming, if somewhat old-fashioned, aspect to his literary productions.[5] This is not to claim, as Melville did of Hawthorne, that at some profound level Irving should be seen as a modernist writer, a darker and more subversive presence than he at first appears; Irving's work resists such univocal definitions, either of the light or the dark. What is more pertinent to consider is the way Irving's style of literary burlesque has been generally misconstrued, just as the aesthetic genre of burlesque itself has been widely ignored or misunderstood. Irving's mode is not so much that of subversion, but of perversion; his work does not radically undermine conventional values, but rather holds them in suspension. Through the double-edged form of burlesque, Irving constructs narratives where dignity and buffoonery, civility and disorder, are brought into a dangerous juxtaposition.

In itself, this doubleness of texture may not be unfamiliar, and may in fact be reminiscent of what Terry Castle, after Bakhtin, has termed the "carnivalization" of literary narratives. For Castle, the carnivalesque appears as a mode that "typically engenders a series of problematic *liaisons dangereuses* by throwing characters into proximity who, if an exhaustive cosmological decorum were truly the goal, would never meet: the high and the low, the virtuous and the vicious, the attached and the unattached."[6] Castle's prime examples of the carnivalesque in eighteenth-century English narrative are drawn from the novels of Richardson, Fielding and Smollett, and it would not be difficult to see how some of Irving's most famous stories might also be understood within this framework. In "The Legend of Sleepy Hollow," for instance, the association between puny schoolmaster Ichabod Crane and energetic yokel Brom Bones introduces a series of reversals in the world of civilized society, as Bones's "Herculean frame and great powers of limb" (1069) put to flight not only Crane's courtship of Katrina but also his general sense of reason: the unfortunate Crane ultimately comes to imagine himself pursued by ghost, goblin, and headless horseman.

There is, however, a crucial distinction to be made here between the carnivalesque and the burlesque. The carnivalesque, as it has been formulated in post-Bakhtinian criticism, connotes some kind of threat to the institutional order; it embodies the voice of a popular culture that is positioned in opposition to the dominant ideology (whether or not that ideology manages to "contain" the carnivalesque is beside the point here). Burlesque, on the other hand, implies no such antagonism; in burlesque, the humorous counterdiscourse runs in parallel with the master narrative, revealing the arbitrariness of its construction, but implicitly supporting, rather than undermining, its established pattern. Whereas the carnivalesque moves toward parody, burlesque generally acquiesces in irony; indeed, the ironic mode of burlesque is predicated upon an audience's recognition of parallels and contiguities between the burlesque scene and familiar social subjects. In this way, burlesque crucially feeds off the preservation of traditional scenarios; in fact, it maintains a vested interest in the preservation of these customary formulas. This is why Irving's work, like that of Austen, may appear conservative in its ideological overtones. But it is also why Irving's texts, again like Austen's, are subtly disorienting in the way their parallel narratives set up a series of reflecting mirrors that grinningly ape the conventions of society.

Irving's own engagement with the intellectual heritage of burlesque has been well documented by Martin Roth in his book, *Comedy and America*. Roth points to Irving's affinities with burlesque writers such as Erasmus (*The Praise of Folly*), Robert Burton (*The Anatomy of Melancholy*), Cervantes, Samuel Butler, Rabelais, and, especially, Laurence Sterne. He also discusses the traditional hostility among literary critics to recognizing burlesque "as a genre or a tradition" in its own right, partly because of its celebration "of madness and obscenity as positive human values," partly because "it is an international tradition and violates the linguistic and territorial agreements we have made in the area of critical nationalism."[7] Both of these factors are relevant to Irving's situation: by describing a human world where the mind is less significant than the body, where what separates people is less relevant than what they have in common, Irving, like Rabelais, negotiates a form of bathetic universalism that brings everybody down to the same level. This, of course, is why Irving's work became marginalized later in the nineteenth century: not only did it seem negligent of mankind's "spiritual" proclivities, it also appeared less than fully committed to the romantic, exceptionalist idea of America as inherently different from other countries.

More immediate manifestations of burlesque in the early nineteenth century were available to Irving in the New York theaters, where he attended English farces frequently. In one of his "Jonathan Oldstyle" letters of 1802, Irving describes the mood of "bathos" (13) associated with a recent play, *The Battle of Hexham, or Days of Old*. In 1807, writing in the first issue of *Salmagundi* under the pen name of "William Wizard," Irving contributed a short essay entitled "Theatrics, containing the quintessence of modern criticism," in which he implicitly proposes the idiom of burlesque as a touchstone for contemporary styles of art. Commenting on a performance of Shakespeare, Irving suggests that Lady Macbeth "would have given greater effect to the night-scene, if, instead of holding the candle in her hand . . . she had stuck it in her night-cap. This would have been extremely picturesque, and would have marked more strongly the derangement of her mind" (57). Shakespeare's plays oscillate between the perspectives of tragic hero and comic fool, but Irving wants to bring everything down to the fool's level, because, like Erasmus, he holds "nobler" forms of heroism to be ultimately self-regarding and self-deluding. In many of these *Salmagundi* pieces, Irving plays with the idea of New York as Gotham City, drawing knowingly on the term's burlesque origins from the days of medieval England, when the wise men of Gotham feigned stupidity and imbecility in order to dissuade King John from establishing a court in their town.[8]

More institutional projections of this world upside down were to come with the commercial development of the burlesque theater in New York City just a few years later. The cornerstone of the Bowery Theater was laid in 1826, and the "anarchic" spirit of that emporium was flourishing by the 1830s. In his account of how burlesque culture emerged in America during the nineteenth century, Robert C. Allen cited an essay entitled "The Age of Burlesque," written by Richard Grant White in 1869. This piece is interesting, because it is one of the few essays seriously to consider burlesque as an aesthetic phenomenon. Describing burlesque as a "monstrous" form of entertainment, White continued:

And by monstrous I do not mean wicked, disgusting, or hateful, but monstrously in-congruous and unnatural. The peculiar trait of burlesque is its defiance both of the natural and the conventional. Rather, it forces the conventional and the natural together just at the points where they are most remote, and the result is absurdity, monstrosity. Its system is a defiance of system. It is out of *all* keeping. . . . burlesque casts down all the gods from their pedestals.[9]

White's analysis illuminates the fundamentally conservative tendencies of bur-lesque, as opposed to the more subversive mode of the carnivalesque. By forcing the conventional and the natural together, as White said, burlesque makes the natural seem conventional and the conventional seem natural. The resultant "absurdity" derives from a sense of defamiliarization, an exposure of the natural as merely conventional; hence, the "natural" is revealed merely as a form of dehistoricized and depoliticized speech. But the implicit conservatism of bur-lesque arises from a simultaneous movement in the opposite direction: as well as making the natural appear conventional, burlesque also makes the conventional appear natural, thus keeping these traditional cultural patterns in place. Whereas the carnivalesque pushes against the normalizing boundaries of political repre-sentation, burlesque, by contrast, feeds off them; indeed, burlesque needs to keep those older paradigms in place so its parodic energies have something to work against. Burlesque, then, sports sardonically, but quietistically, with even the most absurd or repressive social systems. In the carnivalesque, the discourses of high and low intersect antagonistically with each other; but in burlesque, the parallel narratives of high and low, convention and mockery, continue serenely along their self-contained paths, paths that are mutually reflecting, to be sure, but also in the end mutually exclusive.

There are a number of other historical contexts that help illuminate this development of a burlesque, topsy-turvy outlook in Irving's writing. The most obvious of these is the Revolutionary situation itself. In "Rip Van Winkle," the disruptive forces of history intrude upon the idyllic pastoral life of rural New York, so that the hero's world is turned upside down, symbolized by the way the village inn changes its sign from "King George the Third" to "George Washington" (779). Americanist critics of the Cold War era, who used to idealize the virtues of "freedom" at all costs, tended to equate Rip Van Winkle's liberation from his wife with a passage into existential self-fulfillment that was analogous, conceptually, to America's liberation from her European "family"; but, as Donald E. Pease has written, these virtues of feisty independence promulgated by Leslie Fiedler and others find themselves shadowed in Irving's story by a perturbing sense of es-trangement from the past. This in turn generates an equally disturbing experi-ence of alienation from known communities, tensions which, as Pease has said, exemplify the way "many more Americans felt threatened rather than exhilarated by a politically brand-new world." Indeed, it is the insecurity and vulnerability of the early republic, rather than its confident prognosis of the future, which has been highlighted by much recent scholarship.[10]

Another historical correlative to Irving's burlesque style can be found in the significance of travel during this period. Irving shifted countries several times during his literary career, living continuously between 1815 and 1832 in Europe, where he worked as a professional writer and diplomat, and spending another four years in Madrid as minister to Spain during the 1840s. This prolonged sense of exile and deracination provokes in Irving's writing a double discourse of nostalgia and distance, sentimentalism and irony; the narrator in *The Sketch Book* recollects the customs of old New York, but only, as it were, from the outside. This effectively defamiliarizes inherited traditions: the circumstances of life along the Hudson River are framed by a narrative perspective that makes explicit the idiosyncratic nature of these local customs, just as "Rip Van Winkle" and "The Legend of Sleepy Hollow" are typographically and discursively "framed" by prefaces and postscripts commenting sardonically on the veracity of these tales. A similar mood of detachment can be inferred from Irving's description of society's rituals in "The Country Church," where the narrator insists on his status as "a stranger in England" (830), indicating a degree of estrangement from native customs which is reflected formally in the doubled-up style of his art. This combination of empathy and alienation also emerges in *Bracebridge Hall* (1822), when Irving's narrator surveys the English country around the Squire's estate and spots "a fair fresh-looking elderly lady, dressed in an old-fashioned riding-habit, with a broad-brimmed white beaver hat, such as may be seen in Sir Joshua Reynolds' paintings."[11] This represents the category of the picturesque in the purest sense of that term: the English landscape is viewed through the prism of Reynolds' pictures, with Irving's cerebral preconceptions remodeling this local scene to align it aesthetically with the kind of world presented by the eighteenth-century English painter.

This emphasis upon the philosophical implications of distance forms an important strand within Irving's work. He was not simply writing private travelogues but, more importantly, interrogating the wider significance of any kind of local affiliation. Yet it is also crucial to emphasize how, for Irving, travel betokens a mode of alterity, an oscillation between two equally provisional points, rather than a simple passage between the "province" and the "centre."[12] Though the essay "Rural Life in England" praises the "small landscapes of captivating loveliness" (800) which Crayon discovers in the old country, another *Sketch Book* piece, "English Writers on America," finds Crayon hostile to the patronizing and prejudiced tone too often assumed in Britain toward the New World. Thus, it is not easy in this collection to locate any clear social or hierarchical assumptions; indeed, part of Irving's skill lies in his picaresque problematizing of every comfortable conception of "home," his disavowal of any methodological or intellectual center which might reduce other scenarios to a marginal or inferior status. Geoffrey Crayon comes across as a displaced person, a natural loner, and, like other exiles, he finds himself beset by a "roving passion" that it is either his "good or evil lot" to have "gratified" (745). The pertinent epigraph to *The Sketch Book* is taken from Lyly's *Euphues*: "the traveller that stragleth from his owne country is in a short time transformed into so monstrous a shape that he is faine to alter his mansion with his manners, and to live where he can, not where he would" (743). Here traveling is equated with a sense of loss, with the transformation of origins ("his owne country") into radical difference ("so monstrous a shape"). This makes clearer the ways in which Irving's travel fiction relates not just to an American "provincial" consciousness, but also to the broader theoretical matrix of romanticism that was being developed at the turn of the nineteenth century.

Irving, born in 1783, came to intellectual maturity when images of America itself were becoming interwoven with the new, iconoclastic styles of romantic irony. Romantic irony, argues Lilian R. Furst, was concerned to move away from the more straightforward ironic inversions, typical of Augustan satirists, which simply imply the opposite of what is meant. Such reversals presuppose the existence of stable meanings and conscious authorial intentions, whereas in romantic irony neither the writer nor the reader can be so sure of the ground on which he stands. Furst traces the development of romantic irony from the publication of Friedrich von Schlegel's *Lyceum* fragments in 1797, where the German philosopher declares that the finite world is contradictory by definition and so can be justly represented only through an ironic stance. Hence, says Schlegel, "everything that is at once good and great is paradoxical," so that, in literary terms, "Irony is the form that paradox takes."[13] René Wellek in 1965 claimed that such formal irony "is completely absent from the English Romantic writers, even when they laugh or joke or parody"; according to Wellek, these aesthetics of ambivalence and doubling promoted by German theorists like Schlegel and Jean Paul Richter, a critical discourse that "assumes a sinister doubt of the identity of the ego," failed to intrude upon the more sententious and organically unified imaginations of their British contemporaries.[14] But, as we saw in the last chapter, transnational projections of "America" in the works of various British writers of this era did help surreptitiously to introduce alternative vistas into their domestic culture, and this kind of transatlantic reflexivity eventually came to have an important influence on how both British and American cultural traditions came to define themselves. At precisely the time when theories of romantic irony were being developed, America was coming to appear to Europe as a kind of cracked or crazy mirror, wherein the Old World witnessed strangely distorted representations of itself.

The poetry of Oliver Goldsmith represents one of the clearest examples of how this idiom of romantic irony becomes affiliated with fictional projections of America. In "The Deserted Village" (1770), America is represented as a pastoral idea, a haven of retreat from the corruptions of the city. Goldsmith, who never himself crossed the Atlantic, abstractly envisions America as a reversal of British landscapes; unlike the Anglo-Saxon "cooling brook" and "grassy vested green" (360), America is seen as the locale of "blazing suns" (347) and "poisonous fields" (351). For Goldsmith, America is endowed with what Britain lacks: it is a land of wilderness and danger, but also of pristine innocence. This is why he writes of how "half the convex world intrudes between" the two countries (342), since his poetry describes a figurative transition or reflection between these two points.[15] In his earlier poem, "The Traveller" (1764), Goldsmith similarly works with abstract ideas rather than particular times and places, as he outlines the characteristics associated in his mind with various different national types. Thus the Italians are immersed in "sensual bliss" (124); France is the "Gay sprightly land of mirth and social ease" (241); Britons above all prize "independence" (339); while America is associated with a primitivist lack of social order: "Where wild Oswego spreads her swamps around, / And Niagara stuns with thund'ring sound" (411–12).[16] Goldsmith subtitles his poem "A Prospect of Society," and the reader here is given the sense that—as Goldsmith's character, Hardcastle, suggests in *She Stoops to Conquer*—travelling involves witnessing a kind of masquerade. Within this touristic panorama, notions of deep or essential human nature are of less significance than changes of costume. In this sense, Goldsmith's poetry is notable for its radical ambivalence, its refusal to commit itself to any specific entity or point of view. The patriotic conclusion to "The Traveller" appears less of a resolution than a self-ironizing acknowledgment of how the Briton will naturally be attached to British soil, just as the Frenchman is symbiotically intertwined with France. Consequently, Goldsmith's poem "travels" formally as well as thematically, constructing a double-edged discourse in which every possibility becomes balanced off against others. His cerebral peregrinations between England, America, and other nations betoken neither the elevated universalism of the Age of Reason, nor the engaged patriotism of the Age of Revolutions, but something in between: a conceptualization of national identity that is always on the verge of overturning itself, comparatively demystifying its own ideals in relation to alternative kinds of cultural identification or local feeling.

It is significant that Goldsmith was much admired by Washington Irving, who published a biography of the British writer in 1849, declaring him his favorite author.[17] In a discussion of "The Traveller," Irving aligns Goldsmith's double-edged tone with a chameleonic capacity to evoke a sense of the cosmopolitan and the folkish both at once: "A general benevolence glows throughout this poem. It breathes the liberal spirit of a true citizen of the world. And yet how beautifully does it inculcate and illustrate that local attachment, that preference to native land, which, in spite of every disadvantage of soil or climate, pleads so eloquently to every bosom."[18] Goldsmith, in Irving's eyes, combines being a "true citizen of the world" with a sense of "local attachment," and in this light we can see more clearly how the ambiguities inherent within Irving's own aesthetic representations involve an epistemological duality whereby transnational dislocation becomes related philosophically to the dualistic medium of romantic irony. Rather than just lacking "nerve and dagger," Irving, like Goldsmith, projects the idea of transgression—a wandering outside and beyond any given boundary—as something like an ideology. For Irving, significance lies always in the capacity to turn any given conception, including national identity, the other way around.

This spirit of romantic irony works its way through *The Sketch Book*, where Irving follows Schlegel's assumption that the terrestrial world exists in an inherently duplicitous condition which can be described appropriately only through the self-canceling tropes of paradox and contradiction. This is why every kind of legalistic document and practice tends to be given short shrift in Irving's writing: encumbered by a pedantic and dogmatic manner designed to eradicate all traces of irony, such legal forms mistake their own rhetorical prowess for an objective account of the world. Moreover, the interplay between nativity and loss in *The Sketch Book* suggests how Irving's work can be described as "sentimental" in more than a merely casual or derogatory use of that term, since its dialectic of presence and absence fits more precisely with the philosophical definition of sentimentalism propounded by Johann Christoph Friedrich von Schiller in his 1795 essay, "On the Naive and Sentimental in Literature." Here the German scholar describes the sentimental as a kind of double helix, a fusion of the primary "naive" with a belated, secondary style of reflection. Schiller defines the "true genius"—Homer, for instance, or Shakespeare—as enjoying a "naive" unity and empathy with nature; meanwhile, the cerebral sentimentalist, aware of an ontological exile from this happy state, can only yearn consciously to retrieve that lost innocence. Accordingly, Horace, the doyen of classical melancholy, is nominated here as the founder of sentimental poetry.[19]

My point is not, of course, to argue the validity of Schiller's theories. It is, rather, to suggest the way such theories could arise naturally from within the philosophical framework of romantic irony and the relevance they might bear for Irving's parallel narratives. Schiller's acknowledgment of how literary texts alternate between these two concepts—the naive or particular as opposed to the generalized or sentimental—offers a theoretical parallel to the paradoxical structure of Irving's work, where the desire to appropriate any given object is always circumscribed by a recognition of the narrator's necessary alienation and distance from it. In this sense, the author's conception of paradoxology and perverseness involves an interplay between the comic forms of burlesque and these more intellectual, self-reflexive modes of romantic irony. It can be identified as well with a specific historical context, since Irving's transgressive rhetoric also emerges as an aesthetic permutation and repercussion of the American Revolution, in whose aftermath conceptions of national and personal identity were folding in upon themselves in a particularly disorienting manner. It might, in fact, be possible to see the American Revolution within the context of Irving's writing as a kind of "fortunate fall," a traumatic event that allows him aesthetically to negotiate that profound sense of loss which provides the poetic inspiration for his texts.[20]

*   *   *

A History of New York (1809) comprises Irving's most sustained example of a burlesque, deflationary style.[21] The narrative here moves away from teleologies associated with historical progress and nationalist politics so as to delineate ways in which the inconsistencies of human nature tend to frustrate the grander designs of abstract philosophy:

It is a mortifying circumstance, which generally perplexes many a pains taking philosopher, that nature often refuses to second his most profound and elaborate efforts; so that often after having invented one of the most ingenious and natural theories imaginable, she will have the perverseness to act directly in the teeth of his system, and flatly contradict his most favourite positions. (389)

This mode of bathos does not, however, represent a simple siding with the forces of empiricism. *A History of New York* does not univocally privilege "nature" over "system"; instead, it takes delight in foregrounding those processes by which system slides back into something more grossly corporeal or antisystematic. Unlike American romantic writers of a later generation, Irving does not idealize "nature" and use this as a metanarrative instrument with which to castigate lawyers and politicians. As a connoisseur of "perverseness," his concern is rather with sites of self-contradiction, those topsy-turvy scenarios within which human endeavors reveal themselves as fundamentally self-deceiving enterprises.

From this perspective, *A History of New York* involves not so much a Federalist diatribe against Republican administrations but, rather, a subtle elaboration of the conservative imagination, whose burlesque sensibility operates to circumscribe utopian styles of radical will. Appropriately enough, Edmund Burke is cited with approbation in Book IV of the *History* (536). Robert A. Ferguson has called *A History of New York* "the first American book to question directly the civic vision of the Founding Fathers," and this may well be true; but such skepticism works itself out on something more than a straightforwardly satirical or topical level.[22] As Roth observes, burlesque is a universalizing phenomenon, and Irving offers to account for all of human behavior in terms of these patterns of inversion. Hence, his jibes at the "metaphysical jargon" of "William the Testy" (514)—a figure usually identified with Thomas Jefferson—stem from a belief that William's attempts rationally to codify the contradictory structures of human society involve a profound misconception of worldly motivations and possibilities. Like Sterne in *Tristram Shandy*, Irving plays with images of perspective and perception, suggesting how the idealist formulas of the New World have failed sufficiently to acknowledge the obdurate, irreducible energies of human matter:

your amazing acute politicians, are forever looking through telescopes, which only enable them to see such objects as are far off, and unattainable; but which incapacitates them to see such things as are in their reach, and obvious to all simple folk, who are content to look with the naked eyes, heaven has given them. (522)

Diedrich Knickerbocker, the old Dutch historian who acts as Irving's fictional narrator here, emerges in this and other passages as a kind of *homme moyen sensuel*, a genial character who is, as Irving himself put it, an "articulate father of the burly, bluff burlesque . . . of the American tall tale."[23] Knickerbocker's ethnic origins imply another of the conflicts in this *History*, the clash between the cultural tranquility associated with this Dutch-American community in New York and the more manic, potentially destructive power of the Yankees. The sympathies of Knickerbocker (and Irving) with the more passive virtues of the Dutch are clear enough; yet I believe it would be a mistake to suggest, along with Roth, that the Rabelaisian creed practiced by these Dutch-Americans—eating, drinking, gratifying bodily functions—is simply held up by Irving's *History* as a paradigm of worldly goodness. Edward Watts similarly describes this work as a spoof on "the early republic's inflation of history to gospel-like public indoctrination," which is here "enacted as a burlesque of self-absorbed and inflated rhetoric," but this again is to interpret Irving as a veritable champion of the burlesque, intent upon aggressively demystifying any conception of elevated or enlightened idealism.[24] Irving's text, though, is somewhat more sinister, somewhat less obvious, than that. Rather than simply invalidating the idea of transcendence, Irving plays more tricksily with contradictions between transcendence and de-sublimation, civility and burlesque, thus delineating ironic discrepancies between aspirations of the spirit and limitations of the body. Irving does not just identify Dutch-American culture as a form of mythical utopia, any more than he is concerned simply to upbraid the folly of Republican politicians. More tantalizingly, Irving crosses Knickerbocker's tone of burlesque with the self-subverting rhetoric of romantic irony to create a discourse that frames the world within a conceptual structure of paradox or perverseness. Irving's language is predicated upon tropes of alterity, whose destabilizing principle involves a continuous process of transition between different points.

A *History of New York* is self-conscious about the way its chronological narrative is embroiled within this structure of misrecognition. In a discussion of how Manhattan was founded, we are told that the "original name of this beautiful island is in some dispute, and has already undergone a vitiation, which is a proof of the melancholy instability of sublunary things, and of the industrious perversions of modern orthographers" (445). In Schiller's terms, this represents the sentimental attempting to be naive, or rather the reflexive narrative indulging in a form of faux-naïveté, postulating an idea of innocence only for the paradoxical pleasure of lamenting its loss. A similar gesture toward the reconstitution of some original plenitude manifests itself when the narrator confides that he makes it a rule "not to examine the annals of the times whereof I treat, further than exactly a page in advance of my own work; hence I am equally interested in the progress of my history, with him who reads it, and equally unconscious, what occurrence is next to happen" (643).

This introduces, of course, a textual mise-en-abîme: we read Knickerbocker, who is reading the annals, which were themselves an historical interpretation. Irving plays knowingly with these Chinese boxes, and they provide a formal correlative to the romantic ironist's understanding of history as a site of ontological self-contradiction. Discussing the arts of war and diplomacy, for example, Knickerbocker observes how negotiations toward treaties have the effect of gaining time by wasting it; there is, he says, no more effective way of "maintaining peace" than by the "ingenious mode" of "perpetual negociations." Moreover, such diplomatic efforts serve to restore all kinds of polite "coquetries and fondlings" between opposing camps, so that "it may paradoxically be said, that there is never so good an understanding between two nations, as when there is a little misunderstanding" (576). This represents the art of paradoxology in its purest form. The conclusion of formal treaties, proclaims Knickerbocker with an impish flourish, is actually more likely to bring about war than peace:

Treaties at best are but complied with so long as interest requires their fulfillment; consequently they are virtually binding on the weaker party only, or in other words, they are not really binding at all. No nation will wantonly go to war with another if it has nothing to gain thereby, and therefore needs no treaty to restrain it from violence; and if it has any thing to gain, I much question, from what I have witnessed of the righteous conduct of nations, whether any treaty could be made so strong, that it could not thrust the sword through—nay I would hold ten to one, the treaty itself, would be the very source to which resort would be had, to find a pretext for hostilities. (578)

The humor here depends upon the way high abstract conceptions are burlesqued by lower, more material concerns. In that somewhat surreal image of a treaty being ripped apart by the sword, Irving juxtaposes two distinct levels of expression, one theoretical and rationalistic, the other grossly corporeal and self-interested, and he takes artistic delight in the incongruity of the outcome. With "what delightful paradoxes," exclaims Knickerbocker sardonically, "does the modern arcana of political economy abound!" (577). Through the comic persona of his fictional Dutch historian, Irving presents here a perverse history of the world, whose dominant principle is an extended oxymoron, a fundamental principle of reversal.

* * *

This burlesque impetus depends, of course, on the preservation of parallel narratives. As with Jane Austen, Irving's iconoclastic humor always needs a conventional surface against which to play itself off. Also like Austen is the way in which Irving's structure of perverseness comes to involve psychological dissonance. On one level, this kind of mental disturbance simply involves the sense within Irving's American contemporaries of a "division within their identities," as Pease put it, resulting from split loyalties: to Britain and America, to established local customs and a new national citizenship.[25] Such fissures were refracted also in the disjunction between a more mechanistic environment associated with the new print culture and what Christopher Looby has called "the more passionately attached, quasi-somatically experienced nation for which many Americans longed."[26] In this way, Irving's chatty, colloquial style, in The Sketch Book and elsewhere, might be understood as an attempt to subvert the alienating characteristics of modern literary forms so as to move closer to that folksy ambience of oral culture with which provincial America was more comfortable in the eighteenth century. There is, of course, an uncommon irony in America's first professional author achieving success by undermining his own typographical medium in order to reconstitute a simulacrum of more familiar oral genres.[27]

More provocatively, though, Irving takes such ontological divisions into the realms of psychopathology by exploring ways in which his representation of history as paradox correlates with transgressive reformulations of the human body. In particular, he describes a disconcertingly close relationship between the deviant nature of the human body and the more polite forces of social convention. Just as Irving portrays abstract altruism as descending grossly into material self-interest, so he depicts social enlightenment as declining into political factions and parties concerned more for private gain than for the public weal. Such factions are described metaphorically in scatological terms: in New Amsterdam, the two competing parties are known by the names "Square head" and "Platter breech," the latter permitting the narrator to engage in all kinds of playful puns as he describes how adherents to this school are "destitute of genuine courage, or *good bottom*, as it has since been technically termed" (548). This negative principle of political faction is linked by Knickerbocker with certain "ingenious systems" (549) supposedly extrapolated from scientific methods in other fields. Such idiosyncratic formulas once again entwine the promotion of civic virtue with the practice of more grotesque and indecorous customs, as for instance in education, where Knickerbocker extols:

the breechology of professor Higgenbottom, which teaches the surprizing and intimate connection between the seat of honour, and the seat of intellect—a doctrine supported by experiments of pedagogues in all ages, who have found that applications *a parte poste*, are marvellously efficacious in quickening the perception of their scholars, and that the most expeditious mode of instilling knowledge into their heads, is to hammer it into their bottoms! (549)

Though Knickerbocker treats such "breechology" sportively, the burlesque shape of his *History* precisely demonstrates this paradoxical conjunction of mind and body that is epitomized in Higgenbottom's view of a "surprizing and intimate connection between the seat of honour, and the seat of intellect."

Early in his narrative, Knickerbocker outlines the stories of Dutch immigrants "Tough Breeches" and "Thin Breeches," once again punningly relating their characterization to affairs of the body rather than the spirit (443). In the case of another Dutch adventurer, Jacobus Van Zandt, the narrator even more explicitly informs us that his last name, "freely translated, signified from the dirt, meaning, beyond a doubt, that like Triptolemus, Themis—the Cyclops and the Titans, he sprung from dame Terra or the earth!" (442). It is noticeable here how the presence of all these elevated classical allusions serves to recapitulate, on a microcosmic level, the burlesque energies of Irving's style: formally, as well as thematically, high-flown "dame Terra" comes plummeting down to "earth." With respect to the pun on Van Zandt, Knickerbocker's general point is how even America's greatest or richest men "did originally spring from a dung-hill" (442), a notion which on one level might be seen as an agreeably democratic and good-hearted sentiment. In Irving's world, though, this "dung-hill" can never quite be transcended; it always remains a two-way, not a one-way, movement. Great men tend to slide back into the dung-hill, rather than managing to leave it behind entirely. Hence the scatological imagery is commensurate with Irving's ludic strategy of paradox, where the world comes to fold in upon itself and face the other way. In the aftermath of a fractious political independence, where he finds himself confronted by an incoherent and doubled-up version of his familiar world, Irving aesthetically refracts the American Revolution into a topsy-turvy narrative of revisionist history, where what appears normal turns out to be deviant and vice versa.

In this sense, the corporeal inertia of Irving's material domain always tends to frustrate his putative evocation of a new American pastoral spirit. *The Sketch Book* encompasses an affective attachment to conservative traditions which it acknowledges can no longer stand up to the light of reason. Pierre Klossowski said in relation to the representation of the French Revolution in Sade's texts that the "revolutionary community" is always "secretly but inwardly bound up with the moral dissolution of monarchical society, since it is through this dissolution that the members have acquired the force and energy necessary for bloody decisions"; and a similar tone of ambivalence comes through in "Rip Van Winkle," where the new sign of George Washington is inexorably linked in the protagonist's mind with the old sign of King George III.[28] Irving's hero can never quite abandon his affinities with the old ruler and, burdened with the nostalgia endemic to any revolutionary situation, he finds himself torn emotionally between past and present. Caught in the hinge between pre-Revolutionary and post-Revolutionary America, Rip Van Winkle experiences a sense of "bewilderment" as his understanding of selfhood becomes fractured and doubled: "He doubted his own identity, and whether he was himself or another man" (781).

As we saw in relation to the Connecticut Wits, Janine Chasseguet-Smirgel links such forms of rebellion against the father's universe with an "anal-sadistic" consciousness that seeks to turn the world around the other way. This kind of consciousness, however, is always haunted by an implicit sense of inadequacy and a covert respect for the father's law: "at a certain level the anal-sadistic universe of confusion and homogenization constitutes an imitation or parody of the genital universe of the father. . . . if the idea did not exist somewhere in the pervert's mind that the father's universe is the standard by which all values are measured, then he would not need to disguise the anal universe."[29] This kind of ontological ambivalence, a perverse oscillation between alternative postures, permeates the world of *The Sketch Book* at several different levels. From a broad perspective, there is an evident desire here to portray the landscapes of England and America as in some sense continuous, thereby overcoming the political ruptures of the previous decades by projecting a deeper consciousness of rural tranquility and common culture that links the generations together. This is why Irving focuses upon so many evocative historical scenes—the Boar's Head Tavern at Eastcheap, Stratford on Avon, "quaint" English villages (800)—which he claims implicitly as American heirlooms also. But in the early nineteenth century, after the Revolutionary War, such representations of traditional English scenery can no longer appear as an innocent gesture, since from an American point of view this stratified world is fraught with political significance. Consequently, by invoking the past, Irving's narrator is attempting to evade the disruptive and threatening nature of the present. Moreover, Rip Van Winkle's twenty-year sleep can be seen from this perspective as synecdochic of *The Sketch Book* itself, which attempts to arrest time by expelling historical processes from its frozen tableaux of the picturesque.

This quality of the picturesque or statuesque can be seen as an aesthetic corollary to Chasseguet-Smirgel's description of how the passing of time, "as a dimension of life, is rejected by the pervert."[30] When Rip Van Winkle wakes up and sees his grown-up son, a "precise counterpart" (781) of how the confused old fellow imagines himself to be, we are presented with a perfect image of the collapsing of supposedly natural hierarchies, the erasure of differences between generations. And yet, the author implies, such differences cannot be obliterated entirely: Rip Van Winkle himself enjoys an illusory, but not an actual, respite from history. Indeed, one interesting aspect of *The Sketch Book* is how its invocations of a mythic timelessness are always held in check by the narrator's self-mocking style of romantic irony, which implies how the traumas of time and contingency are always lurking dangerously around the margins of the picturesque. Chasseguet-Smirgel observes how "the need to idealize the environment, the scenery, seems to be quite fundamental for the pervert: everything that surrounds the Ego is like a mirror in which it is reflected"; and it is obvious enough how this kind of narcissistic strain manifests itself in Irving's self-absorbed narrator, whose picaresque travels appear to requisition foreign landscapes as extensions of his own lugubrious imagination, while attempting to repress any disturbing note of discord or difference.[31] But again there is a double discourse at work here, for while characters such as Geoffrey Crayon and Rip Van Winkle are drawn compulsively toward the alluring, Lethean rivers of narcissistic timelessness, Irving's multivalent texts box in these reveries through various forms of structural irony that displace their dream worlds and so restore sleep to wakefulness. This is why the whimsical tone of self-mockery is continually breaking into *The Sketch Book*'s sentimental reveries. In Stratford on Avon, for example, Crayon contemplates a chair on which Shakespeare "may many a time have sat when a boy, watching the slowly revolving spit with all the longing of an urchin" (984)—but the point is that he may have sat there, or he may not. The verb implies a note of ambivalence that reflectively draws the narrative back, in Schiller's terms, from the naive to the sentimental, from the innocent to the knowing.

One of the most curious features about Irving's parallel narratives, then, is how their polite, conventional surface goes together with a cultural turbulence and psychological complexity that is difficult to conceptualize in any very specific way. Irving shares with Jane Austen this quality of elusiveness: to read his fictions as conservative and genteel, like Emerson and his followers, is to find them relatively uninteresting because their more iconoclastic and disruptive energies are simply overlooked; but to psychoanalyze Irving's heroes, to interpret Ichabod Crane as an "American Narcissus" or whatever, is to risk attempting to impose cumbersome categories which the elegant wit of Irving's jesting style appears slyly to evade.[32] The double-edged sensibility of Irving, like that of Austen, succeeds in floating more surreptitiously between the orthodox and the deviant, playing off one against the other and never getting caught on either side of the fence.

"The Legend of Sleepy Hollow" perfectly epitomizes these tensions. On one hand, it seems a pleasant enough tale about the schoolmaster, Ichabod Crane, being defeated for the hand of "blooming" Katrina Van Tassel by the "burly, roaring, roystering blade," Brom Van Brunt, otherwise known as Brom Bones (1067–69). On the other hand, the story reverberates with a more uncomfortable psychological subtext, as Crane's pedagogical fondness for the "appalling sound of the birch" (1061) goes hand in hand with his fanciful idealization of the inaccessible Katrina. Impotent when confronted with the redoubtable Brom Bones, Crane finds himself much more at home "enthroned on the lofty stool" (1072) of the schoolroom, and the story generally represents romance and sexuality as attached inextricably to questions of power and domination. Gilles Deleuze, in his essay on Leopold von Sacher-Masoch, describes how Sacher-Masoch's romances present masochistic fantasies as if they were a naturalized aspect of folklore or national custom, and "The Legend of Sleepy Hollow," heavily influenced as it is by the spirit of German romanticism, is engaging with something similar.[33] Irving's story, in fact, blends the sunny charms of American folklore with a more macabre underworld characteristic of German Gothic. In the opening section, the narrator talks of how a "drowsy, dreamy influence seems to hang over" the country of Sleepy Hollow, along the eastern shore of the Hudson, and of how, according to legend, "the place was bewitched by a high German doctor during the early days of the settlement" (1059). Ann Douglas's general observation that the nineteenth-century American picturesque emerged and developed as a debased version of the Germanic sublime is apposite here, since, as Deleuze notes, the work of Sacher-Masoch also incorporates, albeit in eccentric fashion, the ritualistic energies associated with German romanticism, especially in its emphasis on an idealized and abstracted female force encompassing mythic forms of rejuvenation.[34] Irving's narrative embodies similar aspirations, concerned as it is to represent this Dutch-American community in rural New York as a pastoral antidote to the more cerebral agitations of the Yankees.[35] Consequently, many of the qualities attributed by Deleuze to Sacher-Masoch's writings can be found on a more folksy level in Irving's work: both *Venus in Furs* and "The Legend of Sleepy Hollow" feature scenes with "a frozen quality, like statues or portraits," betraying an "intense preoccupation with arrested movement"; both emphasize "waiting and suspense"; both depict a dream world wherein the inaccessible feminine ideal remains suspended in a condition of fantasy.[36]

But it is a mistake, I believe, to see Ichabod Crane as "definitely the enemy" here.[37] Irving's text is not particularly concerned to take sides between Crane and Brom Bones. Rather, by the distancing framework of an epigraph and postscript attributed to "the late Diedrich Knickerbocker" (1058) as well as through those structural ironies introduced by a retrospective narrative style, Irving delineates a conflict between body and mind, the naive and the sentimental, where each side of the equation necessarily implies the other. This is why Crane reimagines Bones as the headless horseman at the end of this tale; Bones, in fact, has no substance except as he appears in the fictional Crane's cranium, just as the self-canceling postscript reveals this legend itself as "hollow": "'I don't believe one half of it myself'" are the storyteller's last words (1088). Having postulated a primitive world of pastoral ritual, Irving proceeds formally to disrupt it. "The Legend of Sleepy Hollow" consequently inscribes a double movement, encompassing a regressive nostalgia for corporeal plenitude, but also indicating an inevitable sense of displacement from that imaginary idyll. As in Sacher-Masoch, the suturing forces of myth and archetype are balanced off against the defiant, even insolent, sense of humor centered around the representation of a masochistically inclined hero who can relate to these atavistic impulses only by proxy.

Hence to see in Ichabod Crane what Albert J. von Frank calls "a portrait of perverse and misdirected sexuality" is, I believe, not especially helpful here. By setting Crane's "perverse and aggressive lust" against a consideration of what might be "socially useful" to "the whole community," von Frank moves toward a clear-cut, moralistic emphasis which Irving's double-edged narrative seems to avoid.[38] The crucial point to emphasize is how Irving's rhetoric of deviance does not work itself out merely at the level of psychological characterization. When Ichabod mounts his horse, Gunpowder, before riding off to meet Katrina, we are told that this animal had "more of the lurking devil in him than in any young filly in the country" and that "Ichabod was a suitable figure for such a steed" (1073). Later, Gunpowder is described as a "perverse old animal" (1082), a fitting counterpart to the character astride him. A similar equation between the diabolical and the perverse is made in *A History of New York*, when Knickerbocker describes the trials of witches in seventeenth-century New England: "Such incredible obstinacy was in itself deserving of immediate punishment," he suggests sardonically, "and was sufficient proof, if proof were necessary, that they were in league with the devil, who is perverseness itself" (595). As in "The Legend of Sleepy Hollow," "perverseness" becomes associated in this narrative with what is sinister, socially heterodox, a threat to the enclosed community; some of the witches, continues Knickerbocker in a vein of grim humor, "even carried their perverseness so far, as to expire under the torture, protesting their innocence to the last" (596). Again, the perverse functions syntactically and culturally as an interactive hinge, a trope oscillating between conformity and subversion: Knickerbocker feigns to share Cotton Mather's values, while simultaneously indicating an ironic distance from them. It is such sliding between different levels of discourse that constitutes, in Irving, an elaborate rhetoric of paradox, and this is why his characterizations cannot be explained simply in terms of psychopathology.

In this light, Ichabod Crane appears in "Sleepy Hollow" not so much as an unwelcome deviant, but rather as a necessary agent of the burlesque, a foreign body whose business is to turn established customs on their head. Therefore, it is entirely appropriate that Crane should mischievously terrify the old Dutch wives in this community by informing them of "the alarming fact that the world did absolutely turn around, and that they were half the time topsy-turvy" (1065). On a more structural level, Knickerbocker's final retraction in the tale's postscript, where he admits the storyteller didn't "believe one half of it" himself, represents another aspect of this process of bouleversement (1088). Such narrative representations of burlesque in "The Legend of Sleepy Hollow" and "Rip Van Winkle" work to illuminate the more implicit, conceptual modes of paradoxology that permeate *The Sketch Book* generally.

For Irving, then, the burdens of exile function figuratively and metaphorically as well as literally. The old landscapes are refracted through a post-Revolutionary perspective that foregrounds the conditions of observation, distance, and exile. *The Sketch Book* disavows notions of both origin and originality; instead, the text situates itself on the boundary between different worlds, between pre-Revolutionary and post-Revolutionary America, between America and Europe, thereby placing itself in a position to represent the various prismatic processes whereby old patterns become refracted into new shapes. In "The Art of Bookmaking," Geoffrey Crayon discusses how the works of "ancient and obsolete writers . . . undergo a kind of metempsychosis and spring up under new forms" (810–11); and, as so often in *The Sketch Book*, this image operates also on a self-reflexive level, since such modes of transposition can be seen as characteristic of Irving's own writing. Similarly, in his piece addressing "Stratford on Avon," Crayon describes how, "Under the wizard influence of Shakespeare," he had mentally "surveyed the landscape through the prism of poetry, which tinged every object with the hues of the rainbow" (1000). *The Sketch Book* is not, then, just about representing the world in a pleasing series of picturesque sketches; it also problematizes the viability of any "natural" world that might exist beyond the purview of the aesthetic imagination, the artist's sketch book. Nothing can be defined except in terms of what it is not. In Irving's eyes, Shakespeare is great because he transgresses against the boundaries of stale academic conventions, rather than, as Schiller argued, because he encompasses human situations in the most complete or "naive" way. Through this idiom of paradox and transgression, Irving's texts work to "naturalize" ideas of the perverse: in "Traits of Indian Character," for example, Geoffrey Crayon deplores those times when a warrior "perversely turns his hostility against his fellow-man," but he then goes on in the next sentence to describe this as "The natural principle of war" (1008), as if laments over such occurrences were only conventional expressions of regret for what was, after all, naturally to be expected. This is perverse history at its most structurally integrated and institutionalized.

A similar naturalization of paradoxology as an intellectual condition manifests itself within the rambling narrative of *Bracebridge Hall*, where Irving's persona encounters "A Village Politician" who, enthused with the radical ideas of William Cobbett, is seeking to make philosophical "converts, or new lights." Much to the chagrin of Squire Bracebridge, who fears this "lean and meagre" troublemaker will turn the parish "into an unhappy, thinking community," the village radical seeks to bring others around to his point of view: "He has convinced and converted the landlord at least half a dozen times; who, however, is liable to be convinced and converted the other way by the next person with whom he talks."[39] The dialectic here is between conversion and perversion: the village politician aspires to reconceptualize the English environment within an idealistic teleology, metamorphosing it into a projection of his own radical state of mind; yet the skeptical tone of Irving's narrative highlights how any such conversion can only be a flimsy phenomenon, since the corporeal nature of English customs and habits will continually interrupt such elevated speculations. Thus any move toward conversion always folds back upon itself, lapses into the more erratic demeanor of perversion, just as the linear teleology of abstract philosophy slides back into the more circuitous peregrinations of travel narratives.

In this way, the idiom of journeying which always underlies the style of Irving's writing betokens in itself an aesthetic of deviation. Eschewing rational sequence and typological significance, Irving allows his tales to focus instead upon random and contingent events, to cast their gaze upon whatever takes their fancy. There is an interesting contrast to be made here with the landscape writings of Timothy Dwight a generation earlier. Dwight, as we saw, was always straining to "convert" New England scenes into emblems of hermeneutic or allegorical meaning, since in his eyes the contingent natural world signified merely a fallen state, a residue of materialism which could not be refined into the higher transcendence of spirit. For Irving, on the other hand, it is the failure of such attempts at radical conversion that generate the diffuse charms of his picaresque narratives, where all quests for millennial resolution have fallen by the wayside. The traveler in *Bracebridge Hall* describes himself oxymoronically as a "busy idler," and it is this rhetoric of self-contradiction that informs all of Irving's narratives.[40]

Hence, we can see that the transvaluation of historical narratives in *A History of New York*, far from being merely a youthful extravagance or folly, actually comes to set the tone for Irving's later work. Irving, like Austen in her "History of England," invents in this early phase an idiom of punitive burlesque, in which claims to objective laws of cause and effect are ridiculed. Later on, Irving and Austen both develop a mature style where external circumstances are no longer simply lampooned, but shown rather to exist only in a contingent relation with the prismatic perspectives that derive from shifting cultural situations. Authority, and the power of judgment that goes with authority, thus become subjectivist and self-gratifying phenomena, not objective imperatives. Just as Austen's juvenilia deconstruct the English feudal hierarchy's lust for dominance, so in *A History of New York* Irving sports mercilessly with the autocratic tendencies of General Von Poffenburgh, self-styled "commander in chief of the armies of the New Netherlands" (598), who orders three prisoners to be "soundly flogged, for the amusement of his visitor, and to convince him, that he was a great disciplinarian" (613). The self-mocking style of Geoffrey Crayon in *The Sketch Book* deliberately rejects this despotic style, but his laxity arises less from any personal feebleness than from an epistemological recognition of the limits of authority. Crayon as a narrator pointedly declines to present himself as the source of authoritative judgment.

Given this idiom of dubiety, it is easy enough to see why Irving has subsequently been marginalized by the annals of American romanticism. Rather than embodying that original force characteristic of "strong poets," in Harold Bloom's phrase, Irving's narrators choose to negotiate with the culture of the past.[41] Instead of engaging empathetically with a relatively unmediated American land-scape, as Emerson or Whitman would have preferred, Irving is content to play with inherited forms, experimenting with different angles of incidence and reflection so as to reconsider the possibilities of the American scene from many different vantage points. Whitman, unimpressed with such subtleties, called Irving's *History of New York* a "shallow burlesque, full of clown's wit."[42] Yet Irving in all of his works scrutinizes romantic assumptions about nature, authenticity, and originality, challenging the proclamations of cultural nationalism that developed alongside such social philosophies. In this way, the inherently duplicitous texts of Austen and Irving offer the reader a complex circuit of civility and deviance, where the masquerade of civilization is silently mocked by the ghosts of alterity.

Such modes of alterity can be related contextually to the aftermath of the American Revolution, the second British Civil War. In the early nineteenth century, American and British culture comprised disturbing mirror images for each other in the light of their newfound separatism. To cross Austen with Irving is to find in both authors a sense of destabilizing and disturbing contingency, where political, ethical, and aesthetic systems come to appear tantalizingly provisional and therefore susceptible of reversal. Both Austen and Irving negotiate with the new naturalizing tone of nationalist discourse, while at the same time implicitly recognizing such discourses as performative codes of enunciation rather than referential truths. Consequently, the works of Austen and Irving participate obliquely in what Homi K. Bhabha calls a postcolonial world of "sly civility," where the mask of authority engenders a reflective "mimicry" from subjects and texts that conform outwardly to cultural imperatives they can never quite believe in.[43] The larger implication of this argument is that representations of literary nationalism in both Britain and the United States during the early nineteenth century emerged not so much as an immediate response to the local environment, but rather through forms of intertextual travesty and mutual misrecognition. Just as Austen's version of rural England is shadowed by the threat of transatlantic insurrection, so Irving's embryonic version of American literature manifests itself as a mode of ontological double vision that relates to its British counterpart through the tropes of paradox and burlesque.

Chapter Seven
Perverse Reflections
Hawthorne and Trollope

The works of Nathaniel Hawthorne and Anthony Trollope have traditionally been seen as embodiments of their native literary traditions. Much of the
best criticism on Hawthorne has emphasized ways in which his texts seek to
engage with the most powerful ideas within American history and culture, from
transcendentalist idealism (Matthiessen) through to liberalism (Bercovitch) or
radical utopianism and the "National Symbolic" (Berlant).[1] None of these critics
suggests that Hawthorne incorporates such notions in an unproblematic way, of
course, but they all imply that his fictions can hardly be understood except
within the framework of particular contexts endemic to American culture. Trollope, similarly, has been normalized and institutionalized by generations of British readers, a process of domestication which has emerged not only from the
more obvious conservative sources but also from oppositional critics like Raymond Williams, who talked of Trollope's "even, easy narrative tone, with a mini-
mum both of analysis and of individual disturbance," which unreflectively takes
the "values [of England] for granted."[2]

My purpose in this chapter, however, is to move away from this specifically
nationalist focus by considering the artistic relationship between Hawthorne and
Trollope in terms of the dynamics of transatlantic exchange. Two generations after
the American Revolution, both Hawthorne and Trollope fondly imagine their
native country in terms of an extended family, where generations are bonded
together within an organic framework of cultural security. At the same time, they
acknowledge how various aspects of cultural incoherence or transnational disturbance continually threaten to throw ironic shadows over these familial designs.
In this sense, the fictions of Hawthorne and Trollope incorporate perverse reflections of British and American culture, according to the theoretical model of
perversion outlined by Julia Kristeva, which "sets up the opposites in human

signification facing each other, with neither synthesis, nor internalization, nor suppression." For Kristeva, "perversion of values," the infraction of particular ideological assumptions and orthodoxies, "establishes the subtle norm of a culture conscious of its reversibilities."[3] The works of Hawthorne and Trollope, I shall argue, internalize this idea of the reversibility of national and psychological identity, with their aesthetic designs being formulated so as to map out the construction of national formations in terms of mutual contradiction. This is to demur from the version of Trollope proffered by Williams or by Henry James, who chose to imagine Trollope as the representative of a unified national culture, epitomizing all the "natural" characteristics of the English race; James claimed that Trollope specifically eschews artistic "perversions," settling instead for what is straight, honest, and true.[4] But the fictions of Hawthorne and Trollope are much less straightforward than this, and, in their attempts to describe the expanding and contracting circumference of national history, they are closer in tone than they might at first appear.

The two novelists were well aware of, indeed fascinated by, each other's work. Hawthorne wrote to James T. Fields from Rome in February 1860 about how his "own individual taste" as a consumer of fiction was "for quite another class of works than those which I myself am able to write," and of how Trollope's "solid and substantial" narratives were particularly to his liking.[5] Trollope was delighted to hear of Hawthorne's approbation and returned the compliment some years later by writing a highly perceptive account of Hawthorne's "lop-sided" sensibility for the *North American Review*. The two writers met each other personally at a dinner in Boston in September 1861, and in his *Autobiography* Trollope paid tribute to Hawthorne as "a brother novelist very much greater than myself . . . whose brilliant intellect and warm imagination led him to a kind of work the very opposite of mine."[6] However, these obvious differences of approach which Trollope and Hawthorne both remarked upon should not conceal their aesthetic compatibility in a more structural sense; in fact, it may have been a recognition of this compatibility at some level that led them to take such a marked interest in each other's work. Hawthorne has too often been read in conjunction with Melville, just as Trollope has normally been considered alongside George Eliot or Dickens, but to disrupt these patterns of national identity by juxtaposing Hawthorne with Trollope is to discover a different kind of Hawthorne and a different kind of Trollope.[7]

One of the strengths of Trollope's critical reading of Hawthorne was acutely to perceive how the peculiar power of these American texts derives from their infraction, rather than their reproduction, of nationalist agendas. Trollope's 1879 essay, "The Genius of Nathaniel Hawthorne," is particularly valuable for the way it introduces an alternative perspective on Hawthorne's work, foregrounding an aspect of devious eccentricity rather than sentimental familiarity:

> There never surely was a powerful, active, continually effective mind less round, more lop-sided, than that of Nathaniel Hawthorne. . . . in no American writer is to be found the same predominance of weird imagination as in Hawthorne. There was something of it in M. G. Lewis—our Monk Lewis as he came to be called, from the name of a tale which he wrote; but with him, as with many others, we feel that they have been weird because they have desired to be so. They have struggled to achieve the tone with which their works are pervaded. With Hawthorne we are made to think that he could not have been anything else if he would. . . . In the true enjoyment of Hawthorne's work there is required a peculiar mood of mind. The reader should take a delight in looking round corners, and in seeing how places and things may be approached by other than the direct and obvious route. . . . the reader must consent to put himself altogether under his author's guidance, and to travel by queer passages, the direction of which he will not perceive till, perhaps, he has got quite to the end of them.[8]

The tone of Trollope's critique here emphasizes defamiliarization and estrangement. Rather than (like Matthiessen or Bercovitch or Berlant) seeing Hawthorne's novels as embodying structural conflicts within the American nation, Trollope fixes on his "lop-sided" and "weird" qualities, his "delight in looking round corners" and his proclivity for exploring "queer passages." Trollope's transnational perspective thus disestablishes any ideological conception of the normative or natural as a basis for reading Hawthorne. Instead, he acknowledges how the American author's texts slide amorphously between the mediation of social ideals and a more grotesque humor, how the structural paradoxes informing his work cause sublimity and bathos to be constantly interfering with each other's assumptions. For Trollope, it is this allure of potential reversibility that constitutes the charm of Hawthorne's art.

Trollope, then, seeks to rediscover a comic or burlesque aspect to Hawthorne's writing. The English novelist's predilection for an idiom of bathos cuts against the more obvious American context of Hawthorne's writing, since many of the latter's famous works were written at a time when his own New England acquaintances were keen to consider how material objects and landscapes might be converted into emblems of patriotic purpose. Indeed, Hawthorne's productions are framed by the legacy of the Puritan conversion narrative, which was reworked by transcendentalism into an affirmation of the romantic sublime, whose providence was underpinned by the desire to establish indigenous nature as the source of all value.[9] In 1840, Emerson confided to his journal that he believed "commerce, law, & state employments" were "now all so perverted & corrupt that no man can right himself in them"; accordingly, he declared, there was nothing left "but to begin the world anew."[10] This Emersonian antithesis, defining a primal innocence against various "perverse" forms of social corruption, is a pattern replicated frequently in the work of other American writers around this time. In *The Oregon Trail* (1849), for instance, Francis Parkman's pastoral idealization of the West works to reduce society to its "original elements" by apotheosizing an unspoiled environment "natural perhaps in early years to every unperverted son of Adam." For Parkman, the perverse becomes demonized within this spectacle as strange and unnatural, in contrast to the scenery of the West, which, he records, "needed no foreign aid."[11] Similar forms of sublimity manifest themselves in Margaret Fuller's essay, "Woman in the Nineteenth Century" (1845), where her emphasis on purity, the inner soul, and "reformation" leads her to scorn any self-reliance "perverted by the current of opinion" or any "mind perverted by flattery from a worthiness of esteem."[12] By imagining an unaffected or regenerate state of nature, Parkman and Fuller position themselves antithetically to represent anything outside that charmed circle as inherently sinister and deviant.

This is not to imply the rhetorical idealism of mid nineteenth-century American writing unproblematically transcended the material world; it is to suggest, though, how Puritan metaphors of conversion continued to reverberate within a secular context, cumulatively engendering agendas of personal and collective improvement that ran in parallel with the ideological imperatives of an American national culture. In her study of "Conversion, Modernity, and Belief," Gauri Viswanathan has argued that religious conversion in the nineteenth century operated as "a subversion of secular power," since, by "undoing the concept of fixed, unalterable identities, conversion unsettles the boundaries by which selfhood, citizenship, nationhood, and community are defined." This representation of conversion as resistance would seem to be more resonant within a British context, where the mobility associated with any kind of personal transformation could be seen as potentially hazardous to the "bureaucratic logic" of the Victorian state.[13] Within the nationalist context of nineteenth-century America, however, the mobility of the conversion experience, in both its theological and in its more broadly cultural manifestations, was enthusiastically appropriated as a narrative of legitimation for the new nation, organized as it was around a rubric of individual and social rejuvenation. As so often in the United States, the rhetoric of protest and dissent became ritually institutionalized as a form of patriotic allegiance.[14]

The Blithedale Romance (1852) represents one of the clearest examples of how Hawthorne's language crosses this kind of secularized conversion narrative with what Trollope called an incongruous, "lop-sided" style. While exploring the

possibilities of his utopian community at Blithedale, the book's narrator, Coverdale, is always slyly detaching himself from its accredited transcendentalist doctrines. After an intense series of valedictions with the inhabitants of this "modern
Arcadia," Coverdale feels himself compelled to repeat the ceremony in a less
elevated milieu:

> I can nowise explain what sort of whim, prank, or perversity it was, that, after all these
> leave-takings, induced me to go to the pig-stye and take leave of the swine! There they lay,
> buried as deeply among the straw as they could burrow, four huge black grunters, the very
> symbols of slothful ease and sensual comfort. . . . They were involved, and almost stifled,
> and buried alive, in their own corporeal substance.[15]

The Blithedale Romance does not simply satirize transcendentalism by invoking
the inescapable nature of "corporeal substance"; more subtly, the text oscillates
perpetually between these two poles, contradicting spiritualism with materialism
and vice versa. This is why Coverdale vacillates between Blithedale and his
comfortable home town, feeling the need of "periodically returning into the
settled system of things" (141); his perverse sensibility betokens a radical ambivalence, an unwillingness finally to decide which side of the line he wants to
inhabit. This kind of psychological and narrative predilection for turning things
around the other way is given metaphorical expression in Coverdale's rumina-
tions after he has returned from Blithedale to his hotel:

> It is likewise to be remarked, as a general rule, that there is far more of the picturesque,
> more truth to native and characteristic tendencies, and vastly greater suggestiveness, in
> the back view of a residence, whether in town or country, than in its front. The latter is
> always artificial; it is meant for the world's eye, and is therefore a veil and a concealment.
> Realities keep in the rear, and put forward an advance-guard of show and humbug. The
> posterior aspect of any old farm-house, behind which a railroad has unexpectedly been
> opened, is so different from that looking upon the immemorial highway, that the spectator
> gets new ideas of rural life and individuality, in the puff or two of steam-breath which
> shoots him past the premises. (149)

The narrator's emphasis here on a "back view" or "posterior aspect," with truth
being located "in the rear," reinforces Trollope's point about Hawthorne's "delight
in looking round corners," his propensity for that "touch of burlesque" which
would stand established structures on their head.[16]

 The Blithedale Romance, then, specifically addresses the idealist trope of
conversion and contemplates how it is liable to slide off into a poetics of perversion. In his manic moral energy, Hollingsworth resembles an early Puritan father
as he sets about attempting to transform his environment; but Coverdale ulti-

mately acknowledges how "Nature . . . converts us to a meaner purpose, when her highest one—that of conscious, intellectual life, and sensibility—has been untimely baulked!" (244). The circuit between conversion and perversion in the novel is analogous to the interaction between soul and body, intellect and sex, which this novel also confronts (and confounds). While Coverdale has been scorned by various critics as "neurotic" and "stunted," the more crucial point is that the structural logic of Hawthorne's narrative demands that he be distanced from the supposedly olympian impersonality of transcendentalist integrity.[17] In reading Hawthorne, American critics have sometimes started out with idealist presuppositions before proceeding tautologically to indict his texts for failing to conform to their own moral concerns: Nina Baym, to take just one example, writes of how "Zenobia's perversities represent, like the perversities of the wizard Maules, the distortions of Eros in civilized life." However, this negative notion of "distortions" requires as its counterpoint a mythic conception of normative nature which *The Blithedale Romance* does not sanction.[18] Instead, the tone of the book points toward secrecy, obstruction, deviation, all of the ways in which, contra Emerson, the axis of vision fails to become coincident with the axis of things.

What I am suggesting here is a reading of *The Blithedale Romance* that underscores its radical aestheticization of the New England landscape. Henry James, still one of Hawthorne's best critics, wrote of how his fellow American novelist treated the "Puritan conscience" as his "national heritage," though "his relation to it was only, as one may say, intellectual; it was not moral and theological. He played with it . . . [from] the poetic and aesthetic point of view, the point of view of entertainment and irony."[19] What James said of Puritanism is true also with respect to transcendentalism: Hawthorne in *The Blithedale Romance* plays with the idea, treats it as a source of irony, and does not see its failures necessarily as grounds for either tragedy or ethical outrage. Hence the libidinal motivations that circulate through Blithedale do not simply subvert or invalidate the utopian community; more subtly, they pervert the community, so that the focus of the text always swings between opposite potentialities, between self-denying philanthropy and self-gratifying indulgence, between social reform and transgressive desire. In this sense, the "lop-sided" element that Trollope discovered in Hawthorne's work can be seen as crucial to the latter's artistic enterprise.

As we have seen, the equation of conversion with what Emerson called "wholesome force" of one kind or another can be seen as a belated, revisionist version of that idealism through which American Puritans associated conversion with regenerate spirit.[20] Not surprisingly, then, understandings of perversion in the nineteenth century were also closely intertwined with discourses of religion, especially with what was seen from Protestant perspectives as the heretical formulas of Roman Catholicism. To be a "pervert" was, quite literally, to have fallen back into the bad old habits of Catholicism, the corrupted faith of the Old World. Harriet Beecher Stowe wrote of listening to a sermon in England by the "celebrated pervert Archdeacon Manning," while the theological "perversion" of John Henry Newman was linked implicitly in the minds of his opponents with a transgression of the orthodox boundaries of gender, the cardinal's supposed predilection for "sexual deviance and 'unspeakable' proclivities." In an 1864 review of Newman's *Apologia pro Vita Sua*, for example, the *British Quarterly Review* maintained that the "instances of perversion to the Romish faith which have come within our knowledge have been nearly all such as may be traced to a womanly weakness in the women, and to the want of a manly courage in the men."[21] Perversion consequently came to be associated with corporeal degeneration as well as with intellectual heresy. Unlike conversion, which exultantly subsumed matter into spirit, perversion denied the possibility of dualistic transcendence by describing instead how the mind was always lapsing back inevitably into the toils of the body, finding itself compromised by the snares of the flesh. Jenny Franchot has emphasized how Catholic modes of thought were crucial for American Protestantism to define itself against during the nineteenth century, and from this perspective the tropes of perversion might be seen as uncomfortable negative counterparts to the teleologies of conversion and salvation that echoed throughout this era. Viswanathan has also observed that Newman's conversion to Catholicism caused particular ructions in Britain because, through its receptiveness to a transnational system of belief, it seemed to challenge the Anglican notion of religious affiliation being based primarily upon national identity.[22] In this sense, we can see how the fall back into sexual and religious "perversion" became associated with an intellectual secession from the guiding authority of the nation state.

Hawthorne's most overt engagement with this religious theme manifests itself in *The Marble Faun* (1860), a novel which emphasizes its transnational agenda by setting itself in Rome and organizing itself around elaborate dialogues between the values of American Puritanism and Italian Catholicism. Rather than simply participating in contemporary discourses of anti-Catholicism or popular American fears about Romish conspiracies, Hawthorne's texts exploit images of Catholicism as the sign of miscegenation and perversion, chronicling the collapse of a rigid Puritan dualism into more heterogeneous systems, where spirit is incarnated within corporeal matter and matter transubstantiated into spirit.[23] A sequence of metaphors plays off the "cold and pure" mentality of cerebral Puritanism against the "colored light" which Miriam sees as "an emanation of herself."[24] Similarly, the sculptor Kenyon contrasts the "angelic purity" of his American companions to the "unspeakable corruption" of "the Roman Church," as epitomized by the stained glass window of a Catholic cathedral:

> "They remind me of that portion of Aladdin's palace which he left unfinished, in order that his royal father-in-law might put the finishing touch. Daylight, in its natural state, ought not to be admitted here. It should stream through a brilliant illusion of Saints and Hierarchies, and old Scriptural images, and symbolized Dogmas, purple, blue, golden, and a broad flame of scarlet. Then, it would be just such an illumination as the Catholic faith allows to its believers. But give me—to live and die in—the pure, white light of Heaven!" (366)

The image of light passing through cathedral windows exemplifies the prism through which transcendental idealism is refracted into multivalent material corruptions. This is why Hilda, the staunch New Englander, describes Catholicism as a form of "perverted Christianity" (412). Yet *The Marble Faun* itself does not simply validate Hilda's point of view, since the novel is not concerned with Catholicism in a theological or religious sense. Instead, Hawthorne aestheticizes Catholicism, just as he aestheticizes American Puritanism, deploying the faith of the Old World as a formal sign of cultural contradiction and ontological perversion.

It is this spirit of cultural contradiction which runs through Hawthorne's work, and which he represents in terms of America's interaction with Anglican Britain as well as Catholic Italy. Writing of *Our Old Home*, Hawthorne's 1863 account of his travels in England, Henry James noted the American author's paradoxical propensity to take delight in various aspects of English life, while "insisting, with a perversity that both smiled and frowned, that they rubbed him mainly all the wrong way." With typical astuteness, James captured the double-edged nature of Hawthorne's sympathies, whose most characteristic feature is an "aloofness wherever he is," a sense of being "outside of everything, and an alien everywhere."[25] In *Our Old Home*, Hawthorne forges a link between psychological notions of strangeness and the exile's condition of foreignness, as he writes about how the physical transgression of national boundaries evokes a sense of estrangement from inherent customs and from systems of local morality:

It may be well for persons who are conscious of any radical weakness in their character, any besetting sin, any unlawful propensity, any unhallowed impulse, which (while surrounded with the manifold restraints that protect a man from that treacherous and life-long enemy, his lower self, in the circle of society where he is at home) they may have succeeded in keeping under the lock and key of strictest propriety—it may be well for them, before seeking the perilous freedom of a distant land, released from the watchful eyes of neighborhoods and coteries, lightened of that wearisome burden, an immaculate name. and blissfully obscure after years of local prominence—it may be well for such individuals to know that, when they set foot on a foreign shore, the long-imprisoned Evil, scenting a wild license in the unaccustomed atmosphere, is apt to grow riotous in its iron cage. It rattles the rusty barriers with gigantic turbulence, and if there be an infirm joint anywhere in the frame-work, it breaks madly forth, compressing the mischief of a lifetime into a little space.[26]

In the preface to *Our Old Home*, Hawthorne records his perennial consciousness of "hereditary sympathies" for England. However, this book does not betray a desire simply to subsume the New World within the Old, but seeks rather to disrupt the assumptions of both by cross-referencing each with the other. He frequently describes the English as cloddish and dogmatically commonsensical, and he suggests the inhabitants of both nations would benefit from a collective change of climate:

For my part, I used to wish that we could annex [England], transferring their thirty millions of inhabitants to some convenient wilderness in the great West, and putting half or a quarter as many of ourselves in their places. The change would be beneficial to both parties. We, in our dry atmosphere, are getting too nervous, haggard, dyspeptic, extenuated, unsubstantial, theoretic, and need to be made grosser. John Bull, on the other hand, has grown bulbous, long-bodied, short-legged, heavy-witted, material, and, in a word, too intensely English. In a few more centuries, he will be the earthliest creature that ever the earth saw.[27]

This passage represents the ideology of exchange at its most apparent. As James said, Hawthorne's writing is never more at home than when describing the "alien everywhere," that process of transition or reversal whereby objects become uprooted and pivoted around the other way.

The same idiom of hybridity permeates Hawthorne's unfinished "American Claimant" manuscripts: "The Ancestral Footstep," "Etherege" and "Grimshawe." In fact, the notion of transatlantic exchange mooted in *Our Old Home* is repeated almost word for word in "Etherege," where the nomadic Lord Brathwaite proposes it as a scheme for national renewal. Again, the overt theme of these last manuscripts is the attempt to bring together England and America through the plot of a family romance, whose hereditary histories are represented "as if they were two points of an electric chain, which being joined, an instantaneous effect must follow." The substance of what Hawthorne writes, though, revolves more upon English and American ideas "brought strikingly into contrast and contact," as he describes it in one of his notebooks: mutual interference and reciprocal antagonism carry more weight here than any imaginary state of transatlantic unity.[28] This comparative perspective runs all the way through the *English Note-*

books, where Hawthorne is forever playing off in his mind the Old World against the New. In 1854, for instance, he visits a "squalid and ugly" village near Rhyl and says to himself: "Just think of a New England rural village in comparison."[29] It is this patriotic sense of cultural separatism that shores up the author's idealized vision of national identity, a vision which made him ultimately unwilling to grant that anyone born outside the United States could participate fully in the virtues of American cultural independence.[30] Nevertheless, Hawthorne chose to focus compulsively during the 1850s on scenes of friction wherein the values of his native culture were liable to reversal and exchange. In this sense, what Frederick C. Crews calls the "incest obsession" in these "American Claimant" manuscripts can be seen to work synecdochically, since the larger concern running through Hawthorne's incestuous family romances is how America and Europe hold up mutually distorting mirrors wherein each other's preoccupations are reconceived in an unfamiliar form.[31]

As in all perverse relations, according to Kristeva's formulation, these figures are the same, but different. Similar enough to be recognizable to each other, these two cultures are yet divergent enough also to be threatening to each other; like the best traitors, they betray their duplicity from within, developing a janus-faced perspective which deviates uncomfortably from that community to which they ostensibly owe allegiance. Again, this conception of betrayal and backsliding carries religious connotations, with *Our Old Home* suggesting how England is, at heart, Catholic: "Catholicism, so lately repudiated, must needs have retained an influence over all but the most obdurate characters."[32] The labyrinthine ways of Catholicism also make up an intricate thread of images in the "American Claimant" manuscripts, as if Hawthorne, in attempting to identify typological differences between America and Europe, were drawn back compulsively to the religious disputes of the sixteenth and seventeenth centuries, when Puritanism came to appear heretical to the Roman Church and vice versa. In this sense, Hawthorne's view of the perverse reflections binding together America and Europe might be said to involve a modernized and secularized version of religious heresies: what in the seventeenth century appeared blasphemous becomes in the nineteenth century perverse. While the historical context changes, the underlying structures of mutual attraction and repulsion, familiarity and betrayal, remain largely the same.

*　　*　　*

Sliding dexterously between conversion and perversion, *The Scarlet Letter* (1850) comprises Hawthorne's most extended and overt meditation on the ways in which the institutional imperatives of American idealism find themselves transgressed and traversed by Old World boundaries. *The Scarlet Letter* is a novel whose abstract projections of national identity become problematized by residual attachments to more complex, hybrid forms of identification. Similarly, indeed analogously, its transcendent textual designs of allegorical spirit come to be circumscribed by the corporeal deviance of the flesh.

For J. Hillis Miller, writing out of an American school of deconstruction, "Hawthorne's fundamental problem as a writer" is "the irreconcilability of spiritual meaning and material embodiment," with the result that meaning within Hawthorne's texts remains perpetually veiled, perpetually deferred. The point to be emphasized here is how Miller's idealist analysis itself replicates that strand of cultural Puritanism within Hawthorne's writing whereby ultimate revelation, like the Reformers' *deus absconditus*, lies mysteriously beyond. Indeed, in an interview attached to his critique of Hawthorne, Miller admitted: "There are certainly traces of my own Protestant heritage there in my insistence on the uniqueness, incommensurability, and privacy of the act of reading."[33] Within *The Scarlet Letter*, obviously enough, such incommensurabilities of interpretation are foregrounded through the multiple meanings clustered around Hester Prynne's "letter A," as well as in that retrospective narrative tone which deliberately seeks distance between the hermeneutic propensities of seventeenth-century Puritanism and the more secular perspectives of nineteenth-century America:

Nothing was more common, in those days, than to interpret all meteoric appearances, and other natural phenomena, that occurred with less regularity than the rise and set of sun and moon, as so many revelations from a supernatural source. Thus, a blazing spear, a sword of flame, a bow, or a sheaf of arrows, seen in the midnight sky, prefigured Indian warfare. . . . Not seldom, it had been seen by multitudes. Oftener, however, its credibility rested on the faith of some lonely eyewitness, who beheld the wonder through the colored, magnifying, and distorting medium of his imagination, and shaped it more distinctly in his after-thought.[34]

Within this Puritan landscape of signs and omens, nature seemingly becomes converted into a source of divine revelation. Objects relinquish their material substance and are reimagined in more abstract terms, as components within some form of providential design.

Hawthorne, then, describes how the community of seventeenth-century Boston sought transcendent meaning through the scriptural process of converting matter into spirit, and he also teases his contemporary readers by appearing to offer a similar hermeneutic framework for interpreting this work of fiction itself.[35] Yet Hawthorne's narrative, through its sense of historical distance and detachment, declines ultimately to validate such sublime maneuvers whereby the human soul might extend its "egotism over the whole expanse of nature" (155) for the purpose of converting itself into an epitome of the divine. As in *The Blithedale Romance* and *The Marble Faun*, the resistance to this kind of abstract idealism is given metaphorical expression by a subtext of Catholicism, which signifies the irruption of an irregular corporeality into the hypothetical realm of disembodied spirit.[36] In this sense, the critical dialectic between deconstruction and materialism, the infinite deferral of history as opposed to its substantial embodiment, is acted out within the structural dynamics of *The Scarlet Letter* itself. In *The Marble Faun*, divergent theological positions are exemplified fairly obviously by the way New England Puritans are situated at the heart of Rome; but in *The Scarlet Letter*, similar debates take place less overtly, as Old World protagonists are transplanted into Boston, one of the symbolic centers of the New World religion. Hester is associated early in the novel with an "image of Divine Maternity," the kind of Madonna figure a "Papist" would have appreciated (56); while later in the narrative her scarlet letter is seen by Governor Bellingham as a "worthy type of her of Babylon" (110), a fitting memento of how American Puritans of this era tended to represent the Roman Church as the Mother of Harlots, the Scarlet Lady of Babylon. As we have seen, perversion originally connoted theological rather than sexual transgression, and, from the point of view of the Puritans in this text these two qualities go together, with Hester's sexual misdeeds being perceived as akin and analogous to the blasphemy inherent in her affiliations with Catholicism.

The key figure within this theological subtext is Hester's daughter, Pearl. Pearl is alleged to be a child of the Lord of Misrule, and she is explicitly equated with the old ghosts of Catholicism, "those naughty elfs or fairies, whom we thought to have left behind us, with other relics of Papistry, in merry old England" (110), as the "venerable pastor" (108), John Wilson, puts it. Others hold that Pearl is "a demon offspring; such as, ever since old Catholic times had occasionally been seen on earth" (99), and this is why she is categorized as an "imp of evil, emblem and product of sin" (93). She is also continually associated with the perverse: of "perversity," indeed, she is said to have "a tenfold portion" (112). The function of Pearl's perverseness is to twist things around the other way, so as to play off etiolated idealisms, of whatever kind, against an idiom of material transgression. In Chapter 10, Chillingworth quizzes Dimmesdale about Pearl's character, asking: " 'Hath she any discoverable principle of being?' " To which the clergyman replies: "None,—save the freedom of a broken law' " (134). In this sense, Pearl epitomizes the novel's projections of transference, whereby energies of all kinds are translated across categories, so that, as by a process of mirroring or reduplication, one thing metamorphoses into another. When Pearl looks at her reflection in the brook in Chapter 19, the "visionary little maid" (168) encounters "another child,—another and the same" (208), with the brook's "mirror" (209) being apprehended in Arthur Dimmesdale's mind as "the boundary between two worlds" (208). It is the ontological condition of Pearl's perversity that she should oscillate between one potential state and another, refusing to be confined to either side of the boundary.

In *The Puritan Origins of the American Self*, Sacvan Bercovitch mentions how seventeenth-century Puritans greatly disliked the production of mirrors during the Renaissance era because such worldly reflections threatened to subvert the autonomy of each individual soul as it meditated inwardly upon its Maker.[37] This highlights the way in which Pearl's propensity for duplicitous reflection itself encompasses an aestheticized version of theology, an association heightened in chapter 19, "The Child at the Brook-side," which works as a parallel to the maidenly visions in various medieval dream poems. When Arthur fancies "that this brook is the boundary between two worlds" and that Pearl, reflected in "the mirror of the brook" (208–9), is forever out of reach on the farther shore, we may be put in mind of the markedly similar allegorical landscapes in Dante's *Divine Comedy* and other medieval dream poems.[38] In this genre, the brook or river traditionally represents a frontier to be traversed between earth and heaven, this world and the next; but in Hawthorne's rewriting of this medieval archetype, the "margin of the stream" (210) creates a "duplicity of impression" (214) that also evokes more worldly kinds of passage. As a dream maiden, Pearl fulfils the traditional role within this poetic genre of appearing as an agent of revelation, a harbinger of the life to come. Thus Hawthorne's Pearl, like Dante's Beatrice, acts analogically in the way she mediates between alternate levels of reality: she is "now like a real child, now like a child's spirit" (204). But what Pearl signifies for Hester is not, as in the medieval poems, celestial bliss, but its earthly equivalent. Hawthorne rewrites Dante's narrative in a secular, even parodic, fashion to represent Pearl as a "bright-apparelled vision" (204) connoting sexual or pagan rather than Christian joy.

Pearl's perverseness, then, introduces an analogical consciousness into a world organized epistemologically around the disjunctive categories of allegory. The idiosyncrasy of Pearl lies in the way she incarnates different possibilities within one body; in a negative or secularized version of Catholic transubstantiation, she mediates in a corporeal manner between the worlds of the Puritan town and the pagan forest, between the New World of America and the Old World of Europe. This Puritan community in Massachusetts Bay is dedicated to working out its destiny under an agenda of separatism, where American spirit is split off from European corruption as rigorously as divine transcendence rises above worldly intelligence. But Pearl's virtuosity consists in bringing these alternate scenarios back into dialogue, so that the Old World and the New come to be seen as refractions of each other's consciousness.

From this point of view, *The Scarlet Letter* is a novel not only about the conversion of tradition and custom from one state to another, but also about ways in which such transformations can operate in reverse, or sometimes, perhaps, not at all. Dimmesdale, Chillingworth and Hester are all clearly described as "English emigrants" (232), and at key points in the story Dimmesdale feels acutely the circumscribed nature of his new geographical location, the way he is being "trammelled" by "regulations" which "hemmed him in" (200). We are told of how his "scholar-like renown still lived in Oxford" (120), and, after his reconciliation with Hester, he turns back to some of this Old World lore in a deliberate attempt to provoke the New England worthies he now finds somewhat narrow-minded. He has it in mind to make "certain blasphemous suggestions . . . respecting the communion-supper," and he laughs to himself "to imagine how the sanctified old patriarchal deacon would have been petrified by his minister's impiety" (218). The word "petrified" is particularly interesting: literally, of course, it means turned to stone, but it may also connote the apostle Peter, legendary founder of the Catholic Church, and of the "Petrine liturgy" that derived from him. Hawthorne's narrator may be punningly implying the rigid, stony-hearted forms of Catholic doctrine, and it seems likely that Dimmesdale's blasphemous ideas concerning the Eucharist are supposed to relate directly to theological debates about its status at the time of the Reformation. In this characteristic Old World manner, Dimmesdale comes to show his "sympathy and fellowship with wicked mortals and the world of perverted spirits" (222). Here, again, the idea of perversion is linked with religious heresy as well as sexual transgression. In the eyes of the strict Puritan fathers, Dimmesdale's Old World attachments raise the specter of both kinds of deviance.

This fear of deviance is all the more marked because the two countries are represented as mirror images of each other. Hawthorne emphasizes that the grimmer forms of Puritan orthodoxy were the product of a later generation in Massachusetts Bay and the landscape of this novel is consequently rife with memories of merry old England. Governor Bellingham maps out his estate along the lines of English custom, with his bond servant wearing the blue coat of English hereditary halls; Bellingham's "heirlooms" have been "transferred hither from the Governor's paternal home" (105); indeed, the inhabitants of Boston generally are said to be "native Englishmen, whose fathers had lived in the sunny richness of the Elizabethan epoch" (230). The narrative accordingly focuses upon how these traditions are refracted and culturally reimagined, how the "hereditary taste" of these Bostonians evokes the "dim reflection of a remembered splendor," a "diluted repetition of what they had beheld in proud old London" (230). This is why the novel's prologue takes us through the customhouse, the boundary between different countries. The usual purpose of a customhouse is to deal with international trade and exchange, and this formal gateway to *The Scarlet Letter* offers a correlative to the book's central concerns, which involve the crossing of frontiers, the transitions between one state and another.

Recent work on *The Scarlet Letter* has tended to relate Hawthorne's text to the cultural frictions that were gathering pace in America during the 1850s. Donald E. Pease describes the author as seeking some antidote to the political turbulence of this era by his strategy of imaginatively describing the "communal purposes in America's republic," returning to the pre-Revolutionary past so as to find "in the Puritans as alternative set of founding fathers."[39] Certainly this myth of national harmony and social homogeneity comprises one crucial strand in the novel, but it is just as important to emphasize how the narrator's perspective on the Revolution looks backward as well as forward. The manuscript contained in an "ancient yellow parchment" (29) that provides the source for this narrative, according to Hawthorne's fictitious preface, is a document from British colonial times said to have been formerly owned by Jonathan Pue, "Surveyor of his Majesty's Customs for the port of Salem" (30). As Hawthorne's persona explains it, this manuscript was accidentally left behind when Pue's Loyalist heirs were obliged to decamp to Halifax, Nova Scotia, at the time of the American Revolution. *The Scarlet Letter* does indeed look to forge a mythic link between pre-Revolutionary and post-Revolutionary generations, as Pease suggests, but the oblique intrusion of the Revolutionary War into the book's preface also introduces a kind of fracture into these symbolic designs.[40] Just as myths of transcendence are held in check by the ironic disjunctions of historical conflict, so Hawthorne's abstract conception of the American ideal must always bear traces and scars of its British ancestor. In "The Custom-House," the narrator talks of how, during the Revolution, the king's officials carried off the records of Puritan America to Nova Scotia; and *The Scarlet Letter* could be seen as engaged in a reciprocal gesture, in the way it seeks to marginalize and knowingly repress this historical context of British-American culture in order to establish "visionary compacts" across the generations in support of a mythic American state.[41] Yet this process of sublimation is constantly contradicted within Hawthorne's text by the residual attachments to Old World culture and theology which permeate the consciousness of these emigrant characters: Hester, for example, always remains liminally cognizant of "that village of rural England" where she grew up, even though it now seems "foreign to her" (80). Hester's form of psychological alienation is thus tied in closely with her situation between two worlds, her defamiliarizing consciousness of the condition of exile: "For years past," we are told, "she had looked from this estranged point of view at human institutions" (199).

Hester's literal transgression, her crossing of the boundary between England and America, is replicated in her sexual transgression, where she traverses the boundary between propriety and misconduct. It is in the very nature of transgression to keep both sides of the dividing line visible: just as in this novel the Old World hovers constantly around the margins of the New, so Hester's sexual lapse has no meaning unless it is played off against what remains on the other side of the line, the probity of Puritan values. This is why Hester cherishes her scarlet letter, preferring the act of transgression to a purer state of emancipation. The often hostile reaction to Hester's duplicitous situation on the part of American critics highlights ways in which this discourse of insurrection remains relatively occluded within the intellectual contexts of American romanticism: Nina Baym, for example, describes Hester as an example of one of Hawthorne's characters "who, in a less repressive society, might be productively creative beings but here turn instead to subversion and perversion."[42] But it might well be argued that Hester's "creative" force is precisely, if paradoxically, dependent upon these authoritarian repressions; the heroine's spirit is not so much romantic or utopian, but, rather, radically perverse in the way it defines itself through a deliberate inversion of cultural assumptions. Hester seems to flourish in the paradoxical condition of a double life, to such an extent that she declines to relinquish the emblem of her social ostracism even when finally invited to do so.[43]

The paradoxical genius of Hawthorne lies precisely in the way he aestheticizes modes of Puritan consciousness, emptying out their substantive authority and reinventing them as theatrical correlatives for affective desire. For all of the major incidents in *The Scarlet Letter*, it is possible—and indeed plausible—to imagine alternative explanations for the characters' actions. For instance, when Hester reverts to wearing her scarlet letter "freely and voluntarily, in order to convert what had so long been agony into a kind of triumph" (227), we sense the classic masochistic pattern of "victory through defeat," predicated upon the kind of contractual masochism that, as Deleuze argues, works to undermine structures of social hierarchy. Within this context, writes Deleuze, masochism involves an "aesthetic" or "plastic" element which, through its self-consciously performative qualities, serves to problematize the strictly coercive aspects of sadism.[44] Such coercive aspects become revealed in their turn as no more than complementary spectacles, linked to various forms of cathectic fulfillment rather than any disinterested vindication of just authority. Hence, Hester's paradoxical "pride" in "what they, worthy gentlemen, meant for a punishment" (54) is matched by the Boston community's ritualistic pleasure at the prospect of her public humiliation, their "peculiar interest in whatever penal infliction might be expected to ensue" (50). The text is shot through with many other paradoxes of this kind: in chapter 17, "The Pastor and His Parishioner," we see, as Berlant notes, Dimmesdale combining his "erotic appeal" with "religious affect," turning what should be a disinterested pastoral exercise into an opportunity for pleasurable flirtation.[45] Christopher Newfield similarly argues that Dimmesdale's "reflexive male masochism" challenges the status of public morality, a morality based upon categorical distinctions between right and wrong, by its dissolution of such polarities within the self-gratifying sensation of private abjection.[46]

The point here is not, of course, simply to superimpose cumbersome psychoanalytical categories on Hawthorne's text, but to suggest how such structural ambiguities cause the narrative to swerve away from stable moral or allegorical identities of any kind. In a formal sense, evidently enough, the text foregrounds issues of transition, the ways in which events become converted into meaning through processes of interpretation. This accords with the book's emphasis upon optics, mirrors, the ways in which different perspectives produce different angles of reflection: the representation in chapter 7 of Hester's scarlet letter in "exaggerated and gigantic proportion" through the "peculiar effect" of a "convex mirror" (106) is only the most visually striking image within this constellation. All of these self-conscious rhetorical figures seek to convert themselves hermeneutically into forms of purpose and meaning, just as the Puritans' favorite trope of conversion sought to transform gross substance into the privileged realms of transcendent spirit. This is why Hester aspires "to convert what had so long been agony into a kind of triumph" (227), to endow the thread of her life with teleological purpose and redemption; it is also why the narrator imitates the manners of this particular historical era as he busily seeks out symbols that might point to an underlying metaphysical providence. As we have observed, though, such aspirations toward transcendence are always circumscribed ironically by the obstinate inconsistencies of worldly affairs, which deny *The Scarlet Letter* any possibility of allegorical closure.

In this sense, the mirror play between conversion and perversion lies along the focal plane of a novel that projects itself within Hawthorne's typical ideological framework of exchange. *The Scarlet Letter*, like Hawthorne's other major work, apprehends its peculiar vision of American national destiny through a comparative structure of transnationalism. It is precisely such processes of comparison that Emerson, with his idealization of individualism and self-reliance, found so disturbing. For Emerson, such comparative consciousness could prove psychologically disorienting and intellectually debilitating, liable to cloud the philosopher's primary focus upon his own integral vision: "never compare your generalization with your neighbor's," he wrote in a journal entry for 1838, "insist on comparing your two thoughts . . . & instantly you are struck with blindness, & will grope & stagger like a drunken man."[47] For Hawthorne, on the other hand, any such integral vision would tend by definition to be self-deluding. Accordingly, his writing systematically develops strategies of reversal associated with comparative perspectives in order to expose the epistemological limitations associated with nationalist versions of transcendentalism, which are always re-illuminated in his texts from an alternative angle of vision.

*   *   *

If Hawthorne uses England in order to aestheticize America, Trollope uses America to aestheticize and relativize the condition of England. Homi K. Bhabha has noted how the idea of national identity is customarily predicated upon the concept of repetition as simultaneity, the conflation of past and present so as to anneal temporal difference by suggesting how history offers identity and continuity rather than disruption.[48] On the face of it, Trollope's fictional world, with its serial repetitions, would appear to be organized around just such an ideology of self-replication. In his 1860 account of a trip to the West Indies, Trollope declares unselfconsciously that "A man from choice will live with those who are of his own habits and his own way of thinking," and his condescension here toward "coloured" people indicates the kind of lofty paternalism and capacity for exclusion all too characteristic of the English Victorian gentleman.[49] Similarly, characters like Sir Omicron Pie and the Duke of Omnium who run through Trollope's serial novels imply an aesthetic of continuity whose chief pleasure involves a recognition of the familiar. The social implications of this formula tend toward conservatism, or perhaps a mild form of liberalism which acknowledges the possibility of change only within the clearly demarcated, existing parameters of society. My argument here, however, is that, as with Hawthorne, nationalist preconceptions can oversimplify our readings of these novels, and that various aspects of transgression and deviance implicit within Trollope's texts can usefully be illuminated by a transatlantic reading of his works. Indeed, America for Trollope often appears as the primum mobile of deviance, introducing specters of alterity into his familiar, homegrown state.

    Within Trollope's fiction, the idea of perversion emerges in his frequent observation of discrepancies between idea and practice. His lengthy narratives delineate stable social patterns of English society which, however, not infrequently find themselves crossed by the more erratic propensities of individual human behavior. In *He Knew He Was Right* (1868–69), this idiom of contradiction becomes expanded into a form of structural division, as Louis Trevelyan obsessively seeks clear evidence of his wife's infidelity: "They who do not understand that a man may be brought to hope that which of all things is the most grievous to him," declares the narrator, "have not observed with sufficient closeness the perversity of the human mind."[50] But this psychological form of perversity, the swerve away from norms of individual probity, does not take place in isolation; instead, it is represented as commensurate with the more general deviation from social and cultural expectations which is a major theme of Trollope's fiction. In *Can You Forgive Her?* (1864–65), for instance, it is precisely because Alice Vavasov's engagement to John Grey appears so eminently satisfactory that she feels profoundly impelled to resist it. The novel goes on to describe Alice's "perverseness of obstinacy" in clinging to her resolution to abandon Grey, "a wish that she might be allowed to undergo the punishment she had deserved."[51] Yet Alice's rejection of her suitor is not, in fact, altogether irrational; John Grey is a dull Cambridgeshire gentleman, whose lack of interest in metropolitan affairs would appear to make him quite incompatible with the more worldly Alice. So what happens here is that Alice interprets her own actions as perverse because she has internalized the norms of society to such an extent that any deviation from them appears to her transgressive. Alice, like other Trollope characters, lacks the strength of will or the sense of personal autonomy that might justify her individual choices; instead, she makes such choices instinctively and then feels guilty because her actions infringe established conventions. Therefore, the perverse in Trollope should be understood as a discrepancy between generic orthodoxy on the one hand and amorphous desire on the other. Alice has been conditioned by her upbringing to such an extent that she can hardly explain to herself why the wealthy and stable Grey appears so unappealing, and this is why she willingly accepts her admonishment from Lady Midlothian, feeling that "she deserved all the lashes she received."[52]

It is this clash between the need to conform and an impulse to rebel, a clash mostly worked out on an unconscious and unformulated level, that helps to account for the vacillating temperaments of so many central characters in Trollope's world. In this sense, the perverse in Trollope is consistently associated with what is foreign, with what deviates from the self-regulating codes of British society. In the Barsetshire novels, it is London that is represented as the threat to rural stability and its tranquil rituals of repetition; as James R. Kincaid notes of *The Small House at Allington*, Lily's suitor, Adolphus Crosbie, is the first powerful invader from the metropolis, and Barset's pastoral world is uncomfortably disrupted by his appearance.[53] The Palliser novels, however, take London life as their focal point, and in these more overtly political texts it is America which frequently represents the intrusive agent, the manifestation of something foreign within the structures of national life. In *The Prime Minister* (1876), for example, the denizens of Wharton Hall believe Emily Wharton to be "perverse and unreasonable" in preferring Ferdinand Lopez to the more solid English virtues of Arthur Fletcher.[54] Lopez is a Portuguese Jew involved with South American trade, and the "perverseness" with which Emily is so often charged in this novel derives from her willingness to disrupt the internal logic of the English class system, an action she later comes self-mortifyingly to regret.

In Trollope's fiction, then, the chameleonic capacities of American culture appear as a threat to the compulsive cycles of English society. The sequential nature of these Barsetshire and Palliser novels itself mimics the ritualistic basis of Trollope's British culture, based upon a recognition of the all too familiar; and, as with all systems of power, the naturalization of social authority and hierarchy here depends upon a kind of fetishistic reenactment of the same. Yet such self-perpetuating nationalist scenarios come to be interrupted by the author's American perspectives, his transcription of alterity and difference. In *The Duke's Children* (1880), the last novel in the Palliser sequence, Lord Silverbridge's choice of a wife lies between an American, Isabel Boncassen, and the quintessentially English Lady Mabel Grex, who feels that such a transatlantic alliance "would be an outrage to all English propriety."[55] This novel can consequently be seen as a subtle exploration of the conflict between the power of rational choice and the presence of irrational attachment. In principle, the Duke of Omnium is open to social change and welcomes the intellectual stimulation of the Boncassen family, but in practice he feels uncomfortable with his son's proposal to take the family beyond national customs and frontiers: "there was an inner feeling in his bosom as to his own family, his own name, his own children, and his own personal self, which was altogether kept apart from his grand political theories. . . . That one and the same man should have been in one part of himself so unlike the other part,—that he should have one set of opinions so contrary to another set,—poor Isabel Boncassen did not understand."[56] This is not hypocrisy, as such, because hypocrisy depends upon the fraudulent inversion of a secure set of beliefs, which is precisely what the duke here does not enjoy. Such internal ruptures are more characteristic of the kind of divided consciousness which, as Kristeva says, "sets up the opposites in human signification facing each other, with neither synthesis, nor internalization, nor suppression." This marks, in Kristeva's words, "the subtle norm of a culture conscious of its reversibilities": the Duke finds himself oscillating ambivalently between conflicting positions, and it is precisely this consciousness of how his native values might be reversed that serves to illuminate the boundaries and assumptions of his inherited state.[57]

Just as the perverse in Hawthorne involves transgressing national ideals and philosophical orthodoxies, so the perverse in Trollope cuts across the margins of British society, complicating its assumptions and values by causing them to be refracted in the dark glass of comparativism. This sense of difference within similarity and similarity within difference causes Britain and America to be defined, in Trollope's later work, as reluctant twins, disturbing reflections of each other. In *The American Senator* (1876–77), Senator Elias Gotobed delivers a public lecture on "The Irrationality of Englishmen" where he argues it is the resemblance of so many aspects within the two cultures—language, laws, cookery, dress—that also produces the most intense disjunctions and frictions.[58] In *The Way We Live Now* (1875), Suffolk gentleman Roger Carbury is cast as a solid upholder of old English virtues and a character who "was prejudiced against all Americans, looking upon Washington much as he did upon Jack Cade or Wat Tyler." Carbury is set in stark contrast to Hamilton K. Fisker, the American financier from the "glorious West," who has schemes for building a railway between Salt Lake City and Vera Cruz, and whose wheeling and dealing is designed to make England part of his empire of multinational capitalism. In a quite straightforward way, one theme of this novel is how traditional English institutions have become unsettled by the development of new communications industries. The shady financier, Melmotte, another character of dubious provenance, has the "telegraph at his command," and so, when investigating Fisker's business schemes, can "make as close inquiries as though San Francisco and Salt Lake City had been suburbs of London."[59] Paul Montague, an Englishman from Oxford, also becomes caught up in these schemes, having himself spent three years with his emigrant uncle in California. Though the novel is still centered on London, Trollope's focus here expands to include an international world, where the rural equivalence between object and value, property and propriety, has elided into a less tangible system of virtual reality. Within this system, credit, speculation, and public image have superseded more traditional guarantees of moral worth.

Yet if Melmotte and Fisher represent the most crass examples of such fraudulence, the novel indicates how such double-dealing is coming to pervade English society as well. The whole business of publishing and book reviewing is revealed as dishonest, with Lady Carbury quite as unscrupulous in her dealings with this world as is Melmotte in his manipulation of the London Stock Exchange. Similarly, Lady Carbury's son, Felix, takes his cue from others at the Bear Garden and comes to excel in cheating at cards. The Bear Garden, a kind of pleasure palace for the wealthy, in fact forms a curious mirror image of the stock exchange, which is presented here as a place where gambling and chicanery have been institutionalized at the heart of British culture. Nor does Trollope's cynicism stop there: when the dim-witted Lord Nidderdale says he cannot understand why Melmotte made him a director of the South Central Pacific and Mexican Railway Company, Montague swiftly provides him with the answer: "'Because you're a lord,'" said Paul bluntly."[60]

The significance of America in this novel, then, lies not simply in the way it represents a meretricious contrast to traditional English values, nor even how it appears as a modernistic projection of how Britain might change and develop under the fortunes of multinational capitalism. More crucially, the violently arbitrary and self-interested energies of America, fueled by a greed masquerading as social altruism, reflect in Trollope's eyes the state of British society as it actually is, and as it has been: the way we live now. As Paul Montague recognizes, especially after his return from California, the aristocratic class system of Britain represents no less of a self-validating sham than the frontier culture of the American West. Despite Roger Carbury's pastoral endeavor to extricate his set of approved English virtues from this circuit of reciprocation and exchange, the implication of Trollope's text is that social hierarchies and class systems are as interchangeable as paper money. From this perspective, America works at a distance to relativize and aestheticize the customs of the country, to display British society as turning on an axis of self-gratifying, ludic formulas rather than being centered around weighty moral imperatives or timeless traditions, as its own public conception of itself would prefer. Trollope's British aristocrats preserve their system of dominance simply because it pleases them, because it is in their interests to do so.

To read Trollope from an Americanist viewpoint, then, is to reconceptualize British society as a matrix of aesthetic patterns and pleasures rather than ethical dilemmas. If psychological deviation in Trollope implies a mode of excess, a failure of corporate system to contain the more erratic energies of corporeal practice, then national identity is similarly subject to fissures and divisions, as Britain (and America) fail to coincide with the more abstract models of their theoretical selves. Yet within Trollope's world, which increasingly moves away from rural tranquility toward international circulation and exchange, the transatlantic dimension also opens up possibilities of alternative perspectives, where personal as well as cultural identities become liable to hybridization. This induces in Trollope's fiction the perverse reflections which destabilize the systemic structures of both cultures by playing them off against each other.

What we consistently find in the narratives of Hawthorne and Trollope, then, is a process of desublimation and reversal, a twisting round of categories. Within the context of the nineteenth century, such aesthetic reversals customarily involve a contamination by the foreign: the irruption of matter into spirit in Hawthorne, the subversion of social stability by alien presences in Trollope. This double-edged discourse transgresses the boundaries of organic coherence, fragmenting the body—both the corporate body of the nation, and the corporeal bodies of its inhabitants—into a series of "lop-sided" deviations, which betoken the lack of any natural "fit" between the particular and the representative. In Trollope, especially, this duplicity extends into the realms of the conscious and unconscious, which often find themselves moving in opposite directions simultaneously. Thus, to establish intertextual relations between Hawthorne and Trollope is to witness an interplay of dialogues between conversion and perversion, spirit and matter, America and Europe. Such oppositions and contradictions necessarily imply how teleologies of cultural and national identity can only be organized around the repression of a fetishistic double bind that, in typical vacillating fashion, states one thing but signifies another. In *The Scarlet Letter*, as we have seen, Hawthorne's narrator tries to repress the memory of the Revolutionary War in order to postulate an essential continuity between the seventeenth-century colony of Massachusetts Bay and his nineteenth-century national community; however, the ghosts of cultural division and transatlantic turbulence are always throwing back disorienting shadows upon these fantasies of family romance. In Trollope's epic sagas, similarly, the exclusion of the United States comes to form a constituent part of the English country heritage in the long aftermath of the American Revolution; but then, like an importunate relative who will never quite disappear, the specter of America keeps recurring in maverick fashion to disturb the established customs of Trollope's fictional homelands. While Hawthorne and Trollope were not exactly "brother" novelists, as the latter suggested in his *Autobiography*, they were at least awkward second cousins whose relationship to their mutual genealogy was both compulsive and troubled.[61]

Conclusion
Transatlantic Perspectives
Poe and Equiano

Within the framework of what Philip Fisher calls "the new American Studies" as it has developed over recent years, the main focus has gravitated toward the Civil War, rather than the Revolution, as the primary site for struggles over national identity and cultural tradition.[1] As we saw in the introduction, F. O. Matthiessen's *American Renaissance*, published in 1941, was pivotal to the initial establishment of American literary study as an academic enterprise, and the key terms in this work are "integrative" and "democratic." Writing, like Emerson, in the "optative" mood, Matthiessen cherished his chosen authors as embodying a spirit of utopian prophecy, as intuitively experiencing "a deep confidence in organic wholeness" that manifests itself in a commitment to the prospects of national community and pastoral renewal.[2] It is, of course, not difficult from our critical vantage point to infer what Matthiessen elides or simply ignores. He selected five white male authors, all from New York or New England, and he diminished the significance of regional and racial conflict to such an extent that, as Jonathan Arac observes, the "Civil War was not even indexed," even though it was literally to tear the United States in half just a few years after the production of the literary works championed there.[3]

Consequently, more recent critics have engaged intertextually with Matthiessen in an effort specifically to incorporate what he omitted. This theoretical pattern involves preserving Matthiessen's equation of democracy with an American spirit, while extending the charmed circle to embrace within its circumference those previously excluded. For instance, Eric J. Sundquist's *To Wake the Nations* (1993) directly addresses the question of "Race in the Making of American Literature"; yet, for all of its radical energy, Sundquist's book is, as Claudia Tate remarked, a reworking of *American Renaissance* in the way it focuses upon an alternative quest for freedom, this time by five black writers—Turner, Douglass,

Delany, Chesnutt, and Du Bois—so as to redefine race as "the founding principle of U.S. literary culture."[4] Eric Lott has similarly written of how "the book that *To Wake the Nations* most often recalls is F. O. Matthiessen's *American Renaissance*," particularly in its invocation of "a democratic faith, nearly synonymous with Americanism." If Sundquist's work "displaces Matthiessen's *American Renaissance*," concluded Lott, "it also follows in its tracks."[5] Also following in Matthiessen's wake, Jane Tompkins's *Sensational Designs* (1985) includes an essay, "The Other American Renaissance," where she examines neglected women's writing of the 1850s, while David J. Reynolds, in *Beneath the American Renaissance* (1988), seeks to recontextualize writers like Whitman by juxtaposing their canonical texts with the "sensational" products of popular culture that a scholar like Matthiessen would never stoop to acknowledge.[6]

My point is that although these (and other) critics have successfully challenged what Eric Cheyfitz has called Matthiessen's "nationalist-formalist version of American exceptionalism," the effect of their revisionist impulse is simply to reinscribe American exceptionalism in a new way.[7] Tompkins, Reynolds and Sundquist offer revised versions of the American cultural heritage, centered around gender, popular culture, and race, but the term not interrogated so rigorously is "America" itself—or, as Lott more accurately put it, "U.S. nationhood."[8] The question begged here is the extent to which any area-based organization of knowledge tends implicitly (if unconsciously) to reproduce the conceptual matrix framing and informing those very categories which it seeks to evade or renew. Sundquist, for example, relocates the moral authority of "American" freedom within slave narratives rather than transcendentalist writings, thereby rotating the axis of Matthiessen's national imaginary from one group of countercultural writers to another. All too often, the progressive model of American studies simply reproduces, in a self-reflexive manner, its own image of liberal idealism within academic considerations of particular objects under its scrutiny. Hence, by a familiar irony of American culture in many of its forms, what starts out appearing radical and iconoclastic becomes oppressively familiar and acculturated, tautologically contained within the established circuits of its own devising. This is why Paul A. Bové writes: "There is no doubt . . . that the strictly 'national' focus of Americanist criticism cannot be sustained," though he also believes that American studies "has not yet reached the point of 'exile' in relation to itself and its nationalist projects."[9]

Such an emphasis within American studies on the ramifications of the Civil War tends to reinforce this nationalist agenda, because the focus on internal fracture signifies an implicit nostalgia for some corresponding state of unity where all divisions might be annealed. This mythologization of the Civil War as

offering the promise of a redemptive national identity, a political paradise re-
gained, was inaugurated by Lincoln's transcendental rhetoric of the early 1860s—
"this nation, under God, shall have a new birth of freedom"—and it has continued to operate powerfully in the twentieth century, even in its negative forms:
for Tompkins and Sundquist, for instance, the point about Lincoln's "new birth of
freedom," as promised at Gettysburg, is precisely that it came to pass only in a
limited and blinkered fashion.[10] Yet, by relocating the provenance of American
literature within an earlier generation, where it emerges as a refraction or travesty
of British culture rather than embodying a house divided against itself, we come
to see how familiar texts within British and American traditions take a paradoxical pleasure in mutual antagonism and interference. In this sense, a comparative
perspective divests these literary works of the teleologies customarily associated with national narratives and suggests instead how ontological contradiction
forms an inherent, if frequently suppressed, component within British-American
literature. Despite subsequent romanticizations of the national imaginary as a
unified and organic phenomenon, British and American literatures each reveal, as
in a crazy mirror, what is lacking in the other.

There were many authors of the eighteenth and nineteenth centuries not
considered here whose work traversed the Atlantic either literally or metaphorically, but I want to conclude by suggesting briefly the symptomatic significance of
transatlantic perspectives within the works of Edgar Allan Poe and Olaudah
Equiano. The writings of Poe might be seen as a fulcrum in any move to dissociate understandings of American literature from the tenets of the "American Renaissance." Excluded from Matthiessen's nationalist synthesis on the grounds of
being "bitterly hostile to democracy" and of not having "the moral depth of
Hawthorne or Melville," Poe positions himself on an eerie dividing line between
British convention and American independence.[11] In "William Wilson" (1839),
this fissure is located specifically within a transatlantic context, as Poe's narrator
tells the story of his youth and upbringing in England, where he found himself
always haunted by a shadow self. Wilson frames this act of doubling through
a pun on constitution, which indicates not only his physical constitution, but
also the political constitution of each country which is mirrored disconcertingly
across this North Atlantic divide: hence, he talks of his own "constitutional
disease," and of how his "parents" were "beset with constitutional infirmities akin
to my own."[12] Wilson also discusses how this split self works to compromise
any conception of autonomy: it is the fragmentation of identity, he says, which
results in "natural rights of self-agency" being "so pertinaciously, so insultingly
denied" (639).

It is not too difficult to relate this constitutional fallibility to what Poe thought of as the fallibility of the American Constitution, grounded as it was upon a Lockeian understanding of cultural independence and natural human rights. Locke's empiricist integrity is counterposed here with Poe's own predilection for what William Wilson calls an "intolerable spirit of contradiction" (630). But this kind of contradiction relates not just to Wilson's own state, nor simply to the epistemological limitations of the American Constitution; it also reflects an alternative view of the British cultural scene from a perspective outside its naturalized environs. Thus, Dr. Bransby, the gentle country cleric, also turns out to be a tyrannical schoolmaster, while the charms of English village life are linked inextricably to the coercive forces symbolized by a "ponderous gate . . . surmounted with jagged iron spikes" (628) that stands at the edge of Bransby's academy. The tranquility of the rural past, as it appears in memory, is haunted by a threat of violence and oppression, as if these placid scenes of English life could never quite conceal the old country's colonial impulse toward domination and mastery. In this sense, the "constitutional infirmities" of the parent do indeed mirror those of its offspring, for if Britain interrogates American claims to the domain of natural rights and self-agency, America in turn unmasks the institutional lust for power implicitly intertwined with Britain's picturesque landscapes.

The narrator in "William Wilson" talks of a "gigantic paradox too utterly monstrous for solution" (627), but in fact paradox for Poe involved something like a psychological and scientific explanation of common phenomena. In *Eureka* (1848), a philosophical treatise he wrote over the last couple of years of his life, Poe extrapolates an overall view of the universe from his understanding of electromagnetism, and, on a "purely geometrical basis," concludes that a circuit of reciprocal contradiction is the fundamental law governing the existence of matter. Poe directly takes issue here with the positivism of John Stuart Mill, as he argues that supposedly rational ideas of "Truth" or "the Steadfast" must inevitably find themselves usurped by this dualistic process governing attraction and repulsion; hence, asserts Poe, "*no such things as axioms ever existed or can possibly exist at all.*"[13] That last statement is, of course, produced with an axiomatic flourish, testifying once again to the author's ingenious capacity for self-contradiction.

This is why the science of contradiction in Poe's world serves to disestablish the idea of authorial self-reliance, in Emerson's sense of that term, and to interrogate the quest for cultural originality and identity. For Poe, the author must not only act, but also react against; consequently, texts become established through overt or covert dialogues with what has gone before. As Jonathan Elmer has argued, Poe's work reveals the social limits of the nation since it suggests "all that America must repress in order to become, or remain, America": as in "William Wilson," the mirror image of Old England forms a potentially disturbing reflection which threatens to splinter the narrator's integrity, to deprive him of his selfhood.[14] To suggest that Poe engages intertextually with British culture is not, of course, to suggest that he was enamored of the more conservative models of English literature. Unlike the James Russell Lowells of this era, who believed American civilization should be seen simply as a variant of its British ancestor, Poe refused what he called the "perfect farce of subserviency to the *dicta* of Great Britain," and he particularly disparaged "the almost exclusive dissemination among us of foreign—that is to say, of monarchical or aristocratical sentiment in foreign books."[15] The absence of any international copyright agreement at this time had the effect of flooding the American market with cheap reprints of novels by Sir Walter Scott and his compatriots, and this would have ensured that Poe's intellectual antagonism toward British traditions was bolstered also by a hard commercial rationale.[16] But such hostility to the colonial mentality did not instinctively lead him, as it led Emerson and Whitman, toward cultural nationalism, which Poe described in 1845 as a "political" rather than "a literary idea."[17] Evading this binary opposition between a genteel, postcolonial conformity and an aggressive American chauvinism, Poe delineates instead an aesthetics of reversal, where the normative and the deviant, the familiar and the *unheimlich*, are always sliding into each other, continually complicating each other's existence.

Such conscious dualisms testify to Poe's incompatibility with the academic assumptions of the American Renaissance. Unlike Whitman, say, who sought harmony between his social and poetic visions, Poe only ever constructs ideals in order to enjoy the frisson of swerving away from them. His work refuses to locate itself "organically" within American culture, as Matthiessen and his successors would have preferred; instead, it positions itself fetishistically on various boundaries: between creation and destruction, spirit and matter, America and Europe. Poe therefore revels in the fetishist's traditional privilege of having it both ways. His texts waver ambivalently across any dividing line they can find, contriving meaning not through naturalized relationships with their environment, but rather through the displacements of mutual mirroring and intertextual transposition. Traditional kinds of American criticism, predicated upon an implicit ideology of romanticism, tend to disparage intertextuality as a weak form of textual self-abasement, a failure to achieve the full sublimity of creative paternity: Harold Bloom, for instance, complained that Poe "fathered precisely nothing."[18] Yet the significance of these mirrors of intertextuality, from a comparative perspective, lies in the way they fracture the hypothetical unity of a national imaginary by collapsing the ethical injunctions inherent within any given culture into a series of performative, aestheticized fictions.

In this sense, comparativism works as an agent of defamiliarization, cutting through those circles of tautology through which the rhetoric of nationalist exceptionalism typically seeks to reproduce itself. One example of this flattening of British-American hybridity into an allegory of American nationalism can be seen in Henry Louis Gates's designation of Olaudah Equiano's autobiography as "the prototype of the nineteenth-century slave narrative," a genre based, according to Gates and Charles T. Davis, upon the "peculiarly *American* quality" of "originality" and romance.[19] Such interpretations have helped Equiano to become institutionalized as an American writer, with a place in the *Anthology of American Literature* published by both Heath and Norton, despite the fact that he was born in Africa, married an Englishwoman and chose to settle finally in London.[20] In his *Interesting Narrative*, first published in 1789, Equiano concludes: "My life and fortune have been extremely chequered, and my adventures various."[21] Being, as he puts it, "of a roving disposition" (171), Equiano crossed the Atlantic many times, visiting the West Indies and Nova Scotia as well as New York, Philadelphia, and Georgia, and continuing to travel widely after purchasing his freedom in 1766. This enabled him to develop international perspectives on the slave trade, knowledge which proved helpful in his subsequent political work for abolition.

In Equiano's *Narrative*, this comparative perspective is modulated formally through odd syntactic constructions, through which incongruous ideas are brought into juxtaposition. En route to Barbados, he speaks of receiving "a salutation in my nostrils" (56) from the stench below decks, as if to introduce a note of parody that indicates a discrepancy between polite social greetings and the gross physical reality with which he is confronted here. Equiano's retrospective vantage point contributes to this process of objectification, where events are not so much recorded experientially but rather framed within a double discourse of displacement and exchange. On board a ship to England, for example, he expresses relief that the crew manage to catch a large shark, "as I thought it would serve the people to eat instead of their eating me" (65). Equiano twists things around with a mordant humor, describing how when he first saw snow in England he thought it was salt, and inscribing a world of transverse identities where the "contrary winds" (73) that drive his American voyage off course to Tenerife become synecdochic of this narrative as a whole.[22]

As Geraldine Murphy has observed, there is a constant thread of self-parody or burlesque in Equiano's *Narrative*.[23] He characteristically invokes the spirit of Columbus, for example, in order to mock his own, more modest seafaring ambitions (208). This burlesque element can also be seen in his representation of racial identity: recounting his attempt to free John Annis, a black man imprisoned by his former West Indian master, Equiano tells of how he "whitened" his face in an attempt to deceive the gentleman of St. Kitts (180). Equiano intimates here how racial identity, like national identity, can appear as a contingent phenomenon, signified by a masquerade of whiteface and thus susceptible of reversal and exchange. Such transgressive aspects to his narrative persona are commensurate with his transnational perspectives, and, as Susan M. Marren has noted, they militate against any conception of essentialist identity in Equiano's writing.[24] In this post-Revolutionary climate of the 1780s, Equiano's burlesque dissociation of racial and national identity from any established sense of natural order could hardly have been more timely, and indeed it suggests, as with Franklin's *Autobiography*, how the shifting sands of national allegiance within a broader historical context contribute to these multiple mutations in the narrator's representation of himself. After the American war ended in 1783, London found itself with a significantly increased black population as Loyalists, in the company of their former slaves, retreated to the mother country, where they were joined by other ex-slaves who had emancipated themselves through an association with British forces during the recent conflict.[25] Again, the American War of Independence did not just change what it meant to be American, but also what it meant to be British.

This apprehension of contingency does not, of course, mean that Equiano seeks simply to elide racial difference into forms of masquerade, or that he remains uncommitted on the issue of slavery. But he insists repeatedly on the "*insanity*" as well as the "injustice" of the slave trade (109), arguing that the "freedom which diffuses health and prosperity throughout Britain" (111) stands as its own indictment of the plantation system. This is the economic argument for abolition which also enticed Franklin and Adam Smith, and it suggests Equiano's particular affiliations with the literary culture of eighteenth-century Britain, the mercantile land of Defoe and Swift. Within this world, adventurous characters embark on expeditions, both real and imaginary, and map out their new territories through various forms of social commerce and intellectual exchange. Indeed, Equiano's *Narrative* was immensely popular in England, going through five editions in as many years after its initial appearance in 1789.[26] Yet, as Paul Gilroy and others have noted, Equiano has been omitted from most twentieth-century accounts of English literary history, just as the significance of transatlantic slavery in general has failed to make an impact upon "the narrow nationalism of so much English historiography."[27] The erasure of Equiano from his British context is symptomatic of a more general tendency to exclude transatlantic dimensions from the privileged circle of British cultural identity, as I have been discussing throughout this book. It is, however, arguable that the American cultural effort to appropriate and integrate Equiano within an alternative national tradition has had the effect of reinforcing this transatlantic divide, rather than traversing and problematizing it in the way Equiano himself would have recognized more clearly.

According to Angelo Constanzo, Equiano "set the pattern for countless narratives—both non-fictional and fictional—that have influenced American literature to the present."[28] But to see Equiano in the way Constanzo does, as a harbinger of self-reliance, is to decontextualize him, to separate him altogether from the British milieu and to imagine him as a precursor of the American Renaissance. Several American critics have elected to focus specifically on the latter part of Equiano's *Narrative*, where he tells of his conversion to Christianity, since this trajectory makes the book conform with conventional American metanarratives of emancipation, where the alienations of entrapment are redeemed by a new vision of freedom. Joseph Fichtelberg, for instance, finds Equiano all at sea (both literally and metaphorically) in the first half of his life story, within a world of "commodities" and empty impersonations: "It is in this context," he argues, "that Equiano's religious conversion makes the most sense, for as an emptiness, a cipher, he is primed to be filled by grace."[29] This is not to misread Equiano, but it is to read him partially, to bring him into line with a mode of national allegory which sublimates the author's chameleonic tendencies into a form of transcendence. Conversion narratives were not in themselves an exclusively American phenomenon, of course, and John Wesley, who as the English founder of Methodism was very influential on both sides of the Atlantic, in fact named Equiano's *Narrative* as one of his favorite works. Moreover, as Helen Thomas has shown, there are important continuities between the elements of radical, dissenting Protestantism in Equiano's writing and their similar manifestation in the work of more celebrated English Romantic writers like Wordsworth, Coleridge, and Blake.[30] My point is, though, that Equiano's style of dissent has taken on an exemplary status within retrospective projections of the American literary tradition, and that this has tended to obscure the various aspects of transatlantic contrariness and topsy-turvydom which are threaded through his *Narrative*.

As recently as 1998, Nancy Ruttenburg's emphasis on cultural nationalism of this kind led her to formulate what she calls an "American aesthetic of innocence, through which democratic personality would be recognized and eventually rehabilitated as the essence of genuine American character and thus the exemplary subject—both representing and represented—of the national literature." The key terms here—"genuine" and "exemplary"—testify to Ruttenburg's belief in the "development of a democratic cultural semiotic" which would continue the task of stripping away false appearances and conventions, an Americanist agenda inaugurated, she believes, by the seventeenth-century Puritans and continued through the work of George Whitefield and James Fenimore Cooper.[31] Just as Matthiessen reinvented transcendentalism in the name of Popular Front communitarianism, so Ruttenburg recuperates a secularized version of Puritanism in the interests of challenging "established and authoritative social and aesthetic forms." Both critics explicitly equate their projects with a vision of national regeneration, and both draw upon the form of the conversion narrative to underwrite a model of what Ruttenburg calls "transferable selfhood," whereby the subject is seen to be susceptible of radical transformation within a new American order.[32] There is a barely suppressed religious ideology at work here, particularly in the association between ancestral American Protestantism and democratic modes of self-renewal, categories both predicated upon an iconoclastic dismantling of arbitrary forms of authority. In this way, both traditional and revisionist accounts of American literature have an inclination to associate national styles of writing with a rhetoric of emancipation, which effectively locks American culture within an exceptionalist circle where the contingent formations of national identity become obscured.

It is, however, easier to see what American literature embraces and omits by comparing it to British literature, just as American literature from a reverse perspective manifests itself as British literature's shadow self, the kind of culture it might have been, but wasn't. As I noted when discussing Alexander Pope and Mather Byles, the utopian visions of Thomas More have exerted a stronger influence on the formation of American literature than Erasmus's famous encomium to folly. What tends to be suppressed in such utopian or millennial accounts of American culture are those elements of paradoxical comedy and material burlesque that lie in the hinterlands of its insurrectionary enterprise. Indeed, to regard classic American literature within this framework of insurrection, rather than self-reliance, is to restore the sense of it as a parallel or doubled-up narrative, which reflects, as in a distorted mirror, the assumptions of its forebears. Traditionally, the Connecticut Wits have been seen as rather dull moral exemplars, self-righteously attempting to stave off the corruptions of Old England, but it is also important to recognize how they became reluctant sponsors of Pope's style of adoxography in the New World. Franklin has been cast as a moral allegorist, rather than being seen also as an Enlightenment satirist involved with duplicitous issues of transnational exchange. Jefferson has become his own icon, the "Jeffersonian image in the American mind," although his intertextual affiliations with Burke and Sterne might suggest ways in which the abstract nature of American revolutionary culture could be disentangled from the circular logic of, in his own phrase, a "self-evident" idealism.[33] By a similar process, an Americanist reading of Richardson or Austen or Trollope can open up vistas which remain obscure when these authors are viewed purely in terms of an English tradition.

For Leo Bersani, writing from a comparative critical position, the power of literature resides not in its capacity to embody the claims of spirit, but in precisely the opposite: in its way of "demystifying the force of argument, argument's claim

to truth." By transmuting ethical issues into aesthetic designs, says Bersani, literature "undoes that security of statement by which we can so easily be seduced, and
possessed." In this way, textual fictions avoid becoming circumscribed within a
normalizing "culture of redemption," as they ascetically dissociate redemptive
teleologies from metaphorical configurations to ensure that the latter can never
be wholly subsumed within the former.[34] By reflecting divergent literary traditions through a glass darkly, the comparative perspective suggests how inherited
assumptions are based upon particular cathectic attachments and emotional affiliations, and not upon any natural sense of order. Rather than proffering a transparent medium of multiculturalism or internationalism, comparativism projects
a prismatic mode of defamiliarization, predicated upon the paradoxical juxtaposition of apparently disparate objects. By disturbing the ethical proprieties associated with native appropriations of cultural identity, the comparative style works
to refract such identities through its medium of diffusion and dispersal.

Notes

Introduction. British-American Literature: Paradoxical Constitutions, Civil Wars

1. David Ramsay, *The History of the American Revolution* (1789), ed. Lester H. Cohen (Indianapolis: LibertyClassics, 1990), 1:53.

2. Simon Gikandi, *Maps of Englishness: Writing Identity in the Culture of Colonialism* (New York: Columbia University Press, 1996), 55–56.

3. Jennifer DeVere Brody, *Impossible Purities: Blackness, Femininity, and Victorian Culture* (Durham, N.C.: Duke University Press, 1998), 18.

4. Edward Watts, *Writing and Postcolonialism in the Early Republic* (Charlottesville: University Press of Virginia, 1998), 2, 17–18.

5. Henry D. Thoreau, *Reform Papers*, ed. Wendell Glick (Princeton, N.J.: Princeton University Press, 1973), 125, 121–22.

6. Gregory Jay, *America the Scrivener: Deconstruction and the Subject of Literary History* (Ithaca, N.Y.: Cornell University Press, 1990), 279. See also Peter Carafiol, *The American Ideal: Literary History as a Worldly Activity* (New York: Oxford University Press, 1991), 3–4.

7. For a survey of American studies in the 1950s, see Donald E. Pease, "New Americanists: Revisionist Interventions into the Canon," *boundary 2* 17 (1990): 1–37.

8. Randolph Bourne, *History of a Literary Radical and Other Essays*, ed. Van Wyck Brooks (1920; rpt. New York: Biblo and Tannen, 1969), 272, 274; Caren Irr, *The Suburb of Dissent: Cultural Politics in the United States and Canada During the 1930s* (Durham, N.C.: Duke University Press, 1998), 30.

9. F. O. Matthiessen, *American Renaissance: Art and Expression in the Age of Emerson and Whitman* (New York: Oxford University Press, 1941); Lawrence Buell, "American Literary Emergence as a Postcolonial Phenomenon," *American Literary History* 4 (1992): 412.

10. F. R. Leavis, "The Americanness of American Literature" (1952), in *Anna Karenina and Other Essays* (London: Chatto and Windus, 1973), 138–51. On the clash between comparative or overseas perspectives and the competing view that "American literature was distinct and separate, only to be understood within the specifics of the social, intellectual, political and cultural context of America itself," see Andrew Hook, "Scottish Academia and the Invention of American Studies," in *The Scottish Invention of English Literature*, ed. Robert Crawford (Cambridge: Cambridge University Press, 1998), 176–77.

11. Ezra Pound, "Provincialism the Enemy," in *Selected Prose, 1909–1965*, ed. William Cookson (London: Faber, 1973), 169.

12. William C. Spengemann, *A Mirror for Americanists: Reflections on the Idea of American Literature* (Hanover, N.H.: University Press of New England, 1989), 161.

13. William C. Spengemann, *A New World of Words: Redefining Early American Literature* (New Haven, Conn.: Yale University Press, 1994), 178–79.

14. Spengemann, *A Mirror for Americanists*, 26, 32; William C. Spengemann, "American Things/Literary Things: The Problem of American Literary History," *American Literature* 57 (1985): 467. For another extended critique of what he calls this "continuities school," see Philip F. Gura, "The Study of Colonial American Literature, 1966–1987," in *The Crossroads of American History and Literature* (University Park: Pennsylvania State University Press, 1996), 50. Gura also makes the point that "literary scholars have been remiss in not focusing on the broad connections between British and British American culture" (52).

15. John M. Murrin, "Beneficiaries of the Catastrophe: The English Colonists in America," in *The New American History*, ed. Eric Foner (Philadelphia: Temple University Press, 1990), 18.

16. On the institutionalization of American literature, see Kermit Vanderbilt, *American Literature and the Academy: The Roots, Growth, and Maturity of a Profession* (Philadelphia: University of Pennsylvania Press, 1986), 263–68, and Gerald Graff, *Professing Literature: An Institutional History* (Chicago: University of Chicago Press, 1987), 209–25. On the Anglican influence in the construction of "English literature," see Brian Doyle, *English and Englishness* (London: Routledge, 1989), 70–83. Doyle records here how gentlemanly values of "taste, tact, and decency" were consistently promoted by the *Review of English Studies* and similar journals in the 1930s (70).

17. Raymond Williams, *The Long Revolution* (London: Chatto and Windus, 1961), 30. For a recent example of the influence of Williams's work in America, see Michael Denning, *The Cultural Front: The Laboring of American Culture in the Twentieth Century* (London: Verso, 1996). Denning's work, which explores conceptions of the "national-popular" during the 1930s and 1940s, provides another example of how the idea of cultural history as a "long revolution" is tied implicitly to forms of organic continuity and national cohesion.

18. Werner Sollors, "Introduction: The Invention of Ethnicity," in *The Invention of Ethnicity*, ed. Werner Sollors (New York: Oxford University Press, 1989), xix, xx; Werner Sollors, *Beyond Ethnicity: Consent and Descent in American Culture* (New York: Oxford University Press, 1986), 13.

19. For a comparative study of earlier British and American literature, see Robin Grey, *The Complicity of Imagination: The American Renaissance, Contests of Authority, and Seventeenth-Century English Culture* (Cambridge: Cambridge University Press, 1997).

20. Robert Weisbuch, *Atlantic Double-Cross: American Literature and British Influence in the Age of Emerson* (Chicago: University of Chicago Press, 1986), 41.

21. Weisbuch, *Atlantic Double-Cross*, xiv, 126.

22. Paul Gilroy, *The Black Atlantic: Modernity and Double Consciousness* (Cambridge, Mass.: Harvard University Press, 1993), 6–7.

23. Paul Gilroy, *"There Ain't No Black in the Union Jack": The Cultural Politics of Race and Nation* (1987; rpt. Chicago: University of Chicago Press, 1991), 49–50. In this work, Gilroy takes issue with Williams's contention that social identity is less a question of "legal definitions" than "long experience." According to Gilroy, "Williams's discussion of 'race' and nation . . . is notable for its refusal to examine the concept of racism which has its own historic relationship with ideologies of Englishness, Britishness and national belonging." It is noticeable that criticisms of Williams in *The Black Atlantic* are much more implicit and muted.

24. Gilroy, *The Black Atlantic*, 34, 28–29, 87.

25. Gilroy, *The Black Atlantic*, 31, 145.

26. The classic statement of the affective ties associated with nation states is Benedict Anderson, *Imagined Communities: Reflections on the Origin and Spread of Nationalism* (London: Verso, 1993).

27. Paul Gilroy, *Against Race: Imagining Political Culture Beyond the Color Line* (Cambridge, Mass.: Harvard University Press, 2000), 2, 334.

28. Myra Jehlen and Michael Warner, eds., *The English Literatures of America, 1500–1800* (New York: Routledge, 1997), 195.

29. Carla Mulford, "What *Is* the Early American Canon, and Who Said It Needed Expanding?" *Resources for American Literary Study* 19, 2 (1993): 172.

30. Jack P. Greene, *Pursuits of Happiness: The Social Development of Early Modern British Colonies and the Formation of American Culture* (Chapel Hill: University of North Carolina Press, 1988), 27.

31. Jack P. Greene and J. R. Pole, "Reconstructing British-American Colonial History: An Introduction," in *Colonial British America: Essays in the New History of the Early Modern Era* (Baltimore: Johns Hopkins University Press, 1984), 7, 13–14.

32. Jim Egan, *Authorizing Experience: Refigurations of the Body Politic in Seventeenth-Century New England Writing* (Princeton, N.J.: Princeton University Press, 1999), 20, 74.

33. René Wellek, *Concepts of Criticism*, ed. Stephen G. Nichols Jr. (New Haven, Conn.: Yale University Press, 1963), 287.

34. For a discussion of the subject's evolution, see Claudio Guillén, *The Challenge of Comparative Literature*, trans. Cola Franzen (Cambridge, Mass.: Harvard University Press, 1993), 3–61.

35. Jonathan Culler, "Comparative Literature and the Pieties," *Profession, 86* (New York: Modern Language Association of America, 1986), 30; Earl Miner, *Comparative Poetics: An Intercultural Essay on Theories of Literature* (Princeton, N.J.: Princeton University Press, 1990), 238.

36. Edward Said, *Culture and Imperialism* (New York: Knopf, 1993), 32, 43.

37. Fredric Jameson, "The State of the Subject (III)," *Critical Quarterly* 29, 4 (1987): 17.

38. Jameson, "The State of the Subject (III)," 25.

39. John Carlos Rowe, *At Emerson's Tomb: The Politics of Classic American Literature* (New York: Columbia University Press, 1997), ix, 247–48.

40. Rowe, *At Emerson's Tomb*, 7, 254, 16.

41. Peter Carafiol, "Commentary: After American Literature," *American Literary History* 4 (1992): 541.

42. Lawrence Buell, "Circling the Spheres: A Dialogue," *American Literature* 70 (1998): 478. Buell's essay consists of an imaginary "conversation" between three Americanists, one of whom proposes this idea.

43. On the implications for identity of such conflicts between nationhood and globalization, see Lauren Berlant, *The Queen of America Goes to Washington City: Essays on Sex and Citizenship* (Durham, N.C.: Duke University Press, 1997), 13–14.

44. Marcus Cunliffe, *Chattel Slavery and Wage Slavery: The Anglo-American Context, 1830–1860* (Athens: University of Georgia Press, 1979), 35.

Chapter One. The Art of Sinking: Alexander Pope and Mather Byles

1. Jay Fliegelman, *Prodigals and Pilgrims: The American Revolution Against Patriarchal Authority, 1750–1800* (Cambridge: Cambridge University Press, 1982), 128–31.

2. George F. Sensabaugh, *Milton in Early America* (Princeton, N.J.: Princeton University Press, 1964), 103, 149.

3. K. P. Van Anglen, *The New England Milton: Literary Reception and Cultural Authority in the Early Republic* (University Park: Pennsylvania State University Press, 1993), 109–27; Keith W. F. Stavely, *Puritan Legacies: Paradise Lost and the New England Tradition, 1630–1890* (Ithaca, N.Y.: Cornell University Press, 1987), 107.

4. Harold Bloom, "In the Shadow of Milton," in *A Map of Misreading* (New York: Oxford University Press, 1975), 144–59, and *The Anxiety of Influence: A Theory of Poetry* (New York: Oxford University Press, 1973).

5. Perry Miller, *Nature's Nation* (Cambridge, Mass.: Harvard University Press, 1967), 1–13; Ralph Waldo Emerson, *Nature*, in *The Collected Works of Ralph Waldo Emerson*, vol. 1, *Nature, Addresses, and Lectures*, ed. Robert E. Spiller (Cambridge, Mass.: Harvard University Press, 1971), 7.

6. Sacvan Bercovitch, *The Rites of Assent: Transformations in the Symbolic Construction of America* (New York: Routledge, 1993), 29–67; Stephen Greenblatt, "Towards a Poetics of Culture," in *The New Historicism*, ed. H. Aram Veeser (New York: Routledge, 1989), 1–14.

7. Vincent Carretta, *George III and the Satirists from Hogarth to Byron* (Athens: University of Georgia Press, 1990), 244.

8. Van Anglen, *The New England Milton*, 49.

9. Michael Warner, "Poetry: The Eighteenth Century," in *The English Literatures of America, 1500–1800*, ed. Jehlen and Warner, 1013.

10. Sensabaugh, *Milton in Early America*, 5.

11. Agnes Marie Sibley, *Alexander Pope's Prestige in America, 1725–1835* (New York: Columbia University Press, 1949), 8, 17–18.

12. Cynthia Dubin Edelberg, "The Shaping of a Political Poet: Five Newfound Verses by Jonathan Odell," *Early American Literature* 18 (1993): 68–69.

13. Sibley, *Alexander Pope's Prestige in America*, 19. For Pope's association with Lord Bolingbroke and their antipathy to Sir Robin Walpole's "Robinocracy," see Isaac Kramnick,

Bolingbroke and His Circle: The Politics of Nostalgia in the Age of Walpole (Cambridge, Mass.: Harvard University Press, 1968), 217–23.

14. Lewis P. Simpson, ed., *The Federalist Literary Mind: Selections from the Monthly Anthology and Boston Review, 1803–1811* (Baton Rouge: Louisiana State University Press, 1962), 191.

15. Sibley, *Alexander Pope's Prestige in America*, 98. In the 1790s, Samuel Taylor Coleridge and Joseph Warton also associated Pope with what Coleridge called the "school of French poetry," and so they deemed him an inappropriate model for the foundation of a native English literary canon. See James Chandler, "The Pope Controversy: Romantic Poetics and the English Canon," *Critical Inquiry* 10 (1984): 491–92.

16. Matthew Arnold, "Thomas Gray," in *The Complete Prose Works of Matthew Arnold*, vol. 9, *English Literature and Irish Politics*, ed. R. H. Super (Ann Arbor: University of Michigan Press, 1973), 190, 202.

17. T. S. Eliot, "John Dryden," *The Listener*, 16 April 1930, 688.

18. Vernon Louis Parrington, ed., *The Connecticut Wits* (1925; rpt. Hamden, Conn.: Archon, 1963), xxv, xi.

19. Matthiessen, *American Renaissance*, 564, 208, 132.

20. Lydia Dittler Schulman, *Paradise Lost and the Rise of the American Republic* (Boston: Northeastern University Press, 1992), 220.

21. "Despite all the hoopla that has accompanied American literary scholarship based in the 'New Historicism,' the study of colonial American literature has remained strangely untouched by it." Philip F. Gura, "Turning Our World Upside Down: Reconceiving Early American Literature," *American Literature* 63 (1991): 104. Gura attributes this deficiency to a lack of "attention" among literary scholars "to what the best historians of colonial America are saying about a region or a period" (ibid.).

22. John P. McWilliams, *The American Epic: Transforming a Genre, 1770–1860* (Cambridge: Cambridge University Press, 1989), 1. For an analysis of how "dominant theoretical definitions of American literature" tend to exclude "major political writers . . . especially eighteenth-century thinkers such as Thomas Paine and the Connecticut Wits," see Russell J. Reising, *The Unusable Past: Theory and the Study of American Literature* (New York: Methuen, 1986), 21.

23. Alexander Pope, *Pope: Poetical Works*, ed. Herbert Davis (London: Oxford University Press, 1966), 337, lines 323–40. Subsequent line references to Pope's poetry, taken from this edition, are given in the text.

24. Helen Deutsch, *Resemblance and Disgrace: Alexander Pope and the Deformation of Culture* (Cambridge, Mass.: Harvard University Press, 1996), 24. Deutsch suggests that Pope's "poetics of deformity" (217) reflect the deformed nature of his own body.

25. William C. Dowling, *The Epistolary Moment: The Poetics of the Eighteenth-Century Verse Epistle* (Princeton, N.J.: Princeton University Press, 1991), 16.

26. Pat Rogers, "Pope and the Social Scene," in *Writers and Their Background: Alexander Pope*, ed. Peter Dixon (Athens: Ohio University Press, 1972), 101.

27. David S. Shields, *Oracles of Empire: Poetry, Politics, and Commerce in British America,*

1690–1750 (Chicago: University of Chicago Press, 1990), 3; Joseph Roach, *Cities of the Dead: Circum-Atlantic Performance* (New York: Columbia University Press, 1996), 139–44.

28. The standard treatment relating Pope to orthodox Roman Catholicism is Francis Beauchesne Thornton, *Alexander Pope: Catholic Poet* (New York: Pellegrini and Cudahy, 1952). More wide-ranging and useful is an essay by Chester Chapin, "Alexander Pope: Erasmian Catholic," *Eighteenth-Century Studies* 6 (1973): 411–30. Other discussions include Patrick Cruttwell, "Pope and His Church," *Hudson Review* 13 (1960): 392–405, and Thomas Woodman, "Pope: the Papist and the Poet," *Essays in Criticism* 46 (1996): 219–33.

29. Samuel Johnson, *Lives of the English Poets*, ed. L. Archer Hind (London: Dent, 1925), 2:149.

30. Emrys Jones, "Pope and Dulness," *Proceedings of the British Academy* 54 (1968): 236.

31. Quoted in Chapin, "Alexander Pope: Erasmian Catholic," 424.

32. Germán Arciniegas, *America in Europe: A History of the New World in Reverse* (1975), trans. Gabriele Arciniegas and R. Victoria Arana (San Diego: Harcourt Brace Jovanovich, 1986), 50, 277.

33. A. R. Humphreys, "Pope, God, and Man," in *Writers and Their Background: Alexander Pope*, ed. Dixon, 90.

34. Michel de Montaigne, *Essays*, trans. J. M. Cohen (Harmondsworth: Penguin, 1958), 394, 405–6, 56.

35. R. A. Sayce, *The Essays of Montaigne: A Critical Exploration* (London: Weidenfeld and Nicolson, 1972), 244.

36. Johnson, *Lives of the English Poets*, 2:151.

37. Johnson, *Lives of the English Poets*, 2:204.

38. *Pope: Poetical Works*, ed. Davis, 239.

39. David B. Morris, *Alexander Pope: The Genius of Sense* (Cambridge, Mass.: Harvard University Press, 1984), 167; Johnson, *Lives of the English Poets*, 2:226.

40. Maynard Mack, *Alexander Pope: A Life* (New Haven, Conn.: Yale University Press, 1985), 736–39.

41. On the significance of Thomist thought within *An Essay on Man*, see Nancy K. Lawlor, "Pope's *Essay on Man*: Oblique Light for a False Mirror," *Modern Language Quarterly* 28 (1967): 305–16.

42. Sibley, *Alexander Pope's Prestige in America*, viii, 26–27; Thornton, *Alexander Pope: Catholic Poet*, 185.

43. Henry F. May, *The Enlightenment in America* (New York: Oxford University Press, 1976), 37.

44. David Lundberg and Henry F. May, "The Enlightened Reader in America," *American Quarterly* 28 (1976): 271.

45. Kenneth B. Murdock, "Mather Byles," *Dictionary of American Biography*, ed. Allen Johnson (New York: Scribner's, 1929), 3:381.

46. C. Lennart Carlson, introduction to Mather Byles, *Poems on Several Occasions*

(1744), ed. C. Lennart Carlson (New York: Columbia University Press, 1940), xxx. Subsequent page references to this edition are given in the text.

47. Arthur Wentworth Hamilton Eaton, *The Famous Mather Byles: The Noted Boston Tory Preacher, Poet, and Wit, 1707–1788* (Boston: Butterfield, 1914), 3.

48. Austin Warren, "To Mr. Pope: Epistles from America," *PMLA* 48 (1933): 70, 72.

49. John Seelye, *Prophetic Waters: The River in Early American Life and Literature* (New York: Oxford University Press, 1977), 320.

50. Benjamin T. Spencer, *The Quest for Nationality: An American Literary Campaign* (Syracuse, N.Y.: Syracuse University Press, 1957), 19–20.

51. Sensabaugh, *Milton in Early America*, 83.

52. Shields, *Oracles of Empire*, 22, 228.

53. Eaton, *The Famous Mather Byles*, 91.

54. For a discussion of this point, see David Harvey, *The Condition of Postmodernity: An Enquiry into the Origins of Cultural Change* (Oxford: Blackwell, 1989), 245.

55. Spengemann, *A Mirror for Americanists*, 32.

56. Bloom, *The Anxiety of Influence*, 5, and *A Map of Misreading*, 63; V. L. Parrington, *Main Currents in American Thought: An Interpretation of American Literature from the Beginnings to 1920* (New York: Harcourt, Brace and Company, 1930), 1:248.

57. For an account of the machinations surrounding the publication of "Eternity," see David S. Shields, *Civil Tongues and Polite Letters in British America* (Chapel Hill: University of North Carolina Press for the Institute of Early American History and Culture, 1997), 245–48. Three weeks after the poem appeared in the *New-England Weekly Journal* of 15 May 1727, Byles published an anonymous tribute to his own poem in the same magazine.

58. Mather Byles, *A Discourse on the Present Vileness of the Body, and It's Future Glorious Change by Christ*, 2nd ed. (Boston: Thomas and John Fleet, 1771), 10–11.

59. Byles, *Discourse on the Present Vileness of the Body*, 6, 14–15, 20, 12.

60. Mather Byles, *A Sermon on the Nature and Necessity of Conversion*, 3rd ed. (Boston: Thomas and John Fleet, 1771), 6, 12, 7–8.

61. Perry Miller and Thomas H. Johnson, *The Puritans* (New York: American Book Company, 1938), 669.

62. Miller and Johnson, *The Puritans*, 690–93.

63. Eaton, *The Famous Mather Byles*, 203, 159.

64. Andrea Juno and V. Vale, eds., *Angry Women* (San Francisco: Re/Search Publications, 1991), 137.

65. Alexander Pope, *Poetry and Prose of Alexander Pope*, ed. Aubrey Williams (Boston: Houghton Mifflin, 1969), 389.

66. Pope, *Poetry and Prose of Alexander Pope*, 391, 408.

67. David S. Shields, "British-American Belles Lettres," in *The Cambridge History of American Literature*, vol. 1, *1590–1820*, ed. Sacvan Bercovitch (Cambridge: Cambridge University Press, 1994), 326, 341.

68. Ezra Pound, *The Cantos* (London: Faber, 1975), 358.

Chapter Two. Topsy-Turvy Neoclassicism: The Connecticut Wits

1. William L. Sachse, *The Colonial American in Britain* (Madison: University of Wisconsin Press, 1956), 164.

2. John C. Shields, "Phillis Wheatley and Mather Byles: A Study in Literary Relationship," *College Language Association Journal* 23 (1980): 377–90.

3. For an example of the attempt to establish Wheatley's radical credentials, see Sondra O'Neale, "A Slave's Subtle War: Phillis Wheatley's Use of Biblical Myth and Symbol," *Early American Literature* 21 (1986): 144–65.

4. Charles Scruggs, "Phillis Wheatley and the Poetical Legacy of Eighteenth-Century England," *Studies in Eighteenth-Century Culture* 10 (1981): 279.

5. J. Saunders Redding, *To Make a Poet Black* (Durham: University of North Carolina Press, 1939), 11; Evert A. Duyckinck and George Duyckinck, eds., *The Cyclopaedia of American Literature* (New York: Charles Scribners, 1856), 1:382, 375.

6. Parrington, *The Connecticut Wits*, 363. On Barlow's "problematical" relationship to the Wits, see William C. Dowling, "Joel Barlow and *The Anarchiad*," *Early American Literature* 25 (1990): 23. For a discussion of how Barlow's "apocalyptic vision" anticipates later themes in American literature, see Emory Elliott, *Revolutionary Writers: Literature and Authority in the New Republic* (New York: Oxford University Press, 1982), 126–27.

7. Kenneth Silverman, *Timothy Dwight* (New York: Twayne, 1969), 22.

8. Parrington, *The Connecticut Wits*, xli, xxi.

9. Annabel Patterson, *Pastoral and Ideology: Virgil to Valéry* (Berkeley: University of California Press, 1987), 194.

10. Timothy Dwight, *The Major Poems of Timothy Dwight*, ed. William J. McTaggart and William K. Bottorff (Gainesville, Fla.: Scholars' Facsimiles and Reprints, 1969), 381. Subsequent line references, taken from this edition, are given in the text.

11. Peter M. Briggs, "Timothy Dwight 'Composes' a Landscape for New England," *American Quarterly* 40 (1988): 361.

12. Lawrence Buell, *New England Literary Culture: From Revolution Through Renaissance* (Cambridge: Cambridge University Press, 1986), 321.

13. Robert Lawson-Peebles, *Landscape and Written Expression in Revolutionary America: The World Turned Upside Down* (Cambridge: Cambridge University Press, 1988), 45.

14. Shirley Samuels, "Infidelity and Contagion: The Rhetoric of Revolution," *Early American Literature* 22 (1987): 186.

15. Colin Wells, "Timothy Dwight's American *Dunciad*: *The Triumph of Infidelity* and the Universalist Controversy," *Early American Literature* 33 (1998): 173–91.

16. William C. Dowling, *Poetry and Ideology in Revolutionary Connecticut* (Athens: University of Georgia Press, 1990), and Christopher Grasso, *A Speaking Aristocracy: Transforming Public Discourse in Eighteenth-Century Connecticut* (Chapel Hill: University of North Carolina Press for the Omohundro Institute of Early American History and Culture, 1999).

17. Briggs, "Timothy Dwight 'Composes' a Landscape for New England," 373.

18. Timothy B. Spears, "Common Observations: Timothy Dwight's Travels in New England and New York," *American Studies* 30, 1 (Spring 1989): 40. Spears notes that in his 1816 essay, "On Light," Dwight discusses ways in which "light is matter, and not a quality of matter" (37).

19. Peter K. Kafer, "The Making of Timothy Dwight: A Connecticut Morality Tale," *William and Mary Quarterly* 47 (1990): 209.

20. Larzer Ziff, *Writing in the New Nation: Prose, Print, and Politics in the Early United States* (New Haven, Conn.: Yale University Press, 1991), 140.

21. Dowling, *Poetry and Ideology in Revolutionary Connecticut*, 7. For classic accounts of how Country ideology in England influenced the American republican tradition, see Bernard Bailyn, *The Ideological Origins of the American Revolution* (Cambridge, Mass.: Harvard University Press, 1967), 66–78, and J. G. A. Pocock, *The Machiavellian Moment: Florentine Political Thought and the Atlantic Tradition* (Princeton, N.J.: Princeton University Press, 1975), 462–92.

22. Silverman, *Timothy Dwight*, 146.

23. Sibley, *Alexander Pope's Prestige in America*, 89.

24. Victor E. Gimmestad, *John Trumbull* (New York: Twayne, 1974), 82.

25. Linda K. Kerber, *Federalists in Dissent: Imagery and Ideology in Jeffersonian America* (Ithaca, N.Y.: Cornell University Press, 1970), 174.

26. Johnson, *Lives of the English Poets*, 2:225. On this general association between "anti-Catholicism" and "homophobia" in eighteenth-century English culture and ways in which Catholics came to appear vulnerable "to exclusion from dominant sexual identities," see Kristina Straub, *Sexual Suspects: Eighteenth-Century Players and Sexual Ideology* (Princeton, N.J.: Princeton University Press, 1992), 76, 78. Rather than seeing Pope as affiliated with this domain of transgression, however, Straub implicates him within the power structures of the dominant ideology, critiquing his "homophobic vision of things gone 'perverse'" (80).

27. Pope, *Poetry and Prose of Alexander Pope*, 426. On Pope's manipulation of structural homologies between flagellation and satire, whose "pleasures are almost always mixed with pain," see Morris, *Alexander Pope*, 216.

28. On carnivalesque in the *Dunciad*, see Peter Stallybrass and Allon White, *The Politics and Poetics of Transgression* (Ithaca, N.Y.: Cornell University Press, 1986), 104–18; on the poem's relation to print culture, see Marshall McLuhan, *The Gutenberg Galaxy: The Making of Typographic Man* (London: Routledge and Kegan Paul, 1962), 255–63.

29. Janine Chasseguet-Smirgel, *Creativity and Perversion* (New York: Norton, 1984), 80.

30. Chasseguet-Smirgel, *Creativity and Perversion*, 1–3, 8.

31. Alexander Cowie, *John Trumbull: Connecticut Wit* (Chapel Hill: University of North Carolina Press, 1936), 197; Edgar Allan Poe, review of *A Fable for Critics*, by James Russell Lowell, in *Essays and Reviews* (New York: Library of America, 1984), 814.

32. The "guiding spirit" behind the *Anarchiad* was David Humphreys, according to Leon Howard, *The Connecticut Wits* (Chicago: University of Chicago Press, 1943), 183.

33. Constance J. Post, "Revolutionary Dialogics in American Mock-Epic Poetry: Double-

Voicing in M'Fingal, *The Anarchiad*, and *The Hasty Pudding*," *Studies in American Humor* NS, 6 (1988): 45–46.

34. *The Anarchiad: A New England Poem* (1786–87), *written in concert by David Humphreys, Joel Barlow, John Trumbull and Dr. Lemuel Hopkins*, ed. Luther G. Riggs (1861; rpt. Gainesville, Fla.: Scholars' Facsimiles and Reprints, 1967), 3, 4. Subsequent page references to this edition are given in the text.

35. Parrington, *Main Currents in American Thought*, 1:248.

36. J. K. Van Dover, "The Design of Anarchy: *The Anarchiad*, 1786–1787," *Early American Literature* 24 (1989): 242.

37. David Hume, *An Enquiry Concerning Human Understanding, and an Enquiry Concerning the Principles of Morals*, ed. L.A. Selby-Bigge (Oxford: Clarendon Press, 1894), 131.

38. Kerber, *Federalists in Dissent*, 21.

39. Pope, *Poetry and Prose of Alexander Pope*, 396.

40. Lewis P. Simpson, "The Satiric Mode: The Early National Wits," in *The Comic Imagination in American Literature*, ed. Louis D. Rubin, Jr. (New Brunswick: Rutgers University Press, 1973), 57.

41. Peter M. Briggs, "English Satire and Connecticut Wit," *American Quarterly* 37 (1985): 28–29.

42. Emerson, *Nature*, 7.

43. Leon Howard, "The Late Eighteenth Century: An Age of Contradictions," in *Transitions in American Literary History*, ed. Harry Hayden Clark (1954; rpt. New York: Farrar, Straus and Giroux, 1967), 86–87, 88, 53.

44. Michel Foucault, "A Preface to Transgression" (1963), in *Language, Counter-Memory, Practice: Selected Essays and Interviews*, trans. Donald F. Bouchard and Sherry Simon, ed. Donald F. Bouchard (Ithaca, N.Y.: Cornell University Press, 1977), 33.

45. John Trumbull, *The Satiric Poems of John Trumbull*, ed. Edwin T. Bowden (Austin: University of Texas Press, 1962), 149. Subsequent line references, taken from this edition, are given in the text.

46. Briggs, "English Satire and Connecticut Wit," 23. On the use of Trumbull's work as conservative propaganda, see Bruce Ingham Granger, "Hudibras in the American Revolution," *American Literature* 27 (1956): 507.

47. Robert A. Ferguson, *Law and Letters in American Culture* (Cambridge, Mass.: Harvard University Press, 1984), 107.

48. Christopher Grasso, "Print, Poetry, and Politics: John Trumbull and the Transformation of Public Discourse in Revolutionary America," *Early American Literature* 30 (1995), 12; Spencer, *The Quest for Nationality*, 20.

49. John Trumbull, *The Meddler* (1769–70) and *The Correspondent* (1770–73), ed. Bruce Granger (Delmar, N.Y.: Scholars' Facsimiles and Reprints, 1985), 39.

50. Trumbull, *The Meddler and the Correspondent*, 14–15.

51. Cowie, *John Trumbull*, 196.

52. Trumbull, *The Meddler and the Correspondent*, 55.

53. Trumbull, *The Meddler and the Correspondent*, 91.

54. Trumbull, *The Meddler and the Correspondent*, 121.

55. Trumbull, *The Meddler and the Correspondent*, 175.

56. Ferguson, *Law and Letters in American Culture*, 101. For Trumbull's opposition to the "New Light" movement, see Bruce Ingham Granger, "John Trumbull and Religion," *American Literature* 23 (1951): 57–79.

57. For similar reasons, Trumbull's earlier poems, like *The Progress of Dulness*, are more influenced by the satirical style of Jonathan Swift. See Howard, *The Connecticut Wits*, 53, 64.

58. Howard, *The Connecticut Wits*, 72, 74–75.

59. Chasseguet-Smirgel, *Creativity and Perversion*, 8.

60. Bruce Ingham Granger, *Political Satire in the American Revolution, 1763–1783* (Ithaca, N.Y.: Cornell University Press, 1960), 157.

61. Vivian Cameron, "Political Exposures: Sexuality and Caricature in the French Revolution," in *Eroticism and the Body Politic*, ed. Lynn Hunt (Baltimore: Johns Hopkins University Press, 1991), 93–96; Lynn Hunt, "Pornography and the French Revolution," in *The Invention of Pornography: Obscenity and the Origins of Modernity, 1500–1800*, ed. Lynn Hunt (New York: Zone Books, 1993), 301–39.

62. Cowie, *John Trumbull*, 39–40.

63. Richard Alsop, preface, *The Echo, with Other Poems* (1807), in *The Poetry of the Minor Connecticut Wits*, ed. Benjamin Franklin V (Gainesville, Fla.: Scholars' Facsimiles and Reprints, 1970), iv.

64. See, for instance, Shields, *Oracles of Empire*, 225–26.

65. Sensabaugh, *Milton in Early America*, 265; Ian Jack, *Augustan Satire: Intention and Idiom in English Poetry, 1660–1750* (London: Oxford University Press, 1952), 45–46. For a different view of *M'Fingal's* fourth canto as "deeply mythological and Miltonic," see Grasso, *A Speaking Aristocracy*, 318.

66. Ferguson, *Law and Letters in American Culture*, 3.

67. William H. Nelson, *The American Tory* (Oxford: Oxford University Press, 1961), 183–84.

68. Kenneth Silverman, *A Cultural History of the American Revolution* (New York: Crowell, 1976), 50, 24, 103.

69. Basil Willey, *The Eighteenth-Century Background: Studies in the Idea of Nature in the Thought of the Period* (London: Chatto and Windus, 1940), 43; John Barrell and Harriet Guest, "On The Use of Contradiction: Economics and Morality in the Eighteenth-Century Long Poem," in *The New Eighteenth Century: Theory, Politics, English Literature*, ed. Felicity Nussbaum and Laura Brown (New York: Methuen, 1987), 121–43.

70. John Bender, *Imagining the Penitentiary: Fiction and the Architecture of Mind in Eighteenth-Century England* (Chicago: University of Chicago Press, 1987), 88.

71. Julia Kristeva, *Strangers to Ourselves* (1989), trans. Leon S. Roudiez (New York: Columbia University Press, 1991), 181.

72. Stallybrass and White, *The Politics and Poetics of Transgression*, 193.

Chapter Three. From Allegory to Exchange: Richardson and Franklin

1. Andrew Delbanco, *The Death of Satan: How Americans Have Lost the Sense of Evil* (New York: Farrar, Straus and Giroux, 1995), 37–38.

2. Giles Gunn, *Thinking Across The American Grain: Ideology, Intellect, and the New Pragmatism* (Chicago: University of Chicago Press, 1992), 131.

3. John Locke, "Conduct of the Understanding," in *The Locke Reader*, ed. John W. Yolton (Cambridge: Cambridge University Press, 1977), 134.

4. David Hume, *A Treatise of Human Nature*, ed. Ernest C. Mossner (Harmondsworth: Penguin, 1969), 490. Subsequent page references to this edition are given in the text.

5. Tom Keymer, *Richardson's Clarissa and the Eighteenth-Century Reader* (Cambridge: Cambridge University Press, 1992), 168; Joseph Epes Brown, *The Critical Opinions of Samuel Johnson* (New York: Russell and Russell, 1961), 376.

6. James D. Hart, *The Popular Book: A History of America's Literary Taste* (New York: Oxford University Press, 1950), 56.

7. Leonard Tennenhouse, "The Americanization of Clarissa," *Yale Journal of Criticism* 11 (1998): 188, 185.

8. Janet Todd, *Sensibility: An Introduction* (London: Methuen, 1986), 137.

9. John Mullan, *Sentiment and Sociability: The Language of Feeling in the Eighteenth Century* (Oxford: Oxford University Press, 1988), 107.

10. Michael McKeon, *The Origins of the English Novel, 1600–1740* (Baltimore: Johns Hopkins University Press, 1987), 378, 363.

11. Samuel Richardson, *Pamela; or, Virtue Rewarded*, ed. William M. Sale Jr. (New York: Norton, 1958), 10.

12. Raymond Williams, *The English Novel from Dickens to Lawrence* (London: Chatto and Windus, 1970), 23.

13. Richardson, *Pamela*, 91.

14. Richardson advertises his preface as being by the book's "editor," using this disguise as "umbrage . . . to screen behind," as he puts it in a 1741 letter. See Richardson, *Pamela; or, Virtue Rewarded*, ed. Peter Sabor (Harmondsworth: Penguin, 1980), 31, 517.

15. On Pamela's capacity for linguistic dexterity and "artful reversal," see Bruce Robbins, *The Servant's Hand: English Fiction from Below* (1986; rpt. Durham, N.C.: Duke University Press, 1993), 82.

16. Herbert R. Brown, "Richardson and Sterne in the *Massachusetts Magazine*," *New England Quarterly* 5 (1932): 68.

17. Markman Ellis, *The Politics of Sensibility: Race, Gender and Commerce in the Sentimental Novel* (Cambridge: Cambridge University Press, 1996), 202.

18. Thomas H. Johnson, "Jonathan Edwards and the 'Young Folks' Bible,'" *New England Quarterly* 5 (1932): 39.

19. Brown, "Richardson and Sterne in the *Massachusetts Magazine*," 67.

20. Mullan, *Sentiment and Sociability*, 107.

21. T. C. Duncan Eaves and Ben D. Kimpel, *Samuel Richardson: A Biography* (Oxford: Clarendon Press, 1971), 314.

22. Robert Newcomb, "Franklin and Richardson," *Journal of English and Germanic Philology* 57 (1958): 27–35.

23. William Beatty Warner, "Staging Readers Reading," *Eighteenth-Century Fiction* 12 (2000): 405. On the eighteenth-century novel's hybrid quality, see also William B. Warner, *Licensing Entertainment: The Elevation of Novel Reading in Britain, 1684–1750* (Berkeley: University of California Press, 1998), and Lennard J. Davis, *Factual Fictions: The Origins of the English Novel* (New York: Columbia University Press, 1983). On the retrospective legitimation of the eighteenth-century novel as a literary genre by nineteenth-century critics, see Homer Obed Brown, *Institutions of the English Novel: From Defoe to Scott* (Philadelphia: University of Pennsylvania Press, 1997), 183.

24. Hannah Webster Foster, *The Coquette*, ed. Carla Mulford (Harmondsworth: Penguin, 1996), 34, and *The Boarding School* (Boston, 1798), 161. See Brown, "Richardson and Sterne in the *Massachusetts Magazine*," 67.

25. Elizabeth Barnes, *States of Sympathy: Seduction and Democracy in the American Novel* (New York: Columbia University Press, 1997), 1–39.

26. Fliegelman, *Prodigals and Pilgrims*, 237.

27. Deborah L. Madsen, *Allegory in America: From Puritanism to Postmodernism* (Basingstoke: Macmillan, 1996), 9.

28. The British view of Richardson's engagement with class issues is central to the more traditional view of him as a sober advocate of middle-class values, as expounded by Ian Watt in *The Rise of the Novel: Studies in Defoe, Richardson and Fielding* (1957; rpt. Harmondsworth: Penguin, 1963). It also emerges in more radical, revisionist accounts: see Terry Eagleton, *The Rape of Clarissa: Writing, Sexuality, and Class Struggle in Samuel Richardson* (Minneapolis: University of Minnesota Press, 1982).

29. Carroll Smith-Rosenberg, "Misprisioning *Pamela*: Representations of Gender and Class in Nineteenth-Century America," *Michigan Quarterly Review* 26 (1987): 19, 25, 22.

30. Fliegelman, *Prodigals and Pilgrims*, 86–89. On "moralizing readings of [*Clarissa*] made by Americans in the late eighteenth century," see also Julia A. Stern, *The Plight of Feeling: Sympathy and Dissent in the Early American Novel* (Chicago: University of Chicago Press, 1997), 119.

31. Cathy N. Davidson, *Revolution and the Word: The Rise of the Novel in America* (New York: Oxford University Press, 1986), 118.

32. Fliegelman, *Prodigals and Pilgrims*, 87.

33. Tennenhouse, "The Americanization of Clarissa," 185.

34. Richardson, *Pamela*, ed. Sabor, 31.

35. Samuel Richardson, *Clarissa; or, The History of a Young Lady*, ed. Angus Ross (Harmondsworth: Penguin, 1985), 727.

36. Terry Castle, *The Female Thermometer: Eighteenth-Century Culture and the Invention of the Uncanny* (New York: Oxford University Press, 1995), 65–66.

37. Nancy Armstrong and Leonard Tennenhouse, *The Imaginary Puritan: Literature, Intellectual Labor, and the Origins of Personal Life* (Berkeley: University of California Press, 1992), 141–42, 196, 202–5.

38. Armstrong and Tennenhouse, *The Imaginary Puritan*, 198.

39. Benjamin Franklin, *Writings*, ed. J. A. Leo Lemay (New York: Library of America, 1987), 1326. Subsequent page references to this edition are given in the text.

40. Karl Marx, *Capital*, trans. Eden Paul and Cedar Paul (London: Dent, 1930), 1:21. For a discussion of how discourses of value in the eighteenth-century English novel are bifurcated between a value associated with finance and a value associated with ethical character, see James Thompson, *Models of Value: Eighteenth-Century Political Economy and the Novel* (Durham, N.C.: Duke University Press, 1996), 1–14.

41. D. H. Lawrence, *Studies in Classic American Literature* (1923; rpt. Harmondsworth: Penguin, 1971), 15, 16. Franklin's description is taken from an epitaph he wrote for himself in 1728.

42. Mitchell Robert Breitwieser, *Cotton Mather and Benjamin Franklin: The Price of Representative Personality* (Cambridge: Cambridge University Press, 1984), 18; Leslie Fiedler, *Love and Death in the American Novel*, 3rd ed. (1982; rpt. Harmondsworth: Penguin, 1984), 63; Fliegelman, *Prodigals and Pilgrims*, 112.

43. Jehlen and Warner, eds., *The English Literatures of America, 1500–1800*, 771, 775.

44. In a letter to Benjamin Vaughan, 24 October 1788. Franklin, *Writings*, 1169.

45. Michael Warner, *The Letters of the Republic: Publication and the Public Sphere in Eighteenth-Century America* (Cambridge, Mass.: Harvard University Press, 1990), 53, 63.

46. Grantland S. Rice, *The Transformation of Authorship in America* (Chicago: University of Chicago Press, 1997), 66, 49.

47. Christopher Looby, *Voicing America: Language, Literary Form, and the Origins of the United States* (Chicago: University of Chicago Press, 1996), 109, 137, 127, 5.

48. Franklin describes these bifocal spectacles in a letter to George Whatley, 23 May 1785: "I have only to move my Eyes up or down, as I want to see distinctly far or near, the proper Glasses being always ready." Franklin, *Writings*, 1109–10.

49. Wayne C. Booth, *The Rhetoric of Fiction* (Chicago: University of Chicago Press, 1961), 319–21.

50. For a discussion of this point, see Joseph J. Ellis, *After the Revolution: Profiles of Early American Culture* (New York: Norton, 1979), 35–36.

51. Breitwieser, *Cotton Mather and Benjamin Franklin*, 200.

52. On Franklin and gamesmanship, see Gary Lindberg, *The Confidence Man in American Literature* (New York: Oxford University Press, 1982), 73–89.

53. For visual representations of Franklin, see Charles Coleman Sellers, *Benjamin Franklin in Portraiture* (New Haven, Conn.: Yale University Press, 1962).

54. Cynthia S. Jordan, *Second Stories: The Politics of Language, Form, and Gender in Early American Fictions* (Chapel Hill: University of North Carolina Press, 1989), 33, 57; Douglas Anderson, *The Radical Enlightenments of Benjamin Franklin* (Baltimore: Johns Hopkins University Press, 1997), 213.

55. Jordan, *Second Stories*, 33.

56. John Bender, "Enlightenment Fiction and the Scientific Hypothesis," *Representations* 61 (Winter 1998): 6–28.

57. For a discussion of how "the overall form of 'The Art of Virtue' is as elastic as its definitions," see Jordan, *Second Stories*, 46.

58. Anderson, *Radical Enlightenments*, 146. Criticism of *A Dissertation on Liberty and Necessity, Pleasure and Pain* has tended generally to underestimate its subversive aspects. While acknowledging Franklin's "denial of a distinction between good and evil," Alfred Owen Aldridge found himself able ultimately to reconcile the author's "necessitarianism" with "assumptions concerning the goodness, omniscience, and omnipotence of God." "Benjamin Franklin and Philosophical Necessity," *Modern Language Quarterly* 12 (1951): 309, 297.

59. Charles L. Sanford, "An American Pilgrim's Progress," *American Quarterly* 6 (1954): 297–310; J. A. Leo Lemay, "Franklin's *Autobiography* and the American Dream," in *Benjamin Franklin's Autobiography: An Authoritative Text*, ed. J. A. Leo Lemay and P. M. Zall (New York: Norton, 1986), 349–60; Kenneth Silverman, "Introduction," in Benjamin Franklin, *The Autobiography and Other Writings*, ed. Kenneth Silverman (New York: Viking Penguin, 1986), xii, ix.

60. Jean-Jacques Rousseau, *Confessions* (1781), trans. J. M. Cohen (Harmondsworth: Penguin, 1953), 378.

61. Roseanne Runte, "La Fontaine: Precursor of the Eighteenth-Century Libertine," *Eighteenth-Century Life* 3 (1976): 49–50.

62. Benjamin Franklin, letter to William Strahan, 27 October 1771, in Franklin, *The Papers of Benjamin Franklin*, vol. 18, ed. William B. Willcox (New Haven, Conn.: Yale University Press, 1974): 236.

63. Franklin, letter to William Strahan, 17 November 1771, *Papers of Benjamin Franklin*, 18: 251; David Hume, letter to Benjamin Franklin, 7 February 1772, in *The Papers of Benjamin Franklin*, vol. 19, ed. William B. Willcox (New Haven, Conn.: Yale University Press, 1975): 75. For the idea of philosophical elitism in Franklin and Hume, see Thomas J. Schlereth, *The Cosmopolitan Ideal in Enlightenment Thought: Its Form and Function in the Ideas of Franklin, Hume, and Voltaire, 1694–1790* (Notre Dame, Ind.: University of Notre Dame Press, 1977). For Hume's "high regard for Franklin," see Melvin H. Buxbaum, "Hume, Franklin and America: A Matter of Loyalties," *Enlightenment Essays* 3 (1972): 93.

64. Robert Darnton, *The Forbidden Best-Sellers of Pre-Revolutionary France* (London: HarperCollins, 1996), 73.

65. David Brion Davis, *The Problem of Slavery in Western Culture* (Ithaca, N.Y.: Cornell University Press, 1966), 380.

66. William H. Shurr, " 'Now, Gods, Stand Up for Bastards': Reinterpreting Benjamin Franklin's *Autobiography*," *American Literature* 64 (1992): 447.

67. For a useful discussion of this aspect of Franklin's writing, see A. Owen Aldridge, *Early American Literature: A Comparatist Approach* (Princeton, N.J.: Princeton University Press, 1982), 114–16.

68. Joseph Fichtelberg, *The Complex Image: Faith and Method in American Autobiography* (Philadelphia: University of Pennsylvania Press, 1989), 113–14. According to Fichtelberg, "The possible perversion of all writing is the aporia at the heart of Franklin's politics" (113).

69. Sacvan Bercovitch, *The Puritan Origins of the American Self* (New Haven, Conn.: Yale University Press, 1975), 134; Watt, *The Rise of the Novel*, 152–271.

70. Michael Seidel, "The Man Who Came to Dinner: Ian Watt and the Theory of Formal Realism," *Eighteenth-Century Fiction* 12 (2000): 193–94.

71. Anderson, *Radical Enlightenments*, 31.

Chapter Four. The Culture of Sensibility: Jefferson, Sterne, and Burke

1. Henry F. May, *The Enlightenment in America* (New York: Oxford University Press, 1976), 287.

2. On Jefferson's Anglophobia, see Michael Durey, *Transatlantic Radicals and the Early American Republic* (Lawrence: University Press of Kansas, 1997), 227–28. Jefferson was deliberately snubbed by King George III when he attended the British court in 1785.

3. Merrill D. Peterson, *The Jefferson Image in the American Mind* (New York: Oxford University Press, 1960), vi.

4. On Jefferson and religion, see Douglass Adair, *Fame and the Founding Fathers*, ed. Trevor Colbourn (New York: Norton, 1974), 143; Daniel J. Boorstin, *The Lost World of Thomas Jefferson* (1948; rpt. Boston: Beacon Press, 1960), 152; Paul K. Conkin, "The Religious Pilgrimage of Thomas Jefferson," in *Jeffersonian Legacies*, ed. Peter S. Onuf (Charlottesville: University Press of Virginia, 1993), 28; James Turner, *Without God, Without Creed: The Origins of Unbelief in America* (Baltimore: Johns Hopkins University Press, 1985), 44.

5. Thomas Jefferson, *Writings*, ed. Merrill D. Peterson (New York: Library of America, 1984), 1085. Subsequent page references to this edition are given in the text.

6. Lester J. Cappon, ed., *The Adams-Jefferson Letters: The Complete Correspondence between Thomas Jefferson and Abigail and John Adams* (Chapel Hill: University of North Carolina Press, 1959), 467.

7. *The Adams-Jefferson Letters*, ed. Cappon, 384.

8. Joseph J. Ellis, *American Sphinx: The Character of Thomas Jefferson* (New York: Knopf, 1997), 283. For a contrast between the relatively indifferent attitude towards religion on the part of the framers of the American Constitution and the fierce resistance by British governments at this time toward any attempt to repeal the Test and Corporation Acts, see Stephen Botein, "Religious Dimensions of the Early American State," in *Beyond Confederation: Origins of the Constitution and American National Identity*, ed. Richard Beeman, Stephen Botein, and Edward C. Carter II (Chapel Hill: University of North Carolina Press for the Institute of Early American History and Culture, 1987), 315–30.

9. *The Adams-Jefferson Letters*, ed. Cappon, 467.

10. Gordon Wood, *The Radicalism of the American Revolution* (New York: Knopf, 1992), 150.

11. Marquis de Sade, "Philosophy in the Bedroom" (1795), in *The Complete Justine, Philosophy in the Bedroom and Other Writings*, ed. Richard Seaver and Austryn Wainhouse (New York: Grove Press, 1966), 296; Drew R. McCoy, *The Elusive Republic: Political Economy in Jeffersonian America* (Chapel Hill: University of North Carolina Press for the Institute of Early American History and Culture, 1980), 67.

12. Leo Marx, *The Machine in the Garden: Technology and the Pastoral Ideal in America* (New York: Oxford University Press, 1964), 120, 139, 125, 141.

13. Jay Fliegelman, "Jefferson, Authorship and Plagiarism," paper presented to the American Studies Association, Costa Mesa, Ca., 7 November 1992, and *Declaring Independence: Jefferson, Natural Language, and the Culture of Performance* (Stanford, Calif.: Stanford University Press, 1993), 3.

14. William Howard Adams, *The Paris Years of Thomas Jefferson* (New Haven, Conn.: Yale University Press, 1997), 126. Jefferson appropriated the *Encyclopaedia*, supposedly for safe keeping during the war, but he was reluctant subsequently to return it to public ownership.

15. Durand Echeverria, *Mirage in the West: A History of the French Image of American Society to 1815* (Princeton, N.J.: Princeton University Press, 1957), 51; Willard Sterne Randall, *Thomas Jefferson: A Life* (1993; rpt. New York: HarperCollins, 1994), 389; Alan Charles Kors, *D'Holbach's Coterie: An Enlightenment in Paris* (Princeton, N.J.: Princeton University Press, 1976), 199, x. On Jefferson's friendships with French intellectuals, see Adams, *Paris Years*, 7, 33.

16. Translated as "the Holbach clique" in Rousseau, *Confessions*, 465.

17. Margaret C. Jacob, *The Radical Enlightenment: Pantheists, Freemasons and Republicans* (London: Allen and Unwin, 1981), 262. See also Norman Hampson, *The Enlightenment* (Harmondsworth: Penguin, 1968), 188.

18. Mark Hulliung, *The Autocritique of Enlightenment: Rousseau and the Philosophes* (Cambridge, Mass.: Harvard University Press, 1994), 26, 20.

19. Darnton, *Forbidden Best-Sellers*, 87–88.

20. Ellis, *American Sphinx*, 100; Adams, *Paris Years*, 296; Darnton, *Forbidden Best-Sellers*, 110–11.

21. Kors, *D'Holbach's Coterie*, 322, 324.

22. Adams, *Paris Years*, 124.

23. Hulliung, *The Autocritique of Enlightenment*, 157.

24. Perry Miller, *The New England Mind: The Seventeenth Century* (New York: Macmillan, 1939); Alan E. Heimert, *Religion and the American Mind, from the Great Awakening to the Revolution* (Cambridge, Mass.: Harvard University Press, 1966).

25. Oscar Kenshur, *Dilemmas of Enlightenment: Studies in the Rhetoric and Logic of Ideology* (Berkeley: University of California Press, 1993), 136; Adams, *Paris Years*, 155. A similar combination of private atheism and public sacerdotalism among political leaders is described by Gibbon in *Decline and Fall of the Roman Empire*.

26. Hulliung, *The Autocritique of Enlightenment*, 93.

27. Henry Steele Commager, *Jefferson, Nationalism, and the Enlightenment* (New York: George Braziller, 1975), 53; Echeverria, *Mirage in the West*, 272, 278. For a discussion of how Jefferson's "polygenetic" theory of evolution, as expounded in *Notes on the State of Virginia*, was "closely associated with atheism" in the intellectual climate of the 1780s, see Alexander O. Boulton, "The American Paradox: Jeffersonian Equality and Racial Science," *American Quarterly* 47 (1995): 480.

28. Gordon Wood, *The Creation of the American Republic, 1776–1787* (New York: Norton, 1969), 47–48.

29. Bruce Burgett, *Sentimental Bodies: Sex, Gender, and Citizenship in the Early Republic* (Princeton, N.J.: Princeton University Press, 1998), 128.

30. Peterson, *Jefferson Image in the American Mind*, 115–22.

31. For Jefferson's theatrical expertise, see Fliegelman, *Declaring Independence*, passim.

32. Wood, *Radicalism of the American Revolution*, 288. On Jefferson's admiration for Cicero, see Saul K. Padover, *A Jefferson Profile* (New York: John Day, 1956), 309–10.

33. Adams, *Paris Years*, 179.

34. Letter to Peter Carr, 10 August 1787, in *Writings*, 902.

35. Hart, *The Popular Book*, 60.

36. Andrew Burstein and Catherine Mowbray, "Jefferson and Sterne," *Early American Literature* 29 (1994): 19.

37. William Hill Brown, *The Power of Sympathy*, ed. Carla Mulford (Harmondsworth: Penguin, 1996), 28.

38. Alan B. Howes, ed., *Sterne: The Critical Heritage* (London: Routledge and Kegan Paul, 1974), 324–25; Brown, "Richardson and Sterne in the *Massachusetts Magazine*," 81.

39. Howes, ed., *Sterne: The Critical Heritage*, 310; Mullan, *Sentiment and Sociability*, 158.

40. Howes, ed., *Sterne: The Critical Heritage*, 18, 138; Mullan, *Sentiment and Sociability*, 172.

41. Howes, ed., *Sterne: The Critical Heritage*, 229.

42. Todd, *Sensibility*, 6, 100; Adams, *Paris Years*, 181.

43. Laurence Sterne, *The Sermons of Mr. Yorick*, ed. Marjorie David (Cheadle: Carcanet, 1973), 32. See also Burstein and Mowbray, "Jefferson and Sterne," 22.

44. Hannah Arendt, *On Revolution* (London: Faber, 1963), 123–27.

45. Pauline Maier, *American Scripture: Making the Declaration of Independence* (New York: Knopf, 1997), 134.

46. Garry Wills, *Inventing America: Jefferson's Declaration of Independence* (Garden City, N.Y.: Doubleday, 1978), 273–81.

47. Laurence Sterne, *The Life and Opinions of Tristram Shandy, Gentleman*, ed. Graham Petrie (Harmondsworth: Penguin, 1967), 96–97.

48. Sterne, *Tristram Shandy*, 95.

49. Jonathan Lamb, *Sterne's Fiction and the Double Principle* (Cambridge: Cambridge University Press, 1989), 120, 113.

50. James Rodgers, "Sensibility, Sympathy, Benevolence: Physiology and Moral Philosophy in *Tristram Shandy*," in *Languages of Nature: Critical Essays on Science and Literature*, ed. L. J. Jordanova (London: Free Association Books, 1986), 117–58.

51. For another indication of how Sterne's novel entered into American public discourse of this era, compare the provocative suggestion that the framers of the American Constitution produced a "novel text" which resembles *Tristram Shandy* in the way it "leaves room for amendment, revision, and reconstruction by its readers," see Thomas Gustafson, *Representative Words: Politics, Literature, and the American Language, 1776–1865* (Cambridge: Cambridge University Press, 1992), 286.

52. Sidney K. Robinson, *Inquiry into the Picturesque* (Chicago: University of Chicago Press, 1991), 93–94, 124. For Jefferson's knowledge of the picturesque, see Lawson-Peebles, *Landscape and Written Expression in Revolutionary America*, 178.

53. Susan Manning, "Naming of Parts; or, The Comforts of Classification: Thomas Jefferson's Construction of America as Fact and Myth," *Journal of American Studies* 30 (1996): 351.

54. Adams, *Paris Years*, 236.

55. Annette Gordon-Reed, *Thomas Jefferson and Sally Hemings: An American Controversy* (Charlottesville: University Press of Virginia, 1997), 157. According to Gordon-Reed: "The evidence of access at the relevant time period . . . is 100 percent with respect to Jefferson. He was there when the event (conception) occurred, and when he was not there, the event did not occur" (101–2). Other evidence for this relationship includes the physical resemblance of Hemings's children to Jefferson, his preferential treatment of them, and the folk memory handed down through the Hemings family. DNA testing in 1998 makes it appear very likely that Jefferson was the biological father of Eston Hemings, Sally's youngest son.

56. Fliegelman, *Prodigals and Pilgrims*, 63, 182.

57. Gilbert Chinard, *Thomas Jefferson: The Apostle of Americanism*, 2nd ed. (1939; rpt. Ann Arbor: University of Michigan Press, 1957), 212; George Green Shackleford, *Thomas Jefferson's Travels in Europe, 1784–1789* (Baltimore: Johns Hopkins University Press, 1995), 2.

58. Edward Gibbon, *The Decline and Fall of the Roman Empire*, ed. Oliphant Smeaton (London: Dent, 1910), 1:77.

59. Robert A. Ferguson, " 'What Is Enlightenment?': Some American Answers," *American Literary History* 1 (1989): 262.

60. Robert Ferguson, "The American Enlightenment, 1750–1820," in *The Cambridge History of American Literature*, ed. Bercovitch, 1:405.

61. Edmund Burke, *Reflections on the Revolution in France*, ed. Conor Cruise O'Brien (Harmondsworth: Penguin, 1968), 152, 90.

62. Thomas Paine, *Rights of Man*, ed. Henry Collins (Harmondsworth: Penguin, 1969), 62, 71, 96.

63. Paine, *Rights of Man*, 76, 71, 68, 161.

64. Edmund Burke, "Speech on Moving His Resolutions for Conciliation with the Colonies," 22 March 1775, in *Edmund Burke: Selected Writings and Speeches*, ed. Peter J. Stanlis (1963; rpt. Gloucester, Mass.: Peter Smith, 1968), 158.

65. Tom Furniss, *Edmund Burke's Aesthetic Ideology: Language, Gender, and Political Economy in Revolution* (Cambridge: Cambridge University Press, 1993), 109–10.

66. David Musselwhite, "Reflections on Burke's *Reflections*, 1790–1990," in *The Enlightenment and Its Shadows*, ed. Peter Hulme and Ludmilla Jordanova (London: Routledge, 1990), 142; Furniss, *Burke's Aesthetic Ideology*, 186.

67. Burke, "Speech on Moving His Resolutions for Conciliation with the Colonies," *Selected Writings*, 159.

68. Burke, *Reflections*, 315.

69. Wills, *Inventing America*, 270.

70. Edmund Burke, *A Philosophical Enquiry into the Origin of Our Ideas of the Sublime and Beautiful*, ed. James T. Boulton (London: Routledge and Kegan Paul, 1958), 45.

71. Burke, *A Philosophical Enquiry*, 159.

72. Burke, *Reflections*, 151, 123.

73. Burke, "Speech on Moving His Resolutions for Conciliation with the Colonies," *Selected Writings*, 184, 167.

74. Paine, *Rights of Man*, 62.

75. Isaac Kramnick, *The Rage of Edmund Burke: Portrait of an Ambivalent Conservative* (New York: Basic Books, 1977), 176, 155.

76. Conor Cruise O'Brien, *The Long Affair: Thomas Jefferson and the French Revolution, 1785–1800* (London: Sinclair-Stevenson, 1996), 148, 116.

77. L. J. Jordanova, Introduction, *Languages of Nature*, 39.

78. Adams, *Paris Years*, 77; L. J. Jordanova, "Naturalizing the Family: Literature and the Bio-Medical Sciences in the Late Eighteenth Century," in *Languages of Nature*, 98–99; Adrienne Koch, *The Philosophy of Thomas Jefferson* (1943; rpt. Chicago: Quadrangle, 1964), 56. For a discussion of the links between sensibility and materialism, see G. J. Barker-Benfield, *The Culture of Sensibility: Sex and Society in Eighteenth-Century Britain* (Chicago: University of Chicago Press, 1992), 1–36.

79. Maier, *American Scripture*, 209–15.

80. *The Adams-Jefferson Letters*, ed. Cappon, 349.

81. See, for instance, various contributions to the "Forum: How Revolutionary was the Revolution? A Discussion of Gordon S. Wood's *The Radicalism of the American Revolution*," especially Barbara Clark Smith, "The Adequate Revolution," and Michael Zuckerman, "Rhetoric, Reality, and the Revolution: The Genteel Radicalism of Gordon Wood," *William and Mary Quarterly* 3rd ser. 51 (1994): 684–702.

82. Durand Echeverria, trans., "Condorcet's *The Influence of the American Revolution on Europe*," *William and Mary Quarterly* 3rd ser. 25 (1968): 92, 101.

83. William Cohen, "Thomas Jefferson and the Problem of Slavery," *Journal of American History* 56 (1969): 503. For a recent analysis of class issues underpinning the institutionalization of racism in Jefferson's Virginia, see Theodore W. Allen, *The Invention of the White Race*, vol. 2, *The Origin of Racial Oppression in Anglo-America* (London: Verso, 1997), 247.

84. Ellis, *The Politics of Sensibility*, 12, 3, 43; Mullan, *Sentiment and Sociability*, 246.

85. Vincent Carretta, ed., *Letters of the Late Ignatius Sancho, an African* (Harmondsworth: Penguin, 1998), 334.

86. Ellis, *The Politics of Sensibility*, 79. For a similar view of how Sterne's "theatrics of bourgeois virtue" signify an implicit conservatism, see Robert Markley, "Sentimentality as Performance: Shaftesbury, Sterne, and the Theatrics of Virtue," in *The New Eighteenth Century*, ed. Nussbaum and Brown, 223.

87. Sterne, *Tristram Shandy*, 578.

88. Julie Ellison, *Cato's Tears and the Making of Anglo-American Emotion* (Chicago: University of Chicago Press, 1999), 98, 123.

89. Winthrop D. Jordan, *White over Black: American Attitudes Toward the Negro, 1550–1812* (Chapel Hill: University of North Carolina Press for the Institute of Early American History and Culture, 1968), 477.

90. Ellis, *The Politics of Sensibility*, 86–87.

91. Ellis, *American Sphinx*, 329, 269.

92. John P. Diggins, "Slavery, Race, and Equality: Jefferson and the Pathos of the Enlightenment," *American Quarterly* 28 (1976): 212, 217.

93. David Morris, *The Culture of Pain* (Berkeley: University of California Press, 1991), 225; Philippe Sollers, *Writing and the Experience of Limits*, ed. David Hayman, trans. Philip Barnard and David Hayman (New York: Columbia University Press, 1983), 191–92.

94. On Sade and d'Holbach, see Jean Leduc, "Les Sources de l'athéisme et de l'immoralisme du marquis de Sade," *Studies on Voltaire and the Eighteenth Century* 68 (1969): 11–19.

95. Malcolm Kelsall, *Jefferson and the Iconography of Romanticism: Folk, Land, Culture and the Romantic Nation* (Basingstoke: Macmillan, 1999).

Chapter Five. *"Another World Must Be Unfurled": Jane Austen and America*

1. David Simpson, *Romanticism, Nationalism, and the Revolt Against Theory* (Chicago: University of Chicago Press, 1993), 57–63.

2. Linda Colley, *Britons: Forging the Nation, 1707–1837* (New Haven, Conn.: Yale University Press, 1992), 137; Marilyn Butler, *Romantics, Rebels and Revolutionaries: English Literature and its Background, 1760–1830* (Oxford: Oxford University Press, 1981), 31.

3. E. P. Thompson, *The Making of the English Working Class*, rev. ed. (Harmondsworth: Penguin, 1968), 144–45, 197.

4. Isaac Kramnick, *Republicanism and Bourgeois Radicalism: Political Ideology in Late Eighteenth-Century England and America* (Ithaca, N.Y.: Cornell University Press, 1990), 66.

5. Colin Bonwick, *English Radicals and the American Revolution* (Chapel Hill: University of North Carolina Press, 1977), 248, 135.

6. James Chandler, *England in 1819: The Politics of Literary Culture and the Case of Romantic Historicism* (Chicago: University of Chicago Press, 1998), 441–80.

7. John Keane, *Tom Paine: A Political Life* (London: Bloomsbury, 1995), xiii. On support for America within Britain from public figures like Richard Price and Thomas Pownall, see Jack P. Greene, *The Intellectual Construction of America: Exceptionalism and Identity from 1492 to 1800* (Chapel Hill: University of North Carolina Press, 1993), 138–39.

8. Gilbert Imlay, *The Emigrants*, ed. W. M. Verhoeven and Amanda Gilroy (New York: Penguin, 1998), 2–3. Despite its appearance in England in 1793 and Ireland in 1794, *The Emigrants* was not published in America until 1964. For an attribution of this exclusion to the novel's "radical ideology," see John Seelye, "The Jacobin Mode in Early American Fiction: Gilbert Imlay's *The Emigrants*," *Early American Literature* 22 (1987): 204–5.

9. Imlay, *The Emigrants*, 79, 108.

10. Patrick C. T. White, *A Nation on Trial: America and the War of 1812* (New York: John

Wiley, 1965), 2–3. On different political interpretations of the "natural," see Claudia L. Johnson, *Equivocal Beings: Politics, Gender, and Sentimentality in the 1790s: Wollstonecraft, Radcliffe, Burney, Austen* (Chicago: University of Chicago Press, 1995), 6.

11. Michael T. Gilmore, "The Literature of the Revolutionary and Early National Periods," in *The Cambridge History of American Literature*, vol. 1, *1590–1820*, ed. Sacvan Bercovitch (Cambridge: Cambridge University Press, 1994), 681.

12. William Cobbett, "The Life and Adventures of Peter Porcupine" (1796), in *Peter Porcupine in America: Pamphlets on Republicanism and Revolution*, ed. David A. Wilson (Ithaca, N.Y.: Cornell University Press, 1994), 171.

13. In 1795, for example, Cobbett wrote a savage critical essay on Susanna Rowson's play, *Slaves in Algiers; or, a Struggle for Freedom*. "A Kick for a Bite," in *Peter Porcupine in America*, 121–36.

14. David A. Wilson, *Paine and Cobbett: The Transatlantic Connection* (Kingston, Ont. and Montreal: McGill-Queen's University Press, 1988), 124.

15. "His principle is repulsion, his nature contradiction. . . . When he is in England, he does nothing but abuse the Boroughmongers, and laugh at the whole system; when he is in America, he grows impatient of freedom and a republic." William Hazlitt, "Mr. Cobbett," in *The Spirit of the Age; or, Contemporary Portraits* (1825; rpt. London: Grant Richards, 1904), 229.

16. Durey, *Transatlantic Radicals and the Early American Republic*, 12–13.

17. William Cobbett, *A Year's Residence in the United States of America* (1819; rpt. Fontwell, Sussex: Centaur Press, 1964), 180.

18. Cobbett, *A Year's Residence*, 18.

19. William Cobbett, *Rural Rides*, ed. George Woodcock (Harmondsworth: Penguin, 1967), 209, 374.

20. Martin Kallich, *British Poetry and the American Revolution: A Bibliographical Survey of Books and Pamphlets, Journals and Magazines, Newspapers and Prints, 1755–1800* (Troy, N.Y.: Whitston, 1988), 1:677. Kallich estimates that approximately 5,600 poems related to the American Revolution were published in Britain between 1755 and 1800, though of course hardly any of these feature in received accounts of "English Literature" (1:xii).

21. William Blake, *The Complete Poems*, ed. Alicia Ostriker (Harmondsworth: Penguin, 1977), 221, 217, 213.

22. Lord Byron, *Don Juan*, ed. T. G. Steffan, E. Steffan, and W. W. Pratt (Harmondsworth: Penguin, 1982), 496, 189.

23. J. G. A. Pocock, "Enlightenment and Revolution: The Case of English-Speaking North America," *Studies on Voltaire and the Eighteenth Century* 263 (1989): 251–52.

24. Simpson, *Romanticism, Nationalism, and the Revolt Against Theory*, 64. For a discussion of how these French wars served the useful purpose for the British government of consolidating a national identity recently threatened by its encounter with America, see J. C. D. Clark, *The Language of Liberty: Political Discourse and Social Dynamics in the Anglo-American World* (Cambridge: Cambridge University Press, 1994), 386.

25. Jonathan Dollimore, *Sexual Dissidence: Augustine to Wilde, Freud to Foucault* (Oxford: Oxford University Press, 1991), 121.

26. On the disruptive influence of America in Europe, see Echeverria, *Mirage in the West*, 63, 156.

27. Edmund Burke, "Letter to the Sheriffs of the City of Bristol on the Affairs of America, 1777," in *Selected Writings and Speeches*, 193.

28. Kallich, *British Poetry and the American Revolution*, 1:xxxi. Pye's diatribe comes from his "Carmen Seculare for the Year 1800."

29. Colley, *Britons*, 143–45.

30. See, for instance, Richard Buel, *Securing the Revolution: Ideology in American Politics, 1789–1815* (Ithaca, N.Y.: Cornell University Press, 1972), 1–49.

31. Karl Marx, *Political Writings*, vol. 2, *Surveys from Exile*, ed. David Fernbach (New York: Random House, 1973), 146–47.

32. Philippe Roger, "A Political Minimalist," in *Sade and the Narrative of Transgression*, ed. David B. Allison, Mark S. Roberts, and Allen S. Weiss (Cambridge: Cambridge University Press, 1995), 91.

33. Michael Kammen, *A Season of Youth: The American Revolution and the Historical Imagination* (New York: Knopf, 1978), 212; Spencer, *The Quest for Nationality*, 124.

34. Cathy N. Davidson, *Revolution and the Word: The Rise of the Novel in America* (New York: Oxford University Press, 1992), 61.

35. Deirdre Lynch, "At Home with Jane Austen," in *Cultural Institutions of the Novel*, ed. Deirdre Lynch and William B. Warner (Durham, N.C.: Duke University Press, 1996), 160.

36. Susan Fraiman, "Jane Austen and Edward Said: Gender, Culture, and Imperialism," *Critical Inquiry* 21 (1995): 807.

37. Marilyn Butler, *Jane Austen and the War of Ideas* (Oxford: Oxford University Press, 1975); Raymond Williams, *The Country and the City* (London: Hogarth Press, 1985), 112–19.

38. Terry Castle, "Sister-Sister," *London Review of Books*, 3 August 1995, 6, and letter, *London Review of Books*, 24 August 1995, 4.

39. Claudia Johnson, letter, *London Review of Books*, 5 October 1995, 4. Johnson develops her argument further in "The Divine Miss Jane: Jane Austen, Janeites, and the Discipline of Novel Studies," *boundary 2* 23, 3 (1996): 143–63.

40. Sandra M. Gilbert and Susan Gubar, *The Madwoman in the Attic: The Woman Writer and the Nineteenth-Century Literary Imagination* (New Haven, Conn.: Yale University Press, 1979), 112, 183.

41. Gilbert and Gubar, *The Madwoman in the Attic*, 161.

42. Mary Poovey, *The Proper Lady and the Woman Writer: Ideology as Style in the Works of Mary Wollstonecraft, Mary Shelley, and Jane Austen* (Chicago: University of Chicago Press, 1984), 172, 44, 182.

43. D. A. Miller, *Narrative and Its Discontents: Problems of Closure in the Traditional Novel* (Princeton, N.J.: Princeton University Press, 1981), 50, 66.

44. Eve Kosofsky Sedgwick, "Jane Austen and the Masturbating Girl," *Critical Inquiry* 17 (1991): 833, 821–22.

45. Joseph Litvak, *Strange Gourmets: Sophistication, Theory, and the Novel* (Durham, N.C.: Duke University Press, 1997), 16, 31, 24.

46. Gilbert and Gubar, *The Madwoman in the Attic*, 183. For a characteristically conservative English reading, see David Cecil, *A Portrait of Jane Austen* (London: Constable, 1978).

47. Tony Tanner, *Jane Austen* (Cambridge, Mass.: Harvard University Press, 1986), 9; Henry James, "The Lesson of Balzac" (1905), in *The House of Fiction: Essays on the Novel*, ed. Leon Edel (London: Rupert Hart-Davis, 1957), 62–63.

48. John Bayley, "The 'Irresponsibility' of Jane Austen," in *Critical Essays on Jane Austen*, ed. B. C. Southam (London: Routledge and Kegan Paul), 8–9.

49. Lionel Trilling, "*Emma* and the Legend of Jane Austen," in *Jane Austen: Emma. A Casebook*, ed. David Lodge (London: Macmillan, 1968), 155; Bayley, "The 'Irresponsibility' of Jane Austen," 9.

50. Miller, *Narrative and Its Discontents*, 66, 76.

51. Jane Austen, *Mansfield Park*, ed. Tony Tanner (Harmondsworth: Penguin, 1966), 91. Subsequent page references to this edition are given in the text.

52. Park Honan, "Jane Austen and the American Revolution," *University of Leeds Review* 28 (1985–86): 188.

53. Jane Austen, *Catharine and Other Writings*, ed. Margaret Anne Doody and Douglas Murray (Oxford: Oxford University Press, 1993), 149.

54. Honan, "Jane Austen and the American Revolution," 183; Edward Said, *Culture and Imperialism* (New York: Knopf, 1993), 80–97.

55. Moira Ferguson, "*Mansfield Park*: Slavery, Colonialism, and Gender," *Oxford Literary Review* 13 (1991): 129. See also Fraiman, "Jane Austen and Edward Said," 812–13. On the "growing visibility of the navy in *Mansfield Park*" and ways in which this "supplements the increasing presence of empire at the edges of Austen's texts," see Suvendrini Perera, *Reaches of Empire: The English Novel from Edgeworth to Dickens* (New York: Columbia University Press, 1991), 43.

56. The most convincing version of *Mansfield Park*'s chronology, taking account of various books mentioned in Austen's narrative, suggests the novel's plot runs from 1810 to 1813. Brian Southam, "The Silence of the Bertrams: Slavery and the Chronology of *Mansfield Park*," *Times Literary Supplement*, 17 February 1995, 13–14.

57. Katie Trumpener, *Bardic Nationalism: The Romantic Novel and the British Empire* (Princeton, N.J.: Princeton University Press, 1997), 174–83. Trumpener argues that Austen, under the influence of Clarkson and others, is concerned deliberately to interrogate "the indirect effects of slavery and the long reach of the plantation system into the heart of England" (175).

58. R. W. Chapman, ed., *Jane Austen's Letters*, 2nd ed. (Oxford: Oxford University Press, 1952), 133; Godwin, *Caleb Williams*, 318.

59. Jane Austen, *Emma*, ed. Ronald Blythe (Harmondsworth: Penguin, 1966), 300. Subsequent page references to this edition are given in the text.

60. Austen, *Catharine and Other Writings*, pp. 244–45. Austen was "an inveterate reader of travel writings," according to Susan Reilly, "'A Nobler Fall of Ground': Nation and Narration in *Pride and Prejudice*," *Symbiosis* 4 (2000): 22. Reilly is one of the few critics

specifically to link Austen's work with "the influence of America and the American Revolution" (28), though she sees this American world as something that the author, in typically conservative fashion, seeks simply to resist.

61. Hunt, "Pornography and the French Revolution," 325; Fliegelman, *Declaring Independence*, 79–94. See also the valuable discussion in Lionel Trilling, *Sincerity and Authenticity* (Cambridge, Mass.: Harvard University Press, 1972), 69. For an analysis of how the "stresses and strains" of the French Revolution work their way into Austen's novels, see Warren Roberts, *Jane Austen and the French Revolution* (New York: St. Martin's Press, 1979), 4.

62. Homi K. Bhabha, *The Location of Culture* (London: Routledge, 1994), 90.

63. Colley, *Britons*, 148.

64. Joseph Litvak, "The Infection of Acting: Theatricals and Theatricality in *Mansfield Park*," *ELH* 53 (1986): 343. See also Joseph Litvak, *Caught in the Act: Theatricality in the Nineteenth-Century English Novel* (Berkeley: University of California Press, 1992), 1–26.

65. Claudia L. Johnson, *Jane Austen: Women, Politics, and the Novel* (Chicago: University of Chicago Press, 1988), 96.

66. Butler, *Jane Austen and the War of Ideas*, 7, 209–10.

67. Pierre Klossowski, *Sade My Neighbor*, trans. Alphonso Lingis (Evanston, Ill.: Northwestern University Press, 1991), 54.

68. Paul Giles, "Gothic Paradoxes in *Pride and Prejudice*," *Text and Context* 2, 1 (1988): 68–75. For the author's description of *Pride and Prejudice*, see Austen, *Letters*, 299.

69. On this point, see the discussion by Joseph Litvak, "Reading Characters: Self, Society, and Text in *Emma*," *PMLA* 100 (1985): 771.

70. Trilling, *Sincerity and Authenticity*, 82.

71. Miller, *Narrative and Its Discontents*, 50.

72. W. J. Harvey, "The Plot of *Emma*," *Essays in Criticism* 17 (1967): 55.

73. Harvey, "The Plot of *Emma*," 57, 52.

74. Sedgwick, "Jane Austen and the Masturbating Girl," 833, 834. For a description of Sedgwick's critique as "required reading for everyone interested in writing and reading about Austen," see Johnson, *Equivocal Beings*, 231.

75. On the association of writing with unruly desire in *Emma*, see Nancy Armstrong, *Desire and Domestic Fiction: A Political History of the Novel* (New York: Oxford University Press, 1987), 145.

76. Nicola J. Watson, *Revolution and the Form of the British Novel, 1790–1825: Intercepted Letters, Interrupted Seductions* (Oxford: Clarendon Press, 1994), 97, 102.

77. Thomas Keenan, "Freedom, the Law of another Fable," *Yale French Studies* 79 (1991): 235. For a commentary on "the remarkable parallels between Sade and Austen," particularly in their proclivity for exposing closely guarded secrets and brutally unmasking the illusions of sentimental consciousness, see John A. Dussinger, "Madness and Lust in the Age of Sensibility," in *Sensibility in Transformation: Creative Resistance to Sentiment from the Augustans to the Romantics*, ed. Syndy McMillen Conger (Rutherford, N.J.: Fairleigh Dickinson University Press, 1990), 97–99, 101.

78. R. F. Brissenden, *Virtue in Distress: Studies in the Novel of Sentiment from Richardson to Sade* (New York: Barnes and Noble—Harper and Row, 1974), 273–94.

79. Austen, *Catharine and Other Writings*, 36.

80. Claudia L. Johnson, "'The Kingdom at Sixes and Sevens': Politics and the Juvenilia," in *Jane Austen's Beginnings: The Juvenilia and Lady Susan*, ed. J. David Grey (Ann Arbor, Mich.: UMI Research Press, 1989), 47–48.

81. Austen, *Catharine and Other Writings*, 36.

82. Austen, *Catharine and Other Writings*, 134.

83. Christopher Kent, "Learning History with, and from, Jane Austen," in *Jane Austen's Beginnings*, ed. Grey, 66.

84. Ellen E. Martin, "The Madness of Jane Austen: Metonymic Style and Literature's Resistance to Interpretation," in *Jane Austen's Beginnings*, ed. Grey, 85; Roger, "A Political Minimalist," in *Sade and the Narrative of Transgression*, ed. Allison et al., 91.

85. Brigid Brophy, "Jane Austen and the Stuarts," in *Critical Essays on Jane Austen*, ed. Southam, 21–38.

Chapter Six. *Burlesques of Civility: Washington Irving*

1. Lewis Leary, "Washington Irving and the Comic Imagination" (1973), rpt. in *Critical Essays on Washington Irving*, ed. Ralph M. Aderman (Boston: Hall, 1990), 199; Joy S. Kasson, *Artistic Voyagers: Europe and the American Imagination in the Works of Irving, Allston, Cole, Cooper, and Hawthorne* (Westport, Conn.: Greenwood Press, 1982), 39.

2. Bhabha, *The Location of Culture*, 143.

3. Jane D. Eberwein, "Transatlantic Contrasts in Irving's *Sketch Book*," *College Literature* 15 (1988): 155, 157.

4. Washington Irving, *History, Tales, and Sketches* (New York: Library of America, 1983), 1049–50. Subsequent page references to this edition are given in the text.

5. Donald A. Ringe, *American Gothic: Imagination and Reason in Nineteenth-Century Fiction* (Lexington: University Press of Kentucky, 1982), 100. For Hawthorne's nineteenth-century reputation as a sentimental novelist, see Jane Tompkins, *Sentimental Designs: The Cultural Work of American Fiction, 1790–1860* (New York: Oxford University Press, 1985), 3–39.

6. Terry Castle, "The Carnivalization of Eighteenth-Century English Narrative," *PMLA* 99 (1984): 908.

7. Martin Roth, *Comedy and America: The Lost World of Washington Irving* (Port Washington, N.Y.: Kennikat Press, 1976), 6.

8. Roth, *Comedy and America*, 88, 93.

9. Robert C. Allen, *Horrible Prettiness: Burlesque and American Culture* (Chapel Hill: University of North Carolina Press, 1991), 52, 25.

10. Donald E. Pease, *Visionary Compacts: American Renaissance Writings in Cultural Context* (Madison: University of Wisconsin Press, 1987), 14–16. On Irving's cultural

insecurity, see also Laura J. Murray, "The Aesthetic of Dispossession: Washington Irving and Ideologies of (De)Colonization in the Early Republic," *American Literary History* 8 (1996): 209.

11. Washington Irving, *Bracebridge Hall, Tales of a Traveller, The Alhambra* (New York: Library of America, 1991), 19.

12. On the significance of the journey as a metaphor for "provincial" American writers, see Susan Manning, *The Puritan-Provincial Vision: Scottish and American Literature in the Nineteenth Century* (Cambridge: Cambridge University Press, 1990), 70.

13. Lilian R. Furst, *Fictions of Romantic Irony in European Narrative, 1760–1857* (London: Macmillan, 1984), 24.

14. René Wellek, *Confrontations: Studies in the Intellectual and Literary Relations Between Germany, England, and the United States During the Nineteenth Century* (Princeton, N.J.: Princeton University Press, 1965), 22–23.

15. Oliver Goldsmith, *Poems and Plays*, ed. Tom Davis (London: Dent, 1975), 189–90.

16. Goldsmith, *Poems and Plays*, 165, 168, 171, 172.

17. Elsie Lee West, Introduction to Washington Irving, *Oliver Goldsmith: A Biography, and Biography of the Late Margaret Miller Davidson*, ed. Elsie Lee West (Boston: Twayne, 1978), xv.

18. Quoted in West, Introduction to *Oliver Goldsmith: A Biography*, xxii. This comes from an essay that Irving wrote in 1825 as the preface to a collection of Goldsmith's works.

19. J. C. Friedrich Schiller, *On the Naive and Sentimental in Literature*, trans. Helen Watanabe-O'Kelly (Manchester: Carcanet New Press, 1981), 28, 34–35.

20. Murray, "The Aesthetic of Dispossession," 219.

21. Irving revised *A History of New York* many times, but I follow James W. Tuttleton in preferring the first edition of 1809, written at a time when Irving was not so renowned and, therefore, not so concerned about giving offense. See the Library of America edition of Irving's *History, Tales, and Sketches*, 1123–24.

22. Ferguson, *Law and Letters in American Culture*, 158.

23. Leary, "Washington Irving and the Comic Imagination," 196.

24. Roth, *Comedy and America*, 143; Watts, *Writing and Postcolonialism in the Early Republic*, 149.

25. Pease, *Visionary Compacts*, 18.

26. Looby, *Voicing America*, 5.

27. For a discussion of this point, see Rice, *The Transformation of Authorship in America*, 72.

28. Klossowski, *Sade My Neighbor*, 52.

29. Chasseguet-Smirgel, *Creativity and Perversion*, 11, 155.

30. Chasseguet-Smirgel, *Creativity and Perversion*, 34.

31. Chasseguet-Smirgel, *Creativity and Perversion*, 95.

32. Edward F. Pajak, "Washington Irving's Ichabod Crane: American Narcissus," *American Imago* 38, 1 (1981): 127–34. There are many treatments of Irving's texts along similar psychoanalytical lines.

33. Gilles Deleuze, "Coldness and Cruelty" (1967), in *Masochism*, trans. Jean McNeil (1971; rpt. New York: Zone Books, 1989), 25.

34. Ann Douglas, *The Feminization of American Culture* (New York: Knopf, 1977), 213, 234.

35. On the regional conflict in "The Legend of Sleepy Hollow," see Donald Ringe, "New York and New England: Irving's Criticism of American Society," *American Literature* 38 (1967): 455–67.

36. Deleuze, "Coldness and Cruelty," 69–70, 133.

37. Roth, *Comedy and America*, 163.

38. Albert J. von Frank, "The Man That Corrupted Sleepy Hollow," *Studies in American Fiction* 15 (1987): 138, 140.

39. Irving, *Bracebridge Hall*, 228–29.

40. Irving, *Bracebridge Hall*, 16.

41. Bloom, *The Anxiety of Influence*, 5.

42. Roth, *Comedy and America*, 12.

43. Bhabha, *The Location of Culture*, 93, 86. On *The Sketch Book* as "a postcolonial text," see Richard V. McLamore, "The Dutchman in the Attic: Claiming an Inheritance in *The Sketch Book of Geoffrey Crayon*," *American Literature* 72 (2000): 31–57.

Chapter Seven. Perverse Reflections: Hawthorne and Trollope

1. Matthiessen, *American Renaissance*, 179–368; Sacvan Bercovitch, *The Rites of Assent: Transformations in the Symbolic Construction of America* (New York: Routledge, 1993), 194–245; Lauren Berlant, *The Anatomy of National Fantasy: Hawthorne, Utopia, and Everyday Life* (Chicago: University of Chicago Press, 1991), 5.

2. Raymond Williams, *The English Novel from Dickens to Lawrence* (London: Chatto and Windus, 1970), 84–86.

3. Kristeva, *Strangers to Ourselves*, 146–47.

4. Sara B. Blair, "Changing the Subject: Henry James, *Dred Scott*, and Fictions of Identity," *American Literary History* 4 (1992): 50, 47.

5. Nathaniel Hawthorne, *The Letters, 1857–1864*, ed. Thomas Woodson et al., *The Centenary Edition of the Works of Nathaniel Hawthorne*, vol. 18 (Columbus: Ohio State University Press, 1987), 229.

6. Anthony Trollope, *An Autobiography*, ed. Michael Sadleir and Frederick Page (Oxford: Oxford University Press, 1980), 144.

7. On Hawthorne's "envious admiration" of Trollope, see Richard H. Brodhead, *Hawthorne, Melville, and the Novel* (Chicago: University of Chicago Press, 1976), 41.

8. J. Donald Crowley, ed., *Hawthorne: The Critical Heritage* (New York: Barnes and Noble, 1970), 514–20.

9. On this theme, see Howard Horwitz, *By the Law of Nature: Form and Value in Nineteenth-Century America* (New York: Oxford University Press, 1991).

10. Ralph Waldo Emerson, *The Journals and Miscellaneous Notebooks*, 7, ed. A.W. Plumstead and Harrison Hayford (Cambridge, Mass.: Harvard University Press, 1969), 342.

11. Francis Parkman, Jr., *The Oregon Trail*, ed. David Levin (New York: Viking Penguin, 1982), 106, 46, 55.

12. Margaret Fuller, *Margaret Fuller: A Selection from Her Writings and Correspondence*, ed. Perry Miller (1963; rpt. Ithaca, N.Y.: Cornell University Press, 1970), 164, 157, 155.

13. Gauri Viswanathan, *Outside the Fold: Conversion, Modernity, and Belief* (Princeton, N.J.: Princeton University Press, 1998), 3, 16.

14. On this point, see R. Laurence Moore, *Religious Outsiders and the Making of Americans* (New York: Oxford University Press, 1986).

15. Nathaniel Hawthorne, *The Blithedale Romance and Fanshawe: The Centenary Edition of the Works of Nathaniel Hawthorne*, vol. 3 (Columbus: Ohio State University Press, 1964), 58, 143–44. Subsequent page references to this edition are given in the text.

16. Crowley, ed., *Hawthorne: The Critical Heritage*, 517.

17. Frederick C. Crews, *The Sins of the Fathers: Hawthorne's Psychological Themes* (New York: Oxford University Press, 1966), 204; Nina Baym, *The Shape of Hawthorne's Career* (Ithaca, N.Y.: Cornell University Press, 1976), 201.

18. Baym, *The Shape of Hawthorne's Career*, 201.

19. Henry James, *Hawthorne*, ed. Tony Tanner (London: Macmillan, 1967), 67–69.

20. Ralph Waldo Emerson, "Fate," in *Complete Works*, vol. 6, *The Conduct of Life* (London: George Routledge, 1903), 35.

21. Jenny Franchot, *Roads to Rome: The Antebellum Encounter with Catholicism* (Berkeley: University of California Press, 1994), 215; Oliver S. Buckton, "'An Unnatural State: Gender, 'Perversion,' and Newman's *Apologia pro Vita Sua*," *Victorian Studies* 35 (1992): 368–69.

22. Viswanathan, *Outside the Fold*, 48.

23. Robert S. Levine, *Conspiracy and Romance: Studies in Brockden Brown, Cooper, Hawthorne and Melville* (Cambridge: Cambridge University Press, 1989), 104–64.

24. Nathaniel Hawthorne, *The Marble Faun: or, The Romance of Monte Beni: The Centenary Edition of the Works of Nathaniel Hawthorne*, vol. 4 (Columbus: Ohio State University Press, 1968), 390, 396. Subsequent page references to this edition are given in the text.

25. Henry James, "Nathaniel Hawthorne" (1879), in *Henry James: The American Essays*, ed. Leon Edel, rev. ed. (Princeton, N.J.: Princeton University Press, 1989), 22–23. This essay, which first appeared in an anthology edited by Charles Dudley Warner, *Library of the World's Best Literature*, is distinct from James's book-length study of Hawthorne, which was also published in 1879.

26. Nathaniel Hawthorne, *Our Old Home, A Series of English Sketches: The Centenary Edition of the Works of Nathaniel Hawthorne*, vol. 5 (Columbus: Ohio State University Press, 1970), 24–25.

27. Hawthorne, *Our Old Home*, 4, 64.

28. Nathaniel Hawthorne, *The American Claimant Manuscripts: The Ancestral Footstep, Etherege, Grimshawe: The Centenary Edition of the Works of Nathaniel Hawthorne*, vol. 12, ed.

Edward H. Davidson, Claude M. Simpson, and L. Neal Smith (Columbus: Ohio State University Press, 1977), 193, 8, 476.

29. Nathaniel Hawthorne, *The English Notebooks, 1853–1856: The Centenary Edition of the Works of Nathaniel Hawthorne*, vol. 21, ed. Thomas Woodson and Bill Ellis (Columbus: Ohio State University Press, 1997), 117.

30. See Hawthorne's journal entry for 2 November 1854: "I do *hate* a naturalized citizen; nobody has a right to our ideas, unless born to them." *The English Notebooks*, 145.

31. Crews, *The Sins of the Fathers*, 250, 267.

32. Hawthorne, *Our Old Home*, 72.

33. J. Hillis Miller, *Hawthorne and History: Defacing It* (Cambridge, Mass.: Blackwell, 1991), 56, 147.

34. Nathaniel Hawthorne, *The Scarlet Letter: The Centenary Edition of the Works of Nathaniel Hawthorne*, vol. 1 (Columbus: Ohio State University Press, 1962), 154–55. Subsequent page references to this edition are given in the text.

35. For associations between *The Scarlet Letter* and "the Protestant sermon," see Stephen Railton, *Authorship and Audience: Literary Performance in the American Renaissance* (Princeton, N.J.: Princeton University Press, 1991), 107.

36. Franchot, *Roads to Rome*, 260–69.

37. Bercovitch, *The Puritan Origins of the American Self*, 14.

38. Dorena Allen Wright, "The Meeting at the Brook-Side: Beatrice, the Pearl-Maiden, and Pearl Prynne," *ESQ* 28 (1982): 112–20.

39. Pease, *Visionary Compacts*, 49, 53.

40. This theme of "crossover" in *The Scarlet Letter* is discussed by George Dekker, *The American Historical Romance* (Cambridge: Cambridge University Press, 1987), 129–85.

41. Pease, *Visionary Compacts*, 46. Significantly, Hawthorne responded to "the dread time of civil war" in America by comparing it to the English Civil War of the 1640s, "where the sovereignty and constitution of England were to be set at stake." In Hawthorne's eyes, it was the failure of America's transcendent political ideals that caused the republic to relapse into the old factional traumas of British history. Hawthorne, "Chiefly about War-matters. By a Peaceable Man," in *Miscellaneous Prose and Verse: The Centenary Edition of the Works of Nathaniel Hawthorne*, vol. 23, ed. Thomas Woodson, Claude M. Simpson, and L. Neal Smith (Columbus: Ohio State University Press, 1994), 404.

42. Baym, *The Shape of Hawthorne's Career*, 210.

43. Michael J. Colacurcio, "Footsteps of Ann Hutchinson: The Context of *The Scarlet Letter*," *ELH* 39 (1972): 484.

44. Deleuze, "Coldness and Cruelty," 69.

45. Berlant, *The Anatomy of National Fantasy*, 124.

46. Christopher Newfield, "The Politics of Male Suffering: Masochism and Hegemony in the American Renaissance," *differences* 1, 3 (Fall 1989): 78.

47. Emerson, *The Journals and Miscellaneous Notebooks*, 7:40.

48. Homi K. Bhabha, "A Question of Survival: Nations and Psychic States," in *Psychoanalysis and Cultural Theory: Thresholds*, ed. James Donald (Basingstoke: Macmillan,

1991), 92. This question is also addressed by Anne McClintock, *Imperial Leather: Race, Gender and Sexuality in the Colonial Contest* (New York: Routledge, 1995), 357.

49. Anthony Trollope, *The West Indies and the Spanish Main* (New York: Carroll and Graf, 1999), 72–73.

50. Anthony Trollope, *He Knew He Was Right*, ed. John Sutherland (Oxford: Oxford University Press, 1985), 364.

51. Anthony Trollope, *Can You Forgive Her?* (London: Oxford University Press, 1948), 2:355.

52. Trollope, *Can You Forgive Her?*, 2:409.

53. James R. Kincaid, *The Novels of Anthony Trollope* (Oxford: Clarendon Press, 1977), 126.

54. Anthony Trollope, *The Prime Minister* (Oxford: Oxford University Press, 1973), 1:145.

55. Anthony Trollope, *The Duke's Children*, ed. Hermione Lee (Oxford: Oxford University Press, 1983), 322.

56. Trollope, *The Duke's Children*, 390–91.

57. Kristeva, *Strangers to Ourselves*, 146–47.

58. Anthony Trollope, *The American Senator*, ed. John Halperin (Oxford: Oxford University Press, 1986), 531.

59. Anthony Trollope, *The Way We Live Now* (New York: Dover, 1982), 355, 401, 47.

60. Trollope, *The Way We Live Now*, 160.

61. Trollope, *Autobiography*, 144.

Conclusion. Transatlantic Perspectives: Poe and Equiano

1. Philip Fisher, "Introduction: The New American Studies," in *The New American Studies: Essays from Representations*, ed. Philip Fisher (Berkeley: University of California Press, 1991), xv.

2. Matthiessen, *American Renaissance*, 593, 3.

3. Jonathan Arac, *Critical Genealogies: Historical Situations for Postmodern Literary Studies* (New York: Columbia University Press, 1987), 165.

4. Eric J. Sundquist, *To Wake The Nations: Race in the Making of American Literature* (Cambridge, Mass.: Harvard University Press, 1993); Claudia Tate, "Reconstructing the Renaissance of U.S. Literature," *American Quarterly* 46 (1994): 594.

5. Eric Lott, "Nation Time," *American Literary History* 7 (1995): 556, 570.

6. Jane Tompkins, *Sensational Designs: The Cultural Work of American Fiction, 1790–1860* (New York: Oxford University Press, 1985), 147–85; David S. Reynolds, *Beneath the American Renaissance: The Subversive Imagination in the Age of Emerson and Melville* (New York: Knopf, 1988), 309–33.

7. Eric Cheyfitz, "What Work Is There for Us To Do? American Literary Studies or Americas Cultural Studies?," *American Literature* 67 (1995): 849.

8. Lott, "Nation Time," 569. For an analysis of how "the field-Imaginary of American Studies" inscribes a particular version of national consensus and ideological hegemony, see Pease, "New Americanists," 11.

9. Paul A. Bové, *In The Wake of Theory* (Hanover, N.H.: University Press of New England, 1992), 60, 63.

10. *The Portable Abraham Lincoln*, ed. Andrew Delbanco (New York: Viking Penguin, 1992), 295.

11. Matthiessen, *American Renaissance*, xii, 115

12. Edgar Allan Poe, *The Complete Poems and Tales* (New York: Modern Library, 1938), 631, 627. Subsequent page references to this edition are given in the text.

13. Edgar Allan Poe, *The Science Fiction of Edgar Allan Poe*, ed. Harold Beaver (Harmondsworth: Penguin, 1976), 229, 216–17.

14. Jonathan Elmer, *Reading at the Social Limit: Affect, Mass Culture, and Edgar Allan Poe* (Stanford, Calif.: Stanford University Press, 1995), 26.

15. On Lowell and anglophilia, see Vanderbilt, *American Literature and the Academy*, 74; Edgar Allan Poe, *Essays and Reviews* (New York: Library of America, 1984), 1027, 1375.

16. Michael Davitt Bell, "Conditions of Literary Vocation," in *The Cambridge History of American Literature*, vol. 2, *1820–1865*, ed. Sacvan Bercovitch (Cambridge: Cambridge University Press, 1995), 14. For a discussion of ways in which the cultural nationalists in the "Young America" movement tried to turn Poe's lifelong support for an international copyright agreement to their own advantage, see Meredith L. McGill, "Poe, Literary Nationalism, and Authorial Identity," in *The American Face of Edgar Allan Poe*, ed. Rosenheim and Rachman, 271–304.

17. Poe, *Essays and Reviews*, 1076.

18. Harold Bloom, Introduction, *Modern Critical Views: Edgar Allan Poe*, ed. Harold Bloom (New York: Chelsea House, 1985), 5.

19. Henry Louis Gates, Jr., *The Signifying Monkey: A Theory of African-American Literary Criticism* (New York: Oxford University Press, 1988), pp. 152–53; Charles T. Davis and Henry Louis Gates, Jr., introduction, *The Slave's Narrative*, ed. Charles T. Davis and Henry Louis Gates, Jr. (New York: Oxford University Press, 1985), xxii.

20. On this anomaly, see Paul Edwards, *Unreconciled Strivings and Ironic Strategies: Three Afro-British Authors of the Georgian Era: Ignatius Sancho, Olaudah Equiano, Robert Wedderburn* (Edinburgh: Edinburgh University Centre of African Studies Occasional Papers No. 34, 1992), 1.

21. Olaudah Equiano, *The Interesting Narrative and Other Writings*, ed. Vincent Carretta (Harmondsworth: Penguin, 1995), 236. Subsequent page references to this edition are given in the text.

22. Gates, *The Signifying Monkey*, 155.

23. Geraldine Murphy, "Olaudah Equiano, Accidental Tourist," *Eighteenth-Century Studies* 27 (1994): 557.

24. Susan M. Marren, "Between Slavery and Freedom: The Transgressive Self in Olaudah Equiano's Autobiography," *PMLA* 108 (1993): 95.

25. Vincent Carretta, Introduction, *Unchained Voices: An Anthology of Black Authors in the English-Speaking World of the Eighteenth Century*, ed. Vincent Carretta (Lexington: University Press of Kentucky, 1996), 10–11.

26. Akiyo Ito, "Olaudah Equiano and the New York Artisans: The First American Edition of *The Interesting Narrative of the Life of Olaudah Equiano, or Gustavus Vassa, the African*," *Early American Literature* 32 (1997): 83. On Equiano's political support for free trade and his reputation as "one of the most intelligent interpreters of the new economic thinking in abolitionist circles," see Keith A. Sandiford, *Measuring the Moment: Strategies of Protest in Eighteenth-Century Afro-English Writing* (Selinsgrove, Pa.: Susquehanna University Press, 1988), 145.

27. Gilroy, *The Black Atlantic*, 12. See also Gilroy, *Against Race*, 121.

28. Angelo Constanzo, *Surprizing Narrative: Olaudah Equiano and the Beginnings of Black Autobiography* (New York: Greenwood Press, 1987), 6.

29. Joseph Fichtelberg, "Word between Worlds: The Economy of Equiano's *Narrative*," *American Literary History* 5 (1993): 473.

30. Helen Thomas, *Romanticism and Slave Narratives: Transatlantic Testimonies* (Cambridge: Cambridge University Press, 2000), 226, 82–124. Thomas describes the close links between Romanticism and abolitionism within the British context.

31. Nancy Ruttenburg, *Democratic Personality: Popular Voice and the Trial of American Authorship* (Stanford, Calif.: Stanford University Press, 1998), 291, 6.

32. Ruttenburg, *Democratic Personality*, 10, 25.

33. Jefferson, *Writings*, 19.

34. Leo Bersani, *The Freudian Body: Psychoanalysis and Art* (New York: Columbia University Press, 1986), 67, and *The Culture of Redemption* (Cambridge, Mass.: Harvard University Press, 1990).

Works Cited

Adair, Douglass. *Fame and the Founding Fathers*. Ed. Trevor Colbourn. New York: Norton, 1974.

Adams, William Howard. *The Paris Years of Thomas Jefferson*. New Haven, Conn.: Yale University Press, 1997.

Aldridge, Alfred Owen. "Benjamin Franklin and Philosophical Necessity." *Modern Language Quarterly* 12 (1951): 292–309.

——. *Early American Literature: A Comparatist Approach*. Princeton, N.J.: Princeton University Press, 1982.

Allen, Robert C. *Horrible Prettiness: Burlesque and American Culture*. Chapel Hill: University of North Carolina Press, 1991.

Allen, Theodore W. *The Invention of the White Race*. Vol. 2, *The Origin of Racial Oppression in Anglo-America*. London: Verso, 1997.

Alsop, Richard. Preface. *The Echo, with Other Poems*. 1807. In *The Poetry of the Minor Connecticut Wits*, ed. Benjamin Franklin V. Gainesville, Fla.: Scholars' Facsimiles and Reprints, 1970. iii–vii.

The Anarchiad: A New England Poem (1786–87), written in concert by David Humphreys, Joel Barlow, John Trumbull and Dr. Lemuel Hopkins. Ed. Luther G. Riggs. 1861. Gainesville, Fla.: Scholars' Facsimiles and Reprints, 1967.

Anderson, Benedict. *Imagined Communities: Reflections on the Origin and Spread of Nationalism*. London: Verso, 1993.

Anderson, Douglas. *The Radical Enlightenments of Benjamin Franklin*. Baltimore: Johns Hopkins University Press, 1997.

Arac, Jonathan. *Critical Genealogies: Historical Situations for Postmodern Literary Studies*. New York: Columbia University Press, 1987.

Arciniegas, Germán. *America in Europe: A History of the New World in Reverse*. 1975. Trans. Gabriele Arciniegas and R. Victoria Arana. San Diego: Harcourt Brace Jovanovich. 1986.

Arendt, Hannah. *On Revolution*. London: Faber, 1963.

Armstrong, Nancy. *Desire and Domestic Fiction: A Political History of the Novel*. New York: Oxford University Press, 1987.

Armstrong, Nancy and Leonard Tennenhouse. *The Imaginary Puritan: Literature, Intellec-*

tual Labor, and the Origins of Personal Life. Berkeley: University of California Press, 1992.

Arnold, Matthew. "Thomas Gray." *The Complete Prose Works of Matthew Arnold.* Vol. 9, *English Literature and Irish Politics.* Ed. R. H. Super. Ann Arbor: University of Michigan Press, 1973. 189–204.

Austen, Jane. *Letters.* Ed. R. W. Chapman. 2nd ed. Oxford: Oxford University Press, 1952.

——. *Mansfield Park.* Ed. Tony Tanner. Harmondsworth: Penguin, 1966.

——. *Emma.* Ed. Ronald Blythe. Harmondsworth: Penguin, 1966.

——. *Catharine and Other Writings.* Ed. Margaret Anne Doody and Douglas Murray. Oxford: Oxford University Press, 1993.

Bailyn, Bernard. *The Ideological Origins of the American Revolution.* Cambridge, Mass.: Harvard University Press, 1967.

Barker-Benfield, G. J. *The Culture of Sensibility: Sex and Society in Eighteenth-Century Britain.* Chicago: University of Chicago Press, 1992.

Barnes, Elizabeth. *States of Sympathy: Seduction and Democracy in the American Novel.* New York: Columbia University Press, 1997.

Barrell, John and Harriet Guest. "On the Use of Contradiction: Economics and Morality in the Eighteenth-Century Long Poem." In *The New Eighteenth Century*, ed. Nussbaum and Brown. 121–43.

Bayley, John. The 'Irresponsibility' of Jane Austen." In *Critical Essays on Jane Austen*, ed. Southam. 1–20.

Baym, Nina. *The Shape of Hawthorne's Career.* Ithaca, N.Y.: Cornell University Press, 1976.

Bell, Michael Davitt. "Conditions of Literary Vocation." In *Cambridge History of American Literature*, vol. 2, *1820–1865*, ed. Bercovitch. 9–123.

Bender, John. *Imagining the Penitentiary: Fiction and the Architecture of Mind in Eighteenth-Century England.* Chicago: University of Chicago Press, 1987.

——. "Enlightenment Fiction and the Scientific Hypothesis." *Representations* 61 (Winter 1998): 6–28.

Bercovitch, Sacvan. *The Puritan Origins of the American Self.* New Haven, Conn.: Yale University Press, 1975.

——. *The Rites of Assent: Transformations in the Symbolic Construction of America.* New York: Routledge, 1993.

——, ed. *The Cambridge History of American Literature.* Vol. 1, *1590–1820.* Cambridge: Cambridge University Press, 1994.

——, ed. *The Cambridge History of American Literature.* Vol. 2, *1820–1865.* Cambridge: Cambridge University Press, 1995.

Berlant, Lauren. *The Anatomy of National Fantasy: Hawthorne, Utopia, and Everyday Life.* Chicago: University of Chicago Press, 1991.

——. *The Queen of America Goes to Washington City: Essays on Sex and Citizenship.* Durham, N.C.: Duke University Press, 1997.

Bersani, Leo. *The Freudian Body: Psychoanalysis and Art.* New York: Columbia University Press, 1986.

——. *The Culture of Redemption*. Cambridge, Mass.: Harvard University Press, 1990.

Bhabha, Homi K. "A Question of Survival: Nations and Psychic States." In *Psychoanalysis and Cultural Theory: Thresholds*, ed. James Donald. Basingstoke: Macmillan-Institute of Contemporary Arts, 1991. 89–103.

——. *The Location of Culture*. London: Routledge, 1994.

Blair, Sara B. "Changing the Subject: Henry James, *Dred Scott*, and Fictions of Identity." *American Literary History* 4 (1992): 28–55.

Blake, William. *The Complete Poems*. Ed. Alicia Ostriker. Harmondsworth: Penguin, 1977.

Bloom, Harold. *The Anxiety of Influence: A Theory of Poetry*. New York: Oxford University Press, 1973.

——. *A Map of Misreading*. New York: Oxford University Press, 1975.

——. Introduction. *Modern Critical Views: Edgar Allan Poe*, ed. Harold Bloom. New York: Chelsea House, 1985. 1–14.

Bonwick, Colin. *English Radicals and the American Revolution*. Chapel Hill: University of North Carolina Press, 1977.

Boorstin, Daniel J. *The Lost World of Thomas Jefferson*. 1948. Boston: Beacon Press, 1960.

Booth, Wayne C. *The Rhetoric of Fiction*. Chicago: University of Chicago Press, 1961.

Botein, Stephen. "Religious Dimensions of the Early American State." In *Beyond Confederation: Origins of the Constitution and American National Identity*, ed. Richard Beeman, Stephen Botein, and Edward C. Carter II. Chapel Hill: University of North Carolina Press for the Institute of Early American History and Culture, 1987. 315–30.

Boulton, Alexander O. "The American Paradox: Jeffersonian Equality and Racial Science," *American Quarterly* 47 (1995): 467–92.

Bourne, Randolph. *History of a Literary Radical and Other Essays*. Ed. Van Wyck Brooks. 1920. New York: Biblo and Tannen, 1969.

Bové, Paul A. *In The Wake of Theory*. Hanover, N.H.: University Press of New England, 1992.

Breitwieser, Mitchell Robert. *Cotton Mather and Benjamin Franklin: The Price of Representative Personality*. Cambridge: Cambridge University Press, 1984.

Briggs, Peter M. "English Satire and Connecticut Wit." *American Quarterly* 37 (1985): 13–29.

——. "Timothy Dwight 'Composes' a Landscape for New England." *American Quarterly* 40 (1988): 359–77.

Brissenden, R. F. *Virtue in Distress: Studies in the Novel of Sentiment from Richardson to Sade*. New York: Barnes and Noble, 1974.

Brodhead, Richard H. *Hawthorne, Melville, and the Novel*. Chicago: University of Chicago Press, 1976.

Brody, Jennifer DeVere. *Impossible Purities: Blackness, Femininity, and Victorian Culture*. Durham, N.C.: Duke University Press, 1998.

Brophy, Brigid. "Jane Austen and the Stuarts." In *Critical Essays on Jane Austen*, ed. Southam. 21–38.

Brown, Herbert R. "Richardson and Sterne in the *Massachusetts Magazine*." *New England Quarterly* 5 (1932): 65–82.

Brown, Homer Obed. *Institutions of the English Novel: From Defoe to Scott*. Philadelphia: University of Pennsylvania Press, 1997.

Brown, Joseph Epes. *The Critical Opinions of Samuel Johnson*. New York: Russell and Russell, 1961.

Brown, William Hill. *The Power of Sympathy*. Ed. Carla Mulford. Harmondsworth: Penguin, 1996.

Buckton, Oliver S. "An Unnatural State: Gender, 'Perversion,' and Newman's *Apologia pro Vita Sua*," *Victorian Studies* 35 (1992): 359–83.

Buel, Richard. *Securing the Revolution: Ideology in American Politics, 1789–1815*. Ithaca, N.Y.: Cornell University Press, 1972.

Buell, Lawrence. *New England Literary Culture: From Revolution Through Renaissance*. Cambridge: Cambridge University Press, 1986.

——. "American Literary Emergence as a Postcolonial Phenomenon." *American Literary History* 4 (1992): 411–42.

——. "Circling the Spheres: A Dialogue." *American Literature* 70 (1998): 465–90.

Burgett, Bruce. *Sentimental Bodies: Sex, Gender, and Citizenship in the Early Republic*. Princeton, N.J.: Princeton University Press, 1998.

Burke, Edmund. *A Philosophical Enquiry into the Origin of our Ideas of the Sublime and Beautiful*. Ed. James T. Boulton. London: Routledge and Kegan Paul, 1958.

——. *Reflections on the Revolution in France*. Ed. Conor Cruise O'Brien. Harmondsworth: Penguin, 1968.

——. *Selected Writings and Speeches*. Ed. Peter J. Stanlis. 1963. Gloucester, Mass.: Peter Smith, 1968.

Burstein, Andrew and Catherine Mowbray. "Jefferson and Sterne." *Early American Literature* 29 (1994): 19–34.

Butler, Marilyn. *Jane Austen and the War of Ideas*. Oxford: Oxford University Press, 1975.

——. *Romantics, Rebels and Reactionaries: English Literature and Its Background, 1760–1830*. Oxford: Oxford University Press, 1981.

Buxbaum, Melvin H. "Hume, Franklin, and America: A Matter of Loyalties." *Enlightenment Essays* 3 (1972): 93–105.

Byles, Mather. *Poems on Several Occasions*. 1744. Ed. C. Lennart Carlson. New York: Columbia University Press, 1940.

——. "Bombastic and Grubstreet Style: A Satire." 1745. In Miller and Johnson, *The Puritans*. 689–94.

——. *A Discourse on the Present Vileness of the Body and It's Future Glorious Change by Christ*. 2nd ed. Boston, 1771.

——. *A Sermon on the Nature and Necessity of Conversion*. 3rd ed. Boston, 1771.

Byron, Lord. *Don Juan*. Ed. T. G. Steffan, E. Steffan and W. W. Pratt. Harmondsworth: Penguin, 1982.

Cameron, Vivian. "Political Exposures: Sexuality and Caricature in the French Revolution." In *Eroticism and the Body Politic*, ed. Lynn Hunt. Baltimore: Johns Hopkins University Press, 1991. 90–107.

Cappon, Lester J., ed. *The Adams-Jefferson Letters: The Complete Correspondence Between Thomas Jefferson and Abigail and John Adams*. Chapel Hill: University of North Carolina Press, 1959.

Carafiol, Peter. *The American Ideal: Literary History as a Worldly Activity*. New York: Oxford University Press, 1991.

———. "Commentary: After American Literature." *American Literary History* 4 (1992): 539–49.

Carlson, C. Lennart. Introduction. Mather Byles, *Poems on Several Occasions*. v–xxxvii.

Carretta, Vincent. *George III and the Satirists from Hogarth to Byron*. Athens: University of Georgia Press, 1990.

———. Introduction. *Unchained Voices: An Anthology of Black Authors in the English-Speaking World of the Eighteenth Century*, ed. Vincent Carretta. Lexington: University Press of Kentucky, 1996. 1–16.

Castle, Terry. "The Carnivalization of Eighteenth-Century English Narrative." *PMLA* 99 (1984): 903–15.

———. *The Female Thermometer: Eighteenth-Century Culture and the Invention of the Uncanny*. New York: Oxford University Press, 1995.

———. "Sister-Sister." *London Review of Books*, 3 August 1995: 3–6.

———. Letter. *London Review of Books*, 24 August 1995: 4.

Cecil, David. *A Portrait of Jane Austen*. London: Constable, 1978.

Chandler, James. "The Pope Controversy: Romantic Poetics and the English Canon." *Critical Inquiry* 10 (1984): 481–509.

———. *England in 1819: The Politics of Literary Culture and the Case of Romantic Historicism*. Chicago: University of Chicago Press, 1998.

Chapin, Chester. "Alexander Pope: Erasmian Catholic." *Eighteenth-Century Studies* 6 (1973): 411–30.

Chasseguet-Smirgel, Janine. *Creativity and Perversion*. New York: Norton, 1984.

Cheyfitz, Eric. "What Work Is There for Us To Do? American Literary Studies or Americas Cultural Studies?" *American Literature* 67 (1995): 843–53.

Chinard, Gilbert. *Thomas Jefferson: The Apostle of Americanism*. 2nd ed. 1939. Ann Arbor: University of Michigan Press, 1957.

Clark, J. C. D. *The Language of Liberty: Political Discourse and Social Dynamics in the Anglo-American World*. Cambridge: Cambridge University Press, 1994.

Cobbett, William. *A Year's Residence in the United States of America*. 1819. Fontwell, Sussex: Centaur Press, 1964.

———. *Rural Rides*. Ed. George Woodcock. Harmondsworth: Penguin, 1967.

———. *Peter Porcupine in America: Pamphlets on Republicanism and Revolution*. Ed. David A. Wilson. Ithaca, N.Y.: Cornell University Press, 1994.

Cohen, William. "Thomas Jefferson and the Problem of Slavery." *Journal of American History* 56 (1969): 503–26.

Colacurcio, Michael J. "Footsteps of Ann Hutchinson: The Context of *The Scarlet Letter*." *ELH* 39 (1972): 459–94.

Colley, Linda. *Britons: Forging the Nation, 1707–1837*. New Haven, Conn.: Yale University Press, 1992.

Commager, Henry Steele. *Jefferson, Nationalism, and the Enlightenment*. New York: George Braziller, 1975.

Conkin, Paul K. "The Religious Pilgrimage of Thomas Jefferson." In *Jeffersonian Legacies*, ed. Peter S. Onuf. Charlottesville: University Press of Virginia. 1993. 19–49.

Constanzo, Angelo. *Surprizing Narrative: Olaudah Equiano and the Beginnings of Black Autobiography*. New York: Greenwood Press, 1987.

Cowie, Alexander. *John Trumbull: Connecticut Wit*. Chapel Hill: University of North Carolina Press, 1936.

Crews, Frederick C. *The Sins of the Fathers: Hawthorne's Psychological Themes*. New York: Oxford University Press, 1966.

Crowley, J. Donald, ed. *Hawthorne: The Critical Heritage*. New York: Barnes and Noble, 1970.

Cruttwell, Patrick. "Pope and His Church." *Hudson Review* 13 (1960): 392–405.

Culler, Jonathan. "Comparative Literature and the Pieties." *Profession*, 86. New York: Modern Language Association of America, 1986. 30–32.

Cunliffe, Marcus. *Chattel Slavery and Wage Slavery: The Anglo-American Context, 1830–1860*. Athens: University of Georgia Press, 1979.

Darnton, Robert. *The Forbidden Best-Sellers of Pre-Revolutionary France*. London: HarperCollins, 1996.

Davidson, Cathy A. *Revolution and the Word: The Rise of the Novel in America*. New York: Oxford University Press, 1986.

Davis, David Brion. *The Problem of Slavery in Western Culture*. Ithaca, N.Y.: Cornell University Press, 1966.

Davis, Lennard J. *Factual Fictions: The Origins of the English Novel*. New York: Columbia University Press, 1983.

Dekker, George. *The American Historical Romance*. Cambridge: Cambridge University Press, 1987.

Delbanco, Andrew. *The Death of Satan: How Americans Have Lost The Sense of Evil*. New York: Farrar, Straus and Giroux, 1995.

Deleuze, Gilles. "Coldness and Cruelty." 1967. *Masochism*. Trans. Jean McNeil. 1971. New York: Zone Books, 1989. 7–138.

Denning, Michael. *The Cultural Front: The Laboring of American Culture in the Twentieth Century*. London: Verso, 1996.

Deutsch, Helen. *Resemblance and Disgrace: Alexander Pope and the Deformation of Culture*. Cambridge, Mass.: Harvard University Press, 1996.

Diggins, John P. "Slavery, Race, and Equality: Jefferson and the Pathos of the Enlightenment." *American Quarterly* 28 (1976): 206–28.

Dixon, Peter, ed. *Writers and Their Background: Alexander Pope*. Athens: Ohio University Press, 1972.

Dollimore, Jonathan. *Sexual Dissidence: Augustine to Wilde, Freud to Foucault*. Oxford: Oxford University Press, 1991.

Douglas, Ann. *The Feminization of American Culture*. New York: Knopf, 1977.

Dowling, William C. "Joel Barlow and *The Anarchiad*." *Early American Literature* 25 (1990): 18–33.

———. *Poetry and Ideology in Revolutionary Connecticut*. Athens: University of Georgia Press, 1990.

———. *The Epistolary Moment: The Poetics of the Eighteenth-Century Verse Epistle*. Princeton, N.J.: Princeton University Press, 1991.

Doyle, Brian. *English and Englishness*. London: Routledge, 1989.

Durey, Michael. *Transatlantic Radicals and the Early American Republic*. Lawrence: University Press of Kansas, 1997.

Dussinger, John A. "Madness and Lust in the Age of Sensibility." In *Sensibility in Transformation: Creative Resistance to Sentiment from the Augustans to the Romantics*, ed. Syndy McMillen Conger. Rutherford, N.J.: Fairleigh Dickinson University Press, 1990. 85–102.

Duyckinck, Evert A. and George Duyckinck, eds. *Cyclopaedia of American Literature*. 2 vols. New York: Charles Scribners, 1856.

Dwight, Timothy. *The Major Poems of Timothy Dwight*. Ed. William J. McTaggart and William K. Bottorff. Gainesville, Fla: Scholars' Facsimiles and Reprints, 1969.

Eagleton, Terry. *The Rape of Clarissa: Writing, Sexuality and Class Struggle in Samuel Richardson*. Minneapolis: University of Minnesota Press, 1982.

Eaton, Arthur Wentworth Hamilton. *The Famous Mather Byles: The Noted Tory Preacher, Poet, and Wit, 1707–1788*. Boston: Butterfield, 1914.

Eaves, T. C. Duncan and Ben D. Kimpel. *Samuel Richardson: A Biography*. Oxford: Clarendon Press, 1971.

Eberwein, Jane D. "Transatlantic Contrasts in Irving's *Sketch Book*." *College Literature* 15 (1988): 153–70.

Echeverria, Durand. *Mirage in the West: A History of the French Image of American Society to 1815*. Princeton, N.J.: Princeton University Press, 1957.

———, ed. and trans. "Condorcet's The Influence of the American Revolution on Europe." *William and Mary Quarterly*, 3rd ser. 25 (1968): 85–108.

Edelberg, Cynthia Dubin. "The Shaping of a Political Poet: Five Newfound Verses by Jonathan Odell." *Early American Literature* 18 (1993): 45–70.

Edwards, Paul. *Unreconciled Strivings and Ironic Strategies: Three Afro-British Authors of the Georgian Era: Ignatius Sancho, Olaudah Equiano, Robert Wedderburn*. Edinburgh: Edinburgh University Centre of African Studies Occasional Papers No. 34, 1992.

Egan, Jim. *Authorizing Experience: Refigurations of the Body Politic in Seventeenth-Century New England Writing*. Princeton, N.J.: Princeton University Press, 1999.

Eliot, T. S. "John Dryden." *The Listener*, 16 April 1930: 688–89.

Elliott, Emory. *Revolutionary Writers: Literature and Authority in the New Republic*. New York: Oxford University Press, 1982.

Ellis, Joseph J. *After the Revolution: Profiles of Early American Culture*. New York: Norton, 1979.

———. *American Sphinx: The Character of Thomas Jefferson*. New York: Knopf, 1997.

Ellis, Markman. *The Politics of Sensibility: Race, Gender, and Commerce in the Sentimental Novel*. Cambridge: Cambridge University Press, 1996.

Ellison, Julie. *Cato's Tears and the Making of Anglo-American Emotion*. Chicago: University of Chicago Press, 1999.

Elmer, Jonathan. *Reading at the Social Limit: Affect, Mass Culture, and Edgar Allan Poe*. Stanford, Calif.: Stanford University Press, 1995.

Emerson, Ralph Waldo. *The Collected Works of Ralph Waldo Emerson*. Vol. 1, *Nature, Addresses, and Lectures*. Ed. Robert E. Spiller. Cambridge, Mass.: Harvard University Press, 1971.

———. *Complete Works*. Vol. 6, *The Conduct of Life*. London: Routledge, 1903.

———. *The Journals and Miscellaneous Notebooks*. Vol. 7, *1838–1842*. Ed. A. W. Plumstead and Harrison Hayford. Cambridge, Mass. Harvard University Press, 1969.

Equiano, Olaudah. *The Interesting Narrative and Other Writings*. Ed. Vincent Carretta. Harmondsworth: Penguin, 1995.

Ferguson, Moira. "*Mansfield Park*: Slavery, Colonialism, and Gender." *Oxford Literary Review* 13 (1991): 118–39.

Ferguson, Robert A. *Law and Letters in American Culture*. Cambridge, Mass.: Harvard University Press, 1984.

———. "'What Is Enlightenment?': Some American Answers." *American Literary History* 1 (1989): 245–72.

———. "The American Enlightenment, 1750–1820." In *Cambridge History of American Literature*, vol. 1, *1590–1820*, ed. Bercovitch. 345–537.

Fichtelberg, Joseph. *The Complex Image: Faith and Method in American Autobiography*. Philadelphia: University of Pennsylvania Press, 1989.

———. "Word Between Worlds: The Economy of Equiano's Narrative." *American Literary History* 5 (1993): 459–80.

Fisher, Philip. "Introduction: The New American Studies." In *The New American Studies: Essays from Representations*, ed. Philip Fisher. Berkeley: University of California Press, 1991. vii–xxii.

Fiedler, Leslie. *Love and Death in the American Novel*. 3rd ed. 1982. Harmondsworth: Penguin, 1984.

Fliegelman, Jay. *Prodigals and Pilgrims: The American Revolution Against Patriarchal Authority, 1750–1800*. Cambridge: Cambridge University Press, 1982.

———. "Jefferson, Authorship, and Plagiarism." Paper delivered to the American Studies Association, Costa Mesa, California, 7 November 1992.

———. *Declaring Independence: Jefferson, Natural Language, and the Culture of Performance*. Stanford, Calif.: Stanford University Press, 1993.

Foster, Hannah Webster. *The Boarding School*. Boston, 1798.

———. *The Coquette*. Ed. Carla Mulford. Harmondsworth: Penguin, 1996.

Foucault, Michel. "A Preface to Transgression." 1963. *Language, Counter-Memory, Practice: Selected Essays and Interviews*. Trans. Donald F. Bouchard and Sherry Simon, ed. Donald F. Bouchard. Ithaca, N.Y.: Cornell University Press, 1977. 29–52.

Fraiman, Susan. "Jane Austen and Edward Said: Gender, Culture, and Imperialism." *Critical Inquiry* 21 (1995): 805–21.

Franchot, Jenny. *Roads to Rome: The Antebellum Encounter with Catholicism.* Berkeley: University of California Press, 1994.

Franklin, Benjamin. *Writings.* Ed. J. A. Leo Lemay. New York: Library of America. 1987.

——. *The Papers of Benjamin Franklin.* Vol. 18. Ed. William B. Willcox. New Haven, Conn.: Yale University Press, 1974.

——. *The Papers of Benjamin Franklin.* Vol. 19. Ed. William B. Willcox. New Haven, Conn.: Yale University Press, 1975.

Fuller, Margaret. *Margaret Fuller: A Selection from Her Writings and Correspondence.* Ed. Perry Miller. 1963. Ithaca, N.Y.: Cornell University Press, 1970.

Furniss, Tom. *Edmund Burke's Aesthetic Ideology: Language, Gender, and Political Economy in Revolution.* Cambridge: Cambridge University Press, 1993.

Furst, Lilian R. *Fictions of Romantic Irony in European Narrative, 1760–1857.* London: Macmillan, 1984.

Gates, Henry Louis, Jr. *The Signifying Monkey: A Theory of African-American Literary Criticism.* New York: Oxford University Press, 1988.

Gates, Henry Louis Jr., and Charles T. Davis. Introduction: "The Language of Slavery." *The Slave's Narrative,* ed. Charles T. Davis and Henry Louis Gates Jr. New York: Oxford University Press, 1985. xi–xxxiv.

Gibbon, Edward. *The Decline and Fall of the Roman Empire.* Ed. Oliphant Smeaton. London: Dent, 1910.

Gikandi, Simon. *Maps of Englishness: Writing Identity in the Culture of Colonialism.* New York: Columbia University Press, 1996.

Gilbert, Sandra M. and Susan Gubar. *The Madwoman in the Attic: The Woman Writer and the Nineteenth-Century Literary Imagination.* New Haven, Conn.: Yale University Press, 1979.

Giles, Paul. "Gothic Paradoxes in *Pride and Prejudice.*" *Text and Context* 2, 1 (1988): 68–75.

Gilmore, Michael T. "The Literature of the Revolutionary and Early National Periods." In *Cambridge History of American Literature,* vol. 1, *1590–1820,* ed. Bercovitch. 539–693.

Gilroy, Paul. *"There Ain't No Black in the Union Jack": The Cultural Politics of Race and Nation.* 1987. Chicago: University of Chicago Press, 1991.

——. *The Black Atlantic: Modernity and Double Consciousness.* Cambridge, Mass.: Harvard University Press, 1993.

——. *Against Race: Imagining Political Culture Beyond the Color Line.* Cambridge, Mass.: Harvard University Press, 2000.

Gimmestad, Victor E. *John Trumbull.* New York: Twayne, 1974.

Godwin, William. *Things as They Are; or, The Adventures of Caleb Williams.* 1794. Ed. Maurice Hindle. Harmondsworth: Penguin, 1988.

Goldsmith, Oliver. *Poems and Plays.* Ed. Tom Davis. London: Dent, 1975.

Gordon-Reed, Annette. *Thomas Jefferson and Sally Hemings: An American Controversy.* Charlottesville: University Press of Virginia, 1997.

Graff, Gerald. *Professing Literature: An Institutional History*. Chicago: University of Chicago Press, 1987.

Granger, Bruce Ingham. "John Trumbull and Religion." *American Literature* 23 (1951): 57–79.

——. "Hudibras in the American Revolution." *American Literature* 27 (1956): 499–508.

——. *Political Satire in the American Revolution, 1763–1783*. Ithaca, N.Y.: Cornell University Press, 1960.

Grasso, Christopher. "Print, Poetry, and Politics: John Trumbull and the Transformation of Public Discourse in Revolutionary America." *Early American Literature* 30 (1995): 5–31.

——. *A Speaking Aristocracy: Transforming Public Discourse in Eighteenth-Century Connecticut*. Chapel Hill: University of North Carolina Press for the Omohundro Institute of Early American History and Culture, 1999.

Greenblatt, Stephen. "Towards a Poetics of Culture." In *The New Historicism*, ed. H. Aram Veeser. New York: Routledge, 1989. 1–14.

Greene, Jack P. *Pursuits of Happiness: The Social Development of Early Modern British Colonies and the Formation of American Culture*. Chapel Hill: University of North Carolina Press, 1988.

——. *The Intellectual Construction of America: Exceptionalism and Identity from 1492 to 1800*. Chapel Hill: University of North Carolina Press, 1993.

Greene, Jack P. and J. R. Pole. "Reconstructing British-American Colonial History: An Introduction." In *Colonial British America: Essays in the New History of the Early Modern Era*, ed. Jack P. Greene and J. R. Pole. Baltimore: Johns Hopkins University Press, 1984. 1–17.

Grey, J. David, ed. *Jane Austen's Beginnings: The Juvenilia and Lady Susan*. Ann Arbor, Mich.: UMI Research Press, 1989.

Grey, Robin. *The Complicity of Imagination: The American Renaissance, Contests of Authority, and Seventeenth-Century English Culture*. Cambridge: Cambridge University Press, 1997.

Guillén, Claudio. *The Challenge of Comparative Literature*. Trans. Cola Franzen. Cambridge, Mass.: Harvard University Press, 1993.

Gunn, Giles. *Thinking Across the American Grain: Ideology, Intellect, and the New Pragmatism*. Chicago: University of Chicago Press, 1992.

Gura, Philip F. "Turning Our World Upside Down: Reconceiving Early American Literature." *American Literature* 63 (1991): 104–12.

——. *The Crossroads of American History and Literature*. University Park: Pennsylvania State University Press, 1996.

Gustafson, Thomas. *Representative Words: Politics, Literature, and the American Language, 1776–1865*. Cambridge: Cambridge University Press, 1992.

Hampson, Norman. *The Enlightenment*. Harmondsworth: Penguin, 1968.

Hart, James D. *The Popular Book: A History of America's Literary Taste*. New York: Oxford University Press, 1950.

Harvey, David. *The Condition of Postmodernity: An Enquiry into the Origins of Cultural Change*. Oxford: Blackwell, 1989.

Harvey, W. J. "The Plot of *Emma*." *Essays in Criticism* 17 (1967): 48–63.

Hawthorne, Nathaniel. *The American Claimant Manuscripts: The Ancestral Footstep, Etherege, Grimshawe*. *The Centenary Edition of the Works of Nathaniel Hawthorne*, vol. 12. Ed. Edward H. Davidson, Claude M. Simpson, and L. Neal Smith. Columbus: Ohio State University Press, 1977.

———. *The Blithedale Romance and Fanshawe*. *The Centenary Edition of the Works of Nathaniel Hawthorne*, vol. 3. Columbus: Ohio State University Press, 1964.

———. "Chiefly about War-matters. By a Peacable Man." 1862. *Miscellaneous Prose and Verse*. *The Centenary Edition of the Works of Nathaniel Hawthorne*, vol. 23. Ed. Thomas Woodson, Claude M. Simpson, and L. Neal Smith. Columbus: Ohio State University Press, 1994. 403–42.

———. *The English Notebooks, 1853–1856*. *The Centenary Edition of the Works of Nathaniel Hawthorne*, vol. 21. Ed. Thomas Woodson and Bill Ellis. Columbus: Ohio State University Press, 1997.

———. *The Letters, 1857–1864*. *The Centenary Edition of the Works of Nathaniel Hawthorne*, vol. 18. Ed. Thomas Woodson et al. Columbus: Ohio State University Press, 1987.

———. *The Marble Faun; or, The Romance of Monte Beni*. *The Centenary Edition of the Works of Nathaniel Hawthorne*, vol. 4. Columbus: Ohio State University Press, 1968.

———. *Our Old Home: A Series of English Sketches*. *The Centenary Edition of the Works of Nathaniel Hawthorne*, vol. 5. Columbus: Ohio State University Press, 1970.

———. *The Scarlet Letter*. *The Centenary Edition of the Works of Nathaniel Hawthorne*, vol. 1. Columbus: Ohio State University Press, 1962.

Hazlitt, William. *The Spirit of the Age; or, Contemporary Portraits*. 1825. London: Grant Richards, 1904.

Heimert, Alan E. *Religion and the American Mind, from the Great Awakening to the Revolution*. Cambridge, Mass.: Harvard University Press, 1966.

Honan, Park. "Jane Austen and the American Revolution." *University of Leeds Review* 28 (1985–86): 181–95.

Hook, Andrew. "Scottish Academia and the Invention of American Studies." In *The Scottish Invention of English Literature*, ed. Robert Crawford. Cambridge: Cambridge University Press, 1998. 164–79.

Horwitz, Howard. *By the Law of Nature: Form and Value in Nineteenth-Century America*. New York: Oxford University Press, 1991.

Howard, Leon. *The Connecticut Wits*. Chicago: University of Chicago Press, 1943.

———. "The Late Eighteenth Century: An Age of Contradictions." In *Transitions in American Literary History*, ed. Harry Hayden Clark. 1954. New York: Farrar, Straus and Giroux, 1967. 49–89.

Howes, Alan B., ed. *Sterne: The Critical Heritage*. London: Routledge and Kegan Paul, 1974.

Hulliung, Mark. *The Autocritique of Enlightenment: Rousseau and the Philosophes*. Cambridge, Mass.: Harvard University Press, 1994.

Hume, David. *An Enquiry Concerning Human Understanding, and an Enquiry Concerning the Principles of Morals*. Ed. L. A. Selby-Bigge. Oxford: Clarendon Press, 1894.

———. *A Treatise of Human Nature*. Ed. Ernest C. Mossner. Harmondsworth: Penguin, 1969.

Humphreys, A. R. "Pope, God, and Man." *Writers and Their Background: Alexander Pope*, ed. Dixon 60–100.

Hunt, Lynn. "Pornography and the French Revolution." In *The Invention of Pornography: Obscenity and the Origins of Modernity, 1500–1800*, ed. Lynn Hunt. New York: Zone Books, 1993. 301–40.

Imaly, Gilbert. *The Emigrants*. Ed. W. M. Verhoeven and Amanda Gilroy. New York: Penguin, 1998.

Irr, Caren. *The Suburb of Dissent: Cultural Politics in the United States and Canada During the 1930s*. Durham, N.C.: Duke University Press, 1998.

Irving, Washington. *History, Tales, and Sketches*. New York: Library of America, 1983.

———. *Bracebridge Hall, Tales of a Traveller, The Alhambra*. New York: Library of America, 1991.

Ito, Akiyo. "Olaudah Equiano and the New York Artisans: The First American Edition of *The Interesting Narrative of the Life of Olaudah Equiano, or Gustavus Vassa, the African*." *Early American Literature* 32 (1997): 82–101.

Jack, Ian. *Augustan Satire: Intention and Idiom in English Poetry, 1660–1750*. London: Oxford University Press, 1952.

Jacob, Margaret C. *The Radical Enlightenment: Pantheists, Freemasons and Republicans*. London: George Allen and Unwin, 1981.

James, Henry. *The House of Fiction: Essays on the Novel*. Ed. Leon Edel. London: Rupert Hart-Davis, 1957.

———. "Nathaniel Hawthorne." 1879. *The American Essays*. Rev. ed. Ed. Leon Edel. Princeton, N.J.: Princeton University Press, 1989. 11–23.

———. *Hawthorne*. Ed. Tony Tanner. London: Macmillan, 1967.

Jameson, Fredric. "The State of the Subject (III)" *Critical Quarterly* 29, 4 (1987): 16–25.

Jay, Gregory. *America the Scrivener: Deconstruction and the Subject of Literary History*. Ithaca, N.Y.: Cornell University Press, 1990.

Jefferson, Thomas. *Writings*. Ed. Merrill D. Peterson. New York: Library of America, 1984.

Jehlen, Myra and Michael Warner, eds. *The English Literatures of America, 1500–1800*. New York: Routledge, 1997.

Johnson, Claudia L. *Jane Austen: Women, Politics, and the Novel*. Chicago: University of Chicago Press, 1988.

———. "'The Kingdom at Sixes and Sevens': Politics and the Juvenilia." In *Jane Austen's Beginnings*, ed. Grey. 45–58.

———. *Equivocal Beings: Politics, Gender, and Sentimentality in the 1790s: Wollstonecraft, Radcliffe. Burney, Austen*. Chicago: University of Chicago Press, 1995.

———. Letter. *London Review of Books*, 24 August 1995: 4.

———. "The Divine Miss Jane: Jane Austen, Janeites, and the Discipline of Novel Studies." *boundary 2* 23, 3 (1996): 143–63.

Johnson, Samuel. *Lives of the English Poets*. Ed. L. Archer Hind. London: Dent, 1925.

Johnson, Thomas H. "Jonathan Edwards and the 'Young Folks' Bible.'" *New England Quarterly* 5 (1932): 37–54.

Jones, Emrys. "Pope and Dulness." *Proceedings of the British Academy* 54 (1968): 231–64.

Jordan, Cynthia S. *Second Stories: The Politics of Language, Form, and Gender in Early American Fictions*. Chapel Hill: University of North Carolina Press, 1989.

Jordan, Winthrop D. *White over Black: American Attitudes Toward the Negro, 1550–1812*. Chapel Hill: University of North Carolina Press for the Institute of Early American History and Culture, 1968.

Jordanova, L. J., ed. *Languages of Nature: Critical Essays on Science and Literature*. London: Free Association Books, 1986.

——. "Naturalizing the Family: Literature and the Bio-Medical Sciences in the Late Eighteenth Century." In *Languages of Nature*, ed. Jordanova. 86–116.

Juno, Andrea and V. Vale, eds. *Angry Women*. San Francisco: Re/Search Publications, 1991.

Kafer, Peter K. "The Making of Timothy Dwight: A Connecticut Morality Tale." *William and Mary Quarterly* 47 (1990): 189–209.

Kallich, Martin. *British Poetry and the American Revolution: A Bibliographical Survey of Books and Pamphlets, Journals and Magazines, Newspapers and Prints, 1755–1800*. 2 vols. Troy, N.Y.: Whitston, 1988.

Kammen, Michael. *A Season of Youth: The American Revolution and the Historical Imagination*. New York: Knopf, 1978.

Kasson, Joy S. *Artistic Voyagers: Europe and the American Imagination in the Works of Irving, Allston, Cole, Cooper, and Hawthorne*. Westport, Conn.: Greenwood Press, 1982.

Keane, John. *Tom Paine: A Political Life*. London: Bloomsbury, 1995.

Keenan, Thomas. "Freedom, the Law of another Fable." *Yale French Studies* 79 (1991): 231–51.

Kelsall, Malcolm. *Jefferson and the Iconography of Romanticism: Folk, Land, Culture and the Romantic Nation*. Basingstoke: Macmillan, 1999.

Kenshur, Oscar. *Dilemmas of Enlightenment: Studies in the Rhetoric and Logic of Ideology*. Berkeley: University of California Press, 1993.

Kent, Christopher. "Learning History with, and from, Jane Austen." In *Jane Austen's Beginnings*, ed. Grey. 59–72.

Keymer, Tom. *Richardson's Clarissa and the Eighteenth-Century Reader*. Cambridge: Cambridge University Press, 1992.

Kerber, Linda K. *Federalists in Dissent: Imagery and Ideology in Jeffersonian America*. Ithaca, N.Y.: Cornell University Press, 1970.

Kincaid, James R. *The Novels of Anthony Trollope*. Oxford: Clarendon Press, 1977.

Klossowski, Pierre. *Sade My Neighbor*. Trans. Alphonso Lingis. Evanston, Il.: Northwestern University Press, 1991.

Koch, Adrienne. *The Philosophy of Thomas Jefferson*. 1943. Chicago: Quadrangle, 1964.

Kors, Alan Charles. *D'Holbach's Coterie: An Enlightenment in Paris*. Princeton, N.J.: Princeton University Press, 1976.

Kramnick, Isaac. *Bolingbroke and His Circle: The Politics of Nostalgia in the Age of Walpole.* Cambridge, Mass.: Harvard University Press, 1968.

——. *The Rage of Edmund Burke: Portrait of an Ambivalent Conservative.* New York: Basic Books, 1977.

——. *Republicanism and Bourgeois Radicalism: Political Ideology in Late Eighteenth-Century England and America.* Ithaca, N.Y.: Cornell University Press, 1990.

Kristeva, Julia. *Strangers to Ourselves.* 1989. Trans. Leon S. Roudiez. New York: Columbia University Press, 1991.

Lamb, Jonathan. *Sterne's Fiction and the Double Principle.* Cambridge: Cambridge University Press, 1989.

Lawlor, Nancy K. "Pope's *Essay on Man*: Oblique Light for a False Mirror." *Modern Language Quarterly* 28 (1967): 305–16.

Lawrence, D. H. *Studies in Classic American Literature.* 1923. Harmondsworth: Penguin, 1971.

Lawson-Peebles, Robert. *Landscape and Written Expression in Revolutionary America: The World Turned Upside Down.* Cambridge: Cambridge University Press, 1988.

Leary, Lewis. "Washington Irving and the Comic Imagination." 1973. In *Critical Essays on Washington Irving,* ed. Ralph M. Aderman. Boston: Hall, 1990. 191–202.

Leavis, F. R. "The Americanness of American Literature." 1952. *Anna Karenina and Other Essays.* London: Chatto and Windus, 1973. 138–51.

Leduc, Jean. "Les Sources de l'athéisme et de l'immoralisme du marquis de Sade," *Studies on Voltaire and the Eighteenth Century* 68 (1969): 7–66.

Lemay, J. A. Leo. "Franklin's *Autobiography* and the American Dream." In *Benjamin Franklin's Autobiography: An Authoritative Text,* ed. J. A. Leo Lemay and P. M. Zall. New York: Norton, 1986. 349–60.

Levine, Robert S. *Conspiracy and Romance: Studies in Brockden Brown, Cooper, Hawthorne and Melville.* Cambridge: Cambridge University Press, 1989.

Lincoln, Abraham. *The Portable Abraham Lincoln.* Ed. Andrew Delbanco. New York: Viking Penguin, 1992.

Lindberg, Gary. *The Confidence Man in American Literature.* New York: Oxford University Press, 1982.

Litvak, Joseph. "Reading Characters: Self, Society, and Text in *Emma*." *PMLA* 100 (1985): 763–73.

——. "The Infection of Acting: Theatricals and Theatricality in *Mansfield Park*." *ELH* 53 (1986): 331–55.

——. *Caught in the Act: Theatricality in the Nineteenth-Century English Novel.* Berkeley: University of California Press, 1992.

——. *Strange Gourmets: Sophistication, Theory, and the Novel.* Durham, N.C.: Duke University Press, 1997.

Locke, John. *The Locke Reader.* Ed. John W. Yolton. Cambridge: Cambridge University Press, 1977.

Looby, Christopher. *Voicing America: Language, Literary Form, and the Origins of the United States.* Chicago: University of Chicago Press, 1996.

Lott, Eric. "Nation Time." *American Literary History* 7 (1995): 555–71.

Lundberg, David and Henry F. May. "The Enlightened Reader in America." *American Quarterly* 28 (1976): 262–93.

Lynch, Deirdre. "At Home with Jane Austen." In *Cultural Institutions of the Novel*. Ed. Deirdre Lynch and William B. Warner. Durham, N.C.: Duke University Press, 1996. 159–92.

Mack, Maynard. *Alexander Pope: A Life*. New Haven, Conn.: Yale University Press, 1985.

Madsen, Deborah L. *Allegory in America: From Puritanism to Postmodernism*. Basingstoke: Macmillan, 1996.

Maier, Pauline. *American Scripture: Making the Declaration of Independence*. New York: Knopf, 1997.

Manning, Susan. *The Puritan-Provincial Vision: Scottish and American Literature in the Nineteenth Century*. Cambridge: Cambridge University Press, 1990.

——. "Naming of Parts; or, The Comforts of Classification: Thomas Jefferson's Construction of America as Fact and Myth." *Journal of American Studies* 30 (1996): 345–64.

Markley, Robert. "Sentimentality as Performance: Shaftesbury, Sterne, and the Theatrics of Virtue." In *The New Eighteenth Century*, ed. Nussbaum and Brown. 210–30.

Marren, Susan M. "Between Slavery and Freedom: The Transgressive Self in Olaudah Equiano's Autobiography." *PMLA* 108 (1993): 94–105.

Martin, Ellen E. "The Madness of Jane Austen: Metonymic Style and Literature's Resistance to Interpretation." In *Jane Austen's Beginnings*, ed. Grey. 83–94.

Marx, Karl. *Capital*. Trans. Eden and Cedar Paul. London: Dent, 1930.

——. *Political Writings*, vol. 2, *Surveys from Exile*. Ed. David Fernbach. New York: Random House, 1973.

Marx, Leo. *The Machine in the Garden: Technology and the Pastoral Ideal in America*. New York: Oxford University Press, 1964.

Matthiessen, F. O. *American Renaissance: Art and Expression in the Age of Emerson and Whitman*. New York: Oxford University Press, 1941.

May, Henry F. *The Enlightenment in America*. New York: Oxford University Press, 1976.

McClintock, Anne. *Imperial Leather: Race, Gender and Sexuality in the Colonial Contest*. New York: Routledge, 1995.

McCoy, Drew R. *The Elusive Republic: Political Economy in Jeffersonian America*. Chapel Hill: University of North Carolina Press for the Institute of Early American History and Culture, 1980.

McGill, Meredith L. "Poe, Literary Nationalism, and Authorial Identity." In *The American Face of Edgar Allan Poe*, ed. Shawn Rosenheim and Stephen Rachman. Baltimore: Johns Hopkins University Press, 1995. 271–304.

McKeon, Michael. *The Origins of the English Novel, 1600–1740*. Baltimore: Johns Hopkins University Press, 1987.

McLamore, Richard V. "The Dutchman in the Attic: Claiming an Inheritance in *The Sketch Book of Geoffrey Crayon*." *American Literature* 72 (2000): 31–57.

McLuhan, Marshall. *The Gutenberg Galaxy: The Making of Typographic Man*. London: Routledge and Kegan Paul, 1962.

McWilliams, John P. *The American Epic: Transforming a Genre, 1770–1860.* Cambridge: Cambridge University Press, 1989.

Miller, D. A. *Narrative and Its Discontents: Problems of Closure in the Traditional Novel.* Princeton, N.J.: Princeton University Press, 1981.

Miller, J. Hillis. *Hawthorne and History: Defacing It.* Cambridge, Mass.: Blackwell, 1991.

Miller, Perry. *The New England Mind: The Seventeenth Century.* New York: Macmillan, 1939.

——. *Nature's Nation.* Cambridge, Mass.: Harvard University Press, 1967.

Miller, Perry and Thomas H. Johnson. *The Puritans.* New York: American Book Company, 1938.

Miner, Earl. *Comparative Poetics: An Intercultural Essay on Theories of Literature.* Princeton, N.J.: Princeton University Press, 1990.

Montaigne, Michel de. *Essays.* Trans. J. M. Cohen. Harmondsworth: Penguin, 1958.

Moore, R. Laurence. *Religious Outsiders and the Making of Americans.* New York: Oxford University Press, 1986.

Morris, David B. *Alexander Pope: The Genius of Sense.* Cambridge, Mass.: Harvard University Press, 1984.

——. *The Culture of Pain.* Berkeley: University of California Press, 1991.

Mulford, Carla. "What Is the Early American Canon, and Who Said It Needed Expanding?" *Resources for American Literary Study* 19 (1993): 165–73.

Mullan, John. *Sentiment and Sociability: The Language of Feeling in the Eighteenth Century.* Oxford: Oxford University Press, 1988.

Murdock, Kenneth B. "Mather Byles." In *Dictionary of American Biography*, vol. 3, ed. Allen Johnson. New York: Scribner's, 1929. 381–82.

Murphy, Geraldine. "Olaudah Equiano, Accidental Tourist." *Eighteenth-Century Studies* 27 (1994): 551–68.

Murray, Laura J. "The Aesthetic of Dispossession: Washington Irving and Ideologies of (De)Colonization in the Early Republic." *American Literary History* 8 (1996): 205–31.

Murrin, John M. "Beneficiaries of the Catastrophe: The English Colonists in America." In *The New American History*, ed. Eric Foner. Philadelphia: Temple University Press, 1990. 3–23.

Musselwhite, David. "Reflections on Burke's *Reflections*, 1790–1990." In *The Enlightenment and Its Shadows*, ed. Peter Hulme and Ludmilla Jordanova. London: Routledge, 1990. 140–62.

Nelson, William H. *The American Tory.* Oxford: Oxford University Press, 1961.

Newcomb, Robert. "Franklin and Richardson." *Journal of English and Germanic Philology* 57 (1958): 27–35.

Newfield, Christopher. "The Politics of Male Suffering: Masochism and Hegemony in the American Renaissance." *differences* 1, 3 (Fall 1989): 55–87.

Nussbaum, Felicity and Laura Brown. *The New Eighteenth Century: Theory, Politics, English Literature.* New York: Methuen, 1987.

O'Brien, Conor Cruise. *The Long Affair: Thomas Jefferson and the French Revolution, 1785–1800.* London: Sinclair-Stevenson, 1996.

O'Neale, Sondra. "A Slave's Subtle War: Phillis Wheatley's Use of Biblical Myth and Symbol." *Early American Literature* 21 (1986): 144–65.

Padover, Saul K. *A Jefferson Profile*. New York: John Day, 1956.

Paine, Thomas. *Rights of Man*. Ed. Henry Collins. Harmondsworth: Penguin, 1969.

Pajak, Edward F. "Washington Irving's Ichabod Crane: American Narcissus." *American Imago* 38, 1 (1981): 127–35.

Parkman, Francis, Jr. *The Oregon Trail*. Ed. David Levin. New York: Viking Penguin, 1982.

Parrington, Vernon Louis, ed. *The Connecticut Wits*. 1925. Hamden, Conn.: Archon, 1963.

——. *Main Currents in American Thought: An Interpretation of American Literature from the Beginnings to 1920*. 3 vols. New York: Harcourt, Brace and Company, 1930.

Patterson, Annabel. *Pastoral and Ideology: Virgil to Valéry*. Berkeley: University of California Press, 1987.

Pease, Donald E. *Visionary Compacts: American Renaissance Writings in Cultural Context*. Madison: University of Wisconsin Press, 1987.

——. "New Americanists: Revisionist Interventions into the Canon." *boundary 2* 17 (1990): 1–37.

Perera, Suvendrini. *Reaches of Empire: The English Novel from Edgworth to Dickens*. New York: Columbia University Press, 1991.

Peterson, Merrill D. *The Jefferson Image in the American Mind*. New York: Oxford University Press, 1960.

Pocock, J. G. A. *The Machiavellian Moment: Florentine Political Thought and the Atlantic Tradition*. Princeton, N.J.: Princeton University Press, 1975.

——. "Enlightenment and Revolution: The Case of English-Speaking North America." *Studies on Voltaire and the Eighteenth Century* 263 (1989): 249–61.

Poe, Edgar Allan. *The Complete Poems and Tales*. New York: Modern Library, 1938.

——. *Essays and Reviews*. New York: Library of America, 1984.

——. *The Science Fiction of Edgar Allan Poe*. Ed. Harold Beaver. Harmondsworth: Penguin, 1976.

Poovey, Mary. *The Proper Lady and the Woman Writer: Ideology as Style in the Works of Mary Wollstonecraft, Mary Shelley, and Jane Austen*. Chicago: University of Chicago Press, 1984.

Pope, Alexander. *Poetical Works*. Ed. Herbert Davis. London: Oxford University Press, 1966.

——. *Poetry and Prose of Alexander Pope*. Ed. Aubrey Williams. Boston: Houghton Mifflin, 1969.

Post, Constance J. "Revolutionary Dialogics in American Mock-Epic Poetry: Double-Voicing in *M'Fingal*, *The Anarchiad*, and *The Hasty Pudding*." *Studies in American Humor* n.s. 6 (1988): 40–51.

Pound, Ezra. "Provincialism the Enemy." *Selected Prose, 1909–1965*. Ed. William Cookson. London: Faber, 1973. 159–73.

——. *The Cantos*. London: Faber, 1975.

Railton, Stephen. *Authorship and Audience: Literary Performance in the American Renaissance*. Princeton, N.J.: Princeton University Press, 1991.

Ramsay, David. *The History of the American Revolution*. 2 vols. 1789. Ed. Lester H. Cohen. Indianapolis: LibertyClassics, 1990.

Randall, Willard Sterne. *Thomas Jefferson: A Life*. 1993. New York: HarperCollins, 1994.

Redding, J. Saunders. *To Make a Poet Black*. Durham, N.C.: University of North Carolina Press, 1939.

Reilly, Susan. "'A Nobler Fall of Ground': Nation and Narration in *Pride and Prejudice*." *Symbiosis* 4 (2000): 19–34.

Reising, Russell J. *The Unusable Past: Theory and the Study of American Literature*. New York: Methuen, 1986.

Reynolds, David S. *Beneath the American Renaissance: The Subversive Imagination in the Age of Emerson and Melville*. New York: Knopf, 1988.

Richardson, Samuel. *Pamela; or, Virtue Rewarded*. Ed. William M. Sale Jr. New York: Norton, 1958.

——. *Pamela; or, Virtue Rewarded*. Ed. Peter Sabor. Harmondsworth: Penguin, 1980.

——. *Clarissa; or, The History of a Young Lady*. Ed. Angus Ross. Harmondsworth: Penguin, 1985.

Rice, Grantland S. *The Transformation of Authorship in America*. Chicago: University of Chicago Press, 1997.

Ringe, Donald A. "New York and New England: Irving's Criticism of American Society." *American Literature* 38 (1967): 455–67.

——. *American Gothic: Imagination and Reason in Nineteenth-Century Fiction*. Lexington: University Press of Kentucky, 1982.

Roach, Joseph. *Cities of the Dead: Circum-Atlantic Performance*. New York: Columbia University Press, 1996.

Robbins, Bruce. *The Servant's Hand: English Fiction from Below*. 1986. Durham, N.C.: Duke University Press, 1993.

Roberts, Warren. *Jane Austen and the French Revolution*. New York: St. Martin's Press, 1979.

Robinson, Sidney K. *Inquiry into the Picturesque*. Chicago: University of Chicago Press, 1991.

Rodgers, James. "Sensibility, Sympathy, Benevolence: Physiology and Moral Philosophy in *Tristram Shandy*." In *Languages of Nature*, ed. Jordanova. 117–58.

Roger, Philippe. "A Political Minimalist." In *Sade and the Narrative of Transgression*, ed. David B. Allison, Mark S. Roberts, and Allen S. Weiss. Cambridge: Cambridge University Press, 1995. 76–99.

Rogers, Pat. "Pope and the Social Scene." In *Writers and Their Background: Alexander Pope*, ed. Dixon. 101–42.

Roth, Martin. *Comedy and America: The Lost World of Washington Irving*. Port Washington, N.Y.: Kennikat Press, 1976.

Rousseau, Jean-Jacques. *Confessions*. 1781. Trans. J. M. Cohen. Harmondsworth: Penguin, 1953.

Rowe, John Carlos. *At Emerson's Tomb: The Politics of Classic American Literature*. New York: Columbia University Press, 1997.

Runte, Roseanne. "La Fontaine: Precursor of the Eighteenth-Century Libertine." *Eighteenth-Century Life* 3 (1976): 47–51.

Ruttenburg, Nancy. *Democratic Personality: Popular Voice and the Trial of American Authorship*. Stanford, Calif.: Stanford University Press, 1998.

Sachse, William L. *The Colonial Writer in Britain*. Madison: University of Wisconsin Press, 1956.

Sade, Marquis de. "Philosophy in the Bedroom." 1795. *The Complete Justine, Philosophy in the Bedroom and Other Writings*. Ed. Richard Seaver and Austryn Wainhouse. New York: Grove Press, 1966. 177–367.

Said, Edward. *Culture and Imperialism*. New York: Knopf, 1993.

Samuels, Shirley. "Infidelity and Contagion: The Rhetoric of Revolution." *Early American Literature* 22 (1987): 183–91.

Sancho, Ignatius. *Letters of the Late Ignatius Sancho, an African*. Ed. Vincent Carretta. Harmondsworth: Penguin, 1998.

Sandiford, Keith A. *Measuring the Moment: Strategies of Protest in Eighteenth-Century Afro-English Writing*. Selinsgrove, Pa.: Susquehanna University Press, 1988.

Sanford, Charles L. "An American Pilgrim's Progress," *American Quarterly* 6 (1954): 297–310.

Sayce. R. A. *The Essays of Montaigne: A Critical Exploration*. London: Weidenfeld and Nicolson, 1972.

Schiller, Friedrich. *On the Naive and Sentimental in Literature*. Trans. Helen Watanabe-O'Kelly. Manchester: Carcanet New Press, 1981.

Schlereth, Thomas J. *The Cosmopolitan Ideal in Enlightenment Thought: Its Form and Function in the Ideas of Franklin, Hume, and Voltaire, 1694–1790*. Notre Dame, Ind.: University of Notre Dame Press, 1977.

Schulman, Lydia Dittler. *Paradise Lost and the Rise of the American Republic*. Boston: Northeastern University Press. 1992.

Scruggs, Charles. "Phillis Wheatley and the Poetical Legacy of Eighteenth-Century England." *Studies in Eighteenth-Century Culture* 10 (1981): 279–95.

Sedgwick, Eve Kosofsky. "Jane Austen and the Masturbating Girl." *Critical Inquiry* 17 (1991): 818–37.

Seelye, John. *Prophetic Waters: The River in Early American Life and Literature*. New York: Oxford University Press, 1977.

——. "The Jacobin Mode in Early American Fiction: Gilbert Imlay's *The Emigrants*." *Early American Literature* 22 (1987): 204–12.

Seidel, Michael. "The Man Who Came to Dinner: Ian Watt and the Theory of Formal Realism." *Eighteenth-Century Fiction* 12 (2000): 193–212.

Sellers, Charles Coleman. *Benjamin Franklin in Portraiture*. New Haven, Conn.: Yale University Press, 1962.

Sensabaugh, George F. *Milton in Early America*. Princeton, N.J.: Princeton University Press, 1964.

Shackleford, George Green. *Thomas Jefferson's Travels in Europe, 1784–1789*. Baltimore: Johns Hopkins University Press, 1995.

Shields, David S. *Oracles of Empire: Poetry, Politics, and Commerce in British America, 1690–1750*. Chicago: University of Chicago Press, 1990.

——. "British-American Belles Lettres." In *Cambridge History of American Literature*, vol. 1, *1590–1820*, ed. Bercovitch. 307–43.

——. *Civil Tongues and Polite Letters in British America*. Chapel Hill: University of North Carolina Press for the Institute of Early American History and Culture, 1997.

Shields, John C. "Phillis Wheatley and Mather Byles: A Study in Literary Relationship." *College Language Association Journal* 23 (1980): 377–90.

Shurr, William H. " 'Now, Gods, Stand Up for Bastards': Reinterpreting Benjamin Franklin's *Autobiography*." *American Literature* 64 (1992): 435–51.

Sibley, Agnes Marie. *Alexander Pope's Prestige in America, 1725–1835*. New York: Columbia University Press, 1949.

Silverman, Kenneth. *Timothy Dwight*. New York: Twayne, 1969.

——. *A Cultural History of the American Revolution*. New York: Crowell, 1976.

——. Introduction. Benjamin Franklin, *The Autobiography and Other Writings*. New York: Viking Penguin 1986. vii–xx.

Simpson, David. *Romanticism, Nationalism, and the Revolt against Theory*. Chicago: University of Chicago Press, 1993.

Simpson, Lewis P. "The Satiric Mode: The Early National Wits." In *The Comic Imagination in American Literature*. Ed. Louis D. Rubin Jr. New Brunswick, N.J.: Rutgers University Press, 1973. 49–61.

——, ed. *The Federalist Literary Mind: Selections from the Monthly Anthology and Boston Review, 1803–1811*. Baton Rouge: Louisiana State University Press, 1962.

Smith, Barbara Clark. "The Adequate Revolution." *William and Mary Quarterly* 3rd ser. 51 (1994): 684–92.

Smith-Rosenberg, Carroll. "Misprisioning *Pamela*: Representations of Gender and Class in Nineteenth-Century America." *Michigan Quarterly Review* 26 (1987): 9–28.

Sollers, Philippe. *Writing and the Experience of Limits*. Ed. David Hayman, trans. Philip Barnard and David Hayman. New York: Columbia University Press, 1983.

Sollors, Werner. *Beyond Ethnicity: Consent and Descent in American Culture*. New York: Oxford University Press, 1986.

——, ed. *The Invention of Ethnicity*. New York: Oxford University Press, 1989.

Southam, Brian C., ed. *Critical Essays on Jane Austen*. London: Routledge and Kegan Paul, 1968.

——. "The Silence of the Bertrams: Slavery and the Chronology of *Mansfield Park*." *Times Literary Supplement*, 17 February 1995: 13–14.

Spears, Timothy B. "Common Observations: Timothy Dwight's Travels in New England and New York," *American Studies* 30, 1 (Spring 1989): 35–52.

Spencer, Benjamin. *The Quest for Nationality: An American Literary Campaign*. Syracuse, N.Y.: Syracuse University Press, 1957.

Spengemann, William C. "American Things/Literary Things: The Problem of American Literary History." *American Literature* 57 (1985): 456–81.

——. *A Mirror for Americanists: Reflections on the Idea of American Literature.* Hanover, N.H.: University Press of New England, 1989.

——. *A New World of Words: Redefining Early American Literature.* New Haven: Yale University Press, 1994.

Stallybrass, Peter and Allon White. *The Politics and Poetics of Transgression.* Ithaca, N.Y.: Cornell University Press, 1986.

Stavely, Keith W. F. *Puritan Legacies: Paradise Lost and the New England Tradition, 1630–1890.* Ithaca, N.Y.: Cornell University Press, 1987.

Stern, Julia A. *The Plight of Feeling: Sympathy and Dissent in the Early American Novel.* Chicago: University of Chicago Press, 1997.

Sterne, Laurence. *The Life and Opinions of Tristram Shandy, Gentleman.* Ed. Graham Petrie. Harmondsworth: Penguin, 1967.

——. *The Sermons of Mr. Yorick.* Ed. Marjorie David. Cheadle: Carcanet, 1973.

Straub, Kristina. *Sexual Suspects: Eighteenth-Century Players and Sexual Ideology.* Princeton, N.J.: Princeton University Press, 1992.

Sundquist, Eric J. *To Wake the Nations: Race in the Making of American Literature.* Cambridge, Mass.: Harvard University Press, 1993.

Tanner, Tony. *Jane Austen.* Cambridge, Mass.: Harvard University Press, 1986.

Tate, Claudia. "Reconstructing the Renaissance of U.S. Literature." *American Quarterly* 46 (1994): 589–94.

Tennenhouse, Leonard. "The Americanization of Clarissa." *Yale Journal of Criticism* 11 (1998): 177–96.

Thomas, Helen. *Romanticism and Slave Narratives: Transatlantic Testimonies.* Cambridge: Cambridge University Press, 2000.

Thompson, E. P. *The Making of the English Working Class.* Rev. ed. Harmondsworth: Penguin, 1968.

Thompson, James. *Models of Value: Eighteenth-Century Political Economy and the Novel.* Durham, N.C.: Duke University Press, 1996.

Thoreau, Henry D. *Reform Papers.* Ed. Wendell Glick. Princeton, N.J.: Princeton University Press, 1973.

Thornton, Francis Beauchesne. *Alexander Pope: Catholic Poet.* New York: Pellegrini and Cudahy, 1952.

Todd, Janet. *Sensibility: An Introduction.* London: Methuen, 1986.

Tompkins, Jane. *Sensational Designs: The Cultural Work of American Fiction, 1790–1860.* New York: Oxford University Press, 1985.

Trilling, Lionel. "*Emma* and the Legend of Jane Austen." In *Jane Austen: Emma. A Casebook,* ed. David Lodge. London: Macmillan, 1968. 148–69.

——. *Sincerity and Authenticity.* Cambridge, Mass.: Harvard University Press, 1972.

Trollope, Anthony. *The American Senator.* Ed. John Halperin. Oxford: Oxford University Press, 1986.

——. *An Autobiography.* Ed. Michael Sadleir and Frederick Page. Oxford: Oxford University Press, 1980.

——. *Can You Forgive Her?* London: Oxford University Press, 1948.

——. *The Duke's Children.* Ed. Hermione Lee. Oxford: Oxford University Press, 1983.

——. *He Knew He Was Right.* Ed. John Sutherland. Oxford: Oxford University Press, 1985.

——. *The Prime Minister.* Oxford: Oxford University Press, 1973.

——. *The Way We Live Now.* New York: Dover, 1982.

——. *The West Indies and the Spanish Main.* New York: Carroll and Graf, 1999.

Trumbull, John. *The Satiric Poems of John Trumbull.* Ed. Edwin T. Bowden. Austin: University of Texas Press, 1962.

——. *The Meddler (1769–70) and The Correspondent (1770–73).* Ed. Bruce Granger. Delmar, N.Y.: Scholars' Facsimiles and Reprints, 1985.

Trumpener, Katie. *Bardic Nationalism: The Romantic Novel and the British Empire.* Princeton, N.J.: Princeton University Press, 1997.

Turner, James. *Without God, Without Creed: The Origins of Unbelief in America.* Baltimore: Johns Hopkins University Press, 1985.

Van Anglen, K. P. *The New England Milton: Literary Reception and Cultural Authority in the Early Republic.* University Park: Pennsylvania State University Press, 1993.

Van Dover, J. K. "The Design of Anarchy: *The Anarchiad,* 1786–1787." *Early American Literature* 24 (1989): 237–47.

Vanderbilt, Kermit. *American Literature and the Academy: The Roots, Growth, and Maturity of a Profession.* Philadelphia: University of Pennsylvania Press, 1986.

Viswanathan, Gauri, *Outside the Fold: Conversion, Modernity, and Belief.* Princeton, N.J.: Princeton University Press, 1998.

Von Frank, Albert J. "The Man That Corrupted Sleepy Hollow." *Studies in American Fiction* 15 (1987): 129–43.

Warner, Michael. *The Letters of the Republic: Publication and the Public Sphere in Eighteenth-Century America.* Cambridge, Mass.: Harvard University Press, 1990.

——. "Poetry: The Eighteenth Century." In *English Literatures of America,* ed. Jehlen and Warner. 1011–13.

Warner, William B. *Licensing Entertainment: The Elevation of Novel Reading in Britain, 1684–1750.* Berkeley: University of California Press, 1998.

——. "Staging Readers Reading." *Eighteenth-Century Fiction* 12 (2000): 391–416.

Warren, Austin. "To Mr. Pope: Epistles from America." *PMLA* 48 (1933): 61–73.

Watson, Nicola J. *Revolution and the Form of the British Novel, 1790–1825: Intercepted Letters, Interrupted Seductions.* Oxford: Clarendon Press, 1994.

Watt, Ian. *The Rise of the Novel: Studies in Defoe, Richardson and Fielding.* 1957. Harmondsworth: Penguin, 1963.

Watts, Edward. *Writing and Postcolonialism in the Early Republic.* Charlottesville: University Press of Virginia, 1998.

Weisbuch, Robert. *Atlantic Double-Cross: American Literature and British Influence in the Age of Emerson.* Chicago: University of Chicago Press, 1986.

Wellek, René. *Concepts of Criticism.* Ed. Stephen G. Nichols Jr. New Haven, Conn.: Yale University Press, 1963.

——. *Confrontations: Studies in the Intellectual and Literary Relations Between Germany, England, and the United States During the Nineteenth Century*. Princeton, N.J.: Princeton University Press, 1965.

Wells, Colin. "Timothy Dwight's American *Dunciad: The Triumph of Infidelity* and the Universalist Controversy." *Early American Literature* 33 (1998): 173–91.

West, Elsie Lee. Introduction. Washington Irving, *Oliver Goldsmith: A Biography, and Biography of the Late Margaret Miller Davidson*. Ed. Elsie Lee West. Boston: Twayne, 1978. xv–xlviii.

White, Patrick C. T. *A Nation on Trial: America and the War of 1812*. New York: John Wiley, 1965.

Willey, Basil. *The Eighteenth-Century Background: Studies in the Idea of Nature in the Thought of the Period*. London: Chatto and Windus, 1940.

Williams, Raymond. *The Long Revolution*. London: Chatto and Windus, 1961.

——. *The English Novel from Dickens to Lawrence*. London: Chatto and Windus, 1970.

——. *The Country and the City*. London: Hogarth Press, 1985.

Wills, Garry. *Inventing America: Jefferson's Declaration of Independence*. Garden City, N.Y.: Doubleday, 1978.

Wilson, David A. *Paine and Cobbett: The Transatlantic Connection*. Kingston and Montreal: McGill-Queen's University Press, 1988.

Wood, Gordon. *The Creation of the American Republic, 1776–1787*. New York: Norton, 1969.

——. *The Radicalism of the American Revolution*. New York: Knopf, 1992.

Woodman, Thomas. "Pope: The Papist and the Poet." *Essays in Criticism* 46 (1996): 219–33.

Wright, Dorena Allen. "The Meeting at the Brook-Side: Beatrice, the Pearl-Maiden, and Pearl Prynne." *ESQ* 28 (1982): 112–20.

Ziff, Larzer. *Writing in the New Nation: Prose, Print, and Politics in the Early United States*. New Haven, Conn.: Yale University Press, 1991.

Zuckerman, Michael. "Rhetoric, Reality, and the Revolution: The Genteel Radicalism of Gordon Wood." *William and Mary Quarterly* 3rd ser. 51 (1994): 693–702.

Index

Acknowledgments

Transatlantic Insurrections has been a long and difficult project to bring to fruition for several reasons. One has been my own transatlantic upheaval, from Portland, Oregon, where the book was begun, to the University of Nottingham, and thence to Cambridge. Another has been the time it took for me, as a modern Americanist by training, to familiarize myself with the literature and culture of early America. Having read the usual wide range of British authors in the English degree at Oxford some years ago, it became obvious to me when teaching American subjects in the United States that conventional narratives of English and American literature had, for various reasons, worked to marginalize each other, and that the role of the American Revolution in the formation of each national literature had been oddly occluded. Consequently, part of my intention in this book has been not just to bring British and American culture into mutual juxtaposition, but also to realign early American with post-Revolutionary literature in an attempt to circumvent the kind of academic separatism which can, I believe, be detrimental to an understanding of each particular area. Like my previous work on Catholic fictions, this book is designed to cast a quizzical eye at some of the ways in which American literature as a professional field has been circumscribed and institutionalized in recent times.

I shall always be grateful to my former colleagues and students in Portland for first engaging me in dialogue about these issues. In particular, I would like to thank the graduate students in my "Theories of the Enlightenment" seminar, especially Jeff Timmons and Katherine Lynes, who acted as a sounding board when these speculations were at little more than a hypothetical stage. I also benefited from a fellowship at the Humanities Research Institute, Dartmouth College, in the summer of 1997, where I got the opportunity to discuss some of these ideas with Donald Pease, William Spengemann, and the other Institute participants. At Nottingham, I had the pleasure of team-teaching an M.A. course on Americanist methods with Richard King, and I am also indebted to David Murray, who gave the whole manuscript a judicious reading at an important time.

At Cambridge, the University Library offered that rare thing in British academe, a first-class research facility in which to finish off this work.

Earlier versions of various parts of this project were offered as talks at the 1996 British Association for American Studies Conference in Leeds, at the University of Leeds, and at Nottingham Trent University; on all of these occasions, members of the audience offered valuable comments and suggestions. I should also like to express my appreciation to the library of the University of Massachusetts at Amherst for their exceptional willingness to loan overseas their microfilm collection of the Byles Family Papers. I am particularly grateful to Jerry Singerman at the University of Pennsylvania Press for his confidence in this project, and to the Press's readers, one of whom was Leonard Tennenhouse, for their helpful and incisive comments. For what Benjamin Franklin would call the "errata" that remain, I, like Franklin, can blame only myself.